EADI BOOK SERIES 24

FOOD AID
AND
HUMAN SECURITY

edited by

EDWARD CLAY and OLAV STOKKE

FRANK CASS
LONDON • PORTLAND, OR
in association with
EADI European Association of Development Research
and Training Institutes, Bonn

First published in 2000 in Great Britain by
FRANK CASS PUBLISHERS
Newbury House, 900 Eastern Avenue
London IG2 7HH, England
1005062070
and in the United States of America by
FRANK CASS PUBLISHERS
c/o ISBS
5804 N.E. Hassalo Street
Portland, Oregon 97213–3644

Website: www.frankcass.com

British Library Cataloguing in Publication Data

Food aid and human security. – (EADI book series; 24)
1. Food relief
I. Clay, Edward J. II. Stoke, Olav
363. 8'83

ISBN 0-7146-5084-6 (cloth)
ISBN 0-7146-8125-3 (paper)

Library of Congress Cataloging-in-Publication Data

Food aid and human security / edited by Edward Clay and Olav Stokke.
    p. cm. – (EADI-book series; 24)
Includes bibliographical references and index.
ISBN 0-7146-5084 (cloth) – ISBN 0-7146-8125-3 (pbk)
    1. Food relief – International cooperation. 2. Food relief – Economic aspects. 3.
Emergency food supply. 4. Security, International. I. Clay, Edward J. II. Stokke, Olav,
1934- III. Series.

HV696.F6 F6263 2000
363.8'83 – dc21   00-043119

Printed in Great Britain by
MPG Books Ltd, Bodmin, Cornwall

Contents

Tables, Figures and Boxes

Introduction:
Food Aid and Human Security

EDWARD CLAY AND OLAV STOKKE

The future role of food aid is in question. This is important because food aid has historically been a major element of development assistance geared to support longer-term development and the primary response to help countries and people in crisis. Doubts about food aid are arising because there is a growing mismatch between the new circumstances produced by rapid political and economic change and the international arrangements and institutions for food aid that are predicated on an earlier reality.

In contrast, the international institutional arrangements for providing food aid have remained much as they were when first established between the 1950s and 1970s. Then food aid represented around a quarter of total official development assistance (ODA). The main challenge was seen to be transforming an additional resource, surplus food in the North, into development in the South. By the mid-1990s, food aid's share had shrunk to under 4 per cent of ODA and had increasingly become an uncertain resource. Meanwhile, even the conceptualisation of food security was changing from assuring the global and national supply of food to assuring access for all. Furthermore, food security should be considered not in isolation but as part of a wider concept of human security. These were circumstances in which the editors of this book felt it worthwhile to revisit the subject of food aid policy within the wider framework of promoting human security.

I. BACKGROUND TO THE PRESENT PROJECT

In 1988, the editors of this volume organised a workshop at Lysebu in Oslo, under the auspices of the European Association of Development Research and Training Institutes (EADI), which resulted in the volume *Food Aid Reconsidered: Assessing the Impact on Third World Countries* [*Clay and Stokke, eds., 1991*]. The editors and most of the contributors to that book were cautious about an enhanced future role for food aid. There were concerns about the appropriateness of and the inflexibility inherent in commodity aid. Issues of its impact on agriculture and its cost-effectiveness were raised: 'To urge an increased role for food in financing the development process implies

1

that food is less costly than financial aid. Even if the juggling of agricultural aid budgets makes that so for some donors, the economic
resource costs for developed countries are now probably not lower,
and may even be higher, than financing food imports or supporting
rural development directly' [*Clay and Stokke, 1991: 32*].

At that time, food aid in kind was still a substantial, and probably a
partly additional, element of development assistance (see Chapter 1,
Table 1.1). Addressing the social consequences of structural adjustment policies through both programme assistance and directly distributed food aid in kind was then a priority. The editors ended up by
speculating: 'If food aid is provided in increasingly flexible ways,
with purchases in developing countries, through monetisation rather
than direct distribution, the distinction between food aid and aid for
food, or financial assistance, will become less important. That is
potentially how much of the conventionally doubly-tied food aid will
gradually disappear during the next decade' [*Clay and Stokke,
1991:32*].

The major changes in the political and economic environment of
food aid, and in aid policy [*Stokke, 1996*], triggered the present new
venture. The concern for aid effectiveness resulted in a series of
major evaluations and policy reviews of food aid and emergency operations in the 1990s [*CMI, 1993; Eriksson et al., 1996; Clay et al.,
1996, 1998; ADAB, 1997; McClelland., 1997; EU Court of Auditors,
1997; Vincent et al., 1998; and Benson and Clay, 1998*]. The evidence emerging from these officially sponsored reports offered an opportunity to synthesise what has been learnt on the role and impact of
food aid and to consider more closely its implications for the future.

II. A FOOD SECURITY AND HUMAN SECURITY PERSPECTIVE

In the early 1990s, the perspective within which food security issues
were to be viewed was broadened, largely as a response to the 'new'
conflict patterns emerging after the end of the Cold War. The
transition period – when the new international order to replace the old
bipolar order that had prevailed since the end of World War II was in
the making – was proving to be ridden by conflicts that caused huge
human suffering. But whereas in the past conflicts were among states,
in the early 1990s there were many low-level conflicts within states,
although some were within a regional framework. Some of these conflicts were extremely intense, involving a high number of civilian
casualties and displacement. Human security was increasingly

recognised as fundamental to human development and the wider development process.

This is recognised in the United Nations Development Programme's *Human Development Report 1994* [*UNDP, 1994*], which introduced a concept of human security having two aspects:

- *safety* from chronic threats such as hunger, disease and repression; and
- *protection* from sudden and hurtful disruptions in the pattern of daily life.

Such security allows people to exercise their expanded choices and develop their capabilities. The absence of such security undermines the processes of development and often leads to social disintegration and humanitarian catastrophe. The range of threats to human security is wide. The categories identified by UNDP include :

- economic security (unemployment, job insecurity, inequality and poverty);
- food security (inadequate availability of food and access by all people);
- health security (communicable diseases and pollution-related illnesses, drug abuse);
- environmental security (degradation of air, water, soil, forests);
- personal security (conflict, terrorism, violence against women and children);
- community security (ethnic clashes); and
- political security (violation of human rights).

This conceptualisation of human security involves a shift in focus from the thinking about security which predominated up to the late 1980s. Up to then the concept of security had been interpreted more narrowly as security of territory from external aggression, as protection of national interests in foreign policy, or as global security – in the first place from the threat of nuclear holocaust. With the end of the Cold War, other aspects of security – always there – came to the fore. Global processes of increasing economic interdependence through trade, investment and the diffusion of technological changes are seen as the motor of economic growth in the traditional sense. The promotion of human security and human development is to protect people against threats that marginalise and exclude them and to enable them to participate in the process of development.

Human security is seen as having four characteristics:

- *Human security is a universal concern,* with differences of intensity between countries and regions.
- *The components of human security are interdependent*: famine, disease, ethnic disputes and social breakdowns are now not usually isolated events restricted within national borders that can be treated as separable problems.
- *Prevention and protection* are easier to undertake and more successful than reactive interventions.
- *Human security is people-centred.*

As Professor Helen O'Neill, in her Presidential Address to EADI in 1996, observed, 'if we differentiate between rich and poor *people* rather than rich and poor *countries,* we find that human insecurities worldwide may look more alike' [*O'Neill, 1998: 24, emphasis added*].

This wider concept of human security, integrating food security concerns, became another point of departure when it was decided to take a new, hard look at the issues of food aid and finance for food almost ten years after the first Lysebu workshop in 1988. In an environment of risks, uncertainty and rapid change, prevailing in the early 1990s, food aid and other assistance have increasingly been organised as part of efforts to assure human security in terms of livelihoods, food, health, a sustainable environment, and personal and political security. However, this multiplicity of goals implies potentially inconsistent, competing claims on the use of quite limited resources for:

- the organisation of an increasing proportion of food aid as part of attempts to *provide human security* in situations of conflict and political and social disintegration;
- using food aid to *counteract both the economic and human effects* of economic shocks, especially transition and structural adjustment as well as natural disasters;
- concentrating food aid on more *limited food security and poverty reduction projects* for vulnerable groups.

To what extent is this ambitious combination of goals realised in practice? To what extent do the modalities and institutional arrangements for aid permit them to be realised?

4

III. A FOCUS ON INTERNATIONAL AGREEMENTS AND INSTITUTIONS

While the political environment of food aid has changed dramatically since 1988, there have been few changes in its institutional arrangements in Europe or internationally. As already noted, most of the basic modalities and arrangements involving food aid and finance for food reflect a process of adaptation in institutional arrangements agreed several decades ago. We therefore decided to focus in this fresh examination of food aid on institutional questions, in particular.

The major institutional arrangements for food aid at present, from a European viewpoint are:

– The World Trade Organisation (WTO), which is now responsible for the monitoring of the follow-up of the Marrakesh Decision of 1994 under the GATT Uruguay Round Agreement. This decision makes commitments to assist low-income countries affected by trade liberalisation and has been the only major institutional development in the 1990s.
– The Food Aid Convention (FAC), agreed in 1967 with substantial modifications, especially in 1981, involving minimum annual commitments of cereals.
– Arrangements related to the European Union (EU) for dividing up responsibilities for food aid between the European Commission and the member states, dating back to 1968.
– The World Food Programme (WFP), established in 1963 to provide food aid through its Regular Programme to development projects and a modest amount of emergency aid. All European members of the OECD Development Assistance Committee (DAC) as well as the EU through the Commission have supported the WFP. Large-scale humanitarian assistance has been provided since 1977 through the International Emergency Food Reserve (IEFR) and humanitarian assistance for Protracted Refugee and Relief Operations (PRRO) in co-operation with the United Nations High Commissioner for Refugees (UNHCR) since 1991. It evolved from a joint UN/FAO programme into an international food aid agency.
– The FAO Consultative Sub-Committee on Surplus Disposal has, since the early 1960s, monitored food aid to ensure that free trade principles are not violated.
– European governments have also been involved in organisations such as the Club du Sahel, established after the drought of the

early 1970s for interfacing with developing countries at a regional level.

There are many other international institutions and arrangements with at least a formal responsibility for some aspect of food security, including notably the UN Office of the Commissioner for Humanitarian Relief (OCHA), UNICEF (children, nutrition and relief), WHO (health and nutrition), the WMO (short-term climatic forecasting) and other UN agencies and international and regional financial institutions such as the IMF, World Bank and IFAD [*Shaw and Clay, 1998*].

IV. THE EADI SETTING OF THIS PROJECT

The present volume results from a research and publishing project under the auspices of EADI's Working Group on Aid Policy and Performance. The proposal to focus again on food aid in the light of the changed political environment and the 'new' perspectives was made ahead of EADI's eighth General Conference, which took place in Vienna in September 1996, and the Working Group decided to take it up. At that time, it had just completed its third major programme, with a focus on evolving North–South relations since the Cold War: aid and political conditionality. Two volumes in the EADI Book Series (Nos. 16 and 18) came out of that effort [*Stokke, ed., 1995; Stokke, ed., 1996*]. Earlier in the 1990s, its second major programme, focusing on evaluation, had been finalised. The outcome was a series of three volumes in the EADI Book Series (Nos. 11, 12 and 14), including the book on food aid previously referred to [*Clay and Stokke, eds., 1991, reprinted 1995; Stokke, ed., 1991; Berlage and Stokke, eds., 1992*]. Previously the group had examined the aid policies of European countries, a task completed in 1984 with the publication of two volumes in the EADI Book Series (No. 4) [*Stokke, ed., 1984a and b*]. Its most recent publication, resulting from a project on policy coherence in development co-operation, was published in the EADI Book Series (No. 22) in 1999 [*Forster and Stokke, eds., 1999*].

Over the years, the EADI Working Group on Aid has established a method of working. A project design is prepared by the Convenor(s), and pre-eminent researchers in the field are invited to comment. These consultations are followed by invitations to specialists to contribute component studies. The draft studies are presented at an international workshop also involving a selected group of experts in the specific field. Revised and refined versions of selected drafts, scrutinised through this process, are finally published. Before publication, contributions have also to be refereed by the EADI committee on publications, which decides whether to include the volume in the EADI Book Series.

This method of working has, by and large, been followed here. Drafts of 11 of the papers included in this volume were presented and scrutinised at an international workshop in April 1998, held again at Lysebu. Several bilateral and multinational agencies and NGOs participated, sharing their insights on the subject. Some 'gaps' were identified, which were filled afterwards by four additional chapters by Uwe Kracht, Nita Pillai, Alain Mourey and Wenche Barth Eide – in addition to the concluding chapter by the editors.

V. OUTLINE OF THE BOOK

In Chapter 1, the *editors* reflect on the changing role of food aid in kind and finance for food, taking as their point of departure the many changes that have taken place in the political and economic environment in the 1990s. They explore the language used by major actors and identify some of the consequences of different definitions, *inter alia*, for the statistics. Many actors are involved in providing food aid, including the OECD DAC group of donors, international agencies and NGOs, thus giving rise to considerable institutional complexity. Policy coherence, therefore, emerges as a major challenge.

The following three chapters focus on *aid resources, global food prospects and commitments.* In Chapter 2, *Rajul Pandya-Lorch* looks into the twenty-first century assessing the food prospects and potential imports of low-income countries. Her contribution is based on a comprehensive report she co-authored as part of the International Food Policy Research Institute's 2020 Vision initiative [*Pinstrup-Andersen et al., 1997, 1999*].

In Chapter 3, *Panos Konandreas, Ramesh Sharma and Jim Greenfield* make an attempt to identify the difficulties food-importing developing countries face as a result of the implementation of the Uruguay Round, with particular reference to least developed countries (LDCs) and net food-importing developing countries (NFIDCs). They then examine the role of food aid as a response to these difficulties, since food aid, according to the Marrakesh Decision, is one means of helping countries that may be adversely affected during the reform process envisaged by the Uruguay Round.

The Food Aid Convention (FAC) commits signatories to provide specified minimum tonnages of 'wheat equivalent' food aid with the objective of providing a guaranteed minimum flow of food aid to developing countries. It is intended as a safety net to protect recipient countries, from both financial and nutritional perspectives, against potential downward fluctuations in annual shipments of food. In Chapter 4, *Charlotte Benson* examines the role the FAC has played in determining actual flows of food aid and the implications for future ways of assuring resources for relief and combating food insecurity.

The following four chapters focus on *the realities, the role and the effects of food aid*. In Chapter 5, *Uwe Kracht* directs attention to challenges posed by the growing number of conflicts throughout the world in the 1990s. He identifies and discusses four issues that are both conflict- and food-security-related: the changing emergency environment; the food-security consequences of conflicts; the nature of conflicts (does food insecurity represent a causal factor?); and conflict prevention, food and humanitarian aid and conflict resolution, and post-conflict peace building. In Chapter 6, *Jeremy Shoham, Fiona O'Reilly and Jane Wallace* explore another aspect of the international response to humanitarian crisis and conflict: food assistance and nutritional security. It is frequently taken as axiomatic that food for relief is a good thing, and the authors probe the reality behind this assumption drawing upon extensive evidence from relief operations in sub-Saharan Africa. In Chapter 7, the perspective is shifted to humanitarian crises and natural disasters with particular reference to the SADC region of southern Africa. The economies of the region are particularly susceptible to food crises, because of their geographical position, the high proportion of people dependent on rain-fed agriculture for their livelihoods, and the strong links between agriculture and the rest of the economy. The traditional view of humanitarian crises caused by droughts has been that of sudden and widespread famine and starvation, requiring large inflows of food aid. *Roger Buckland, Graham Eele and Reggie Mugwara* look at whether this view is any longer valid in the light of the rapid and dramatic changes that have taken place in the region over the past ten years, which have resulted in much lower risk of famine. In Chapter 8, *Nita Pillai* reviews the literature on the impact and effectiveness of development food aid. Two types of food aid transactions are used for developmental purposes, namely programme and project food assistance. The evidence on the developmental impacts of both these forms is reviewed in terms of resource transfer efficiency and effectiveness in addressing poverty, food insecurity and promoting human resource development.

The following three chapters focus on *institutions and policies*, particularly the World Food Programme (WFP) and European-based NGOs, with an emphasis on the development role of food aid. In

Chapter 9, *Just Faaland, Diana McLean and Ole David Koht Norbye*, focusing on the WFP's performance as a development agency, present a summary of the findings, main critique and recommendations of their evaluation of the WFP, the so-called tripartite evaluation initiated by the governments of Canada, the Netherlands and Norway [*CMI, 1993*]. They proceed to review the follow-up by the WFP of the issues raised in that evaluation.

In a complementary essay (Chapter 10), *Jens H. Schulthes* poses and addresses the questions: Is there a future for the WFP as a development agency and does food aid still have a comparative advantage? His point of departure is that donors will only be prepared to continue supporting the WFP if they are persuaded that food aid still has a comparative advantage as a development resource, even after the disappearance of burdensome surpluses. In Chapter 11, *Marie-Cécile Thirion* considers the role of NGOs in food aid, interacting through a complex set of arrangements with the European Commission acting as a food aid donor.

The following three chapters focus on efforts to establish *a normative basis for* improving and safeguarding food security and human security. The authors are insiders, who in various capacities and ways have been actively involved in the process of establishing the norms they are describing and analysing. In Chapter 12, *Robin Jackson* describes and assesses efforts to develop a charter for food aid in the Sahel region. In the following chapter, *Alain Mourey* describes the code of conduct for the Red Cross and NGOs in disaster relief and assesses how it is followed up, and in Chapter 14, *Wenche Barth Eide* describes the efforts to promote a human rights perspective on food security. Documentation is provided. The full text of the Food Aid Charter for the Sahel appears as an appendix to Chapter 12, and the full text of the Code of Conduct for the International Red Cross and Red Crescent Movement and Non-Governmental Organisations (NGOs) in disaster relief (with annexes) is included as an appendix to Chapter 13.

The concluding chapters focus on policy, especially the institutional implications of the marginalisation of food aid within development co-operation. In Chapter 15, *Martin Doornbos* revisits the food aid debate and takes a closer look at the institutional factor. He identifies strategies used by institutions under threat of losing their key functions because of declining and uncertain resources. In Chapter 16, *the editors* summarise and conclude. Their brief answer is that institutional reform is long overdue. Radical reform of food aid institutions is deemed necessary and should take as its point of departure a wider concept of human security.

IV. ACKNOWLEDGEMENTS

This research and publishing programme benefited from much help and goodwill. The Norwegian Ministry of Foreign Affairs has generously contributed to the project by covering the major expenses involved in organising the international workshop at Lysebu in Oslo, also in producing camera-ready copy, and covering some of the research costs of the Norwegian Institute of International Affairs (NUPI). We are also indebted to the United Kingdom Department for International Development (DFID) for contributing to the research costs of the Overseas Development Institute (ODI). The Danish Ministry of Foreign Affairs (DANIDA) has also contributed by financing the component study by Jeremy Shoham and his colleagues on food aid and nutritional security in areas of conflict. These grants are gratefully acknowledged. This project would not have been possible without them.

We are also indebted to all the institutes and organisations which the authors of the component studies included here are associated with. For many, this implied support 'in kind'. Thanks also go to a number of bilateral and multilateral agencies and international organisations for the interest they took in the project by participating in the workshop at Lysebu. The fertile interaction between administrators and researchers at that workshop resulted in a significant strengthening of almost all the papers presented in this volume. In addition to those contributing chapters to the book, the following people all actively participated in the workshop: Bob Bell, Erik Berg, Pascale Crapouse, Niels Dabelstein, Bernard Dreesman, Roland Fox, Jean-Jacques Gabas, Charles E. Hanrahan, Ruth Haug, Hugo Herm, Gerd Holmboe Ottesen, Raul Hopkins, Kaisa Karttunen, Helge Kjekshus, Ragne Birte Lund, Frans Makken, Manfred Metz, David Morton, T. J. Ryan, Arvid Solheim, Atle Sommerfeldt and Dianne Spearman.

From the very beginning, the project has had the privilege of being integrated in the research programmes of the Overseas Development Institute in London and the Norwegian Institute of International Affairs in Oslo, with which the two project directors are associated. It has benefited from their institutional support and discussion with present and former colleagues, including at ODI Simon Maxwell, John Borton, Sanjay Dhiri and Nick Leader and at NUPI Sverre Lodgaard. Vibeke Lindeberg Sand assisted in making the Lysebu workshop run smoothly. The project has, in its final stages, benefited from the editorial support of Eilert Struksnes and the efficient and pleasant secretarial support of Liv Høivik, who has produced the camera-ready copy. Ros Schwartz translated the chapter by Marie-Cécile Thirion and Terry Henson processed several of the chapters. Warm thanks also go to Margaret Cornell for her invaluable assistance in editing the present volume, including language revision and indexing.

REFERENCES

ADAB, 1997, *Report of the committee of review on the Australian overseas aid programme* (The Simons Report), Canberra: Australian Development Assistance Bureau (April).

Benson, C. and E. J. Clay, 1998, 'The Impact of Drought on Sub-Saharan African Economies: A Preliminary Examination', *World Bank Technical Paper*, No. 401, Washington DC: World Bank.

Berlage, L. and O. Stokke, eds., 1992, *Evaluating Development Assistance: Approaches and Methods*, London: Frank Cass.

Clay, E. J. and O. Stokke, 1991, 'Assessing the Performance and the Economic Impact of Food Aid', in Clay and Stokke, eds.

Clay, E. J. and O. Stokke, eds., 1991, *Food Aid Reconsidered: Assessing the Impact on Third World Countries*, London: Frank Cass.

Clay, E. J., S. Dhiri and C. Benson, 1996, *Joint Evaluation of European Union Programme Food Aid: Synthesis Report*, London: Overseas Development Institute.

Clay, E. J., N. Pillai and C. Benson, 1998, *The Future of Food Aid: A Policy Review*. London: Overseas Development Institute.

CMI, 1993, *Evaluation of the World Food Programme: Final Report*, Bergen: The Chr. Michelsen Institute. (In Chapter 9: Governments of Canada, the Netherlands and Norway, 1994, *Evaluation of the World Food Programme: Main Report*, Ottawa: Canadian International Development Agency; Netherlands: Ministry of Foreign Affairs; Royal Norwegian Ministry of Foreign Affairs.)

Eriksson, J. et al., 1996, *The International Response to Conflict and Genocide: Lessons from the Rwanda Experience. Joint Evaluation of Emergency Assistance to Rwanda. Synthesis Report*, Copenhagen: Ministry of Foreign Affairs.

EU Court of Auditors, 1997, 'Special Report No. 2/97 concerning humanitarian aid from the European Union between 1992 and 1995 together with the Commission's replies', *Official Journal*, C143, Brussels (12 May).

FAO, 1996, *Rome Declaration on World Food Security and World Food Summit Plan of Action*, Rome: Food and Agriculture Organisation of the United Nations.

Forster, J. and O. Stokke, eds., 1999, *Policy Coherence in Development Co-operation*, London: Frank Cass.

McClelland, D. G., 1997, 'Food Aid and Sustainable Development – Forty Years of Experience', Washington DC: Center for Development Information and Evaluation, USAID (July).

O'Neill, H., 1998, 'Globalisation, Competitiveness and Human Security: Challenges for Development Policy and Institutional Change', Presidential Address to the 8th EADI General Conference in Vienna 11–14 September 1996, in *Proceedings of the 8th EADI General Conference*, Geneva: EADI Secretariat and Vienna: VIDC.

Pinstrup-Andersen, P., R. Pandya-Lorch and M. Rosegrant, 1997, *The World Food Situation: Recent Developments, Emerging Issues and Long-term Prospects'*, Washington DC: International Food Policy Research Institute.

Pinstrup-Andersen, P., R. Pandya-Lorch and M. Rosegrant, 1999, *World Food Prospects: Critical Issues for the Early Twenty-First Century'*, Washington DC: International Food Policy Research Institute.

Shaw, D.J. and E.J. Clay, 1998, 'Global Hunger and Food Security after the World Food Summit', *Canadian Journal of Development Studies*, Vol. 19, Special Issue, pp. 55–76.

Stokke, O., 1996, 'Foreign Aid: What Now?', in Stokke, ed.

Stokke, O., ed., 1984a, *European Development Assistance: Policies and Performance*, Volume 1, Tilburg: Executive Secretariat of the EADI, EADI Book Series No. 4.

Stokke, O., ed., 1984b, *European Development Assistance: Third World Perspectives on Policies and Performance*, Volume 2, Tilburg: Executive Secretariat of the EADI, EADI Book Series No. 4.

Stokke, O., ed., 1991, *Evaluating Development Assistance: Policies and Performance*, London: Frank Cass.

Stokke, O., ed., 1995, *Aid and Political Conditionality*, London: Frank Cass.

Stokke, O., ed., 1996, *Foreign Aid Towards the Year 2000: Experiences and Challenges*, London: Frank Cass.

UNDP, 1994, *Human Development Report 1994,* New York and Oxford: Oxford University Press.

Vincent, B. *et al.*, 1998, *Food Aid Performance Review: Performance Report*, Ottawa: Canadian International Development Agency.

The Changing Role of Food Aid and Finance for Food

EDWARD CLAY AND OLAV STOKKE

I. INTRODUCTION

1. *A Changed Environment: The International System and Trends in Aid Policy*

The last decade has seen fundamental changes taking place in international relations. The international system which is gradually replacing the bipolar system of the post-Second World War period is still in the making. Although important features may be identified, the emerging picture is complex and contains ambiguities. The situation is characterised by mounting globalisation, particularly in the economic field, driven by a revolution in technology and communications. Within some fields, military power in particular, the US hegemonic status has become more transparent and more widely recognised than before. Although a hegemony within this core area will have a spill-over to other areas of international politics, this is the case only to a certain degree. Much of the so-called globalisation materialises within regional confines. An important characteristic of regionalism is that it tends to countervail global hegemony by a single power.

The end of the Cold War has not led to a more stable world system – removing tensions and violent conflicts. Indeed, to a certain degree, the opposite appears to have been the case. Although the old bipolar system tended to extend the East–West conflict to the South through the support provided by the superpowers to their clients, fuelling violent conflicts (often conflict by proxies), the opposite was also the case: because of the fear of escalation, conflicts were prevented from erupting into violence. With the disintegration of the Soviet bloc and its hegemonic power, old conflicts that had been contained within the bipolar system surfaced, often with a cultural basis (ethnic nationalism). 'New' conflict patterns have come to the fore: whereas previously conflicts between states attracted most attention, a large number of low-level conflicts within states, some of a high intensity, have become the focus of attention. Intra-state war is increasingly seen as a major threat to development and human security. As noted, experiences – in Europe and in the South – have demonstrated that violent conflicts may, in the course of weeks, destroy material resources that have taken generations to build, cause immense human suffering, make millions of innocent people refugees in their own or neighbouring countries, cause states to collapse and wreck societies [*Stokke, 1997: 196*].[1]

Economically, aspects of globalisation include the continuing liberalisation of international trade and the rapid growth of global financial markets. All are underpinned by the minimally regulated communications system that permits 24-hour trading and quickly spreads news of extreme events – economic shock, natural disaster, political violence. The liberalisation process also involves a shift to more wholly market-based economic activity, with declining state intervention at the national level. These changes have been more far-reaching in many developing countries of the 'South' and the 'economies in transition' of the former Soviet bloc. Institutionally, the process of liberalisation has been given form in the ratification of the GATT Uruguay Round. That agreement resulted in the transformation of GATT into the World Trade Organisation (WTO), which had its first meeting in Singapore in December 1996. The full implications of these changes are yet to become clear in terms of the breadth of the liberalisation process or the full impact on inter-state economic relationships.

Another trend is the search by Western industrial countries for greater policy coherence *vis-à-vis* the developing countries. These efforts go beyond the field of development co-operation; they include macroeconomic policies, trade, export credits, direct investments, agriculture, the environment, migration (including policy on refugees), the arms trade and drugs. The issue was put strongly on the agenda by the high-level meeting of the Development Assistance

---

1. For an overview of violent conflicts during the period 1990–95, see Smith *et al.* [*1997*], who counted 93 wars, involving 70 states, with about 5.5 million people killed. They observed that these wars only rarely produced disasters that take a whole nation to despair and destruction. Wars simply continue; it is difficult to know when they have begun and when they ended. Cease-fires and peace agreements are more often made than honoured. Most wars are fought with relatively low technology, and most casualties are civilians – about three-quarters. As we all have observed (not least in the former Yugoslavia), there are exceptions to this general picture! See also Chapter 5.

Committee (DAC) of the Organisation of Economic Co-operation and Development (OECD) in 1991 [*OECD, 1992:31 ff*]. However, centrifugal forces are also at play, related, in particular, to conflicting interests within and between states and regions [*Forster and Stokke, 1999*].

This transformation of the international system is also affecting *aid policy* in various important ways. One of the previous superpowers has disappeared as a provider of development assistance, with serious consequences for its clients in the South who, in addition, have lost both political support and a market for their exports. The disintegration of the USSR has transformed several of its component units into aid recipients, competing with the South for shrinking aid resources. As for the other superpower, an important component of its rationale for providing development assistance has disappeared: as noted, US aid had from the very beginning been driven by security interests [*Griffin, 1991; Lancaster, 1993; Zimmerman and Hook, 1996*]. This may explain the decline of US development assistance from a level that already in the 1980s was low compared with other OECD countries, in terms of official development assistance (ODA) as a percentage of GNP. However, as argued elsewhere [*Stokke, 1996*], for some Western small and middle powers, developmental objectives have been, and still remain, the primary motive for providing aid. Such objectives are closely related to the humanitarian imperative, as expressed in relief operations. Consequently, their ODA has not declined to the same extent – if at all. However, 'the ethical imperative' has also always been an important basis for the remaining superpower in providing development assistance beyond its rhetoric. Nevertheless, the general trend in the 1990s has been one of declining total ODA – in absolute and relative terms.

In the 1990s, development assistance increasingly became an instrument for promoting policy reform in developing countries. To some extent, aid has always been used as an instrument for promoting the national interests of the donor country; as noted, this used to apply, in particular, to the major powers. In the 1980s, intervention in the domestic politics of developing countries, using aid as a tool, was no longer restricted to the major powers. Gradually the whole donor community adopted this approach, with particular reference to first generation conditionality: reform of economic policy was set, openly and transparent, as a condition for aid. The Bretton Woods institutions were in the driving seat. In the 1990s, triggered by the disintegration of 'the Second World', the scope has broadened. Second generation conditionality has brought systemic reforms as well as reforms within major policy areas to the fore as conditions for providing aid [*Stokke, 1995*]. This trend towards growing intervention in the internal policy of developing countries has been highly controversial from both normative and instrumental perspectives. However, although the parallel emphasis on 'participation' and 'ownership' may indicate the opposite, this approach has dominated the aid policy of bilateral and multilateral donors in the 1990s and rules the ground into the new millennium.

In the early 1990s, a change gradually took place in the objectives set for aid and the emphasis given to the various concerns. Whereas 'traditional' objectives – economic and social development, with an emphasis on poverty alleviation – were predominant in the early 1980s, with 'the ecological imperative' added in the second part of the decade ('sustainable development'), the 1990s experienced a proliferation of aid objectives: promotion of human rights, democracy, good governance. These 'new' objectives were brought to the fore, and were pursued through the policy of aid conditionality as well as through so-called positive measures: support for internal processes and purposes within developing countries that were assumed to attain these objectives. The traditional development objectives were in no way discarded; poverty alleviation has never before been given so much emphasis in the rhetoric of most if not all bilateral and multilateral providers of development assistance. The new concerns were simply added. In a situation where total aid was declining, this was bound to influence the actual distribution of aid negatively from the perspective of the 'traditional' objectives [*Stokke, 1995, 1996*].

Humanitarian action is a complex and highly controversial subject area. It includes issues such as protection and peacekeeping that are outside the scope of this volume, which focuses primarily on food related concerns. Humanitarian aid, more narrowly defined, with the primary objective of meeting immediate needs resulting from manmade and natural disasters, has from the very beginning been part of the official development assistance (ODA) or aid as defined and reported. However, the implementation of humanitarian aid, usually categorised as relief or emergency aid, has to some extent been administered by institutions separate from those responsible for longer-term development co-operation. The crises and conflicts of the 1990s affected quite substantially the balance between aid for 'development' and 'relief': a large and growing proportion was allocated to humanitarian aid, relief operations and refugees in particular. The so-called 'complex emergencies', involving also peacekeeping and even peace-restoring operations, affected this balance. Also the need for rehabilitation and reconstruction after a violent conflict has been contained tends to shift attention and resources away from 'traditional' long-term development objectives [*Stokke, 1997*].

2. The Changing Policy Context and Evolving Food Aid

Food aid has been a significant aspect of international humanitarian aid and development co-operation since the post-Second World War Marshall Plan [*Clay, 1995*]. Because food aid involves issues of trade and aid, and agricultural policy in donor as well as aid-recipient countries, it gave rise to international institutional arrangements that have grown more complex as the humanitarian aid objective has grown in importance. Apart from its own intrinsic significance as an aspect of aid policy and practice, it provides an important entry point for a far-reaching exploration of the implications of system transformation and change in aid policy.

Although food aid has been heavily affected by these changes, the general approach appears, as discussed below, to have been one of adaptation to immediate needs and 'practical problems' as they emerge. The more fundamental analysis of what these changes may imply for the theory and strategies underpinning food aid has more or less been absent from official policy discussion. The pressing need for institutional reform is part of this problematic. This represents one of the most important challenges with which food aid is confronted today.

The formulation and promotion of the concept of human security has been an important way in which the international community has sought to address broadening its agenda for development co-operation to include physical safety and a range of basic needs couched in terms of the human right to be free from insecurity [*UNDP, 1994*]. Food security, now usually understood to imply assuring both access to food and nutritional status, has been incorporated into this wider conceptualisation of security for vulnerable people. Human security therefore provides a framework within which both the humanitarian and developmental objectives of aid can be considered together. The underlying assumption of this re-examination of food aid is that the focus needs to be broadened to include the wider concept of human security of which food security constitutes an important part.

In the wake of the transformation of the international system, human security has been affected in many different ways, with a direct bearing on food security and food aid policy:

(i) Both human security and food security more narrowly have been affected by the disintegration of the former Soviet bloc and its core power: this applies, in particular, to several of the former Soviet republics and Russia itself, Eastern Europe and, most recently, North Korea. The more or less immediate response from multilateral and bilateral aid agencies has been the provision of large-scale humanitarian assistance, food aid in particular.

(ii) The 1990s have experienced violent conflicts of a magnitude and a cruelty that have shocked the whole world. In many of these, traditional sources of conflict have been reinforced by cultural dimensions (ethnicity, religion). Millions have been able to watch these events directly on their television screens. The human suffering caused by conflicts in Africa (the Great Lakes region, the Sudan, the Horn of Africa, and Liberia) has been displayed. Similar horrors have been transmitted from other continents, including Europe, where events in the former Yugoslavia have attracted most attention. The response from the international community to these man-made catastrophes has been the supply of humanitarian aid, including food aid, but also intervention with peacekeeping and peace-enforcing forces. These complex emergencies have confronted those who have intervened with challenges that they were ill prepared to tackle. In 'traditional' conflicts between states, the parties to the conflict could easily be identified and the leadership approached. In contrast, in these new conflicts the conflicting parties were not easily identified and their structures including those of their leadership were often fragmented.

(iii) An increasing share of total development assistance has, consequently, been provided as humanitarian aid – for relief operations and refugees in particular. This also affected the balance between food aid for development and food aid for relief: a growing share has gone to relief operations. Natural disasters, such as those associated with El Niño events in 1991/92 and again in 1997/98, further reinforced this trend.

(iv) As noted, aid programmes came under severe budgetary pressure in the 1990s. Some donor countries reduced their aid; this included countries that traditionally have been the main providers of food aid, the US in particular. Canada and Australia also cut back on their food aid commitments. These developments, when combined with a price spike for cereals in 1995/96, resulted in a sharp decline in food aid, whether measured in volumetric (tonnes of food) or value terms, to the lowest levels since the Marshall Plan began in 1947/48.

Finally, there is an attempt to find fresh institutional arrangements as part of the wider move to increase the accountability and transparency of aid in general and, as noted, to base international public action on human rights [*ODI, 1999a;1999b*]. These moves are themselves part of a global tendency to emphasise the responsibilities of governments and their need for accountability, in which civil society institutions, and formal charters of rights and good practice are important [*e.g. Gellner, 1992*].

3. The Challenges Ahead

In this chapter, we seek to identify the main challenges ahead. During the last six to seven years, concern about the impact and efficiency of food aid and finance for food has resulted in a considerable accumulation of evidence, including joint donor and individual agency-sponsored studies.[2] Several of the authors contributing to this volume have been associated with these evaluations and the follow-up. The combination of all these changes and the evaluative evidence offers an opportunity for synthesising experience and exploring the implications for the role of food aid and other ways in which the international community finances food assistance, and to consider more closely the implications for future institutional arrangements.

The main challenge, identified above, may be split into the following more specific questions:

(i) In the 1990s, what major changes have taken place in the international food aid policy, as stated and implemented, including the financing of food aid?

(ii) To what extent are these changes a temporary phenomenon or of a more lasting nature, reflecting fundamental changes in the international policy environment and, in particular, changes that have taken place within aid policy as such?

---

2. These include in particular the Tripartite Evaluation of the World Food Programme by Canada, the Netherlands and Norway [*Chr. Michelsen Institute, 1993*], the Joint Evaluation of EU Programme Food Aid for the Working Group of EU Evaluators, 1996 [*Clay et al., 1996*], the Joint Evaluation of the Rwanda Relief Operation by DANIDA and others [*Eriksson et al., 1996*]. In addition, there have been important evaluations by the European Commission, several European bilateral agencies as well as the Australian Development Assistance Bureau [*ADAB, 1997*], the Canadian International Development Agency [*Vincent et al., 1998*] and USAID [*McClelland, 1997*]. There have also been reviews of other major emergency operations including several on responses to the southern African drought in 1992/93 [*Benson and Clay, 1998b*] and of the European Commission Humanitarian Office by the EU Court of Auditors [*1997*]. The response to Hurricane Mitch devastation in the Caribbean in 1998 is, at the time of writing, about to unleash another round of evaluations, audits and assessment meetings.

(iii) To what extent have institutions established to meet past challenges, particularly the international organisations and arrangements within this particular area, been adapted to the new policy environments? Is there a need for fundamental institutional reform?

In Section II, the language used is briefly explained. As noted in our previous joint effort to analyse some major issues within this policy area [*Clay and Stokke, 1991: 1*], words may mean different things, varying with the context and the user. The main concepts and definitions are explained and some of the confusions involved identified. The changes within this high-profiled policy area have taken place so fast and are therefore not yet widely appreciated. In Section III, a documentation of the major changes is therefore provided. This serves as the basis both for the description and discussion that follow in this chapter and as a common reference framework for the discussions taking place in other chapters of the present volume. In Section IV, it is noted how food aid has become an increasingly uncertain resource. In Section V, it is argued that institutional reform, with particular reference to the international delivery system, is long overdue.

II. CONCEPTS, DEFINITIONS AND POLICY

So far food aid and food assistance have been discussed as if these were fully understood concepts with no ambiguities. But that is far from the case. The World Food Programme's Interfais and the Food and Agriculture Organisation (FAO) have international responsibility for reporting food aid flows in physical terms (tonnes of food) and the OECD Development Assistance Committee (DAC) reports food aid as an aid resource in monetary terms. These bodies have all experienced increasing difficulty in reporting food aid as a separate category of aid, which indicates the need to give careful consideration to what is meant by food aid, food assistance, food security or human security (see Box 1.1). Our intention here is to identify how the main actors are defining the core concepts involved, with particular reference to variations in their language, and not to establish the ultimate concepts.

Box 1.1
Is This Food Aid?

Three examples of food-related aid to three recipient countries from three donors illustrate the problem of determining what is food aid and the ambiguity of official food aid statistics.

Bangladesh. The European Commission uses its Food Security, formerly Food Aid, budget lines to support Bangladesh's Integrated Food Assisted Development Project (IFADP) in three ways. The IFADP is itself part of wider donor support to the nationwide Food-for-Work (FFW) programme. EU aid meets some of IFADP costs with financial aid. Imported wheat is also supplied to the Ministry of Food which makes available an equivalent quantity, part of which is sold to meet IFADP costs and part released to be distributed directly as FFW wages. FAO and the WFP report only the imported wheat as food aid, and thus the EU switch to financial support for Bangladesh's major food assistance programme is recorded statistically as a decline in food aid tonnage.

Burkina Faso. A Deutsche Gesellschaft für Technische Zusammenarbeit (GTZ) food security project finances the local purchase of grains to replenish a government food security reserve from which grains are sold. The WFP reports this as project food aid at the time of purchase. FAO in its statistical publications reports only international food shipments as food aid and so the switch from donor-funded imports to local purchases is reflected as a decline in food aid.

Zimbabwe. In 1992–93, the World Bank financed drought-related maize imports by making an International Development Association (IDA) Emergency Recovery Loan. The Maize Marketing Board was required to tender openly for each import contract under IDA procurement rules. DAC, FAO and the WFP do not report these transactions as food aid.

The ways in which food aid is defined have important policy implications in terms of objectives and outcomes, as well as for donor public expenditure. For countries eligible for development aid, there are also resource-transfer, budgetary and programmatic implications. The definitions adopted also have profound implications for policy analysis.

The objectives of international development co-operation within this policy area have broadened, first of all from providing food as a development resource to supporting *wider notions of food security.* This wider concept implies ensuring not only availability and stability of supply but also access to food. The shift in emphasis is fully signalled in the declarations of recent international meetings convened by the UN, notably the World Food Summit in 1995 [*FAO, 1996a*].[3] It is also reflected in the academic literature [*Maxwell, 1996*]. These declarations are described more fully from a human rights perspective by Wenche Barth Eide in Chapter 14.

Severe local or national short-term threats to food availability, usually a crisis at national level, or to vulnerable groups' access to food, are problems of *acute* food insecurity. These problems may be *transitory*, that is, associated with an environmental or economic shock, or may persist as a so-called continuing emergency, especially in a conflict situation. *Chronic* food insecurity is a continuing long-term problem caused by the inability of vulnerable households to have access to adequate levels of food for normal bodily functioning and human development. This problem is fundamentally intertwined with problems of poverty and inadequate livelihoods.[4]

In an environment of risks, uncertainty and rapid change in the 1990s, food aid and other assistance are, as noted above, increasingly organised as part of efforts to assure *human security* in terms of *livelihoods, food, health, a sustainable environment and personal and political security.* That is why this volume adopts the wider framework of human security rather than a narrower food security concept for examining the role of *food aid.* But as the editors recognised in the introduction to the previous volume, it is also critically important to be clear about what is meant by food aid [*Clay and Stokke, 1991: 1*].

A frequent source of confusion in writing about food aid is the need to distinguish between *interventions* that involve providing food directly or subsidising food purchases and food aid as a form of *aid transfer.* For that reason the FAO [*1996b*], in one of its background

---

3.   The definition of food security adopted by the World Food Summit, reflecting the current widely accepted emphasis on access rather than availability and food as a right rather than a 'need', is: 'the right of everyone to have access to safe and nutritious food, consistent with the right to adequate food and the fundamental right of everyone to be free from hunger.' Maxwell and colleagues [*Smith et al., 1992*] identified around two hundred definitions or implied definitions of food security since the concept first became widely used in the mid-1970s, underlining the ambiguous and evolving nature of this construct and the issues being addressed.
4.   The distinctions between acute, transitory and chronic food insecurity were first made in the widely cited study of poverty and hunger by the World Bank [*1986*].

papers for the World Food Summit (WFS), makes an explicit distinction between *food assistance* and international *food aid.*

Food assistance has historically provided, and continues to provide, a way of addressing both transitory and chronic food insecurity. This assistance may involve the direct provision of food to be consumed on-site, such as intensive or supplementary feeding and school meals, or take-home food or wages in kind as well as rations. The United States, uniquely amongst developed industrialised countries, uses Food Stamps, coupons exchangeable for a range of food purchases, as its major form of social assistance [*Gough et al.,1997*], and this form of intervention has been followed in a few developing countries. Food assistance also includes subsidisation linked to food, such as fair price shops and canteens, and more indirectly through market interventions to influence prices and assure supplies to consumers. It may be largely internally funded as in India, or supported by internationally sourced food and financial aid as in Bangladesh or Ethiopia. The role of food assistance in providing relief in an emergency, and in the rehabilitation of affected peoples and regions, is generally accepted; such actions are supported by internationally sourced food and financial aid from public funds and private charities. The role of food assistance in combating chronic food insecurity and thereby contributing to poverty reduction or promoting human development, involving both direct and indirect forms, is more controversial. For example, the FAO's main background paper for the World Food Summit envisaged a quite restricted role for food assistance in complementing other poverty reduction and agricultural development measures to address world hunger [*FAO, 1996b*]. In contrast, the WFP in a separate background paper for the WFS envisaged a considerably wider role for food assistance and food aid, because of the special advantages of food in targeting the 'hungry poor' and women in particular [*WFP, 1996*].

Food aid, as conventionally defined and reported as part of the activities of bilateral development co-operation agencies, multilateral institutions and NGOs, is commodity aid used to support food assistance actions in aid-eligible countries and also to fund general development through the provision of balance-of-payments support by substituting for commercial imports or budgetary support from sales revenue. Such aid may, therefore, be only indirectly related to or, some might argue, not intended to assist specific groups or consumers more generally through the medium of food. Most controversially, it may be politically motivated to a conflict-immersed regime, as during the Vietnam War [*Wallerstein, 1980*] or Central America in the 1980s

[*Garst and Barry, 1990*]. Food aid transfers meet the DAC criteria for official development assistance – grants or loans with at least 25 per cent concessionality, intended for developmental or humanitarian purposes and organised by development co-operation agencies. In addition, the historical origins of food aid in agricultural surplus disposal have resulted in further regulatory and definitional complexities. Food aid, for the purposes of the Food Aid Convention (FAC) and reporting to the FAO Committee on Surplus Disposal [*FAO, 1980*], implies that the donor or its agent acquires the commodities at some point in the transfer process. Food aid as currently defined therefore includes three forms of commodity aid: *direct aid* – food acquired on the donor's internal market or internationally on open markets; *triangular transactions* where the food is acquired from developing country sources other than the beneficiary country or country of use; and *local purchases* where the donor's agent acquires food for humanitarian or developmental purposes in the country of use.

A second source of confusion is the distinction between food aid in kind and financial aid to fund food assistance or food security activities. Currently the DAC and Food Aid Convention (FAC) definitions of food aid include all of the above categories but exclude financial aid tied to importing food, such as the World Bank Emergency Recovery Loans (see Box 1.1), or financing additional food import costs by countries drawing on the International Monetary Fund's (IMF) Commodity Contingency Financing Fund (CCFF). Food imports financed by credits from the exporting governments and their agents, such as the US Export Enhancement Programme or EU export restitutions, are also normally excluded.[5] Some analysts, for example, Shaw and Singer [*1996*], have argued that all such transactions should be regarded as 'grey' food aid because of the substantial element of concessionality involved. With some exporters providing both food aid and export credits, often in packages of assistance blended with a mix of humanitarian, developmental, foreign policy and trade motives, there is undoubtedly a considerable grey area. This is an important issue when considering the wider economic developmental implications of food aid and also the food security implications, where both food aid as conventionally defined and concessional agricultural exports have

---

5. In exceptional circumstances where these agricultural budget lines have been used to provide assistance on a wholly grant basis, for instance, EU exports to the former Soviet republics in the early 1990s, these transactions have been reported by the WFP and FAO, but not the DAC, as aid [*Benson and Clay, 1998a*]. However, there has been concern about the legality of such actions [*European Court of Auditors, 1994*]. See also Box 1.3 on US food aid.

supported direct food assistance (rationing), as well as indirect assistance through price subsidisation and stock measures.

Recognising that there are different transactions constituting food aid, these can, in practice, be grouped into three broad categories:

– *Relief food aid*, which is targeted and freely distributed to victims of natural and man-made disasters. This aid is also variously called emergency or humanitarian food aid.
– *Programme food aid*, which involves commodities provided directly to a recipient government or its agent for sales on local markets to generate local-currency counterpart funds (CPFs), usually under the control of the recipient government but with some form of agreement with the donor about their management and use.
– *Project food aid*, which is provided on a grant basis to targeted groups to support specific developmental activities.

These categories are widely accepted, as reflected in the reporting of food aid by the WFP's Interfais, the primary data source for food aid operations [*Jost, 1991*]. Both relief and project food aid are usually, but not necessarily, channelled by donor governments through the WFP or international NGOs.

Monetisation, involving the sale of imported commodities to generate local currency, is a term often used to describe actions undertaken by NGOs or the WFP as part of projects in which sales proceeds are used either for specific non-food project expenditures or in-country costs of handling and delivering food aid. Some projects supported by the receipts from food aid sales also do not involve any form of direct *food assistance* to targeted beneficiaries.[6] The boundary lines between such actions and programme aid are contingent and institutionally defined, and not based on theoretically clear distinctions.

The categorisation of individual food aid actions and their aggregation at donor agency level (Appendix Table A1.1) or for recipient countries (Appendix Table A1.2) depend on donor declarations in reporting. For example, the food security actions by the GTZ in Sahelian countries are reported as project aid (see Box 1.1 and also Chapter 12). The large-scale and long-term supply of dairy commodities under Operation Flood in India involved sales to the Indian National Dairy Development Corporation, but because the use of the

---

6. In financial year 1998 almost 40 per cent of US development food aid as channelled through NGOs was monetised, making this use of project food aid a substantial element of official support for the development activities of the US based voluntary sector [*USAID, 1999*].

funds was restricted to dairy development this was reported as 'project food aid' rather than sectoral or programme aid.[7]

The distinction between relief aid and programme aid is also sometimes unclear. A case in point is North Korea where the government controls food distribution in one of the few remaining centrally planned economies. Emergency aid is being provided over several years in response to a 'continuing crisis'[*Bennett, 1999*]. Statistical reporting reflects the way in which donors choose to channel and report their aid to North Korea, as bilateral programme aid in the case of China and Japan or through the WFP as relief aid in the case of South Korea and the United States (Appendix Tables A1.1 and A1.2).

Part of the increasing difficulty in categorising food aid arises from the attempts to achieve more flexibility in its uses as tied commodity aid or finance tied by the funding agency to food to be acquired by an operational agency such as the WFP or a NGO. The WFP developed the practice of commodity exchanges or *swaps*, where it organised the import of food for emergency or project use. The imported food was then either exchanged by a barter arrangement or sold and the proceeds used to purchase food for use in assistance schemes [*Relief and Development Institute, 1990*]. US private voluntary organisations (PVOs or NGOs) have even, by means of lobbying, obtained the possibility of third country monetisation in which funds generated by sales in one country can be used for development activities in another country. These actions are categorised as food aid to the country in which the funds are spent.

This brief survey conveys, first of all, that there is no agreed definition of the core concept involved. Several actors are involved, each with a perspective, an agenda and a method of working of its own. These particulars tend to influence not only the language but also definitions. Even global statistics is affected: as noted, what is reported as food aid varies from one agency to another. That is why it is necessary to distinguish between the various actors and their different foci as well as between the various forms of assistance that are subsumed under the notion of food aid. The subtlety of some of the concepts established, even involving major agencies, is not easily grasped by 'outsiders'; thus, when FAO [*1996b*] distinguishes

---

7. Doornbos *et al.* [*1991*] provide a brief account of Operation Flood, whilst an in-depth analysis of this large and complex aid-assisted programme for dairy development is provided in Doornbos *et al.* [*1990*]. The only element of food assistance that the prices of dairy products ranging from fresh milk to ice cream were *de facto* almost continuously subsidised for consumers, a large proportion of whom were urban and middle income households; and this became a subject of criticism in donor evaluations.

between 'food assistance' and 'food aid', it could create confusion in the broader community concerned with development co-operation, where 'aid' and 'assistance' are used more or less synonymously. However, it is highlighting a central distinction between actions or interventions which are limited to food intended to assist specific categories of people and food as commodity aid, which may be provided for a variety of purposes which the donor declares to be 'developmental' or humanitarian. When using the core concept of food aid, its various forms and contexts therefore become important. Instead of attempting to come up with an 'ultimate' definition of the concept, we have chosen to describe these various contexts and main forms. When using the core concept ourselves, care is taken to provide the context if a need for precision is deemed necessary, with particular reference to 'food aid in kind' and 'finance for food' and the purposes for which that aid is provided.

For this reason we have explicitly recognised the broad range of humanitarian and developmental purposes for which food aid and finance for food may be provided − human security rather than food security. Humanitarian assistance and the ways in which it is provided necessarily involve issues of personal security (see Chapters 5, 6, 13 and 15). The issue of food security cannot be divorced from that of livelihood security, poverty and health. There are issues of differential access, bound up with culture, gender and age. Even food security as defined and translated into broad goals for action by the World Food Summit is concerned not just with hunger and undernutrition [*FAO, 1996a*], but with issues of choice which are socio-culturally influenced. These complex and overlapping concerns were reflected in the UNDP's promotion of the concept of human security [*UNDP, 1994*].

III. FOOD AID IN DECLINE

This policy area has always had a high profile. This can be explained by the media interest in humanitarian disasters, caused by man or nature, and in the response of the international community in the form of relief operations and humanitarian assistance. It can also be explained by the fact that the US has been a major donor of food aid and that this type of aid has accounted for a large share of its development assistance; the policy and activities of a superpower attract particular attention by the media. From the Marshall Plan era up to the early 1970s, food aid accounted for around 25 per cent of US development assistance. However, since the early 1970s, food aid as a share of total ODA has declined, in recent years quite dramatically, from around 16

TABLE 1.1
FLOW OF FINANCIAL RESOURCES AND FOOD AID TO DEVELOPING COUNTRIES
($ BILLION)

	Total ODA	Total food aid	Food aid as % of ODA
1965	5.9	1.5	25
1975	13.6	2.2	16
1985	29.4	3.1	11
1995	58.9	2.3	4

Source: OECD, Development Co-operation Reports (various).

per cent of total aid to about 4 per cent by the mid-1990s (Table 1.1). In part, this decline can be explained by the general reduction in ODA by the US. A downward trend is also discernible in EU Community Action food aid: this declined from 26 per cent of total EU aid organised by the Commission in 1986 to 11 per cent in 1995. However, when food aid and humanitarian aid, which included much of what was previously reported as food aid, are combined, their share had fallen only from 29 to 26 per cent of EU aid during this period [*Cox and Koning, 1997*].

Several factors affect the volume of food aid – in terms of food deliveries and finance for food – as measured by traditional parameters, tonnes and value in US dollars, and its relative share (percentage of ODA) within a donor country as well. Some of these factors are related to the international environment, others to developments within the donor country concerned. Some factors are related to the demand side; however, most belong to the supply side. These various concerns are interwoven, and the rhetoric of the main actors on the donor side is seldom the best guide to the real concerns involved. As indicated, food aid is also part and parcel of the foreign and trade policy of the donor country and used as an instrument to attain long-term foreign policy objectives that belong to different policy areas, as well as immediate declared objectives of relief and development.

Changes in the volume of food aid in kind related to *the supply side* reflect the donor's agricultural policy, and the wider international trade regime as well as climatic variability. For some individual donors such as the US, Japan and Norway, domestic agricultural policy is a separable, relatively unambiguous construct. However, the EU involves one Community-funded and 15 national food aid programmes, all within a single market and within the framework of the Common Agricultural Policy, but national governments still have, as discussed below, some flexibility on levels and sources of food aid. The dominant market position of the US makes it difficult to separate domestic and international influences as mediated through prices. The donors are largely Northern, temperate zone agricultural economies in which weather patterns are, according to current understanding, only weakly related to the dominant forcing mechanism affecting most poor, Southern countries, the El Nino-Southern Oscillation (ENSO) phenomenon. But the important exceptions not affected by ENSO include China, India and Russia, potentially the largest importers, so there could be supply-demand interactions.

There is the further difficulty in knowing when, in the late Alec Cairncross's phrase, 'a bend is a trend'. Except with the benefit of hindsight, it is difficult to distinguish when analysing recent changes those that reflect short-term influences clearly expressed through international price variability, as discussed below especially in Chapter 4, from more sustained developments that may be shaped by declining agricultural protection implied in the GATT-WTO process (Chapter 3).

These comments have taken a single donor country as the point of departure, focusing on economic processes and market mechanisms. Foreign policy concerns of a donor country may 'overrule' domestic agricultural policy and market mechanisms. Thus, if a partner in a security policy arrangement is affected by a crisis that threatens the well-being of its people (or the position of a friendly government), food aid may be supplied by partners almost regardless of the costs involved. Similarly with other crises that involve human misery, caused by conflicts or natural disasters; donor governments will act on their own or may be pressed to act by humanitarian organisations and a public opinion that is informed through the media and demands immediate action.

It follows that *the demand side* also affects the volume of food aid. As noted, man-made and natural disasters do not necessarily appear with any regularity; this type of demand-driven food aid will therefore vary over time. However, in some regions and countries, human security is increasingly recognised as a more or less permanent concern. Food scarcity and undernutrition loom high in this context, but also conflicts that flare up from time to time add to the misery. 'Small' conflicts in the periphery seldom attract the attention of international media and if they occasionally should catch the headlines, they do not remain there for long. Donors are therefore not reminded of the need for humanitarian assistance, including food aid, to the same extent as for the more spectacular disasters. And there is some support for this view from statistical and budgetary analysis of the way a few major crises have influenced food aid volumes [*Benson and Clay, 1998a*].

However, the institutionalisation of food aid in kind may contribute to a more 'stable' demand side request involving, in particular, international agencies and private voluntary organisations with an emphasis on development activities rather than relief operations.

Against this background therefore, and emphasising the always provisional nature of any answers, we pose the questions: what changes have taken place in international food aid in recent years and how can they be explained?

1. Variability and Then a Steep Decline in Food Aid in the Mid-1990s

First there was the era (prior to 1972) when US food aid programmes were generally also major instruments for agricultural market management and surplus disposal. Then in the 1970s there was a massive decline during the 'World Food Crisis' and afterwards a recovery also involving Europe and Japan to a greater extent as donors. Food aid to developing countries was relatively stable during the 1980s (Figure 1.1). Fluctuations reflected a combination of price effects on the US and Canadian programmes in particular, which are budgeted well ahead in financial rather than physical commitments. From the late 1970s other instruments, in particular Export Enhancement Programmes, came to play the major role in surplus disposal and market management. Globally food aid, including transfers to Eastern Europe and the former Soviet republics, peaked again in the early 1990s. These actions coincided with crisis measures in favour of sub-Saharan Africa, and the prevalence of easy market conditions and large stocks.

In the mid-1990s food aid levels declined far more sharply than those of development aid more generally, making food aid now a relatively marginal feature of development co-operation overall, perhaps 4 per cent of aid from the OECD countries collectively and within the budgets of most individual DAC members.[8] Even countries such as Canada and the US have seen the share of their aid budgets attributable to food aid decline significantly between the mid-1980s and mid-1990s, from 15 per cent and 19 per cent to 9 per cent and 12 per cent respectively. In these circumstances the future of food aid has appeared to be in question. Certainly, as discussed below, overall levels seem uncertain.

---

8. There are problems of completeness and double counting in individual donor reporting of food aid expenditure, especially emergency aid and finance for developing country purchases and attribution of EU Community Action, and these estimates must be regarded as highly approximate [*Clay et al., 1996*].

FIGURE 1.1

SHIPMENTS OF CEREALS FOOD AID, 1970/71–1998/99 (IN MILLION TONNES)

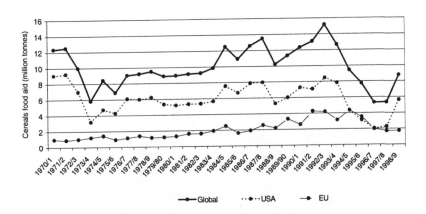

2. From Programme Aid to Relief

Historically programme aid has been dominant, accounting for around three-quarters of all food aid in the 1960s and close to 60 per cent in terms of cereal commodities up to the mid-1990s (Figure 1.2). Levels then dropped precipitately. This was due in part to tighter commodity availability. But policy changes, especially on the part of the EU and its member states as well as Canada, to give lower priority to this form of aid, are reflected in reduced levels and some countries putting an end to programme food aid. By 1998, only the US and Japan (the latter because of North Korea) were substantial providers of programme food aid (see Appendix Table A1.1). Project aid represented around 20 per cent of food aid, largely provided by the WFP and the US or internationally based NGOs, and constituting a relatively stable element in the picture. In the mid-1990s, quantities of project aid also contracted.

Food aid provided for relief has fluctuated with specific major crises, but has increased progressively in absolute quantities and relative terms over the last decade to become the major component of food aid. Reality and wider public perceptions have therefore converged, since media attention and press releases have always focused on the role of food aid in natural disasters and humanitarian crises.

31

FIGURE 1.2
GLOBAL FOOD AID DELIVERIES 1988–98

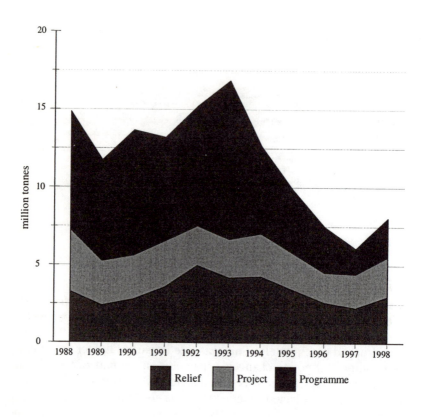

The WFP is the distributor of virtually all multilateral food aid. Its activities have mirrored the general trend of increasing emergency operations, and in consequence it has become operationally the single most important institution through its three functions: providing food aid, handling other donors' food aid and co-ordinating emergency logistics within this field. In contrast, its Regular Programme of development projects has declined steadily since the late 1980s (Figure 1.3).

FIGURE 1.3
DISTRIBUTION OF FOOD AID THROUGH THE WFP

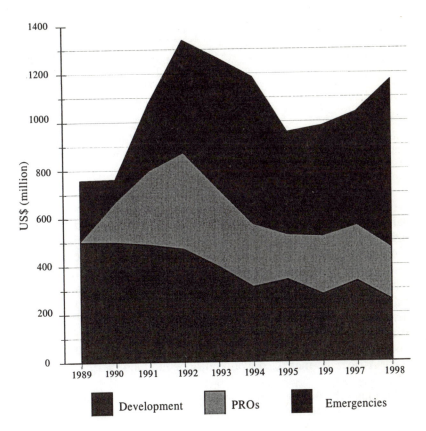

3. The Geographical Focus on 'Countries-in-Crisis'

Geographically, the focus of food aid shipments gradually shifted from Asia to sub-Saharan Africa during the 1980s and early 1990s (Table 1.2). This was in line with the increasing domestic cereal production of the larger Asian economies and their ability to finance imports commercially. In contrast, sub-Saharan Africa has experienced continuing prospects of problems in sustaining food production growth to keep pace with the population. Many countries in the region in which there is a potential gap in production and nutrition-related consumption needs are likely to find the funding of additional imports difficult (see Chapter 2).

TABLE 1.2
REGIONAL DISTRIBUTION OF FOOD AID ('000t – CEREALS IN GRAIN EQUIVALENT)

	SSA	NA/ME	S/E Asia	LA/Carib.	NIS/Eur.	Total
1989	2824	2701	3209	1995	359	11088
1993	3565	1149	1885	1913	7860	16372
1996	2532	728	2032	756	1441	7489
1998	2940	347	2920	980	846	8032

Note: SSA: Sub-Saharan Africa; NA/ME North Africa and Middle East; S/E Asia: South and East Asia; LA/Carib.: Latin America and the Caribbean; and NIS/Eur.: Newly Independent States and Europe.
Source: WFP Interfais.

Eastern Europe and the former Soviet republics were for a time the main recipients in the early 1990s, and the Balkans and Caucasus regions have continued to receive conflict-related humanitarian aid. Equally striking was the association of the end of civil conflicts in Central America, notably El Salvador, with a decline in US food aid to the regimes that it supported, and in EU food aid to Nicaragua. The response to Hurricane Mitch in 1998 is too recent to be fully documented as a possible temporary upward blip in food aid to Central America. All regions were affected by the general downward trend in food shipments in the mid-1990s and, apart from the Middle East and North Africa, the increased availability of food aid in 1998/99 (Table 1.2).

Although the discourse on international development aid often focuses on broad differences between regions in continental terms, Latin America or sub-Saharan Africa, a focus on individual recipient countries provides a more meaningful picture of food aid. Between the mid-1980s and early 1990s, the major part of global food aid has been provided to a relatively small number of recipients, with over 60 per cent going to just ten countries and a large number receiving small quantities (Table 1.3 and Appendix Table A1.2). This situation has remained relatively unchanged despite the decline in total aid since 1994. The only apparent discernible tendency is a slight decline in the significance of the largest recipients, with a smaller volume of aid being spread more thinly over more recipients.

TABLE 1.3
TOP TEN RECIPIENTS OF GLOBAL CEREAL FOOD AID

1985/86 Country	'000t	1990/91 Country	'000t	1996 Country	'000t	1998 Country	'000t
Egypt	1799	Egypt	1864	Bangladesh	678	Bangladesh	851
Bangladesh	1287	Bangladesh	1356	Ethiopia	477	Korea, DPR	711
Sudan	904	Ethiopia	894	Korea, DPR	476	Ethiopia	630
Ethiopia	793	Poland	742	Rwanda	339	Indonesia	500
Pakistan	384	Jordan	481	India	296	India	350
Sri Lanka	366	Romania	480	Georgia	283	Peru	262
China	290	Mozambique	454	Ex-Yugoslavia	227	Rwanda	250
El Salvador	278	Sudan	453	Armenia	215	Mozambique	239
India	257	Peru	371	Angola	207	Angola	220
Mozambique	252	Tunisia	348	China	170	Bolivia	217
Top 10 as a percentage of global tonnage	61		60		51		53
Total number of recipients	96		97		111		102

Sources: FAO; WFP Interfais.

The allocations to major recipients reflect, more clearly than wider regional trends, both recent and current emergencies and changes in donor political priorities (Table 1.3). Some long-term major recipients, notably Egypt, for 35 years the largest recipient, Sri Lanka and Tunisia have been almost phased out. In 1996, North Korea, the former Yugoslavia (including Bosnia), Rwanda, Armenia and Georgia were major recipients. In 1998, the effects of recent natural disasters are discernible in increased food aid to Bangladesh because of floods and to Bolivia because of drought-related El Niño. The US also responded to the economic crisis in Indonesia with programme food aid [*Poh et al., 1999*]. These major recipients also indicate smaller coherent regions in crisis – the Great Lakes region of Africa or the Caucasus – within which food aid is targeted on some countries for a combination of humanitarian and political reasons.

There are also some more consistently substantial recipients – Bangladesh, Ethiopia and India. In these countries, starting with crisis responses between 1966 and 1977, food aid for development has become institutionalised through both WFP project aid sustained by many bilateral donors and US-supported PVO projects over an extended period. It is not surprising, therefore, that a substantial part of the evaluation literature and other research studies concern project food aid in these three countries (see Chapter 8).

The large number of minor recipients is partly the consequence of the WFP's widespread portfolio which included over 80 countries in 1998, as well as the activities of US-based PVOs for which food aid has been the major public resource, and, to a lesser extent, European NGOs. These many minor recipients include a complex of different categories involving programme, project and humanitarian relief operations that are on a modest scale globally but are important regionally or locally for small countries. In sub-Saharan Africa programme aid is relatively important, for example, to Cape Verde, Comoros, Djibouti and Eritrea. Elements of the international humanitarian operation in the Great Lakes–Central African region occur in Tanzania, Uganda and Zambia as well as Rwanda (Appendix Table A1.2).

4. A Partial Shift from Commodity Aid to Finance for Food

There have also been changes in the sourcing of food aid. The trend of increased procurement of commodities in developing countries, which began in the 1980s [*Clay and Benson, 1991*], continued in the 1990s (Table 1.4). This form of procurement, as either triangular transactions or local purchases, doubled globally from 11 to 22 per cent of all deliveries between 1990 and 1996. North European donors are the main funders of developing country purchases. The European Commission also almost doubled its purchases from developing countries, the share increased from 11 to 27 per cent between 1990 and 1996. In contrast, major cereal exporters – Australia, Canada, France and the US – have continued to provide what is effectively tied food aid, sourcing their food aid directly on domestic markets. The provisions of the World Trade Agreement allow such tying of food aid (see Chapter 3).

The coming into force of the EU Single Market in the early 1990s has been an important factor in encouraging the shift from direct aid in kind (food deliveries) to developing country acquisition (partly combined food aid/finance for food) [*Clay et al., 1996*]. The regulations based on the Act require Community-wide tendering for larger contracts, and the scope for specific food industry interests to influence product selection is thus much reduced. For example, Denmark ceased to be a supplier of a range of processed animal products, shifting to WFP selecting commodites which are still tied to Danish sourcing [*Colding and Pinstrup-Andersen, 1999*]. Effectively tying aid can also continue, as in French cereals aid, by means of devices such as the narrow specification of commodities and stating the port of loading in a tender.

TABLE 1.4
FOOD AID DELIVERIES BY MODE OF DELIVERY

Donor	Direct Transfer ('000t)	%
Canada:		
1990	1010	97
1996	373	95
Denmark: (a)		
1990	na	na
1996	61	79
EU Community Action: (a)		
1990	1855	89
1996	1123	73
France:		
1990	127	96
1996	194	98
Germany: (a)		
1990	252	70
1996	31	11
Netherlands: (a)		
1990	24	19
1996	9	6
Norway: (a)		
1990	na	na
1996	14	30
Sweden: (a)		
1990	9	90
1996	5	6
UK: (a)		
1990	37	67
1996	11	10
USA:		
1990	5571	100
1996	3291	99
Global: (a)		
1990	9718	89
1996	5820	78

Note:
(a) There are discrepancies in the published data between the volume given for total food aid and those reported by delivery mode which are apparently incomplete.
Sources: WFP Interfais; FAO.

5. Emphasis on Human Security

Within this context, a number of potentially contradictory policy tendencies are observable for the use of quite limited resources. First, an increasing proportion of food aid is used as part of attempts to *provide human security* in situations of conflict and social breakdown, as in the Great Lakes region or the former Yugoslavia. Second, there is the well-established practice of using food aid as part of the response to natural disasters, such as drought, flood and hurricane, that disrupt food supply or create problems of access for affected people. Third, food aid is used to *counteract both the economic and human effects* of economic shocks, especially transition and structural adjustment, as in the cases of Indonesia and North Korea in the late 1990s. Fourth, there are attempts to concentrate food aid on more limited food security and poverty reduction projects for vulnerable groups, which all the major bilateral donors and the WFP have declared to be a high priority, for example in their statements to the 1996 World Food Summit.

IV. AN UNCERTAIN RESOURCE

Food aid is subject to two sources of uncertainty. First, there is the general uncertainty of aid being dependent on donor priorities. These reflect trends or fashions in aid, such as the decline during the 1990s in support for public sector agricultural research [*Pinstrup-Andersen and Pandya-Lorch, 1996; Bie, 1994*] and the return to favour of multi-component rural development projects [*Carney, 1999*] and the rise of micro-credit [*Marr, 1999*].

There is a second and specific source of uncertainty because of the strong connection of food aid with the agricultural supply situation in donor countries and international food market conditions. Supply-side fluctuations in availability may be anticipated, but they are difficult to predict with any precision, as is demonstrated by Konandreas and others in Chapter 3, and Benson in Chapter 4.

The Food Aid Convention (FAC) seeks to address these uncertainties by setting minimum annual obligations and rules for major cereal exporters and other DAC donors. The wider agricultural trade context of the Convention is considered in Chapters 3 and 4 and is only highlighted here. The FAC provided a floor well below actual food aid shipment levels between the mid-1970s and the early 1990s. After lower commitments were announced unilaterally by some signatories to the Convention, notably the US and Canada in 1995, overall shipments fell to, if not below, that floor in 1996/97 (Table 1.5). That year probably saw the lowest level of shipments in 50 years, and in 1997/98 total shipments of food aid remained close to minimum obligations.

TABLE 1.5
CEREALS FOOD AID SHIPMENTS AND FAC MINIMUM CONTRIBUTIONS

	FAC min contrib 1986–95 ('000t)	Cereals food aid as % of min contrib 1988/89–93/94 (%)	FAC min contrib 1995–1998 ('000t)	Cereals food aid as % of min contrib		
				1995/96 (%)	1996/97 (%)	1997/98 (%)
Canada	600	158	400	116	93	87
EU (of which):	1670	232	1755	156	112	97
Community Action	920	301	920	195	117	94
National Actions (a)	750	149	835	113	106	100
Norway	30	150	20	95	160	220
Sweden (a)	40	290	–	–	–	–
USA	4470	156	2500	124	81	90
Global	7517	175	5350	145	99	100

Note: (a) From 1995/96 Sweden plus Austria and Finland are included in EU National Actions.
Sources: IGC and WFP Interfais.

A major feature of food aid is the considerable short-term fluctuation in levels in line with cereal price movements, which is analysed in Chapter 4. This is largely an *ex post* phenomenon because some major donors, notable the US and Canada, budget in financial terms. Others like the EU have failed to compensate for higher indicative prices when making quantitative commitments for future years.[9] Now the widely recognised, and so partly predictable, relationship between grain prices and food aid shipments appears to have weakened further. This change appears to be partly a result of *ex ante* budgetary cuts [*Benson and Clay, 1998a*]. There is a shift in resources from commodity aid to financial assistance for food security, particularly by the European Commission under its 1996 policy reform which allows the use of food aid budget lines to provide finance for food security [*European Commission, 1996*].

What of other resources for financing food assistance in emergencies or in support of human development? These have not been subject to systematic assessment and cannot be readily quantified. Nevertheless, there is a discernible increase in willingness on the part of international and bilateral agencies to meet some of the additional food import costs of a natural disaster or economic shock with financial aid. The World Bank used highly concessional IDA Emergency Recovery Loans and agreed to reallocate already committed funds for

---

9.   See Benson and Clay [*1998a*] for a recent re-examination of this relationship. Benson in Chapter 4 confirms the past weakness of the link between FAC commitments and food aid levels.

this purpose in southern Africa in 1992/93 (see Chapter 7). The IMF's CCFF is little used because of its high costs and difficulties of access. The WTO process through the Marrakesh Decision draws attention to the role of food aid and other possible means of meeting additional food import costs of trade liberalisation, but so far there has been little that is new (see Chapter 3). Only by a survey of all programme aid and international financial institution operations for specific countries would it be possible to gain a clearer appreciation of the proportion of aid used to meet the public expenditure costs of food imports and supporting food assistance schemes. Because of problems of fungibility and other well-known difficulties in examining patterns of and trends in public expenditure, it will be difficult to find conclusive answers [*White, 1996*]. The available evidence suggests that assistance to food imports is overall usually a relatively small part of aid. There are two important exceptions: very small highly food import-dependent countries, and countries recently and severely affected by conflict or natural disaster [*Clay et al., 1996*].

There is a substantial food-related component in humanitarian assistance associated with logistics and protection as well as the actual food purchases regarded as food aid. Where there is a large, high-profile, politically significant emergency, the enhanced levels of resources are eventually, if not immediately, forthcoming [*Eriksson et al., 1998*]. The most recent examples in 1998 and 1999 were the responses to Hurricane Mitch and the Kosovo humanitarian crisis. Overall levels of such assistance are, therefore, sensitive to the scale and character of the major humanitarian crises of the moment. Thus there appears to have been a downward trend in overall relief expenditure in the mid-1990s reflecting the phasing down of some major operations that were part of the legacy of the collapse of communist regimes, ex-Yugoslavia included (Figure 1.4). The politically contingent and narrowly crisis-related nature of most humanitarian aid implies an additional element of uncertainty in resources for agencies preparing against future emergencies. There is a second problem of the financing of reconstruction or continuing relief for those displaced by crisis, which comes out of different budget lines and even from different agencies, as discussed by Kracht in Chapter 5 and Shoham *et al.* in Chapter 6.

These developments are indicative of an increasingly difficult situation in which many of the humanitarian and development activities supported historically can no longer be resourced with international food aid. Issues of international commitments and priorities have to be resolved either constructively by co-operation, or by default, as the aggregate of individual bilateral donor decisions. The appropriate basis for such decisions would appear to be a careful consideration of the cumulative body of evidence on where food aid has or has not been effective. Is food aid in kind a comparatively efficient way of addressing specific needs for international assistance? What are the nature and likely scale of the problems that it could efficiently and effectively address? These issues are taken up by Shoham *et al.* for humanitarian aid (Chapter 6), Pillai for project aid (Chapter 8), and Faaland *et al.* (Chapter 9) and Schulthes (Chapter 10) focusing on the WFP.

FIGURE 1.4
TOTAL DAC EMERGENCY AID 1990–97

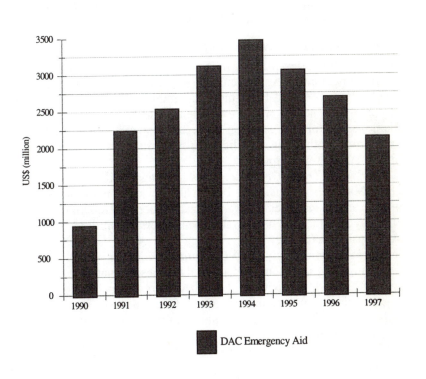

V. INSTITUTIONAL ARRANGEMENTS FOR FOOD AID

There have been few changes in the institutional arrangements of food aid, in Europe or internationally, despite all these changes in the political environments, its sources and use, and the increasing scrutiny of performance. Most of the basic modalities and arrangements reflect a process of adaptation in the institutional arrangements agreed between 1950 and 1970, when food aid was both a major element of development co-operation (Table 1.1) and a considerable part of agricultural trade.[10] The time is therefore ripe for institutional reform.

What are the main challenges? We will start with a brief overview of the major international institutional arrangements for food aid: the Food Aid Convention, the WFP, the FAO and the WTO. The institutional arrangements of the US within this policy area – traditionally the main provider of food aid, food aid in kind in particular – need particular attention. It is a picture of a complex and fragmented food aid delivery system that is appearing from this brief overview. Policy coherence emerges as the greatest challenge.

1. The Major International Institutions and Arrangements

The Food Aid Convention (FAC) was agreed in 1967 as part of the International Grains Agreement. There were extensive modifications, especially in 1980 and 1995, involving minimum annual commitments of cereals defined in wheat equivalent. The latest 1999 Convention implies some further reduction in cereals food aid commitments, but a broadening of the range of eligible commodities to include vegetable oil and sugar (see Chapter 4).

The World Trade Organisation is now responsible for overseeing of the Marrakesh Decision of 1994 which makes commitments to low-income countries affected by the trade liberalisation of the GATT Uruguay Round. This new arrangement offers possibilities for change as discussed in Chapter 3.

The FAO Consultative Sub-Committee on Surplus Disposal, established in 1955, has monitored food aid to ensure that export interests are not harmed. Historically it has been largely concerned with programme aid, because relief and project food aid were considered to be additional to the 'usual marketing requirements' of food-importing recipient countries [*FAO, 1980*].

The World Food Programme was established in 1963 to provide food aid through its Regular Programme of development projects and

---

10. Between 1954 and 1969 food aid under PL480 accounted for 23 per cent of US agricultural exports by value [*OECD, 1971*].

a modest amount of emergency aid. All the European members of DAC, as well as the European Union through the Commission, have supported the WFP. Large-scale humanitarian assistance has been provided through its International Emergency Food Reserve (IEFR) since 1977 and humanitarian assistance for Protracted Refugee and Relief Operations (PROs) in co-operation with the UNHCR since 1991. It evolved from a joint UN/FAO programme into an international food aid agency as confirmed by changes in its regulations in 1992. It has been engaged in a review of its development role setting itself, in 1999, two years to reconstruct its portfolio [*WFP, 1999*]. Faaland *et al.* consider this further in Chapter 9.

In addition, there is a further overlapping set of *international institutional mandates and responsibilities* for food aid and in relation to food security, summarised in Box 1.2. These complex arrangements make international action difficult to achieve beyond statements of problems, declarations of responsibility and setting global targets [*Shaw and Clay, 1998*]. This is one of the areas in which the need for change in global governance has been widely recognised [*ODI, 1999a*].

Box 1.2
Mandates and Responsibilities: The Issue of Coherence

Various aspects of food aid policies and their implementation are considered in parallel in different forums. Minimum commitments under the Food Aid Convention are monitored by a *Food Aid Committee* of donor countries, with the International Grains Council in London acting as Secretariat. The FAO *Committee on World Food Security* (CFS) in Rome provides a general framework for food security policy. The FAO *Consultative Sub-Committee on Surplus Disposal* in Washington DC monitors food aid to ensure that free trade principles are not violated. This is now also a *WTO* issue. The WFP *Executive Board* (in Rome) also has a mandate to consider wider food aid policy issues. *UNICEF* (New York), the UN *High Commissioner for Refugees* (in Geneva) and the *Office of the Co-ordinator for Humanitarian Affairs (OCHA)* within the UN Secretariat (Geneva and New York) have an interest in aspects of food aid and convene international meetings in relation to their wider responsibilities. There is no single forum or body through which a major international or national crisis would automatically be considered or overall policy reviewed and negotiated.

There are also *regional intergovernmental consultative arrangements* which have a food security aspect. In sub-Saharan Africa perhaps the two most effective groups are CILSS (la Comité inter-états de lutte contre la sécheresse dans le Sahel) and the Southern African Development Community (SADC). The Club du Sahel, the OECD-based donor group which interfaces with CILSS, was established after the drought of the early 1970s, and has been responsible for developing a Charter for Food Aid to the Sahel (see Chapter 12). SADC's role in an evolving food security strategy for Southern Africa is considered in Chapter 7.

2. Donor Complexity: The United States and the European Union

Complex institutional arrangements are also found at the level of bilateral donors of food aid. Here, several ministries – and interest groups interacting closely with these ministries – are usually involved, most prominently the ministries of foreign affairs and agriculture. Several agencies are involved in one or more components of the food aid, typically the aid agency, but also several other official and semi-official institutions, like the national FAO committee, institutions representing export interests, and others representing human rights and relief concerns. These ministries and agencies, in turn, relate to international institutions in the field, particularly those identified above but also a large number of international non-governmental organisations (INGOs) active in the field of food aid or more broadly in humanitarian assistance. An increasing share of ODA has been channelled through INGOs (such as the Red Cross and Save the Children federations) and multilateral programmes and institutions with a humanitarian mandate (such as the UNHCR, the UNICEF and the WFP). Bilateral agencies are also interacting with a large number of governments of developing countries with which the donor country has established close development co-operation relations and beyond, since humanitarian aid is often channelled to countries outside that group.

The arrangements of the largest bilateral donor of food aid, the US, and the EU illustrate the complexity involved. We will not explore here the coherence problematic involved in any detail or depth,[11] but

---

11. For an exploration of the policy coherence problematic, with particular reference to development co-operation and, more broadly, policies of OECD countries that affect developing countries and North–South relations, see Forster and Stokke [*1999*]. The authors distinguish between four frameworks: coherence within the particular policy area (development co-operation), the national policies of a donor country *vis-à-vis* developing countries, the policies of the donor community towards developing countries and, finally but not least important, coherence between donor and recipient policies. Forster and Stokke [*eds., 1999*] include several component studies that focus on policy coherence within the first two frameworks identified.

just sketch out the institutional jungle that exists. Co-ordination of activities, within and between the various bilateral and multilateral aid-providing agencies, has generally been poor, if existing at all; this has been particularly strongly exposed in some major international relief operations.

The US situation is complex but relatively transparent. This is because the government structure involves a division of powers that makes it necessary for the executive to have a detailed legislative basis for its actions and afterwards to be able to account to Congress for every dollar. The landmarks in US food aid are therefore intensively negotiated Farm Bills for agriculture and agricultural trade and aid agreed for a fixed period; in between, even the international negotiating position of the US government is severely circumscribed [*Hanrahan and Leach, 1994; Hanrahan, 1998; Ruttan, 1993*]. The next of these bills is scheduled for 2001. The legislation-based arrangements for US food aid are summarised in Box 1.3.

There is an added layer of complexity for the EU which has arrangements dating back to 1968 for dividing up responsibilities as a signatory to the Food Aid Convention between the European Commission and the then six (now 15) member states. This provides for 'Community Action' organised by the Commission and 'national actions' of the member states, resulting in effect in 16 separate food aid programmes. The management of this arrangement involves a Working Group of the European Council of Ministers and a Food Aid Committee chaired by the Commission. Community action provides both humanitarian and developmental food aid, and there is also extensive NGO involvement, as described by Thirion in Chapter 11. There are, therefore, extensive liaison and management arrangements simply for the food aid provided by the Commission which have been the source of considerable operational problems and, in 1999, were again in the process of reorganisation.[12]

Possibly the most important long-term adaptation has been in the greater flexibility with which finance is provided for food aid. This is reflected in the increase in triangular transactions and local purchasing since the early 1980s. Changes in the Food Aid Convention rules facilitated such flexibility over sources. The EU's 1996 Regulation for Food Aid is the latest major development in that direction [*European Commission, 1996*]. There has been a parallel adaptation on the

---

12. The uncertainties surrounding food aid in particular are exemplified by the extended attempt involving the Commission and NGOs to renegotiate the contractual relationship of EuronAid as the emergency and development food procurement logistics organisation of European NGOs [*EuronAid, 1999*].

agricultural export side as the US and the EU, in particular, found a range of alternatives to food aid for subsidising agricultural exports and the disposal of surpluses.

Box 1.3
The US Food Aid Programme

Food aid had its origins in the Marshall Plan. However, the basis for food aid in a developmental and humanitarian context is US Public Law 480 in 1954.

Title I of the Food for Peace Program (PL480) 'Trade and Development Assistance'. This is a government-to-government concessional sales programme to developing countries, administered by the US Department of Agriculture (USDA). The loans offer terms of 10 to 30 years, with a 7-year grace period and low rates of interest. In 1998 it provided economic support to crisis-affected Indonesia.

Title II of the Food for Peace Program (PL480) 'Emergency and Private Assistance'. This is a grant programme, administered by USAID on behalf of the State Department. Food aid provided under this programme may be used for emergency purposes, but also for non-emergency purposes through PVOs, co-operatives and international agencies (WFP). Commodities supplied may be monetised by PVOs to provide support for development activities.

Title III of the Food for Peace Program (PL480) 'Food for Development'. This is a multi-year bilateral grant programme to provide economic development and food security, also administered by USAID. The food aid can be sold, with the CPFs generated used for development activities or directly in feeding programmes. Previously a major programme, operations were reduced to $300 million in Financial Year (FY) 1995.

Section 416 (of the Agricultural Trade Act of 1949). This is a grant programme, administered by the USDA, entailing donations of surplus food, acquired by the Commodity Credit Corporation (CCC) of USDA to developing countries, emerging democracies and intergovernmental relief operations bilaterally or through PVOs. Not available in FY1997 or FY1998, but substantial 'emergency', programme-aid type grants, were made in FY1999 to Bangladesh, Indonesia and North Korea.

Food-for-Progress Programme. This is an independently authorised usually grant aid programme that uses commodities, Title I funds or CCC funds in support of countries which have made commitments to introduce or expand free enterprise elements in their agricultural economies.

Food Security Commodity Reserve. A reserve of 4 million tonnes of cereals was created in 1980 to help fulfil PL480 commitments where US supplies were short or to meet unanticipated emergency needs. The Reserve (now renamed a trust) may be replenished with CCC-owned commodities or appropriated funds [*Hanrahan, 1998*].

VI. WHERE FROM HERE?

The institutional arrangements which the international community has inherited reflect a very different world: then, food aid in kind was assumed to be a major feature of development and humanitarian relief. This resource was to some considerable extent additional to other aid, but involved all sorts of inflexibilities. The challenge then was how to use it to best effect, as Schulthes explains in Chapter 10. This was an agenda for localised optimisation within a highly constrained policy situation, but involving considerable resources. Once the period of postwar reconstruction was over and the reintegration of the world economy had begun, the comparative inefficiency of food aid in kind was never in question [*Schultz, 1960*]. The quest to use what were then clearly perceived to be additional resources, was the reason for the establishment of the WFP [*Singer et al., 1987*]. The other major change has been from a world of closely regulated food systems and administered agricultural trade to liberalisation both internationally (Chapter 3) and internally in many developing countries, for example in southern Africa, as Buckland *et al.* explain in Chapter 7.

Food aid (in kind and finance for food assistance) is now relatively a marginal and uncertain aspect of development co-operation, as shown above in sections III and IV. Two primary policy questions, we suggest, are raised in these circumstances by the process of change and institutional adaptation which has been briefly outlined. First, when is food assistance in kind an appropriate intervention for government or civil society institutions in low-income developing countries and in a humanitarian crisis elsewhere? Second, when is food aid in kind an appropriate way of providing international support for such actions? This way of posing the questions implies that there is no axiomatic link between problems of hunger and malnutrition, food insecurity and food aid in kind or in terms of finance for food. Human security rather than food security or conceivably poverty has been deliberately chosen as the framework for the reassessment of food aid and finance for food aid. This wider framework is considered to be more appropriate for taking account of the many goals and concerns that actually impinge on food aid. The usefulness of this wider framework is explored in this volume.[13]

REFERENCES

Australian Development Assistance Bureau (ADAB), 1997, 'Report of the Committee of Review on the Australian Overseas Aid Program' (*The Simons Report*), Canberra: AusAid (April).

Bennett, J., 1999, 'North Korea: the Politics of Food Aid', *RRN Network Paper*, No. 28, London: Overseas Development Institute.

Benson, C. and E.J. Clay, 1998a, 'Additionality or Diversion? Food Aid to Eastern Europe and the Former Soviet Republics and the Implications for Developing Countries', *World Development*, Vol. 26, No. 1, pp. 31–44.

Benson, C. and E.J. Clay, 1998b, 'The Impact of Drought on Sub-Saharan African Economies: A Preliminary Examination', *World Bank Technical Paper*, No. 401, Washington DC: World Bank (March).

Bie, S.B., 1994, 'Global Food: Agricultural Research Paradigms', *Forum for Development Studies*, No. 2, Special issue on North–South Relations and Development Co-operation, Oslo: NUPI.

Carney, D., 1999, 'Approaches to Sustainable Livelihoods for Rural Poor', *ODI Poverty Brief*, No. 2, London: Overseas Development Institute.

Chr. Michelsen Institute, 1993, *Evaluation of the World Food Programme: Final Report*, Bergen.

Clay, E.J., 1995, 'Conditionality and Programme Food Aid: From the Marshall Plan to Structural Adjustment', in Stokke, ed.

Clay, E.J. and C. Benson, 1991, 'Triangular Transactions, Local Purchases and Exchange Arrangements in Food Aid: a Provisional Review with Special Reference to Sub-Saharan Africa,' in Clay and Stokke, eds.

Clay, E.J. and O. Stokke, 1991, 'Assessing the Performance and Economic Impact of Food Aid', in Clay and Stokke, eds.

Clay, E.J., S. Dhiri and C. Benson, 1996, 'Joint Evaluation of European Union Programme Food Aid', *Synthesis Report*, London: Overseas Development Institute.

Clay, E.J. and O. Stokke, eds., 1991, *Food Aid Reconsidered: Assessing the Impact on Third World Countries* (EADI Book Series 11), London: Frank Cass.

Colding, B. and P. Pinstrup-Andersen, 1999, 'A six-fold increase in the impact of food aid: Denmark's contribution to World Food Programme', *Food Policy*, Vol. 24, No. 1, pp.93–108.

Cox, A. and A. Koning, 1997, 'Understanding European Community Aid. Aid Policies, Management and Distribution Explained', London: Overseas Development Institute and European Commission.

Doornbos, M. *et al.*, 1990, *Dairy Aid and Development: India's Operation Flood*, New Delhi and London: Sage.

---

13. This wider framework is taken from the UNDP's definition of human security in its 1994 *Human Development Report* [*UNDP, 1994*]. It was also taken as the point of departure by EADI for its 1996 triennial conference [*O'Neill, 1998*].

Doornbos, M., L. Gertsch and P. Terhal, 1991, 'Dairy Aid and Development: Current Trends and Long-Term Implications of the Indian Case,' in Clay and Stokke, eds.
Eriksson, J. et al., 1996, *The International Response to Conflict and Genocide: Lessons from the Rwanda Experience. Joint Evaluation of Emergency Assistance to Rwanda. Synthesis Report*, Copenhagen: Ministry of Foreign Affairs.
EuronAid, 1999, *Annual Report for 1998*, The Hague: Euronaid.
European Commission, 1996, 'Programme communautaire de sécurité et d'aide alimentaire', Brussels: Directorate General for Development, Food Security and Food Aid Unit.
European Court of Auditors, 1994, 'Annual Report concerning the financial year 1993 together with the institutions' replies', *OJ*94/C 327/01, Brussels (Nov.).
European Court of Auditors, 1997, 'Special Report No. 2/97 concerning humanitarian aid from the European Union between 1992 and 1995 together with the Commission's replies', *OJ* C143, Brussels (12 May).
FAO, 1980, 'Principles of Surplus Disposal', Rome: Food and Agriculture Organisation of the United Nations.
FAO, 1996a, *Rome Declaration on World Food Security and World Food Summit Plan of Action*, Rome: Food and Agriculture Organisation of the United Nations.
FAO, 1996b, 'Food Security and Food Assistance', *Technical Background Documents*, No. 13, World Food Summit, Rome (13–17 Nov.), Rome: Food and Agriculture Organisation of the United Nations.
Forster, J. and O. Stokke, 1999, 'Coherence of Policies Towards Developing Countries: Approaching the Problematique', in Forster and Stokke, eds.
Forster, J. and O. Stokke, eds., 1999, *Policy Coherence in Development Co-operation*, London: Frank Cass.
Garst, R. and T. Barry, 1990, *Feeding the Crisis: US Food Aid and Farm Policy in Central America*, Lincoln, NE: University of Nebraska Press.
Gellner, E., 1992, *Civil Society and Its Enemies*, Harmondsworth: Penguin.
Gough, I. et al., 1997, 'Social Assistance in OECD Countries', *Journal of European Social Policy*, Vol. 7, No. 1, pp. 17–43.
Griffin, K., 1991, 'Foreign Aid after the Cold War', *Development and Change*, No. 4, London: Sage Publications.
Hanrahan, C.E., 1998, 'The Food Security Commodity Reserve: The Replenishment Issue', *CRS Report for Congress* 98-398 ENR, Washington DC: Congressional Research Service, Library of Congress.
Hanrahan, C.E. and I. Leach, 1994, 'PL480 Food Aid: History and Legislation, Programs and Policy Issues', *CRS Report for Congress* 94-3035, Washington DC: Congressional Research Service, Library of Congress.
Hook, S.W., ed., 1996, *Foreign Aid Toward the Millennium*, London: Lynne Rienner Publishers.
Jost, S., 1991, 'An Introduction to the Sources of Data for Food Aid Analysis with Special Reference to Sub-Saharan Africa', in Clay and Stokke, eds.
Lancaster, Carol, 1993, 'Governance and Development: The Views from Washington', *IDS Bulletin*, Vol. 24, No. 1.
Marr, A., 1999, 'The Poor and Their Money', *ODI Poverty Brief*, No. 4.
Maxwell, S.M., 1996, 'Food security: a post-modern perspective', *Food Policy*, Vol. 21, No. 2, pp. 155–70.
McClelland, D.G., 1997, 'Food Aid and Sustainable Development – Forty Years of Experience', Washington DC: Center for Development Information and Evaluation, USAID (July).
ODI, 1997, 'Global Hunger and Food Security after the World Food Summit', *Briefing Paper* 1997 (1), London: Overseas Development Institute.
ODI, 1999a, 'Global Governance: an Agenda for the Renewal of the United Nations', *Briefing Paper* 1999 (2), London: Overseas Development Institute.
ODI, 1999b, 'What can we do with a rights-based approach to development?', *Briefing Paper* 1999 (3), London: Overseas Development Institute.

OECD, 1971, *Development Co-operation, 1971 Review,* Paris: Organisation for Economic Co-operation and Development.

OECD, 1992, *Development Co-operation, 1992 Report,* Paris: DAC, OECD.

O'Neill, H., 1998, 'Globalisation, Competitiveness and Human Security: Challenges for Development Policy and Institutional Change', *Proceedings of the 8th EADI General Conference, Vienna, 11-14 September 1996,* Geneva: EADI (March) (Presidential Address to EADI).

Pinstrup-Andersen, P. and R. Pandya-Lorch, 1996, 'Using Modern Science to Assure Food Security', *IFPRI Report,* Washington DC: International Food Policy Research Institute.

Poh, L.K. *et al.,* 1999, 'Manufacturing a crisis: the politics of food aid to Indonesia', *Development Report* 13, Oakland: Institute for Food and Development Policy.

Relief and Development Institute, 1990, 'A Study of Commodity Exchanges in WFP and other Food Aid Operations,' *WFP Occasional Paper,* No. 12, Rome: World Food Programme.

Ruttan, V.W., 1993, *Why Food Aid.?* Baltimore: Johns Hopkins University Press.

Schultz, T.W., 1960, 'Impact and Implications of Foreign Surplus Disposal on Underdeveloped Economies: Value of U.S. Farm Surpluses to Underdeveloped Countries', *Journal of Farm Economics,* Vol. 42, No. 4, pp.1019–30.

Shaw, D.J. and E.J. Clay, 1998, 'Global Hunger and Food Security after the World Food Summit', *Canadian Journal of Development Studies,* Vol. 19, Special Issue, pp. 55–76.

Shaw, D.J. and H.W. Singer, 1996, 'A future food aid regime: implications of the final act of the Uruguay Round', *Food Policy,* Vol. 21, No. 4/5, pp.447–60.

Singer, H.W., J. Wood and T. Jennings, 1987, *Food Aid: The Challenge and the Opportunity,* Oxford: Oxford University Press.

Smith, D. *et al.,* 1997, *The State of War and Peace Atlas,* London: Penguin.

Smith, M., J. Ponting and S. Maxwell, 1993, *Household Food Security: Concepts and Definitions: an annotated bibliography,* Brighton: Institute of Development Studies.

Stokke, O., 1995, 'Aid and Political Conditionality: Core Issues and State of the Art', in Stokke, ed.

Stokke, O., 1996, 'Foreign Aid: What Now?', in Stokke, ed.

Stokke, O., 1997, 'Violent Conflict Prevention and Development Co-operation: Coherent or Conflicting Perspectives?', *Forum for Development Studies,* No. 2, Oslo: NUPI.

Stokke, O., ed., 1995, *Aid and Political Conditionality,* London: Frank Cass.

Stokke, O., ed., 1996, *Foreign Aid Towards the Year 2000 – Experiences and Challenges* (EADI Book Series 16), London: Frank Cass.

UNDP, 1994, *Human Development Report 1994,* New York: Oxford University Press.

USAID, 1999, *US International Food Assistance Report,1998,* Washington DC: United States Agency for International Development, Bureau of Humanitarian Response.

Vincent, B. *et al.,* 1998, *Food Aid Performance Review: Performance Report,* Ottawa: Canadian International Development Agency.

Wallerstein, M., 1980, *Food for War – Food for Peace: US Food Aid in a Global Context,* Cambridge, MA: MIT Press.

WFP, 1996, *Tackling Hunger in a World Full of Food: Tasks Ahead for Food Aid,* Rome: World Food Programme, Public Affairs Division.

WFP, 1999, *Time for Change: Food Aid and Development,* Rome: World Food Programme (April).

White, H., 1996, *Evaluating Programme Aid,* The Hague: Institute of Social Studies.

World Bank, 1986, *Poverty and Hunger: Issues and Options for Food Security in Developing Countries,* Washington DC: World Bank.

Zimmerman, R. F. and S. W. Hook, 1996, 'The Assault on U.S. Foreign Aid', in Hook, ed.

APPENDIX

TABLE A1.1

FOOD AID DELIVERIES IN 1998 BY DONOR AND CATEGORY OF USE

Donor	Relief	Project	Programme	Total
		(as per cent of total)		('000 t)
Australia	36	62	2	274
Canada	14	71	15	403
China	1	0	99	102
EU (of which):				
Community Action	53	37	10	1004
National Actions	49	29	21	1044
Japan	32	1	67	671
Korea	100	0	0	54
NGOs	95	5	0	99
Norway	22	78	0	66
USA	31	32	37	4077
Other (a)	63	25	12	238
Total	37	32	31	8032

Note: (a) Other comprises those donors contributing less than 50,000t and includes India, Pakistan and Switzerland.
Source: WFP Interfais.

TABLE A1.2
FOOD AID DELIVERIES IN 1998 BY RECIPIENT AND CATEGORY OF USE

Recipient Region/Country	Total food aid (in tonnes)	Relief	Project	Programme
		(as a percentage of total food aid)		
GLOBAL TOTAL	8,032,453	37	32	31
SUB-SAHARAN AFRICA	2,940,296	54	26	20
Angola	219,588	53	0	47
Benin	25,972	0	78	22
Burkina Faso	49,569	1	87	12
Burundi	295	94	6	0
Cameroon	13,481	38	62	0
Cape Verde	69,417	0	35	65
Cen. Afr. Rep.	1,933	0	81	19
Chad	16,722	20	56	24
Comoros	4,184	0	14	86
Congo	14,032	2	12	86
Congo, D.R.	12,891	76	8	17
Côte d'Ivoire	26,293	0	12	88
Djibouti	14,212	50	29	21
Eq. Guinea	1,890	0	100	0
Eritrea	110,105	5	22	73
Ethiopia	630,139	73	26	1
Gambia	7,676	0	100	0
Ghana	60,376	0	94	6
Guinea Bissau	9,030	100	0	0
Guinea	22,376	64	5	31
Kenya	139,009	55	30	15
Lesotho	7,018	0	100	0
Liberia	123,910	98	2	0
Madagascar	30,128	11	60	30
Malawi	48,232	12	53	35
Mali	21,977	38	25	37
Mauritania	13,744	0	53	47
Mozambique	239,285	4	65	32
Niger	55,912	5	81	15
Rwanda	249,752	89	2	9
Sao Tome/Principe	3,400	0	12	88
Senegal	11,767	10	36	53
Sierra Leone	92,175	100	0	0
Somalia	42,222	98	2	0

South Africa	18,046	0	100	0
Sudan	210,024	90	9	0
Tanzania	102,216	59	2	39
Togo	7,008	0	0	100
Uganda	130,213	92	7	1
Zambia	27,872	41	55	4
Zimbabwe	56,203	0	16	84
N. AFRICA/	*346,722*	*23*	*27*	*50*
MIDDLE EAST				
Algeria	16,072	92	8	0
Egypt	66,621	0	32	68
Gaza/W. Bank	25,778	46	54	0
Iran	12,946	100	0	0
Iraq	48,307	75	24	2
Jordan	119,471	1	5	93
Lebanon	958	100	0	0
Morocco	244	0	100	0
Syria	20,430	3	97	0
Tunisia	64	0	100	0
Yemen, Rep. of	35,832	7	49	45
LATIN AM./	*979,693*	*3*	*52*	*45*
CARIBBEAN				
Bolivia	217,472	0	46	54
Brazil	121	0	100	0
Chile	75	0	100	0
Colombia	7,010	0	100	0
Cuba	19,191	9	39	52
Dominican Rep.	7,130	3	97	0
Ecuador	21,126	2	48	50
El Salvador	20,352	0	81	19
Guatemala	70,515	1	59	40
Guyana	59,446	0	4	96
Haiti	157,457	0	64	36
Honduras	27,125	15	82	3
Nicaragua	87,128	28	24	48
Panama	1,518	0	100	0
Peru	262,227	0	66	34
Surinam	21,800	0	0	100

EUROPE AND CIS	846,166	49	0	51
Albania	29,065	3	0	97
Armenia	117,637	23	0	77
Azerbaijan	68,133	43	0	57
Bosnia	68,216	93	0	7
Bulgaria	10,706	83	17	0
Croatia	1,335	100	0	0
Georgia	114,865	35	0	65
Kazakhstan	7,000	100	0	0
Kyrgyzstan	38,370	11	0	89
Lithuania	30,000	0	0	100
Moldova	59,400	2	0	98
Russia	16,440	100	0	0
Tajikistan	114,304	67	0	33
Ukraine	39,866	19	0	81
Uzbekistan	420	0	100	0
Ex-Yugoslavia	130,409	99	1	0
ASIA	2,919,576	29	41	30
Afghanistan	51,831	100	0	0
Bangladesh	851,091	7	65	28
Bhutan	4,754	0	100	0
Cambodia	36,867	100	0	0
China	89,200	0	100	0
India	349,602	2	98	0
Indonesia	499,781	25	0	75
Korea, DPR	710,906	72	12	15
Laos	8,600	74	26	0
Mongolia	21,340	0	0	100
Myanmar	4,255	89	0	11
Nepal	49,143	59	33	8
Pakistan	57,580	2	29	69
Papua/N. Guinea	3,303	100	0	0
Philippines	72,048	0	12	88
Sri Lanka	37,591	25	4	71
Thailand	10,942	100	0	0
Viet Nam	60,742	1	99	0

Source: Taken from WFP website (www.wfp.org).

2

Food Prospects and Potential Imports of Low-income Countries in the Twenty-first Century

RAJUL PANDYA-LORCH

I. INTRODUCTION

During the next quarter century the world will produce enough food to meet the demands of those who can afford to buy it, and real food prices will continue to decline. However, while the global community continues with business as usual, prospects for food security will be bleak for millions of people and degradation of natural resources will continue. In many developing economies food production is unlikely to keep pace with the increase in the demand for food by growing populations. The 'food gap' – the difference between production and demand for food – could more than double in the developing world during the next 25 years, increasing dependence on imports from developed countries. For those countries with sufficient foreign currency reserves, this should not be cause for alarm. However, many low-income economies, including most of those in sub-Saharan Africa, will not be able to generate the necessary foreign exchange to purchase needed food on the world market. And many poor people within these countries will not be able to afford the food to meet their needs fully.

Humanity is entering an era of volatility in the world food situation. Several factors have emerged that could lead to larger fluctuations in food availability and access in various regions and countries around the world, making the poor even more vulnerable to hunger. These factors include low grain stocks and declining food aid, which

This chapter draws extensively on *The World Food Situation: Recent Developments, Emerging Issues, and Long-Term Prospects,* by Per Pinstrup-Andersen, Rajul Pandya-Lorch and Mark W. Rosegrant, 2020 Vision Food Policy Report, Washington DC: International Food Research Institute, 1997.

have reduced a key buffer at times of food shortages; growing scarcity of water, which is likely to reduce its availability for agricultural uses; weather fluctuations such as those induced by El Niño and global warming, which affect production in ways difficult to predict; and civil strife and political and social instability, which are both a cause and a result of hunger.

Policy-makers, researchers, and others must take proactive steps to minimise uncertainty in the future world food situation in order to achieve food security for all people. In developing countries, policy-makers need to ensure that their policies promote broad-based economic growth, especially agricultural growth, so that their countries can produce enough food to feed themselves or enough income to buy the necessary food on the world market. Policy-makers in developed countries should consider reversing the decline in aid flows and redirecting aid to the most vulnerable developing countries. A world of food-secure people is within our reach, if we take the necessary actions.

II. PROSPECTS FOR GLOBAL FOOD SECURITY

Prospects of a food-secure world – a world in which each and every person is assured of access at all times to the food required to lead a healthy and productive life – remain bleak if the global community continues with business as usual. The International Food Policy Research Institute (IFPRI) has developed a global economic model, the International Model for Policy Analysis of Agricultural Commodities and Trade (IMPACT), that permits projections to the year 2020 of world food demand, supply and trade as well as child malnutrition under different scenarios. IMPACT[1] projects that, under the most

---

1. IMPACT is a global food model that divides the world into 37 countries or country groups. Its baseline version represents the most realistic set of assumptions according to the model team which is led by Dr Mark Rosegrant of IFPRI. IMPACT covers 18 cereal, meat, and roots and tubers commodities. The base data used in this version are averages of the 1992–94 annual data from the FAO Statistical Database. Since each of the 37 country groups produces and/or consumes at least some of each commodity, literally thousands of supply and demand parameters have to be specified (income, price, and cross-price elasticities of demand; production parameters including crop area, yield growth trends, and herd size and productivity; price response parameters; initial levels and trends in feed conversion; trade distortion parameters; and so on). Parameter estimates were drawn from econometric analysis, assessment of past and changing trends, expert judgment, and synthesis of the existing literature. The myriad assumptions are too detailed to report here, but more information can be found in Rosegrant, Agcaoili-Sombilla and Perez [*1995*]; Rosegrant *et al.* [*1997a, 1997b*]; Rosegrant, Leach and Gerpacio [*1998*] and Rosegrant and Ringler [*1998*]. The model is solved on an annual basis by linking each country model to the rest of the world

likely or baseline scenario, 150 million children – one out of four children under the age of six – will be malnourished in 2020, just 20 per cent fewer than in 1993 (Table 2.1).[2] Child malnutrition is expected to decline in all major developing regions except sub-Saharan Africa, where the number of malnourished children could increase by 45 per cent between 1993 and 2020 to reach 40 million. In South Asia, home to half of the world's malnourished children in 1993, the number of malnourished children is projected to decline by more than 30 million between 1993 and 2020, but the incidence of malnutrition is so high that, even with this reduction, two out of five children could remain malnourished in 2020. With more than 70 per cent of the world's malnourished children, sub-Saharan Africa and South Asia are expected to remain 'hot spots' of child malnutrition in 2020.

TABLE 2.1
MALNOURISHED CHILDREN, 1993, 2010 AND 2020

	Number of malnourished children (million)			% of malnourished children		
	1993	2010	2020	1993	2010	2020
South Asia	99.8	83.9	67.0	56.9	46.6	40.0
China and South-East Asia	40.5	29.3	27.5	22.0	18.2	16.5
Sub-Saharan Africa	27.4	37.4	39.9	28.2	26.7	24.9
Latin America	10.1	8.6	6.7	16.5	13.9	11.0
West Asia and North Africa	7.6	8.0	6.8	12.8	11.4	9.6

Source: IFPRI, IMPACT simulations [*1997*].

---

through commodity trade. The market-clearing condition solves for the set of world prices that clears international commodity markets, so that the total imports of each commodity equal total exports. World prices of commodities thus act as the equilibrating mechanism and maintain the model in equilibrium. When an exogenous shock is introduced in the model, such as an increase in crop yields from higher investment in crop research, the world price will adjust and each adjustment is passed back to the effective producer and consumer prices. Changes in domestic prices subsequently affect the supply and demand of the commodities, necessitating their iterative readjustments until world supply and demand are in balance and world net trade again equals zero. Projections from the IMPACT model are middle of the road in outlook and neither pessimistic nor bullish.
2. Malnourished children are those whose weight-for-age is more than two standard deviations below the weight-for-age standard set by the US National Center for Health Statistics and adopted by many United Nations agencies in assessing the nutritional status of persons in developing countries.

Projections by FAO on the number of food-insecure people paint a similarly mixed picture.[3] FAO projects that 680 million people, 12 per cent of the developing world's population, could be food-insecure in 2010, down from 840 million in 1990–92 [*FAO 1996a*]. Food insecurity is expected to diminish rapidly in East Asia and to a lesser extent in South Asia and Latin America, but it could accelerate substantially in sub-Saharan Africa, West Asia and North Africa. Sub-Saharan Africa and South Asia, home to a projected 70 per cent of the world's food-insecure people in 2010, will be the locus of hunger in the developing world. In fact, sub-Saharan Africa's share of the world's food-insecure population is projected to almost quadruple between 1969–71 and 2010 from 11 to 39 per cent [*ibid.*]. By 2010, every third person in sub-Saharan Africa is likely to be food-insecure, compared with every eighth person in South Asia and every twentieth person in East Asia. These disturbing figures reflect widespread poverty and poor health.

Worldwide, per capita availability of food is projected to increase by around 7 per cent between 1993 and 2020, from about 2,700 calories per person per day in 1993 to about 2,900 calories. Increases in average per capita food availability are expected in all major regions, with China and East Asia projected to experience the largest increase, and West Asia and North Africa the smallest (Table 2.2). The projected average availability of about 2,300 calories per person per day in sub-Saharan Africa is barely above the minimum required for a healthy and productive life. Since available food is not distributed equally to all, a large proportion of the region's population is likely to have access to less food than is needed.

TABLE 2.2
DAILY PER CAPITA CALORIE AVAILABILITY, 1993 AND 2020

	1993	2020
East Asia	2,760	3,157
West Asia and North Africa	3,073	3,135
Latin America	2,692	2,967
South Asia	2,356	2,714
Sub-Saharan Africa	2,210	2,311

Source: IFPRI, IMPACT simulations [*1997*].

---

3. FAO classifies these people as chronically undernourished; that is, their access to per capita food supplies is less than 1.55 times the basal metabolic rate.

Related to this is an increasing gap between food demand and production in several parts of the world. Demand for food is influenced by a number of forces, including population growth and movements, income levels and economic growth, human resource development, and lifestyles and preferences. In the next several decades, population growth will contribute to increased demand for food. The United Nations recently scaled back its population projections, but even with these reduced estimates, almost 80 million people are likely to be added to the world's population each year during the next quarter century, increasing world population by 35 per cent from 5.69 billion in 1995 to 7.67 billion by 2020 [*UN, 1996*]. More than 95 per cent of the increase is expected to be in developing countries, whose share of global population is projected to increase from 79 per cent in 1995 to 84 per cent in 2020. Over this period, the absolute population increase will be highest in Asia, but the relative increase will be greatest in sub-Saharan Africa, where the population is expected to almost double by 2020. At the same time, urbanisation will contribute to changes in the types of food demanded. Much of the population increase in developing countries is expected in the cities; the developing world's urban population is projected to double over the next quarter century to 3.6 billion [*UN, 1995*].

People's access to food depends on income. Currently, more than 1.3 billion people are absolutely poor, with incomes of a dollar a day or less per person, while another 2 billion people are only marginally better off [*World Bank, 1997a*]. Income growth rates have varied considerably between regions in recent years, with sub-Saharan Africa and West Asia and North Africa struggling with negative growth rates while East Asia, until recently, was experiencing annual growth rates exceeding 7 per cent [*World Bank, 1997b*]. Prospects for economic growth during the next quarter century appear favourable, with global income growth projected to average 2.7 per cent per year between 1993 and 2020 (Table 2.3). The projected income growth rate for developing countries as a group is almost double that for developed countries.

The long-term effects of the financial and economic crisis that engulfed many South-East Asian countries in 1997 and is still continuing today are uncertain. The expected growth rates of the region's economies have been revised sharply downward, and in most instances are now negative. The declining growth rates may significantly influence food insecurity and child malnutrition, the nature and level of food demand, and patterns of trade and growth in the region and the rest of the world. IFPRI projections suggest that in a severe Asian crisis scenario (where the income growth rates drop to half the pre-crisis levels), the number of malnourished children in developing countries could be 10 per cent higher than in the baseline scenario [*Rosegrant and Ringler, 1998*].

Under the baseline scenario, IMPACT projects global demand for cereals to increase by 41 per cent between 1993 and 2020 to reach 2,490 million tonnes, for meat to increase by 63 per cent to 306 million tonnes, and for roots and tubers to increase by 40 per cent to 855 million tonnes.[4] Most of these increases are projected to occur in developing countries, which will account for more than 80 per cent of the increase in global cereal demand, nearly 90 per cent of the increase in meat demand, and more than 90 per cent of the increase in demand for roots and tubers.

Demand for cereals for feeding livestock will increase considerably in importance in coming decades, especially in developing countries, in response to strong demand for livestock products. Between 1993 and 2020, developing countries' demand for cereals for animal feed is projected to double, while demand for cereals for food for direct human consumption is projected to increase by 47 per cent. By 2020, 24 per cent of the cereal demand in developing countries will be for feed, compared with 19 per cent in 1993. However, in absolute terms, the increase in cereal demand for food will be higher than for feed. In developed countries, however, the increase in cereal demand for feed will outstrip the increase in cereal demand for food in both absolute and relative terms.

TABLE 2.3

PROJECTED AVERAGE ANNUAL INCOME GROWTH RATES, 1993–2020 (%)

China and South-East Asia	6.2
South Asia	5.3
West Asia and North Africa	3.6
Sub-Saharan Africa	3.5
Latin America	2.9
Eastern Europe and the former Soviet Union	1.6
Developing countries	4.3
Developed countries	2.3
World	2.7

Source: IFPRI, IMPACT simulations [*1997*].

---

4. All tonnes in this chapter are metric tons.

TABLE 2.4
ANNUAL GROWTH IN CEREAL YIELDS, 1967–82, 1982–94, 1993–2020 (%)

	1967–82	1982–94	1993–2020
Developing countries	2.87	1.87	1.20
Developed countries	1.69	1.30	0.94
World	2.24	1.51	1.06

Source: IFPRI, IMPACT simulations [*1997*].

Because of substantial increases in demand for livestock products, especially in developing countries where maize and other coarse grains are used primarily for animal feed, demand for maize is projected to increase faster than for other cereals in both developed and developing countries. Global demand for maize is projected to grow at an annual rate of 1.4 per cent between 1993 and 2020, followed by wheat at 1.3 per cent and rice at 1.2 per cent. In China and India, for instance, demand for maize and other grains for feed is projected to increase by around 3 per cent per year between 1993 and 2020.

How will the expected increases in cereal demand be met? Not by expansion in cultivated area. IMPACT projections indicate that the area under cereals will increase by only 5.5 per cent or 39 million hectares between 1993 and 2020, almost two-thirds of which will be in sub-Saharan Africa. Since growth in cultivated area is unlikely to contribute much to future cereals production growth, the burden of meeting increased demand rests on improvements in crop yields. However, the annual increase in yields of the major cereals is projected to slow down during 1993–2020 in both developed and developing countries (Table 2.4). This is worrying, given that yield growth rates were already on the decline.

With the projected slowdowns in area expansion and yield growth, cereal production in developing countries as a group is also forecast to slow to an annual rate of 1.5 per cent during 1993–2020, compared with 2.3 per cent during 1982–94. This figure is still higher, however, than the 1.0 per cent annual rate of growth projected for developed countries during 1993–2020.

Cereal production in developing countries will be insufficient to meet the expected increase in demand. As a group, developing countries are projected to more than double their net imports of cereals (the difference between demand and production) between 1993 and 2020. With the exception of Latin America, all major developing

61

regions are projected to increase their net cereal imports: the quadrupling of Asia's net imports will be driven primarily by rapid income growth, while the 150 per cent increase forecast for sub-Saharan Africa will be driven primarily by its continued poor performance in food production. While wheat is expected to constitute the bulk of the developing world's net cereal imports in 2020, the share of maize is forecast to increase sharply from 19 per cent in 1993 to 27 per cent, primarily because of the rapid increase in demand for meat. Trade in rice is forecast to remain negligible. With an almost 60 per cent projected increase in net cereal exports between 1993 and 2020, the United States is expected to capture a large share of the increased export market for cereals. Australia is forecast to almost double its net cereal exports during this period. It is also noteworthy that, under the baseline scenario, Eastern Europe and the former Soviet Union are expected to shift from being significant net cereal importers to significant net exporters by 2020.

Net imports are a reflection of the gap between production and market demand. For many of the poor, the gap between food production and human needs is likely to be even wider than that between production and demand, because many of these people are priced out of the market, even at low food prices, and are unable to exercise their demand for needed food. The higher-income developing countries, notably those of East Asia, will be able to fill the gap between production and demand through commercial imports, but the poorer countries may be forced to allocate foreign exchange to other uses and thus may not be able to import food in needed quantities. It is the latter group of countries, including most of those in sub-Saharan Africa and some in Asia, that will remain a challenge and require special assistance to avert widespread hunger and malnutrition.

III. SOURCES OF VOLATILITY IN THE WORLD FOOD SITUATION

1. Cereal Prices

The rising cereal prices of 1995–96 were a short-run phenomenon and not the beginning of a permanent upswing in prices or the forerunner to another world food crisis, as feared by some. With the rebound in cereal production in 1996/97 and 1997/98, and the slowdown in demand resulting from the Asian financial crisis, international prices are now at their lowest levels for many years. The long-term trend is for cereal prices to continue to decline, although at slower rates than in the past. Real wheat prices will decrease only slightly up to 2010, maize prices are expected to stagnate, and rice prices are projected to increase (Table 2.5). After 2010, the continued fall in the rate of population growth and the declining propensity to consume cereals as incomes rise (that is, declining income elasticity of demand for cereals) will combine to reduce growth in demand, and cereal prices are projected to drop by 11 per cent between 2010 and 2020. Meat prices are projected to decline by only 5 per cent between 1993 and 2010, and thereafter by another 1 per cent to 2020.

Concerns are growing that cereal prices may be more volatile than in the past [*FAO, 1996b*]. Reduced stocks and uncertainties associated with developments in China and the former Soviet Union, among other factors, could increase price instability. On the other hand, market liberalisation in developing countries, policy reform in developed countries, and more consistent and transparent stock-holding and trade policies will make producers more responsive to price changes and could reduce price instability. How these factors play out will determine whether cereal prices will be more volatile in coming years. In addition to price fluctuations in the international market, many low-income food-insecure developing countries suffer from large domestic price fluctuations, owing to inadequate markets, poor roads and other infrastructure, and inappropriate policies and institutions. Even small changes in production resulting from better or poorer growing conditions may cause large fluctuations in food prices.

TABLE 2.5

REAL WORLD PRICES FOR CEREALS AND MEATS, 1993, 2010, AND 2020 (US$ PER TONNE)

	1993	2010	2020
Rice	286	305	260
Wheat	148	145	128
Maize	126	126	121
Meat (per 100 kg)	158	150	148

Source: IFPRI, IMPACT simulations [*1997*].

2. Feeding China

With one-fifth of the world's population and one of the fastest growing and most rapidly changing economies in the world, China has the potential to affect global food security significantly, depending on the extent of its future demand for cereals, its capacity to meet its needs through production, and the degree to which it enters world markets to satisfy its unmet needs [*Rozelle and Rosegrant, 1997*]. Views on the size and dominance of China's food economy in the twenty-first century vary widely, with some forecasting that China will be a major cereal exporter [*Chen and Buckwell, 1991; Mei 1995*] and others cautioning that China might become a major cereal importer, if not the world's largest importer [*Garnaut and Ma, 1992; Carter and Funing, 1991; Brown, 1995*]. IMPACT projections indicate that, in the baseline scenario, total cereal demand in China will increase by 42 per cent, to 490 million tonnes, between 1993 and 2020, and cereal production by 31 per cent, to 449 million tonnes. At 41 million tonnes, China's net cereal imports in 2020 would represent 18 per cent of the developing world's projected net cereal imports. While sizeable, China's projected imports are unlikely to pose an intolerable burden on the global food situation.

Alternative simulations suggest that only with extraordinarily rapid income growth, severe resource degradation, and failure to invest in agriculture would China's net cereal imports increase substantially and have a significant effect on world cereal prices [*Rozelle and Rosegrant, 1997*]. For instance, should there be no increase in government investment in the agriculture sector in China, cereal production could be 19 per cent lower in 2020 relative to the baseline scenario (Table 2.6). This could lead to net cereal imports of 85 million tonnes in 2020, more than double the volume forecast in the baseline scenario, which would cause world cereal prices to increase by 10 per cent relative to the baseline scenario. However, should China increase its government investment in agriculture by 5 per cent annually in real terms, domestic production is forecast to increase to 573 million tonnes in 2020, 28 per cent higher than production levels in the baseline scenario. China would then become a net exporter of as much as 31 million tonnes of cereals in 2020, easing pressure on world markets and causing prices to decline by 11 per cent. If the Chinese government adopts policies to promote the attainment of 100 per cent self-sufficiency in cereals, world cereal prices are forecast to be 6 per cent lower in 2020 relative to the baseline scenario. China's cereal production would be higher relative to the baseline scenario, while demand would be lower (Table 2.6). By definition, there would be no net trade in cereals under this scenario. And should the Chinese government pursue a policy of 95 per cent self-sufficiency in cereals, world cereal prices would be only slightly higher relative to the baseline scenario [*Fan and Sombilla, 1997*]. However, should the structural transformation in the Chinese livestock sector be accompanied by technical changes that promote efficiencies in the use of animal feed, total cereal demand in 2020 is projected to be about 4 per cent lower than in the baseline scenario, while net cereal imports would be 36 per cent lower.

TABLE 2.6
CHINA'S PROJECTED PRODUCTION, DEMAND AND NET TRADE IN CEREALS, 1993 AND 2020, VARIOUS SCENARIOS

Year/scenario	Production (million tonnes)	Demand	Net trade[a]	World price (US$/t)
1993	343.3	344.3	-0.9	164
2020				
Baseline scenario	448.9	490.1	-41.1	147
Zero increase in government investment in agriculture	362.9	448.2	-85.2	162
5% annual increase in government investment in agriculture	572.8	541.6	31.2	131
100% self-sufficiency in cereals	469.5	469.5	0.0	138
95% self-sufficiency in cereals	457.2	481.8	-24.5	152
Structural change in livestock sector without technical change[b]	488.1	557.1	-69.0	162
Structural change in livestock sector with technical change[b]	477.8	474.1	-26.3	154

Source: Fan and Sombilla [*1997*].
Notes: (a) Negative sign denotes net imports; positive sign denotes net exports.
(b) Structural change refers to the shift from 'backyard' to commercial livestock production. Technical change refers to more efficient feed use.

China is already a significant player in world food markets and is likely to become increasingly important. However, it does not represent a major threat to world food markets.

3. Feeding India

With a population of 930 million in 1995, India is the second most populous country in the world after China [*UN, 1996*]. Like China more than a decade ago, India is in the midst of major economic reform. If it succeeds, incomes in India will rise much faster than they have done in recent decades, with profound effects on food demand and food security. In the baseline scenario, India is projected to have an average annual economic growth rate of 5.5 per cent during 1993–2020. With this growth rate, the number of malnourished children is projected to decline from 76 million in 1993 to 49 million in 2020, while the proportion of children who are malnourished is projected to decline from 60 to 43 per cent. Daily per capita calorie availability is projected to increase from around 2,400 calories to 2,780 calories.

As incomes increase, will Indians greatly increase their consumption of livestock products, or will they remain more or less vegetarian, as the country's history and cultural traditions would suggest? Views are mixed. In the baseline scenario, demand for livestock products is projected to increase by 4.6 million tonnes between 1993 and 2020 to 8.5 million tonnes (the corresponding increase in meat demand in China is 51 million tonnes to 89 million tonnes in 2020). Given the extremely low initial levels of livestock consumption in India, rapid growth in absolute demand for livestock would require a dramatic change in eating patterns. In a scenario modelling the effects of such a change in diets, India's demand for meat products is forecast to increase almost tenfold from 3.8 million tonnes in 1993 to 36.4 million tonnes in 2020. This increase would have to be met through trade, as meat production is not projected to increase beyond the 8.5 million tonnes shown in the baseline scenario for 2020. India's projected net meat imports of 28 million tonnes under this scenario are a far cry from the less than 0.5 million tonnes forecast in the baseline scenario. This increase in Indian net imports would increase world meat prices by 21 per cent in 2020 relative to the baseline scenario and by 13 per cent relative to 1993. If India attempts to meet potentially large increases in livestock demand through domestic production rather than imports, thereby raising demand for feed grain, the implications for global livestock and cereals trade and prices would be dramatically different from those predicted by the scenario that relies primarily on livestock imports to meet demand.

4. Transition in Eastern Europe and the Former Soviet Union

The fall of the Berlin Wall and the associated political changes in Eastern Europe and the former Soviet Union brought great promise for rapid economic growth in that part of the world. Many projected that food production in a number of countries affected, including Ukraine and the Russian Federation, would expand rapidly and significantly, causing Eastern Europe and the former Soviet Union to switch quickly from being net importers of grain to being significant net exporters [Tyers, 1994]. Although net grain imports by the former Soviet Union have fallen dramatically, this optimistic scenario has not materialised [FAO, Food Outlook various years]. There is still a great deal of uncertainty regarding future food production and demand in these countries.

Many of the countries of Eastern Europe and the former Soviet Union have tremendous agricultural potential that is as yet underutilised. Appropriate changes in institutions and policies (including property rights), increased market and trade liberalisation, and investment in rural infrastructure could result in rapid increases in production, but such changes have been extremely slow. European Union (EU) membership by some East European countries could accelerate agricultural transformation in these countries with resulting expansions in food production.

IMPACT's baseline scenario projects that Eastern Europe and the former Soviet Union will become major net exporters of cereals by 2020, on the order of about 33 million tonnes. Cereal production is projected to increase by almost 40 per cent between 1993 and 2020 to 341 million tonnes, while demand is projected to increase by 12 per cent to 308 million tonnes. However, if incomes in Eastern Europe and the former Soviet Union grow faster than the baseline projection and crop productivity increases at a slower pace than forecast, these countries would remain net importers. For example, with an increase in income growth of 30 per cent and a drop in production growth of two-thirds, crop production would increase by only 12 per cent between 1993 and 2020 to 278 million tonnes while demand would increase to 304 million tonnes, resulting in net cereal imports of 26 million tonnes in 2020 – a very different outcome. Slow crop production in Eastern Europe and the former Soviet Union could cause world cereal prices to be higher in 2020 relative to the baseline scenario. Changes in cereal production and demand in Eastern Europe and the former Soviet Union can have significant effects on the world food situation, but it would take very large declines in productivity growth in this region to drive cereal prices up dramatically.

5. Fragile Recovery in Sub-Saharan Africa

In sub-Saharan Africa, the population growth rate has exceeded the rate of growth in food production since the early 1970s and the gap is widening, resulting in declining per capita food production. Simple extrapolations of the trends in population and food production growth since 1961 show a further increase in the gap between population and food production. This is exactly the gap predicted by Malthus.[5] However, several recent developments suggest that Malthus's shadow over sub-Saharan Africa could finally be waning.

First, Malthus's predictions grossly underestimated the potential of productivity-increasing technology. Where such technology has been effectively developed and utilised, as in Asia, food production has expanded much faster than population. In sub-Saharan Africa, the potential of appropriate productivity-increasing technology has yet to be realised. Maize yields for Africa and Asia were virtually the same in 1961, but since then they have tripled in Asia and quintupled in China while they have remained stagnant at around 1 tonne per hectare in Africa [FAO, 1997a; Byerlee and Eicher, 1997]. However, there are encouraging signs that productivity-increasing technology is beginning to accelerate yield growth of African food crops [CGIAR, 1997].

Second, after a number of years of low or negative growth, sub-Saharan Africa is experiencing economic recovery. However, this recovery is fragile. Some of the factors that contributed to it are short-term in nature and cannot be expected to persist; these include higher commodity prices and favourable weather conditions. Other factors, such as policy reforms, an improved macroeconomic environment, and social and political stability, can have a more lasting effect on economic growth, if properly nurtured. Moreover, economic growth rates will have to be substantially higher if they are to make a dent in sub-Saharan Africa's poverty; per capita incomes have fallen so much that even if economic growth were to continue at the current pace (about 5 per cent per year), it would still take at least a decade to recover to the levels prevailing in 1980 [CGIAR, 1997].

---

5. Thomas Malthus's basic argument was that the world's natural resources could not guarantee expansions in food supply to match population growth. Region after region has disproved his prediction. He postulated that the population would grow geometrically and food production would grow arithmetically. To date, except for sub-Saharan Africa, region after region has disproved his prediction.

If Malthus is to be proved wrong in sub-Saharan Africa, a much greater effort must be made to ensure that farmers have access to appropriate production technology and that policies are conducive to expanded productivity in staple food crops. Besides new initiatives and increased support for agricultural development, more must also be done to reduce population growth. Sub-Saharan Africa's annual population growth is projected to decline between 1993 and 2020. Yet the number of people added to the region's population every year is projected to increase until at least 2020, a consequence of the past high rates of population increase. Moreover, the projected annual population growth rate of 2.33 per cent during 2015–20 will be more than double the growth rates in other regions [*UN, 1996*]. Population growth of this magnitude will severely constrain efforts to increase income and improve welfare, while at the same time it will greatly increase the need for food.

6. Weather Fluctuations and Climate Change

With the recent resurgence of El Niño, followed by the relatively weaker La Niña, major weather fluctuations are under way or imminent in many parts of the world. These fluctuations could lead to sizeable food production shortfalls and deterioration in food security in many parts of the world. The 1982–83 El Niño caused severe flooding in Latin America, droughts in parts of Asia, declines in fish stocks, and other weather-related damage estimated at over US$10 billion [*FAO, 1997b, 1997c*]. The 1991–92 El Niño resulted in severe drought in southern Africa that caused cereal production to drop by 60 per cent or more in several countries, and imports and food aid had to increase to meet more than half of the cereal consumption in at least five countries [*Pinstrup-Andersen et al., 1997*].

The 1997–98 El Niño far surpassed the previous two major El Niños in severity, causing severe drought in South-East Asia, flooding in the Andean countries of South America, and drought in a wide swath across Eastern Africa, and in general diminishing agricultural production around the globe. El Niño adds a major element of uncertainty to agricultural production and livelihoods worldwide. And concerns are growing that El Niños may become more frequent and more severe in the future as a result of climate changes.

Although the trend of global warming is becoming increasingly clear, its effects on food production are still uncertain. Some research suggests that growing conditions will deteriorate in current tropical areas (where many of the developing countries are located) and improve in current temperate areas (where many of the developed countries are located) [*Rosenzweig and Parry, 1994; Fischer et al., 1996*]. However, effects on productivity and production will occur over a long period of time and will be very small in any given year. It is therefore reasonable to believe that policies and technologies can be developed to prevent or counter the negative productivity effects of global warming. Failure by the public sector to act, and failure by the market and the private sector to respond, could result in significant long-term effects on food supply. Such a scenario might include reduced food production in tropical and subtropical countries and increased production in temperate countries. Whether these opposing effects will cancel each other out through expanded international trade, with little or no effect on total world food supply, is yet to be determined.

7. Growing Water Scarcity

Unless properly managed, fresh water may well emerge as the key constraint to global food production. While supplies of water are adequate in the aggregate to meet demand for the foreseeable future, water is poorly distributed across and within countries and between seasons. And, with a fixed amount of renewable water resources to meet the needs of a continually increasing population, per capita water availability is declining steadily. Today, 28 countries with a total population exceeding 300 million people face water stress.[6] By 2025, their number could increase to about 50 countries with a total population of about 3 billion people [*Rosegrant et al., 1997a; Population Action International, 1995*].

Demand for water will continue to grow rapidly. Since 1970, global demand for water has grown by 2.4 per cent per year [*Rosegrant et al., 1997a*]. Projections of water demand[7] to 2020 indicate that global water withdrawals will increase by 35 per cent between 1995 and 2020 to reach 5,060 billion cubic meters. Developed countries are projected to increase their water withdrawals by 22 per cent, more than 80 per cent of the increase being for industrial use. Developing countries are projected to increase their withdrawals by 43 per cent over the same period and to experience a significant structural change in their demand for water, reducing the share for agricultural use. Failure to address the gap between tightening supplies and increasing demand for water could significantly slow growth in food production.

---

6. Their annual internal renewable water resources are less than 1,600 cubic meters per person per year.
7. Approximated by water withdrawals because of a lack of consistent data on consumptive use of water at national or regional levels.

8. Declining Soil Fertility

Improved soil fertility is a critical component of the drive of low-income countries to increase sustainable agricultural production. Past and current failures to replenish soil nutrients in many countries must be rectified through the balanced and efficient use of organic and inorganic plant nutrients and through improved soil management practices. Although some of the plant nutrient requirements can be met through the application of organic materials, these are insufficient to replenish the nutrients removed from the soils and thus to expand crop yields further. But the use of chemical fertilisers has decreased worldwide during the last few years, particularly in the developed countries and in parts of Asia. Although reduced use of fertilisers is warranted in some locations because of negative environmental effects, it is critical that fertiliser use be expanded in countries where soil fertility is low and a large share of the population is food-insecure. Fertiliser consumption in these countries is generally low because of the high prices, insecure supplies, and the greater risk associated with food production in marginal areas. For example, on average, fertiliser consumption in sub-Saharan Africa is about 14 kg per hectare compared with about 200 kg per hectare in East Asia [*World Bank, 1997a*]. Expanded use of fertilisers in sub-Saharan Africa would help alleviate current production shortfalls as well as serious soil degradation.

9. Conflicts and Food Security

Widespread local, national, and regional instability and armed conflicts contribute to the persistence of poverty, food insecurity, and natural resource degradation. While relief agencies around the world are well aware of the disastrous effects of conflicts on people's capacity to assure their food security, opportunities for preventing or resolving conflict through improvements in food security and more sustainable use of natural resources have received little attention until recently. It is becoming increasingly clear that poverty, food insecurity, and natural resource degradation contribute to the initiation or prolongation of instability or conflicts. Poor, food-insecure people may, in desperate circumstances, perceive no option but to engage in conflict to secure their access to resources that will guarantee future well-being. Of course, not all poor, food-insecure people engage in conflict, but the probability of instability or conflict rises in circumstances where people are pushed to the limit to meet even their most fundamental needs. The complex, mutually reinforcing relationship between poverty, food insecurity, and natural resource degradation, on the one hand, and social and political instability and conflict, on the other, has not been fully recognised or acknowledged.

Yet, 57 per cent of the countries considered by the United Nations to have low human development (low life expectancies at birth, low levels of education, and low incomes) were gripped by conflict during 1990–95, compared with 14 per cent of the countries considered to have high human development (high life expectancies at birth, high levels of education, and high incomes) [*Smith, 1997*]. And more than half of the 17 sub-Saharan African countries currently suffering from food emergencies are also suffering from civil strife or armed conflict [*FAO, 1997d*]. Conflicts in countries such as Burundi and Rwanda are frequently characterised as resulting from tribal or political issues when, in fact, the underlying or catalytic causes are natural resource degradation, extreme poverty, and widespread food insecurity. Such conflicts, in turn, breed further food insecurity, poverty, and natural resource degradation, continuing the vicious circle of hunger and instability.

IV. IMPLICATIONS FOR POLICY AND RESEARCH

During the next 25 years, food production will not keep pace with increases in food demand in developing countries. For those with growing economies, this increased demand can be met by imports, mainly from developed countries. However, many of the low-income, slower-growth countries, including most of those in sub-Saharan Africa, may not be able to fill the gap between food demand and production through commercial imports. Greater risks and larger fluctuations in food availability and prices will exacerbate their precarious food security situation. Unless new action is taken, the gap between food needs and availability in many low-income countries will widen, resulting in increasing food insecurity, hunger and malnutrition.

The actions needed are comprehensively described in action plans from the World Food Summit and IFPRI's 2020 Vision initiative [*FAO, 1996b; IFPRI, 1995*]. The focus of agricultural research and policy aimed at reducing poverty and food insecurity should be on the low-income developing countries, and particularly on their small farmers. Continued low productivity in agriculture not only contributes to food gaps in these countries, but also prevents attainment of the broad-based income growth and lower unit costs in food production needed to help fill the gap and improve food security. While efforts to improve long-term productivity on small-scale farms must be accelerated, more emphasis must also be placed on research and policy that will help farmers, communities, and governments to cope better with expected increases in risks resulting from poor market integration, dysfunctional or poorly functioning markets, climatic fluctuations, and a host of other factors. All appropriate scientific tools, including bioengineering, should be mobilised to help solve the problems facing small-scale farmers in developing countries. Current investments are extremely low and must be expanded.

The agricultural productivity increases needed to lift the populations of low-income developing countries out of poverty and food insecurity without doing irreparable damage to natural resources will be possible only if appropriate government policies are pursued and investments in the rural areas are expanded. The specific policy measures must be designed within each country. Most low-income developing countries will need to review their trade and macroeconomic policies, as well as policies that concern their sound economy and environment. The latter cover issues such as water management and allocation, property rights to land and other natural resources, agricultural input and output markets, income-earning opportunities and social safety nets for low-income families, infrastructure, financial markets, and various other incentives for small farmers, including those needed to adjust to and benefit from further trade liberalisation. Governments should also review their current allocation of public sector resources to primary education, health care, agricultural research and extension, rural infrastructure, and other public goods needed to accelerate broad-based growth within and outside agriculture. Developed countries should consider reversing the downward trend of official development finance, particularly to the most vulnerable developing countries. Failure to take appropriate action will result in continued low economic growth and rapidly increasing food insecurity and malnutrition in many low-income developing countries, forgone opportunities for expanded international trade, widespread conflict and civil strife, and an unstable world for all.

REFERENCES

Brown, L., 1995, *Who Will Feed China?* New York: W. W. Norton.
Byerlee, D. and C. K. Eicher, eds., 1997, *Africa's Emerging Maize Revolution*, Boulder, CO: Lynne Rienner.
Carter, C. and Z. Funing, 1991, 'China's Past and Future Role in the Grain Trade', *Economic Development and Cultural Change*, Vol. 39.
CGIAR (Consultative Group on International Agricultural Research), 1997, 'Phenomenal Increase in Maize Production in West and Central Africa', *CGIAR News*, Vol. 4, No. 2.

Chen, L. Y. and A. Buckwell, 1991, *Chinese Grain Economy and Policy*, Wallingford, UK: CAB International.

Fan, S. and M. A. Sombilla, 1997, 'China's Food Supply and Demand in the 21st Century: Baseline Projections and Policy Simulations'. Paper prepared for the postconference workshop on 'China's Food Economy in the 21st Century' at the American Agricultural Economics Association Annual Meeting, Toronto, 31 July.

FAO (Food and Agriculture Organisation of the United Nations), 1996a, *Investment in Agriculture: Evolution and Prospects*, World Food Summit Technical Background Document 10, Rome.

FAO, 1996b, *Rome Declaration on World Food Security and World Food Summit Plan of Action*, Rome.

FAO, various years, *Food Outlook*, Rome.

FAO, 1997a, FAOSTAT database http://faostat.fao.org/default.htm, accessed August and Sept.

FAO, 1997b, *Special Report: El Niño's Impact on Crop Production in Latin America*, Rome.

FAO, 1997c, *Special Report: The Impact of El Niño and Other Weather Anomalies on Crop Production in Asia*, Rome.

FAO, 1997d, *Food Supply Situation and Crop Prospects in Sub-Saharan Africa*, No. 3 (Aug.), Rome.

Fischer, G., K. Frohberg, M. L. Parry and C. Rosenzweig, 1996, 'Impacts of Potential Climate Change on Global and Regional Food Production and Vulnerability', in T.E. Downing, ed., *Climate Change and World Food Security*, NATO ASI Series, Vol. 37, Berlin: Springer Verlag.

Garnaut, R. and G. Ma, 1992, *Grain in China: A Report*, Canberra: Department of Foreign Affairs and Trade, East Asian Analytical Unit.

IFPRI (International Food Policy Research Institute), 1995, *A 2020 Vision for Food, Agriculture, and the Environment: The Vision, Challenge, and Recommended Action*, Washington DC.

Mei, F., 1995, 'China Can Feed Its Population', *China Daily*, 29 April.

Pinstrup-Andersen, P., R. Pandya-Lorch and S. Babu, 1997, 'A 2020 Vision for Food, Agriculture, and the Environment in Southern Africa', in Lawrence Haddad, ed., *Achieving Food Security in Southern Africa: New Challenges, New Opportunities*, Washington DC: IFPRI.

Population Action International (PAI), 1995, *Sustaining Water: An Update*, Washington DC: PAI.

Rosegrant, M.W., M. Agcaoili-Sombilla and N.D. Perez, 1995, *Global Food Projections to 2020: Implications for Investment.* Food, Agriculture, and the Environment Discussion Paper 5, Washington DC: IFPRI.

Rosegrant, M.W., C. Ringler and R.V. Gerpacio, 1997a, 'Water and Land Resources and Global Food Supply', paper prepared for the 23rd International Conference of Agricultural Economists, Sacramento, CA, 10–16 August.

Rosegrant, M.W., M.A. Sombilla, R.V. Gerpacio and C. Ringler, 1997b, 'Global Food Markets and U.S. Exports in the Twenty-First Century', paper presented at the Illinois World Food and Sustainable Agriculture Program Conference 'Meeting the Demand for Food in the Twenty-First Century: Challenges and Opportunities for Illinois Agriculture', Urbana-Champaign, 27 May, Washington DC: IFPRI.

Rosegrant, M.W., N. Leach and R.V. Gerpacio, 1998, 'Alternative Futures for World Cereal and Meat Consumption', Washington DC: IFPRI. Mimeo.

Rosegrant, M. W. and C. Ringler, 1998, 'Economic Crisis in Asia: A Future of Diminishing Growth and Increasing Poverty?', 2020 Vision Brief No. 57, Washington DC: IFPRI.

Rosenzweig, C. and M.L. Parry, 1994, 'Potential Impact of Climate Change on World Food Supply', *Nature*, Vol. 367 (Jan.).

Rozelle, S. and M.W. Rosegrant, 1997, 'China's past, present, and future food economy: Can China continue to meet the challenges?', *Food Policy*, Vol. 22, No. 3.

Smith, D., 1997, *The State of War and Peace Atlas*, new rev. 3rd ed., London/ Harmonsworth: Penguin.

Tyers, R., 1994, *Economic Reform in Europe and the Former Soviet Union: Implications for International Food Markets*, Research Report No. 99, Washington DC: IFPRI.

UN (United Nations), 1995, *World Urbanization Prospects: The 1994 Revisions*, New York.

UN, 1996, *World Population Prospects: The 1996 Revisions*, New York.

World Bank, 1997a, *1997, World Development Indicators*, Washington DC.

World Bank, 1997b, *World Development Report 1997*, Oxford: Oxford University Press.

3

The Uruguay Round, the Marrakesh Decision and the Role of Food Aid

PANOS KONANDREAS, RAMESH SHARMA
AND JIM GREENFIELD

I. INTRODUCTION

Six years have passed since the conclusion of the Uruguay Round (UR) and the World Trade Organisation (WTO) has expanded to include more than 130 countries, with most of the new members being developing countries. Discussions on the continuation of the reform process in agriculture were scheduled to begin in 1999, as called for by Article 20 of the Agreement on Agriculture, and it is considered highly desirable that developing countries, especially the least developed among them, participate fully in this process. Yet, several issues hang over these developments, having to do with commitments made under the Uruguay Round, and, for a particular group of countries, the Marrakesh Ministerial Decision on Measures Concerning the Possible Negative Effects of the Reform Programme on Least Developed and Net Food Importing Developing Countries is of particular importance.

The Uruguay Round, being the product of multilateral trade negotiations involving a number of commodities and sectors, implied that some commodity sectors in some countries would gain and some would lose. Overall, however, it was expected that the sum of the gains would exceed the sum of the losses.[1] As regards basic foodstuffs, most studies projected that their prices would rise on the world market compared with what they would otherwise have been. For several developing countries which depend heavily on imports of

---

The views expressed in this chapter are those of the authors and do not necessarily represent the position of FAO.
1.   This is borne out by such studies as those by the OECD/World Bank and GATT which estimate annual net gains to world income of over US$200 billion, although there is a wide variation, ranging from less than US$100 bn to as much as US$500 bn [*Goldin et al., 1993; GATT, 1994*].

basic food commodities, this could translate into higher food import bills, at least in the short term.

The possibility of such adverse effects was the main rationale for the Marrakesh Decision mentioned above which was negotiated as an integral part of the Final Act of the trade negotiations. The Decision calls for certain remedies in the form of assistance, should the reform process result in negative effects for the least developed (LDCs) and net food-importing developing countries (NFIDCs) (see Annex 3.1). Despite the obvious difficulties that these groups of countries have experienced in the past few years, not necessarily ascribed to the Uruguay Round, little action under this Decision has so far materialised.

This chapter looks in some detail at the nature of the difficulties food-importing developing countries may face as a result of the implementation of the Uruguay Round and examines the role of food aid in response to these difficulties, food aid being one of the means of assistance under the Decision. First, it reviews various aspects of the impact of the Round on world food markets and attempts to clarify these effects on the basis of analytical and empirical judgments. Section III then analyses how the food supply situation in the LDCs and NFIDCs has evolved in the recent past and how these countries have managed to meet their cereal needs especially during the period of high world prices experienced in 1995/96. Section IV discusses how food aid may respond to the needs of these countries as called for by the Decision and the final section draws some overall conclusions.

II. LIKELY IMPACTS OF THE URUGUAY ROUND

This section takes stock of the various effects of the Uruguay Round on world food markets and related food security issues.

1. Higher World Market Prices?

The first expectation of the Uruguay Round was an increase in the world market prices of temperate zone food commodities, which enjoyed considerable support in the developed countries in the past. Reduction of that support as a result of the Round was expected to lead to a decrease in output and exportable surpluses and thus boost world prices of these commodities at least in the short term. Several models attempted to ascertain *ex ante* the magnitude of this effect on world market prices [*FAO, 1995; UNCTAD, 1995; Goldin and Mensbrugghe, 1995*]. The consensus was for moderate price increases, compared with underlying trends, as a result of the trade policy reforms under way (Table 3.1).

TABLE 3.1

CHANGES IN WORLD MARKET PRICES OF AGRICULTURAL PRODUCTS DUE TO THE URUGUAY
ROUND (% CHANGE FROM BENCHMARK LEVELS AT THE END OF IMPLEMENTATION PERIOD)[a]

Products	WFM	ATPSM		RUNS	
		I: Without policy response	II: With policy response	I: 1982–93 base	II: 1991–93 base
Wheat	6.9	8.6	1.0	1.2	6.3
Rice	7.3	9.6	0.7	-1.5	0.8
Coarse grains	4.4	9.0	3.2	0.1	3.2
Fats and oils	4.2	5.9	2.5	-0.6	3.9
Oil seeds	-	7.7	3.8	-	-
Bovine meat	8.0	10.1	5.3	0.2[b]	1.4[b]
Pig-meat	10.4	6.3	2.7	-0.9[b]	-0.1[b]
Sheep meat	9.9	10.2	5.5	0.2[b]	1.4[b]
Poultry	8.4	9.3	4.9	-0.9[b]	-0.1[b]
Dairy products	7.6	7.9	4.5	-1.3	2.3
Sugar	-	11.3	4.5	-1.0	2.5
Coffee	-	-	-	-1.7	-1.4
Cocoa	-	-	-	-1.3	-0.6
Tea	-	-	-	-1.6	-1.2
Wool	-	-	-	-1.1	0.5
Cotton	-	-	-	-1.3	-0.3

[a] These are 2000 for WFM and ATPSM, and 2002 for RUNS.
[b] In RUNS, there are only two meat groups, bovine/sheep meats, and pig-meat/poultry meats.

Sources: WFM [*FAO, 1995*]; ATPSM [*UNCTAD, 1995*]; RUNS [*Goldin and Mensbrugghe 1995*]. ATPSM I refers to a scenario where domestic markets in non-OECD countries are assumed not to respond to changes in world market prices while ATPSM II assumes that they do. RUNS I simulates the Uruguay Round reform from the 1982–93 average base protection level, while RUNS II uses the 1991–93 base period. (WFM=World Food Model; ATPSM=Agricultural Trade Policy Simulation Model; RUNS=Rural-Urban North-South).

International prices of most agricultural commodities, measured in constant dollar values, have been falling over the longer term (Figure 3.1), although it is sometimes difficult to be sure when comparing recent prices with those in the mid- to late 1980s, when export subsidies were rife and actual import prices were therefore often well below quoted prices for many importing countries. Some analysis suggests that a levelling off of world prices started in the late 1980s [*Vanzetti, 1998*], a finding that, if anything, is strengthened by the fact that world prices in the late 1980s and early 1990s overstated their true level because of the widespread use of export subsidies. One has to be cautious therefore in assuming that the decline in the real prices of major food commodities will continue. In the medium term, they are likely to be above their historically declining trend, and they will perhaps remain at the levels reached in the early 1990s.

FIGURE 3.1
REAL PRICE TRENDS OF AGRICULTURAL COMMODITIES (1980 = 100)

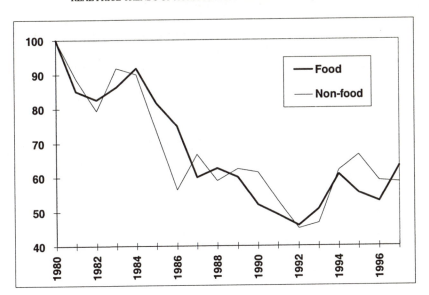

Source: Commodities and Trade Division, FAO

2. Higher World Price Variability?

Equally uncertain is the extent to which world market price instability may be affected in the future. In general, although there have been no strong trends in world price instability in the past [*Sarris, 1997*], this cannot be a reliable guide for the future. Several fundamental parameters have changed considerably, some of which would be expected to contribute to greater and some to less instability [*FAO, 1990, 1996*].

Factors that may contribute to increasing instability, especially in the important cereals sector, include, *inter alia*:

– lower levels of global cereal stocks;
– UR-related shifts in the location of production to regions more prone to instability, although the likely effect would be very small;
– greater vertical integration in the livestock industry, in some cases making demand for feedstuffs less responsive to price changes;

79

- increased pressure of financial funds in international commodity markets, although their effect would be mainly on increased within-year price variability; and
- uncertainties with respect to adjustments under way in the transition economies and the integration of China and countries of the former USSR into the world agricultural trading system.

On the other hand, factors that may reduce instability include, *inter alia*:

- market liberalisation, including the UR agreements, regional trading arrangements and unilateral initiatives, which should lead to greater price responsiveness;
- increased transparency and consistency on the part of governments in their stockholding and trade policies;
- the larger share of private stocks within a reduced total, which would be more responsive to price developments; and
- advances in feed technology, in some cases making the sector more flexible in responding to price changes.

It is not possible to come to a conclusion with any certainty on the net impact on instability of this complex set of developments. The path to the new more liberalised market environment is unsettled and instability is likely to be greater in the transitional period than when the system has fully adjusted.

3. Higher and Unstable Domestic Prices?

Changes in the domestic prices of importing countries depend not only on the changes in world prices but also on the degree of transmission of these world prices to the domestic market. This transmission is largely dependent on the extent of trade liberalisation carried out by the importing countries themselves [*Colman, 1993, 1995*].

There can be no generalisation on the direction of change in the domestic price. In cases where the tariff reduction was zero, the domestic price would increase following a rise in the world price, if the country traded at world prices. In other cases, the change in the domestic price could be positive or negative depending on the extent of reduction in the tariff rate and the increase in the world market price.

The main conclusion from the above is that it is not necessarily the case that the Uruguay Round would result in an increase in the domestic price of an importing country, even though there may be an increase in the world market price; a decrease in the domestic price is also possible, depending on the initial level of protection and the reduction in that protection by the importing country.[2] It also follows that, since the domestic price can move in the opposite direction from that of the world price, instability in the world market does not necessarily have to be fully transmitted to the domestic market.

4. Higher Food Import Bills?

The expectation of higher food import bills as a result of the Uruguay Round is a direct consequence of the expected higher world market prices discussed above. A FAO estimate of the projected impact of the Uruguay Round on food import bills [*Greenfield et al., 1996*] indicated that on the whole developing countries would spend some US$3.6 billion more in 2000 as a result of the Round, or about 15 per cent above their projected food import bill for that year.

The impact on individual importing countries would depend on the extent to which price changes are transmitted to the domestic market, and how consumption and, more importantly, production respond to these changes.[3] Taking cereals as an example and assuming supply and demand elasticities of 0.3 and -0.2, and a transmission elasticity of 0.8, then only countries with a self-sufficiency ratio (SSR) below about 67 per cent would be likely to face higher cereal import bills (Figure 3.2). On the other hand, when there is not much response, that is, the transmission, demand and supply elasticities are much smaller, then even countries with much higher SSRs are likely to be adversely affected by higher prices. For example, assuming values of the related elasticities half the above levels, then even countries with an SSR as high as 90 per cent are likely to face higher cereal import bills as a result of higher world prices.[4]

---

2. In practice, this is also affected by changes in the exchange rate.
3. Formally, the food import bill (M) is the product of the world price (P_w) and the import volume which, in the absence of stock variations, is the difference between total domestic consumption (D) and domestic production (Q), that is,

$M = P_w (D - Q)$

Assuming a simple transmission equation of the world market price to the domestic market of the form:

$P_d = a \, P_w^\tau$

where τ is the transmission elasticity, it follows that the elasticity of the food import bill with respect to the world market price (e_m) would be:

$e_m = 1 + \tau \, e_d + \tau \, (e_d - e_s) \, SSR/(1-SSR),$

where e_d and e_s are the price elasticities of domestic demand and supply respectively, and SSR is the food self-sufficiency ratio of the importing country.
4. In all cases the net purchasers of food commodities in a net food importing country (for instance urban households) would be adversely affected by higher domestic prices, and internal or international transfers may be needed to compensate them.

FIGURE 3.2
THE PRICE ELASTICITY OF THE IMPORT BILL

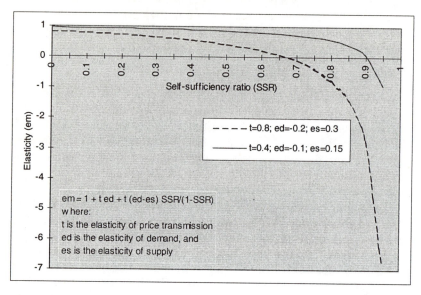

Two important conclusions can be derived from the above. First, the more a country transmits the world price to the domestic market and the greater the demand and supply response, the smaller the impact of a higher world price on its food import bill. Second, the possibilities for adjustment have a limited effect in countries which depend heavily on food imports. For the LDCs and NFIDCs as a group, their average (1994–96) SSR is about 82 per cent (90 per cent for the LDCs and 72 per cent for the NFIDCs).[5] However, there are considerable differences between countries (Figure 3.3). One-quarter of these countries have an SSR below 25 per cent, half of them have an SSR below 65 per cent and three-quarters of them below 90 per cent. Therefore, with low SSRs, a large number of these countries are located in the left part of Figure 3.2, where the price elasticities of the import bill are positive. Moreover, these countries have generally low agricultural potential to respond to higher prices (low e_s) and their food consumption levels are already low and thus cannot be adjusted further without undue hardship (low e_d). Clearly, therefore, a large number of the LDCs and NFIDCs would be able to reduce the volume of imports only modestly through adjustments in domestic production and consumption. An increase in their cereal import bills as a result of higher world prices is therefore inevitable.

5. The SSR of the developing countries as a whole is about 89 per cent.

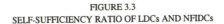

FIGURE 3.3
SELF-SUFFICIENCY RATIO OF LDCs AND NFIDCs

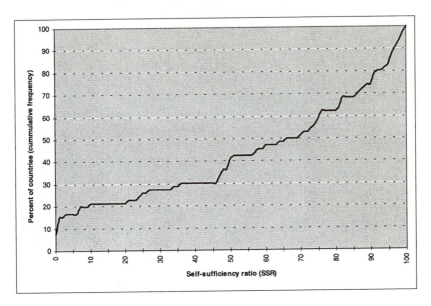

III. THE ACTUAL SITUATION IN THE LDCS AND NFIDCS

The above somewhat theoretical exposition leaves the possibility for a wide range of effects, the impact of which for individual countries would depend on their specific situation. For a more concrete picture we need to focus on specific groups of countries and base the analysis on actual data. An appropriate list of countries to consider are clearly those eligible for assistance under the Marrakesh Decision (see Annex 3.1).[6]

1. The Food Security Situation in the LDCs and NFIDCs

The LDCs and NFIDCs are clearly distinct from the rest of the developing countries. The 48 LDCs had a population of 588 million in 1995, growing at 2.9 per cent per annum. Their average per capita income was US$235 in 1995 and for 24 of them, for which data are available, it was declining during the period 1985–95. The NFIDCs numbered 18, with a total population of 368 million in 1995, growing at 2.6 per cent per annum. Average per capita income was US$920

---

6. This section is based on an initial study undertaken by FAO [*FAO, 1997*] which is updated here to include more recent data.

and it was rising for 16 of them over the period 1985–95. Together, these two groups of countries accounted for 21 per cent of the population of developing countries but contained one-third of the undernourished. The percentage of undernourished population has barely changed since the early 1970s – at about 40 per cent for the LDCs and 20 per cent for the NFIDCs. Given the serious extent of undernourishment, even small variations in year-to-year supply can have considerable implications for the nutritional situation in these countries.

The performance of their domestic food production has not been encouraging. In the case of cereals, which account for 52 per cent of total dietary supplies in LDCs and 45 per cent in NFIDCs, per capita production showed a declining trend in the period 1980–96 – falling in 29 of the 42 cereal-producing LDCs and in 13 of the 18 NFIDCs. At between 170 to 180 kg per annum, per capita cereal production in both the LDCs and the NFIDCs is over 100 kg less than in the rest of the developing countries (Figure 3.4). Moreover, the coefficient of variation of cereal production exceeded 10 per cent in 26 of the LDCs and in 11 NFIDCs, thus contributing to sharp fluctuations in cereal imports. The burden of such fluctuations in import requirements is larger, the greater the dependence on cereal imports.

This dependence is highest for the NFIDCs. On average this group of countries imports close to 30 per cent of the total cereals consumed (Figure 3.5). For the LDCs the dependence on imports is 10 per cent, about the same level as that of the rest of the developing countries. Cereals dominate the food import bills of these countries, accounting for roughly 40 per cent of the total for both LDCs and NFIDCs during recent years, followed by vegetable oils and oilseeds at about 20 per cent (Figure 3.6). The food import composition for LDCs and NFIDCs differs considerably from that of the remaining developing countries, where the share of both cereals and vegetable oils is much smaller (at 28 and 15 per cent respectively). This is largely a reflection of the higher average income levels of the latter countries which can afford to import other higher value commodities such as meat and dairy products, and fruits and vegetables.

Another characteristic of the LDCs and NFIDCs has been their heavy dependence on food aid and other concessional sales. Especially during the 1980s, a considerable share of their import needs was met by food aid (as much as 64 per cent for the LDCs and about 22 per cent for the NFIDCs) and this trend continued well into the 1990s although at much reduced levels (Figure 3.7).

FIGURE 3.4
PER CAPITA CEREAL PRODUCTION (KG/ANNUM)

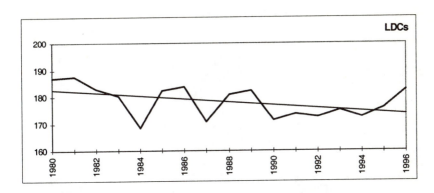

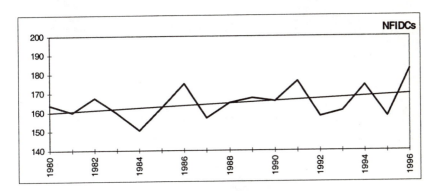

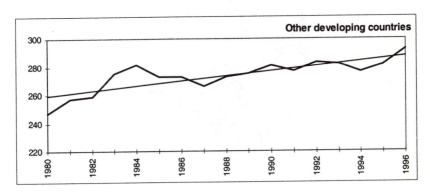

FIGURE 3.5
DEPENDENCE ON FOOD IMPORTS FOR CEREALS (%)

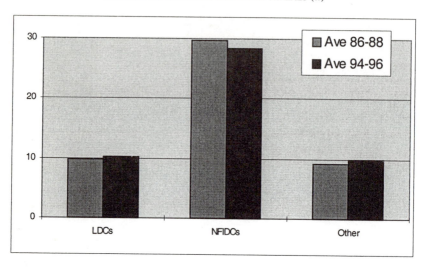

FIGURE 3.6
COMPOSITION OF FOOD IMPORTS, 1993–95 (%)

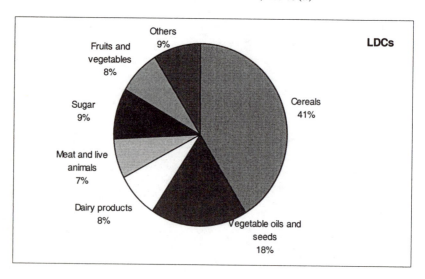

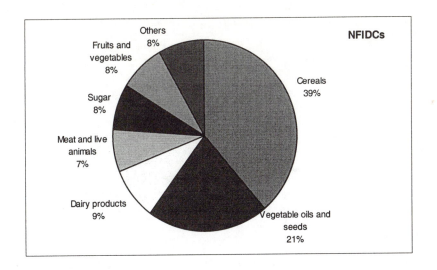

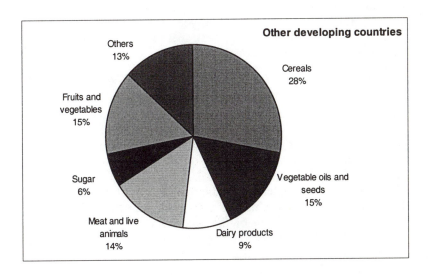

FIGURE 3.7
RATIO OF FOOD AID TO TOTAL CEREAL IMPORTS

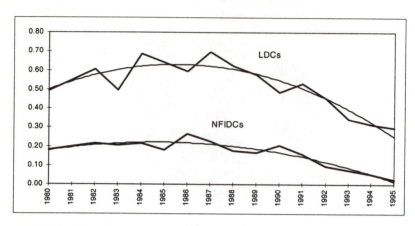

The overall conclusion of the above is that the LDCs and the NFIDCs are clearly differentiated from the rest of the developing countries. Their slow food production growth and high production variability remain a major problem and this contributes to high levels of chronic and transitory undernutrition. In turn, they have a high dependence on imports (as well as sharp year-to-year fluctuations in their cereal import bills), which in the past were met to a considerable degree by food aid and other concessional sales.

2. Trends in Cereal Import Bills of LDCs and NFIDCs since 1995

Given the relatively high import dependence of the LDCs and NFIDCs, their experience in the post-Uruguay Round period (since 1995) is of particular importance in view also of the substantial increase in the world price of basic foodstuffs during part of this period. Table 3.2 provides details of the cereal import bills of the LDCs and NFIDCs on an annual basis for the marketing years 1993/94 to 1998/99. Clearly, the high price year 1995/96 was a shock for these countries.[7] Taking the two years prior to 1995 as a benchmark (that is, the average of the two marketing years 1993/94 and 1994/95), the increase in the cereal import bills in 1995/96 was over 60 per cent for the two groups of countries taken together. Nearly all of this increase was due to increases in the *per unit cost* of imported cereals as volumes changed only marginally.

---

7.   Wheat prices (US No. 2 hard winter) increased from US$143/tonne in 1993/94 to US$216/tonne in 1995/96. The corresponding prices for maize (US No. 2 yellow) were US$113/tonne and US$159/tonne, and for rice (Thai, 100 per cent, 2nd grade) US$250/tonne and US$336/tonne.

TABLE 3.2
CEREAL IMPORTS OF LDCs AND NFIDCs (1993/94 TO 1998/99)

	1993/ 94	1994/ 95	Average 1993/94– 94/95	1995/ 96	1996/ 97	1997/ 98	Average 1996/97– 97/98	Preliminary 1998/99
Values ($ 1000)								
LDCs	1188	2037	1613	2787	2058	2833	2446	2538
NFIDCs	3510	4011	3760	5822	5483	5107	5295	4038
LDCs+NFIDCs	4698	6048	5373	8609	7542	7940	7741	6577
% change over 1993/94–94/95				60.2	40.4	47.8	44.1	22.4
Volumes (1000 tonnes)								
LDCs	11172	13307	12240	12337	10556	14039	12297	14077
NFIDCs	25502	25958	25730	26078	27694	31044	29369	27706
LDCs+NFIDCs	36674	39265	37969	38416	38249	45082	41666	41783
% change over 1993/94–94/95				1.2	0.7	18.7	9.7	10.0
Per unit cost ($/tonnes)								
LDCs	106	153	130	226	195	202	198	180
NFIDCs	138	155	146	223	198	165	181	146
LDCs+NFIDCs	128	154	141	224	197	176	187	157
% change over 1993/94–94/95				58.9	39.8	24.9	32.3	11.6
Nominal export price ($/tonnes) Wheat (US No. 2 hard winter)	143	157	150	216	181	142	162	118
% change over 1993/94–94/95				44.0	20.7	-5.3	7.7	-21.3

Source: FAO. Figures for 1998/99 are preliminary

As the world price has returned to more normal levels since then, have the cereal import bills also improved? The answer to this question is yes but only moderately (Figure 3.8). Although lower than the 1995/96 peak, cereal import bills are now at a much higher plateau than they were prior to 1995. To get an idea of the reasons behind this shift to a higher plateau, Table 3.2 compares the two years following 1995/96 (that is, the average of marketing years 1996/97 and 1997/98) with that of the pre-UR situation. Average cereal imports of these two groups of countries during the 1996/97–97/98 marketing years are estimated at about 42 million tonnes, compared with an average of 38 million tonnes during the 1993/94–94/95 marketing years. This amounts to a volume increase of about 10 per cent. During the same period, the cost of the imported cereals increased by some 44 per cent. In other words, out of the total increase of their cereal import bill

89

between these two periods, less than 25 per cent is due to volume increase and over 75 per cent is due to an increase in the *per unit cost* of cereal imports. In fact, the per unit cost of cereal imports has increased by about 32 per cent between 1993/94–94/95 and 1996/97–97/98 (from \$141/tonne to \$187/tonne) compared with an increase in the nominal export price of wheat during the same period of only 8 per cent. Therefore, the increase in the cost of the cereal import bills of LDCs and NFIDCs during this period is partly due to volume increases (roughly 23 per cent) and partly due to nominal price increases (roughly 18 per cent), leaving close to 60 per cent of the total increase due to the drastic change in the financial terms of imports (Figure 3.9).

FIGURE 3.8
EVOLUTION OF CEREAL IMPORT BILLS

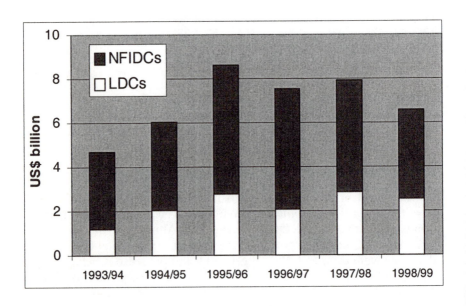

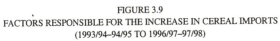

FIGURE 3.9
FACTORS RESPONSIBLE FOR THE INCREASE IN CEREAL IMPORTS
(1993/94–94/95 TO 1996/97–97/98)

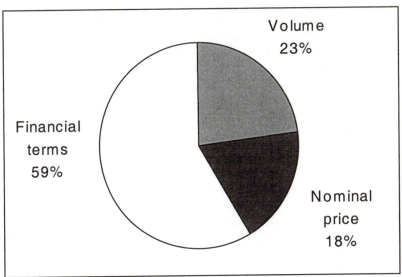

Thus, despite the substantial decline in nominal cereal prices since the 1995/96 spike, cereal import bills persist at relatively high levels. One of the main reasons is that the contribution of concessional imports which played a major role in the past in meeting the cereal import needs of these countries has substantially diminished in recent years. For example, during 1997/98, food aid in cereals accounted for 23 per cent of the LDCs' cereal imports compared with 36 per cent in 1993/94 and 64 per cent in the mid-1980s. The decline in the relative contribution of food aid to cereal imports of the NFIDCs is even sharper, from 22 per cent in the mid-1980s to 7.6 per cent in 1993/94, down to 2 per cent in 1997/98. These drastic changes in the contribution of food aid to the cereal import burden of these countries reflect the substantial reduction in the global volume of food aid in cereals to about 5 million tonnes per annum in 1997/98,[8] the lowest level since the beginning of the food aid programmes in the mid-1950s.[9] A similar

---

8.   Moreover, increasingly a larger share of food aid is now used to meet emergency needs, in both developing and developed countries, and less is left for countries facing structural food deficits.
9.   For the 1998/99 season, food aid is likely to significantly rebound to about 9 million tonnes of cereals and it is forecast that LDCs and NFIDCs could receive about

dramatic reduction has been seen for the other component of food assistance to these countries, namely subsidised sales which have virtually vanished since 1995/96.

The implication of both these trends, though largely expected in the context of the new policy environment under the Uruguay Round, is that a much greater volume of cereals now has to be imported by LDCs and NFIDCs under *commercial* terms, whereas before a large part of the total volume imported consisted of food aid and subsidised sales. Together with an increase in underlying cereal deficits, this has led these countries into facing significantly higher cereal import bills since 1995 than before.

IV. POSSIBLE ROLE OF FOOD AID UNDER THE WTO DECISION

Food aid has been an important resource in assisting food-deficit countries to meet their food needs. Requirements for food aid continue to be large, both for balance-of-payments support and to meet the growing emergency needs and supplementary feeding programmes. In addition, food aid has been called to play a role in the implementation of the Marrakesh Decision. Food aid is one of the instruments to help LDCs and NFIDCs that may be adversely affected during the reform process under the Uruguay Round. These old and new demands on food aid resources necessitate some innovative approaches on how various instruments already available or to be developed could better respond to needs.

1. The Requirements for Food Aid

In general, more rapid, and more broadly based, economic growth will enable more people to enter the market-place to satisfy their nutritional needs. Conversely, slow and uneven economic growth would constrain consumption and increase the numbers of food-insecure people. Although progress is continuously being made in improving food security in all countries, this is a long-term process and by all accounts the food import requirements of low-income food-deficit

---

4.6 million tonnes which is some 50 per cent higher than what they have received in each of the previous two years. At that level, food aid would amount to about 11 per cent of their cereal imports compared with 7.4 per cent in the previous two years. But the cereal import bills of these countries in 1998/99 are projected to be some 22 per cent higher than the average of 1993/94–94/95. In particular the per unit cost of cereal imports will continue to be some 12 per cent higher, despite the fact that nominal export cereal prices continue to decline (as shown in Table 3.2, wheat prices in 1998/99 are projected to be some 21 per cent lower than in 1993/ 94–94/95).

countries are projected to continue to be large in the future. The usual claims on food aid are not therefore likely to diminish.[10]

An uncertain part of the requirements for food aid is also that which may be attributable to the reform programme under the Uruguay Round. The Marrakesh Decision calls on donors to review food aid levels under the Food Aid Convention and to establish a level of food aid commitments sufficient to meet the *legitimate needs of developing countries during the reform programme*, but it does not define these needs. One *narrow* interpretation of legitimate needs would be those that relate to the reform process itself, that is, needs that are over and above those that would have emerged in the absence of the reform programme. Clearly, this interpretation would require establishing a counterfactual scenario, that is, what would have been the case in the absence of the UR. Attempts to quantify a counterfactual scenario face many problems and it would be difficult to substantiate legitimate needs on the basis of such an approach.[11]

A second, *broader* definition of legitimate needs would be one that does not limit them to those strictly linked to the reform programme. In that sense, such needs could be defined as those that would be required to supplement supplies so that countries would be able to maintain adequate levels of food consumption during the reform process. Such an interpretation would be valid if the aim of the Decision were to alleviate any undue hardship which, if left unattended, could compromise the success of the reform programme. However, again it is unlikely that the intention of the signatories of the Decision would have been to address needs that would be so encompassing and loosely defined.

---

10. Traditional uses of food aid include assistance to people with inadequate purchasing power (that is, requirements for emergencies and targeted nutritional intervention projects) and assistance to governments for balance-of-payments support. There are no strong reasons why assistance for balance-of-payments problems (and to some extent for the other needs as well) have to be met by food aid. Financial aid appropriately targeted could equally well satisfy these requirements, if such aid were available. However, identification of assistance needs in kind may help somewhat in making such assistance *available*, in view of the humanitarian and food security considerations involved which weigh more than other considerations on the part of donors and often in the past have resulted in *additional* resources.

11. One approach, however, that goes some way to meeting this 'narrow' requirement is to define a world *price trigger level*, above which a country would be eligible for assistance under the Decision for a proportion of its food import bill. To be realistic, the price trigger would have to be based on a percentage above a base period, beyond which price increases would be considered unreasonably high. Elsewhere in the Agreement on Agriculture, the unit values of imports in the base period 1986–88 have been used as the point of departure. Alternatively, the average unit values for the three-year period before the beginning of the implementation of the Uruguay Round – say 1992–94 – could be used. Another possibility is a moving average.

In summary, the definition of legitimate needs under the Decision is unclear. As already mentioned, these needs would also depend critically on possibilities for adjustment in consumption and, more importantly, on how food production in the countries affected might respond to price changes as a result of the reform process itself.

2. The Supply of Food Aid

Food aid flows are influenced by a multiplicity of factors, including humanitarian considerations and development assistance objectives, the level of public stocks in donor countries, the world prices of commodities provided as food aid, and the institutional commitments of donors. Food aid flows in the past have been sensitive to these factors and changing situations in agricultural markets.[12]

Traditionally the level of programme food aid, and to some extent project food aid, has been inversely related to the opportunity cost of that resource from the perspective of the donors.[13] Several factors may provide an explanation for this inverse relationship. When stocks are high food aid also tends to be high, and vice versa. Second, donors usually fix their food aid budgets in fiscal terms, so that when international prices increase, the volume of food aid tends to decline.

These observations, when combined with the on-going changes in the policy environment in the donor countries, suggest that the tightening of food aid in recent years may possibly become one of its permanent features.[14] In all major donors there has been a tendency to limit public stockholding operations. The Uruguay Round is likely to reduce further the structural surpluses of main foodstuffs in the major donor countries. Finally, there is a shift in the perception in the donor community as to whether food aid donations are the most appropriate form of assistance under circumstances of tight (and non-additional) resources.[15]

The conclusion from the above observations is that maintaining food aid flows sufficient to respond to all potential requirements is

12. See Konandreas [1987] on estimates of the relative importance of the various factors.
13. See Ram and Konandreas [1991]. Emergency food aid has generally been spared from such considerations and is largely linked to humanitarian relief needs.
14. One of the signs that point to a possible tightening of food aid availability in the future is the substantial reduction in the minimum annual commitment of donor countries under the 1995 Food Aid Convention, further reduced in the 1999 Convention. The overall FAC commitment under the 1999 Convention stands at 4.9 million tonnes (in wheat equivalent), down from the 7.52 million tonnes level under the 1986 Convention. (See Chapter 4 for further discussion.)
15. In other words, a reduction of food aid due to these trends is not likely to be substituted by cash or other types of assistance.

likely to become more difficult in the future. Thus, the challenge would be, first, to find ways which would increase resources committed to this type of assistance (that is, increasing the level of food aid) and, second, to make more efficient and effective use of the resources already made available (that is, increasing the flexibility of food aid).

3. Broadening Donors and Donatable Foodstuffs

The first consideration, that is, increasing the level of food aid, would also respond to some extent to the recommendation of the first WTO Ministerial Conference in connection with broadening the *range of donors and donatable foodstuffs*. To the extent that food aid resources are additional to other transfers, and given absorptive capacity for commodities other than basic foodstuffs, there are several good reasons for broadening the food aid commodity basket. First, food deficits in needy countries go well beyond grains. To the extent that such basic commodities would have been imported commercially, providing them as food aid is essentially equivalent to providing grains. Second, broadening the basket of donatable commodities would allow the participation of those potential donors who may not have grains to contribute but have other desirable food commodities. Finally, and perhaps more importantly, it would allow donors to respond more rationally to food aid needs as their considerations would be in relation to actual needs and not in relation to meeting an inflexible commodity-specific target.

One argument against expanding the food aid commodity basket is that some commodities may not be of priority from the food security point of view, that is, are not primarily consumed by the poor. There could be some remedies to this problem. The first one could be by the donors who could maintain a minimum commitment under the Food Aid Convention in basic foodstuffs only (with the definition of basic foodstuffs perhaps expanded to include, in addition to cereals and pulses, vegetable oils, dairy products and sugar). Donations in non-basic foodstuffs could be made above that minimum commitment. The second concerns the recipient country itself. To the extent that it would otherwise have imported commercially the non-basic foodstuff commodity it receives as food aid, it could, in turn, undertake an obligation to import commercially an equivalent value of the basic foodstuffs it needs.

4. Possible Instruments to Increase Responsiveness to Variable Needs

Together with broadening the donor and commodity base in order to increase the level of food aid, there is also a need to increase the flexibility of food aid so that it can respond better to variable needs. This is particularly important for meeting the needs under the Decision, as such needs in aggregate would normally vary in an inverse relationship to the overall availability of food aid. In fact, the factor that is responsible for increasing assistance under the Decision (increasing world market price) is also responsible for a reduced availability of food aid. Therefore, new instruments to deal with the variable needs under the Decision would need to be considered and existing mechanisms strengthened. In general, such instruments should aim to add a time flexibility in the provision of food aid and to exploit possible complementarities with other non-food aid mechanisms (that is, financial facilities).

One existing mechanism to deal with variable food aid needs is the International Emergency Food Reserve (IEFR). An improvement in the IEFR would be to supplement it with stand-by resources to be drawn upon when needed. Such stand-by resources could be institutionalised under the FAC, whereby donors would make a pledge to contribute a certain amount of resources (on a stand-by basis) over a period of, say, five years, that could be drawn upon at any time during that period to meet exceptional needs as and when they arose.

Another mechanism to enhance flexibility could take the form of carrying forward or calling forward resources, as needs dictate. This would imply an increase or decrease in the following year's commitments by the amounts carried or called forward.

A significant potential contribution of limited food aid resources could be made if they were used in conjunction with a financial facility. The Decision also recognises that affected countries may be eligible to draw on financing facilities to purchase food from the world market in years of high world prices. However, making funds available during such years is likely to lead to even higher prices. One way to avoid this could be by setting up physical reserves in the donor countries themselves, under national food reserve systems, earmarked for use under the Decision. In years of high prices, these supplies would be made available to countries eligible for assistance, including those that received additional resources from compensatory financing facilities. This would avoid a self-defeating syndrome, namely that the 'cure' (extra finance) aggravated the 'illness' (higher prices).

5. Use of Instruments Based on the Nature of Variable Needs

How could all these instruments work together to respond to variable needs? To illustrate possible appropriate responses, four distinct sets of circumstances of ordinary emergency needs and needs under the

Decision are identified. These are based on possible combinations between low/high prices in the world market (corresponding to low/high needs under the Decision) and low/high domestic food production in the developing countries (corresponding to high/low ordinary emergency needs).

Case A: Low world price/high domestic production: In this case, needs under the Decision would be zero while ordinary emergency needs would also be relatively low. Such emergency needs would easily be met. As food aid levels may be relatively high and the overall needs low, donors should be encouraged in such years to make contributions towards a physical reserve and carry-forward arrangements.

Case B: Low world price/low domestic production: Again needs under the Decision would be zero while ordinary emergency needs would be moderately high as the low world market prices would permit the affected countries to respond partly from their own resources. Again, food aid resources above emergency and project needs should be contributed towards physical reserves and carry-forward arrangements.

Case C: High world price/high domestic production: As the volume of imports of developing countries would be below normal, the needs under the Decision might not be large. At the same time, low needs for ordinary emergencies would free up food aid resources to meet needs under the Decision. Use could also be made, as needed, of stand-by resources and calling-forward arrangements.

Case D: High world price/low domestic production: The needs in this case would be high for both ordinary emergencies and under the Decision. This is the most difficult case and would normally require the use of all possible regular and complementary resources. Beyond drawing on regular and stand-by IEFR resources, calling forward is likely to be needed, as well as releases from any food-aid-supported reserves.

V. CONCLUSIONS

Of great significance for many developing countries in the continuation of the reform process in agriculture is giving adequate consideration to non-trade concerns and especially food security, which is explicitly mentioned in the preamble to the Agreement on Agriculture. The Uruguay Round agreements accorded special and differential treatment to developing countries in a number of areas of concern to them. These provisions, in the form of special concessions, were designed to take account of the constraints faced by many developing countries in taking advantage of trading opportunities and in adjusting to the new trading environment, because of structural problems, the low level of industrialisation, limited access to advanced technologies or the non-availability of adequate infrastructure.

In the view of a number of developing countries, these special provisions have fallen short of affording them any real advantages so far. Hence many of them emphasise that a high priority should be given to addressing the existing imbalances and the problems of implementing the relevant provisions and decisions adopted during the Uruguay Round negotiations.

The situation of the LDCs and NFIDCs raises some concern. All the relevant statistics clearly differentiate these two groups from the rest of the developing countries as regards food availability and capacity to import. It is true that the food security problems faced by them are of a long-term nature and do not represent a situation that has been created by the trade liberalisation process *per se*. Yet, it can be argued that the trade liberalisation process has suddenly introduced certain difficulties for these countries by altering the status quo. Distortions in the world food markets had persisted for so long that many importing countries had become used to taking them as given and forming their long-term food security strategy and their investment decisions accordingly. In a sense, the removal of past distortions has revealed a reality which is considerably different from what these countries were used to in the past and they have consequently suffered initial damage and are obliged to make major adjustments to overcome the difficulties they now face. In this connection, implementation of the Marrakesh Decision, which was precisely meant to address such difficulties, is long overdue.

Food aid is one of the means included in the Decision to help LDCs and NFIDCs adjust to the new realities and policy changes ushered in by the Uruguay Round. To the extent that it is an additional development assistance resource, food aid in commodities for which absorptive capacity exists has a role to play in this regard, especially if it becomes a more flexible resource than in the past in order to respond better to variable needs. But the Decision goes well beyond food aid. Other types of assistance called for under the Decision may often be more appropriate in addressing the food security concerns of countries, especially over the long term, including, in particular, technical and financial assistance to increase agricultural productivity in the countries themselves.

REFERENCES

Colman, D., 1993, *Price Transmission from International to African Agricultural Prices — Policy Implications*, ESC/93/2, Rome: FAO.

Colman, D., 1995, 'Problems of Measuring Price Distortion and Price Transmission: A Framework for Analysis', *Oxford Agrarian Studies*, Vol. 23, No. 1.

FAO, 1990, *The Effects of Trade Liberalization on Levels of Cereal Stocks*, CCP:GR 90/3, Rome: FAO.

FAO, 1995, *Impact of the Uruguay Round on Agriculture*, Rome: FAO.

FAO, 1996, *Agricultural Price Instability*, Report of a Meeting of Experts, Rome: FAO.

FAO, 1997, *The Food Situation in the Least Developed Countries (LDCs) and the Net Food Importing Developing Countries (NFIDCs)*, Rome: FAO.

GATT, 1994, *The Results of the Uruguay Round of Multilateral Trade Negotiations*, Geneva: GATT.

Goldin, I., O. Knudsen and D. van der Mensbrugghe, 1993, *Trade Liberalization: Global Economic Implications*, Paris: OECD and Washington DC: World Bank.

Goldin, I. and D. van der Mensbrugghe, 1995, 'The Uruguay Round: An Assessment of Economy-wide and Agricultural Reforms', in W. Martin and L. Alan Winters, eds., *The Uruguay Round and the Developing Economies*, World Bank Discussion Paper No. 307, Washington DC: World Bank.

Greenfield, J., M. de Nigris and P. Konandreas, 1996, 'The Uruguay Round Agreement on agriculture: food security implications for developing countries', *Food Policy*, Vol. 21, No. 4/5, Sept./Nov.

Konandreas, P., 1987, 'Responsiveness of Food Aid in Cereals to Fluctuations in Supply in Donor and Recipient Countries', in M. Bellamy and B. Greenshields, eds., *Agriculture and Economic Instability*, Aldershot: Gower.

Ram, S. and P. Konandreas, 1991, 'An Additional Resource? A Global Perspective on Food Aid Flows in Relation to Development Assistance', in E. Clay and O. Stokke, eds., *Food Aid Reconsidered: Implications for Developing Countries*, EADI Book Series II, London: Frank Cass.

Sarris, A., 1997, *The Evolving Nature of International Price Instability in Cereals Markets*, Rome: FAO.

UNCTAD, 1995, *Report on Evaluating the Outcome of the Uruguay Round Agricultural Agreement using the Agricultural Trade Policy Simulation Model*, Consultancy Report to ITP by O. Gulbrandsen, Geneva: UNCTAD.

Vanzetti, D., 1998, *Global Stocks, Price Stability and Food Security*, Copenhagen: Danish Institute of Agricultural and Fisheries Economics.

ANNEX 3.1
LIST OF LDCs AND NFIDCs

LDCs	NFIDCs
Afghanistan	Barbados
Angola	Botswana
Bangladesh	Côte d'Ivoire
Benin	Dominican Rep.
Bhutan	Egypt
Burkina Faso	Honduras
Burundi	Jamaica
Cambodia	Kenya
Cape Verde	Mauritius
Central Afr. Rep.	Morocco
Chad	Pakistan
Comoros	Peru
Congo Dem. Rep.	St. Lucia
Djibouti	Senegal
Eq. Guinea	Sri Lanka
Eritrea	Trinidad & Tobago
Ethiopia	Tunisia
Gambia	Venezuela
Guinea	
Guinea-Bissau	
Haiti	
Kiribati	
Laos	
Lesotho	
Liberia	
Madagascar	
Malawi	
Maldives	
Mali	
Mauritania	
Mozambique	
Myanmar	
Nepal	
Niger	
Rwanda	
Samoa	
São Tomé and Príncipe	

ANNEX 3.1
LIST OF LDCs AND NFIDCS

LDCs	*NFIDCs*
Sierra Leone	
Solomon Islands	
Somalia	
Sudan	
Tanzania	
Togo	
Tuvalu	
Uganda	
Vanuatu	
Yemen	
Zambia	

4

The Food Aid Convention:
An Effective Safety Net?

CHARLOTTE BENSON

The Food Aid Convention (FAC) is an international agreement under which signatories are legally committed to provide specified minimum tonnages of 'wheat equivalent' food aid, with the objective of providing a guaranteed minimum flow of food aid to developing countries.[1] Historically, the principal objective of the Convention has been to provide a safety net protecting recipient countries, from both financial and nutritional perspectives, against potential downward fluctuations in annual shipments of food aid.

This chapter examines the role that the FAC has played in determining actual flows of food aid. It finds that the floor on levels of food aid flows set by the FAC has been so low as to have had only a negligible impact on actual shipments, both globally and from most individual donors. Indeed, on only two occasions in almost 30 years – in 1973/74 and 1996/97 – has the Convention been likely to have prevented an even greater decline in shipments of food aid than that actually experienced. These findings raise serious questions about the credibility of the Convention in establishing a safety net and the most appropriate form of international commitments for protecting the food security of developing countries.

This chapter is an expanded version of a background paper prepared as part of the study funded by the UK's DFID (Project No. R6985) [*Clay et al., 1998*].
1.   In checking food aid shipments against FAC minimum commitments, cereals are quantified in wheat, rather than grain, equivalent. However, in the past, levels of food aid shipments reported to the Food Aid Committee, which monitors compliance with the FAC, have under-estimated total food aid flows as some donors, particularly the USA, have not always reported all of their food aid, as defined by the Development Assistance Committee. Moreover, in the real world recipient countries are more interested in actual tonnages of food aid received than in their wheat equivalent values. For the purposes of this chapter, FAC minimum commitments have therefore been compared against food aid shipments in cereals equivalent, as the more meaningful and conventional norm practised by FAO, WFP and others in reporting cereals food aid shipments.

I. THE ORIGINS AND HISTORY OF THE FAC

The first FAC in 1967 originated as a form of international burden-sharing for supporting food aid as part of the Kennedy Round of GATT negotiations [*Wallerstein, 1980*]. There were 18 signatories to the initial Convention, including all of the then major wheat-exporting countries and one grain-exporting developing country, Argentina, and some of the most important grain importers [*IWC, 1991*]. The European Union's obligation was undertaken as a joint and collective commitment which was then apportioned by the European Council between the Commission and the member states. Minimum commitments were based on complex calculations involving donor countries' grain production and consumption and per capita GDP. Food aid commitments could be met in the form of wheat, coarse grains or grain products fit for human consumption and acceptable to recipients. Alternatively, cereal-importing donors were allowed to provide cash for the purchase of grains.

Further FACs were signed in 1971, 1980, 1986, 1995 and 1999 (Table 4.1), although with certain changes to membership, commodity coverage, eligible recipient countries and principles. Minimum annual food aid commitments of 4.3 million tonnes were made under the first Convention, with a marginal decline to 4.2 million tonnes under the second. Minimum annual commitments were increased significantly under the third Convention of 1980, rising to 7.6 million tonnes. This increase reflected commitments to provide 10 million tonnes of food aid annually made at the World Food Conference in 1974, itself held in response to the crisis of 1972–74.[2] A significant part of the increase was accounted for by a 2.6 million tonnes increase in US minimum commitments. Both global and national minimum annual commitments remained broadly unchanged under the subsequent fourth Convention of 1986, standing at 7.5 million tonnes as only Australia reduced its commitment – by 100,000 tonnes. However, minimum annual commitments dropped sharply, to 5.4 million tonnes, under the fifth Convention of 1995. This decline again largely reflected changes in US minimum commitments, which fell by 44 per cent or 2.0 million tonnes. Canada also reduced its commitment by 33 per cent or 200,000 tonnes. Despite this decline, the list of recipient countries to which shipments could be counted against FAC minimum

---

2. A resolution of the Conference had recommended that '... all donor countries ... make all efforts to provide commodities and/or financial assistance that will ensure in physical terms at least 10 million tons of grains as food aid a year' (cited in IWC, 1991).

commitments was also extended under the fifth Convention to include those former COMECON countries which had been given developing country status by the Development Assistance Committee.

TABLE 4.1

MINIMUM CONTRIBUTIONS OF FOOD AID UNDER SUCCESSIVE FOOD AID CONVENTIONS, 1968/69–99/02 ('000 TONNES)

	July 68– June 71	July 71– Dec. 72	Jan. 73– June 73	July 73– June 80	July 80– June 86	July 86– June 95	July 95– June 99	July 99– June 02
EU[a]	1,287	1,035	1,161	1,287	1,670	1,670	1,670	1,320 [e]
of which Community actions	330 [b]	439 [c]	464	580	920	920	920	
National actions[a]	957	596	697	707	750	750	750	
Canada	495	495	495	495	600	600	400	420
USA	1,890	1,890	1,890	1,890	4,470	4,470	2,500	2,500
Global	4,259	3,974	4,100	4,226	7,612	7,517	5,350 [d]	4,895

Notes

(a) Includes the six original member states (Belgium, France, Germany, Italy, Luxembourg and the Netherlands) and six more recent members (Denmark, Ireland and the UK, who all joined in 1973; Greece, which joined in 1981; and Portugal and Spain, which joined in 1986. The three most recent members (Austria, Finland and Sweden) are not included except in the figure indicated under the most recent (1999) convention.

For ease of comparison of changes in commitments under successive conventions, the commitments of the 12 member states included in the date are included in the EU totals from 1968 onwards, regardless of when they joined the convention.

The EU's obligation is undertaken as a joint and collective commitment which is then apportioned by the European Council between the Commission and member states. This is an internal EU matter, of no concern to the FAC.

(b) FAC obligations to be met from Community actions were increased from 301,000 tonnes in 1968/69 to 336,900 tonnes in 1969/70 and 353,140 tonnes in 1970/71. The figure reported in the table is an average of these three levels.

(c) FAC obligations to be met from Community actions were increased from 414,000 tonnes in 1971/72 to 464,000 tonnes in 1972/73. The figure reported in the table is an average of these two levels.

(d) Total FAC obligations fell by 50,000 tonnes, to 5,3 million tonnes, in July 1998 as a consequence of a reduction in Australia's minimum annual FAC commitment from 300,000 to 250,000 tonnes.

(e) The EU committed an additional 130 m ecus in value terms, part of which is expected to be expended on commodities as well as transportation and other operational costs.

Sources: FAO and IGC, various.

In 1997 negotiations were begun for a further Convention, with a new agreement coming into effect in July 1999. During the negotiations, Australia unilaterally reduced its contribution for 1998/99 by 50,000 tonnes, to 250,000 tonnes, because of other aid commitments. Under the 1999 Convention, donors are permitted to express their commitments in tonnage or value terms, or in a combination of the two. Commitments in value terms can be used to meet transport and other operational costs associated with the food aid operations as well as the purchase of commodities. Tonnage commitments fell to 4.9 million tonnes in wheat equivalent under this new Convention but the EU, which is the only signatory so far to have expressed any commitment in value terms, agreed to provide an additional ecus 130 million in value terms. Using the indicative wheat price indicated in the 1999 Convention, the ecus 130 m commitment is equivalent to some 0.6 million tonnes of cereals, bringing total commitments to 5.5 million tonnes and so implying little change from the previous Convention.[3] Indeed, the EU has indicated that its flow of commodities under the 1999 FAC will not be less than its minimum commitment under the previous Convention and will probably be more. However, the change could imply a further decline in the total quantity of food aid provided under future Conventions.

With regard to commodities covered, the Convention has gradually become more and more flexible in terms of the way in which commodities are acquired and the recipient country actions which can be counted against signatories' obligations. Commodity coverage was formally expanded to include rice as well as wheat products and coarse grains under the 1980 Convention. Another change concerned a switch in the system of evaluating cash equivalent contributions from a fixed rate to 'prevailing market prices'. This adjustment was made in order to reflect the price variability experienced in grain markets. However, a 20 per cent limit was placed on the level of movement allowed from one year to the next. Moreover, only a small proportion of food aid provided under the FAC is given in the form of cash commodities, implying quite limited implications for annual fluctuations in wheat equivalent flows. Further changes occurred under the 1986 Convention, which allowed cereals food aid purchased within recipient countries for emergency operations and food security

---

3. According to figures reported in the 1999 Convention, the EU commitment of 1.32 million tonnes of food aid (in wheat equivalent) and ecus 130 m in value terms has a total indicative value of ecus 422 m [*Food Aid Committee, 1999*]. This implies a wheat price of ecus 221 per tonne. In volume terms, the EU's value commitment of ecus 130 m is therefore equivalent to 0.6 million tonnes of food aid in wheat equivalent.

reasons to be counted against obligations.[4, 5] Since 1995 donors have also been able to count pulses provided for relief purposes against fulfilment of up to 10 per cent of their overall obligation. Furthermore, substantive changes occurred under the 1999 Convention, with the list of eligible products widened to include limited quantities of edible oil, root crops, skimmed milk powder, sugar, seed for eligible products and products which are a component of the traditional diet of vulnerable groups or of supplementary feeding programmes. The 10 per cent restriction on the provision of pulses was also lifted.

As of 1999, there were 23 signatories to the FAC, including the European Union represented by the Commission and its now 15 member states [*Food Aid Committee, 1999*].

II. EFFECTIVENESS OF THE FAC

The Agricultural Committee of the World Trade Organisation (WTO) submitted a number of recommendations to the Singapore Ministerial Conference of the WTO in December 1996. In the light of these recommendations, WTO Ministers asked that action be initiated in 1997 within the framework of the Food Aid Convention to develop proposals with a view to the establishment of a level of food aid commodities sufficient to meet the legitimate needs of developing countries during the implementation of agricultural trade liberalisation as agreed under the Uruguay Round of the GATT Agreement. During a meeting in June 1998, the Food Aid Committee also indicated that a major focus of the negotiations for the forthcoming sixth FAC was to seek an increase in the effectiveness of food aid provided by donor governments. These concerns resulted in a substantive revision of the Convention, including new articles on the needs of recipients and on effectiveness and impact as well as a more general increased emphasis on promoting local agricultural development in recipient countries.

However, these tasks are complicated by the fact that the FAC still does not require systematic evaluation of individual donor or overall performance in relation to objectives and, thus, that no systematic assessments have ever been undertaken of the effectiveness or efficiency of the Convention. This chapter therefore attempts to address

---

4.　FAO data on food aid shipments do not include commodities acquired through local purchase (see Chapter 1).
5.　Since the first FAC in 1967 it has been possible for donors to count commodities purchased in one developing country for use in another against their FAC commitment.

part of that gap by analysing the achievements of past FACs at their broadest level, in providing a food aid safety net and contributing towards the attainment of international food security.

Relatively early on in its existence, during the world food crisis of 1972–74, the FAC played an important role in maintaining food aid flows. As the IWC [*1991:6*] notes, following a very poor Soviet crop and the consequent depletion of world grain stocks, 'non-FAC food aid and concessional sales almost disappeared, falling to only 2 million tonnes in 1973/4 ... [but] ... aid under the FAC remained steady at around 4 million tonnes as donors continued to honour their minimum tonnage obligations'.

FIGURE 4.1

TRENDS IN GLOBAL CEREALS FOOD AID AND FAC MINIMUM COMMITMENTS, 1970/71–97/98

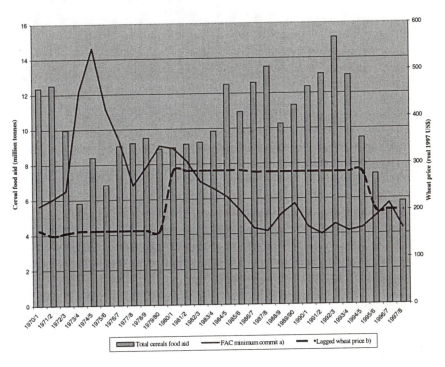

(a) Global minimum obligations rose from 3,974 to 4,100 thousand tonnes at the beginning of 1973.

(b) US No. 2 hard winter ordinary wheat in real 1997 prices, lagged 6 months.

FIGURE 4.2
TRENDS IN EU CEREALS FOOD AID AND FAC MINIMUM COMMITMENTS, 1970/71–97/98

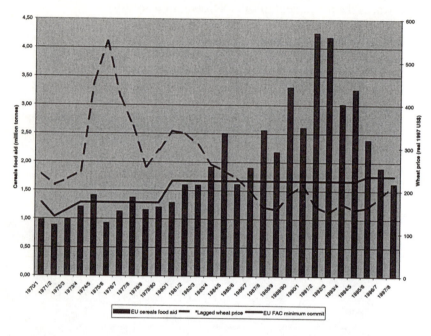

(a) EU minimum obligations rose from 1,035 to 1,161 thousand tonnes at the beginning of 1973.

(b) US No. 2 hard winter ordinary wheat in real 1997 prices, lagged 18 months.

However, the extent to which the FAC has subsequently continued to provide an effective safety net during tighter world cereal market conditions is less clear-cut. An initial comparison of FAC minimum commitments and flows of food aid indicates that, despite the Convention, annual global flows have varied by up to 20–25 per cent between years. The FAC appears to have had little impact in eliminating such wide fluctuations, in part because actual flows have often exceeded minimum commitments by considerable amounts, particularly in the early 1970s and late 1980s through to the early 1990s (Figure 4.1). Only in the two most recent years for which data are available, 1996/ 97 and 1997/98, have FAC commitments barely been met (see below). Thus, FAC minimum commitments may have been set too low to provide an effective floor preventing downward fluctuations in food aid shipments following poorer harvests in donor countries. Unsurprisingly, this pattern also appears to have been replicated at the level of individual donors (Figures 4.2, 4.3 and 4.4). This is also demonstrated by reviewing three-yearly average cereals food aid shipments as a percentage of FAC minimum contributions (Table 4.2).

FIGURE 4.3
TRENDS IN US CEREALS FOOD AID AND FAC MINIMUM COMMITMENTS, 1970/71–97/98

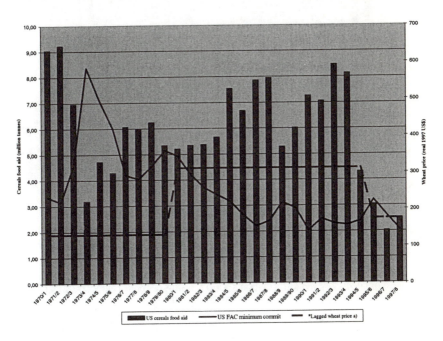

However, wide inter-annual fluctuations *per se* may not mean that the Convention has been entirely unsuccessful in helping to promote national food security. Such a conclusion rests partly on the nature of the factors underlying that variability. Have the fluctuations reflected changing needs, such as being determined by the scale of conflict or the intermittent occurrence of severe drought? Or have they reflected changing world cereal market conditions and donor budgetary factors? The answer clearly has important implications. If fluctuations have been driven by changes in demand or need, then they may have reflected an efficient and effective use of aid resources. However, if they have reflected supply factors, then the FAC may indeed have failed to protect low-income food-deficit countries from the vagaries of international cereal markets.

FIGURE 4.4
TRENDS IN CANADIAN CEREALS FOOD AID AND FAC MINIMUM COMMITMENTS, 1970/71–97/98

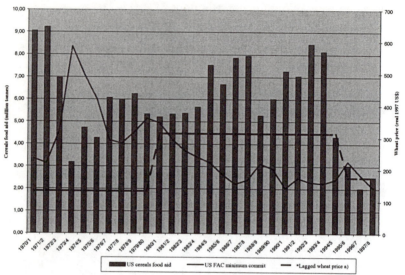

(a) US No. 2 hard winter ordinary wheat in real 1997 prices, lagged 0 months.

TABLE 4.2
THREE-YEARLY AVERAGE CEREALS FOOD AID SHIPMENTS AS PERCENTAGE OF FAC
MINIMUM COMMITMENTS

	1971/72– 73/74	1976/77 – 78/79	1981/82– 83/84	1986/87– 88/89	1995/96– 97/98 [(a)]
EU[(b)]	88	95	102	133	118
of which					
Community action	77	108	98	123	132
National actions[(b)]	101	84	107	144	101
Canada	173	188	126	193	97
USA	341	323	122	157	101
Global	230	219	124	161	115

Notes:
(a) Data on food aid shipments in 1997/98 are provisional.
(b) See note a) for Table 4.1.

Sources: FAO and IGC, various.

III. QUANTITATIVE ANALYSIS

The remainder of this chapter considers the role of supply factors in more detail, exploring the extent to which the FAC has protected food-importing developing countries against fluctuations in world cereals market conditions as well as its role in determining the scale of annual flows of food aid. Multiple regression techniques (in logarithmic form) were used to explore the impact of the FAC on both international food security and annual flows of food aid more formally, focusing on the period 1970/71–97/98. Separate regressions were undertaken for global food aid and for the European Union, EU Community actions, EU member state national actions, Canada and the United States. These donors together provided 87 per cent of global food aid between 1970/71 and 1997/78.

A widely accepted test of the effect of food aid on global food security is whether the volume of commodities provided is positively or negatively correlated with movements in world market prices (for example, see Taylor and Byerlee [1991]). Three explanatory variables were therefore tested: a wheat price series[6] and dummy variables to take account of changing levels of FAC commitments and two extra-ordinary relief programmes in 1984/85 and 1992/93, both in response to droughts in sub-Saharan Africa.[7] Two FAC dummies were included: to capture, first, the substantial upward revision in minimum commitments under the FAC in 1980/81 and, second, the major downward revision that occurred in 1995/96.[8] If the FAC had played a significant role in stabilising annual flows of food aid by providing an effective floor, then food aid flows were expected to be correlated positively with the first FAC dummy variable and negatively with the

---

6. The price series was based on that for US No.2 Hard Winter (ordinary) wheat in US dollar terms, deflated using the US GDP deflator to put prices in real 1997 terms. This price series was selected following earlier discussions with the IGC. No account was taken of movements in other currencies against the US dollar, although this could have had implications for levels of food aid flows from non-US donors. Since wheat constitutes the single most important commodity within total cereals food aid, and, with the notable exception of rice, movements in the price of cereals are generally highly correlated, this price series was considered a reasonable proxy for a more general cereals price series.
7. The emergency dummy was assigned a value of 1 in 1984/85 and 1992/93 and 0 in other years.
8. The first FAC dummy variable assumed values of 0 in 1970/71–1979/80 and again in 1995/96–97/98 and of 1 in 1980/81–94/5. The second assumed values of 0 in 1970/71–94/95 and of 1 in 1995/96–97/98. For purposes of the analysis of EU food aid (including separate analysis of Community actions and member state national programmes) the first FAC dummy variable was amended to assume values of 1 for the full period 1980/81–97/98 as EU minimum commitments were not revised under the 1995 FAC.

second. *Ex ante*, it was also hypothesised that annual levels of food aid shipments would be negatively correlated with the wheat price series – that is, the higher the wheat price, the smaller the flow of food aid. In other words, it was postulated that fluctuations in shipments of food aid accentuated the impact of price variability, with food aid flows declining and therefore necessitating increased commercial imports during periods of higher prices. Finally, food aid flows were expected to be positively correlated with the emergency dummy.

A number of regressions were also run to test a range o price lags in recognition of the varying intervals between the programming and shipment of aid provided by different donors. In the US case, for example, food aid is largely budgeted in value rather than volume terms. As a result, inter-yearly fluctuations in volume were expected to be highly correlated with real price movements in the same year. By contrast, over the period of analysis the European Commission's food aid programme has been subject to considerable delays between programming and shipping of food aid actions, as reflected in best-fit estimations for the wheat price series lagged 24 months.

The results, including the best-fit lag for each donor, are indicated in Table 4.3. Regressions were first undertaken on the wheat price alone; then on the wheat price and the emergency dummy variable; and finally on the wheat price, the emergency dummy and FAC dummy variables.

The findings indicate a strongly significant positive correlation between food aid shipments and the FAC dummy both for the EU overall and also for Community and member state actions.[9] This suggests that the upward revisions in minimum commitments under the FAC in 1980/81 resulted in higher flows of food aid during the 1980s and early 1990s. However, except in the case of Community action, in regressions including the FAC dummy as a dependent variable a strong negative correlation was also found with the wheat price series, indicating that wheat prices have also played an important role in determining annual flows of food aid (Table 4.3). In other words, the FAC did not prevent large inter-yearly fluctuations in EU member

---

9. Additional regressions were also run taking actual food aid shipments expressed as a percentage of minimum food aid commitments as the dependent variable and again using the same wheat price series and emergency and FAC dummy variables as before, as the independent variables. The FAC dummies were included to capture major shifts in the base against which food aid shipments were being measured. The results obtained were very similar to those reported above, including a typically strong negative correlation between the dependent variable and both the wheat price series and also, in the case of the USA, Canada and globally, the first FAC dummy.

state food aid actions in response to changing world market conditions, essentially because EU food aid flows followed a gradual upward trend during the 1980s and early 1990s, as a consequence of which the EU's minimum commitments under the Convention played an increasingly ineffective role. The fact that annual levels of Community action were not correlated with the wheat price series, once the role of upward revisions in the FAC had been accounted for, reflects the fact that the budget for this food aid is fixed in volume, rather than value terms, with additional budgetary allocations in response to major emergencies.

The results for flows of Canadian and US food aid were more surprising. They suggested that, although the wheat price series was typically strongly negatively correlated with the volume of food aid flows, FAC minimum commitments had had little influence on levels of shipments. Indeed, although coefficients for the first food aid dummy, which was intended to capture the upward revision in the two donors' minimum commitments under the 1980/81 FAC, were statistically significant, they indicated a negative rather than positive correlation with food aid flows. In other words, for any given wheat price, food aid flows were lower over the period 1980/81–94/95 than over the earlier period 1970/71–79/80, despite increases in the two donors' minimum commitments under the Convention.

This finding appears partly to reflect the scale of Canadian and US food aid flows during the 1970s relative to subsequent FAC minimum commitments under the third and fourth FACs of 1980/81 to 1994/95. In the case of the USA, in eight out of the ten years 1970/71 to 1979/80 annual food aid shipments were higher than subsequent minimum commitments under the third and fourth Conventions of 1980/81–1994/95. Similarly, annual Canadian food aid shipments during the 1970s exceeded subsequent minimum commitments under the third and fourth Conventions in every single year between 1970/1 and 1979/80. Thus, the upward revision in minimum US and Canadian FAC commitments from 1980 perhaps reflected less an undertaking to increase levels of food aid than an increase in commitments to levels commensurate with actual food aid shipments over the previous decade.

TABLE 4.3
REGRESSION RESULTS – FACTORS EXPLAINING VARIATION IN ACTUAL SHIPMENTS OF CEREALS FOOD AID

Donor	Wheat price lag	Period of regression	Constant	Regression coefficients				F	Adjusted R^2	Durbin–Watson statistic
				Wheat price	Emergency dummy	FAC dummy 1	FAC dummy 2			
EU total	18 months	1971–80	2.681	0.147 (0.90)				0.81	0.00	1.80
		1981–98	5.506	-0.934 (-4.65)**	0.136 (1.88)*			13.54**	0.60	1.20
		1971–98		-0.836 (-4.55)**	0.198 (1.87)*			14.02**	0.49	0.75
		1971–98		-0.449 (-2.60)**	0.153 (1.82)*	0.218 (4.05)**		20.59**	0.69	1.00
EU Community action	24 months	1971–80	1.549	0.428 (0.64)				0.41	0.00	0.95
		1981–98	5.695	-1.105 (-3.52)**	0.134 (1.09)			7.43**	0.43	1.28
		1971–98	5.624	-1.126 (-3.03)**	0.254 (1.14)			6.14**	0.28	0.49
		1971–98	3.737	-0.448 (-1.28)	0.168 (0.93)	0.426 (3.78)**		11.04**	0.53	0.73
EU Member states	12 months	1971–80	3.465	-0.264 (-2.68)*				7.20*	0.41	1.58
		1981–98	3.717	-0.343 (-2.28)**	0.102 (0.83)*			4.33**	0.28	1.80
		1971–98	3.873	-0.417 (-5.02)**	0.117 (2.34)*			17.17**	0.58	1.57
		1971–98	3.574	-0.308 (-3.18)**	0.102 (2.12)*	0.062 (1.95)*		13.99**	0.59	1.82
Canada	0 months	1971–80	4.496	-0.614 (-3.10)**				9.59*	0.49	1.52
		1981–98	3.284	-0.176 (-0.43)	0.028 (0.20)			0.12	0.00	0.23
		1981–98	3.837	-0.385 (-1.61)	-0.048 (-0.59)		-0.382 (-5.56)**	10.54**	0.63	1.06
		1971–98	3.065	-0.067 (-0.35)	0.000 (0.00)			0.06	0.00	0.34
		1971–98	4.183	-0.490 (-3.05)**	-0.050 (-0.69)	-0.104 (-1.92)*	-0.491 (-6.39)**	11.70**	0.61	1.21
USA	0 months	1971–80	6.266	-0.989 (-8.45)**				71.40**	0.89	2.00
		1981–98	4.055	-0.147 (-0.37)	0.181 (1.34)			1.00	0.00	0.46
		1981–98	4.654	-0.374 (-2.20)*	0.099 (1.74)		-0.413 (-8.48)**	27.75**	0.83	3.05
		1971–98	4.164	-0.179 (-0.92)	0.146 (1.21)			1.39	0.03	0.51
		1971–98	5.422	-0.656 (-5.22)**	0.092 (1.60)	-0.120 (-2.82)**	-0.546 (-9.07)**	26.43**	0.79	2.57

TABLE 4.3

REGRESSION RESULTS – FACTORS EXPLAINING VARIATION IN ACTUAL SHIPMENTS OF CEREALS FOOD AID

Donor	Wheat price lag	Period of regression	Constant	Regression coefficients					F	Adjusted R^2	Durbin–Watson statistic
				Wheat price	Emergency dummy	FAC dummy 1	FAC dummy 2				
Global	6 months	1971–80	5.448	-0.596* (-3.94)*					15.50**	0.62	2.97
		1981–98	4.786	-0.346 (-1.30)	0.148 (1.70)				2.30	0.13	0.35
		1981–98	5.094	-0.458 (-4.40)**	0.098 (2.85)**		-0.268 (-9.23)**		38.51**	0.87	2.83
		1971–98	4.785	-0.340 (-2.69)**	0.134 (1.81)*				6.01**	0.27	0.62
		1971–98	5.269	-0.524 (-6.07)**	0.097 (2.47)*	-0.023 (-0.83)	-0.293 (-7.39)**		28.98**	0.81	2.81

Notes: T-statistics are given in parentheses. T-statistics and F-statistics which are statistically significant at the 5 per cent level of significance are indicated by ** (using one-tailed t-test in the case of t-statistics). See main text for explanation of the emergency and FAC dummy variables. Statistics are for agricultural trade years. July 1970–June 1971 are reported as 1971 etc.

A second factor perhaps contributing to the negative correlation between flows of US and Canadian food aid shipments and the first FAC dummy has been a statistically significant change in the relationship between food aid shipments and wheat prices between the 1970s and 1980/81–97/98. Regressions for the respective donors over the two periods separately indicate statistically significant lower coefficients of determination on wheat prices in the latter period.[10] In other words, for a given price of wheat, the resulting volume of food aid shipped by the USA and Canada was higher in the 1970s than in the latter period (Table 4.3). The apparently negative correlation between food aid flows and the FAC dummy for 1980/81–94/95 could therefore partly reflect the fact that the FAC dummy has acted as a proxy for factors contributing to this change in relationship.

Meanwhile, the second FAC dummy variable was, unsurprisingly, strongly negatively correlated with the volume of both US and Canadian food aid flows. This reflected the downward revision in commitments which the two donors made to reflect reductions in their food aid programmes.

---

10. Chow F tests were run to test the stability of the estimated relationships, comparing the results for 1970/71–79/80 and for 1980/81–97/98 with those for the full period 1970/71–97/98. These revealed statistically significant changes between the two periods which the first FAC dummy variable failed to explain sufficiently.

Finally, in terms of global food aid, the regression results indicated that the substantial increase in FAC commitments in 1980 had no significant impact on the volume of global food aid shipments. Basically, the positive relationship between EU food aid shipments and FAC minimum commitments was negated by the negative correlation between the two respective variables for the USA and Canada. Meanwhile, a strong, negative correlation continued to prevail between food aid shipments and world cereals prices.

IV. CONCLUSION: IMPLICATIONS FOR THE FUTURE OF THE FAC

The results of the quantitative analysis indicate that the food aid commitments provided by donors under the FAC over the past two or three decades have failed to prevent a strong, statistically significant negative correlation between fluctuations in food aid flows and trends in international wheat prices. In other words, the Convention has contributed little to international food security. Had FAC minimum commitments reached the target level of 10 million tonnes recommended by the 1974 World Food Conference, then the Convention might have been more effective in stabilising food aid levels. Instead, cereal-importing developing countries have been left potentially vulnerable to simultaneous increases in the cost of commercial cereal imports (assuming no downward adjustment in the volume of imports) and declines in food aid receipts.[11]

---

11. Two other analyses support the findings of a strong statistically significant correlation between food aid flows and world cereals prices. First, Shapouri and Missiaen [*1990*] conducted a similar analysis of domestic factors determining total volumes of food aid provided by each of the USA, the European Community and Canada. In the case of the USA, they differentiated between food provided under PL480 Title II, other PL480 programme food aid and total food aid. Multiple regressions using an ordinary least squares estimation in linear form were run, with grain stocks, grain price, government budget agricultural outlays and a dummy variable to take account of extraordinary relief operations in recipient countries as explanatory variables. In the case of the USA, a dummy variable was also used to represent the political party of the incumbent president. Regressions were run for 1961–86 for the USA and 1970–86 for the EC and Canada. Overall, strong relationships were found.

Second, Eggleston [*1987*] also undertook a statistical analysis of the factors determining levels of US food aid over the period 1955–79. He found a positive correlation between the level of, or changes in, US agricultural surpluses and levels of PL480 aid, with an R^2 of 0.67. The other two explanatory variables, per capita food agricultural production in recipient countries and a dummy variable indicating the party of government in the USA, were not found to be significant.

Related analysis was also undertaken by Benson and Clay [*1998*] to explore the extent to which food aid flows to Eastern Europe and the former Soviet republics were additional to flows to traditional food aid recipients. The analysis presented here, which also models the determinants of fluctuations in food aid flows, effectively draws on this earlier analysis.

This pattern was effectively institutionalised under the 1995 FAC. Under this Convention, minimum commitments were reduced from 7.6 to 5.35 million tonnes, allowing substantial reductions in shipments in the immediate wake of an increase in international cereals prices to levels not seen since the early 1980s. The fact that the FAC existed may have prevented an even greater decline in food aid in 1996/97, in view of the world market circumstances, and may at least have held up levels of support for WFP development activities. Nevertheless, the fact that commitments had already been cut, in part as a short-term response to tighter market conditions as well as to the budgetary difficulties of certain major donors, effectively reduced the potential role that the FAC might have played in support of international food security. Moreover, even then, donors were unable to fulfil even their much reduced obligations in 1996/97, with a combined minimum contribution of 5.3 million tonnes reported to the Convention. This shortfall was principally due to a 0.48 million tonne deficit in US contributions, the second time in three years that the US had failed to fulfil its obligation; in 1994/95, there had been a 0.15 million tonne shortfall in the US contribution. Indeed, in recent years US minimum levels appear to have been determined more by commitments made in the US legislature rather than by their international obligations under the FAC. Australia's unilateral implementation of a 50,000 tonne reduction in its obligation in 1998/99 raised further questions about the degree of donor commitment to the Convention.

The apparent failure of the FAC to meet its objective raises questions about whether there is a continuing role for minimum levels of food aid. Admittedly, the objectives of the most recent, 1999, Convention are somewhat different from earlier ones. The latter focused specifically on securing specified minimum levels of food aid, whereas the 1999 Convention has far broader objectives, seeking ' to contribute to world food security and to improve the ability of the international community to respond to emergency food situations and other food needs of developing countries'. Moreover, in its Preamble the latest Convention states that 'the ultimate objective of food aid is the elimination of the need for food aid itself'. However, in the shorter term the primary function of the FAC remains the securing of minimum levels of food aid. As such, it is worth considering whether there is a continuing role for minimum food aid commitments.

Although the current level provides some floor, much of it is effectively accounted for by programmed commitments of relief and project aid and multi-year commitments to some recipients. This leaves little flexibility to respond to any substantial new emergencies. Thus, it might be more appropriate to rethink obligations in terms of the two generally agreed areas of need for continuing food aid: the food aid requirements of those affected by emergencies, refugees and displaced persons and the food assistance required to prevent the situations of highly food-insecure groups degenerating into crisis. This would require a definition of needs in terms of groups rather than balance sheets, perhaps linked to commitments to make the necessary funding available rather than to provide legally binding quantitative minimum obligations.[12]

The recent change permitting the expression of commitments in value as well as, or instead of, tonnage terms represents a positive step in this direction to the extent that a more people-centred approach to food aid can be associated with higher-cost food aid operations. Previously, all contributions, whether provided on a f.o.b. basis or including delivery costs up to the point of distribution, were treated equally in terms of fulfilment of FAC obligations. This implied substantial variations in cost per tonne of food aid, ranging from perhaps US$150 to $800 per tonne [*Clay et al., 1998*]. However, further mechanisms need to be introduced to help ensure that needs, rather than commitments, are met.

A shift in emphasis of the FAC away from a minimum quantitative commitment, whether in tonnage or value terms, towards some form of obligation linked to need may also be more appropriate, in view of the decline in the use of food aid as a means of agricultural surplus disposal. Food aid increasingly competes directly with other forms of assistance for donor funding. As such, it needs to be justified as an effective use of resources. Higher minimum commitments, regardless of higher or lower levels of need in a particular year, might be difficult to justify.

Finally, mechanisms need to be introduced to ensure continual assessment of the impact of the FAC, both in terms of international food security and of other factors. For example, some commentators have suggested that the FAC may limit the choice of commodities available in many relief situations, in turn leading to adverse nutritional consequences (see Chapter 6). However, no study has been undertaken to investigate such statements or, indeed, any other aspect of the impact of the FAC.

---

12. In this vein, during negotiations for the 1999 Convention, WFP proposed a reformulation of the FAC towards a more people-centred approach, concentrating a greater proportion of food aid on the most vulnerable people in the poorest regions of developing countries [*WFP, 1997*]. It further suggested that a combination of incentives and discounts might be incorporated within the FAC to encourage the best use of food aid.

REFERENCES

Benson, C. and E.J. Clay, 1998, 'Additionality or Diversion? Food Aid to Eastern Europe and the Former Soviet Republics and the Implications for Developing Countries', *World Development*, Vol. 26, No. 1, pp. 31–44.
Clay, E.J., N. Pillai and C. Benson, 1998, *The Future of Food Aid*, London: Overseas Development Institute.
Eggleston, R. C., 1987, 'Determinants of the Levels and Distribution of PL 480 Food Aid, 1955–79', *World Development*, Vol. 15, No. 6.
Food Aid Committee, 1999, *Food Aid Convention, 1999*, London: International Grains Council.
IWC, 1991, 'The Food Aid Convention of the International Wheat Agreement: A Note by the Secretariat of the International Wheat Council', London: International Wheat Council (May).
Shapouri, S. and M. Missiaen, 1990, 'Food Aid: Motivation and Allocation Criteria', *Foreign Agricultural Economic Report* 240, Washington DC: United States Department of Agriculture.
Taylor, D. and D. Byerlee, 1991, 'Food Aid and Food Security: A Cautionary Note', *Canadian Journal of Agricultural Economics*, Vol. 39, pp. 163–75.
Wallerstein, M., 1980. *Food for War – Food for Peace. United States Food Aid in a Global Context*, Cambridge: The MIT Press.
WFP, 1997, 'WFP Submission to the Food Aid Committee', Rome: World Food Programme (June).

5

Humanitarian Crises: Food Security and Conflict Prevention

UWE KRACHT

The hopes for world peace and stability raised by the end of the Cold War have been replaced by the reality of many fresh and many persistent conflicts throughout the world, which pose difficult new challenges for the international community, and divert a substantial share of human and financial resources, national and international, from long-term development to relief operations. Armed conflict is linked with food insecurity in a vicious circle of cause and effect. The most obvious effect of conflict is the acute deprivation, malnutrition and famine it causes in the short term, often combined with protracted post-conflict food insecurity following the destruction of the production base and related infrastructure. It is this aspect in particular of the food insecurity/conflict relationship which prompted the 1996 World Food Summit to call, under the first objective of its action plan for food security,[1] for the strengthening of conflict prevention and resolution mechanisms [*World Food Summit, 1996*]. Less well understood is the impact that food insecurity may have on the causes of conflict or, inversely, how food security can contribute to conflict prevention.

Against this background, this chapter addresses four conflict- and food-security related aspects:

- the changing emergency environment;
- the food-security consequences of conflicts;
- understanding the nature of conflicts – food insecurity as a causal factor?
- conflict prevention, food and humanitarian aid and conflict resolution, and post-conflict peace-building.

---

1. The WFS Action Plan contains seven broad commitments with a total of 27 objectives and 182 action proposals; for a synthesis of these see Kracht [*1999a*].

On this basis, the chapter concludes with a proposal for a holistic approach to dealing with conflicts before, when and after they occur, and its implications for international co-operation.

I. THE CHANGING EMERGENCY ENVIRONMENT

Changes have occurred on several fronts in the global emergency environment since the end of the Cold War. For a period, emergencies resulting from natural calamities gave way in relative importance to humanitarian crises induced by violent conflicts, and the nature of the conflicts also changed. In particular, armed conflicts within states now outnumber the 'traditional' international conflicts. The fighting that takes place in *intra*-state conflicts is generally not of the 'symmetric' nature of organised armies confronting each other in *inter*-state wars. Frequently, internal conflicts degenerate into some form of 'gang warfare' and primitive revenge processes.

Increasingly, it is civilians rather than combatants who are the victims of armed conflicts. In the First World War, for example, there was an estimated one civilian casualty for every 20 military casualties. In the Second World War, the ratio was 50/50, while more recent wars commonly cause ten civilian casualties for every one military casualty [*UNDP/ DHA, 1996: 22*]. The distinction between civilians and combatants becomes more and more blurred, however. Civilians are often the main targets, and civilians participate in the perpetration of violence. It is because of these complexities that contemporary conflicts are often referred to as 'complex humanitarian emergencies'. These have been defined as combining 'internal conflicts with large-scale displacements of people and fragile or failing economic, political and social institutions… random and systematic violence against noncombatants, infrastructure collapse, widespread lawlessness, and interrupted food production and trade' [*Weiss and Collins, 1996: 4*]. Natural disasters may be an exacerbating factor [*World Conference on Religion and Peace, 1994*].

During the period 1989–97, a total of 103 armed conflicts of varying intensity were registered. Their number increased with the end of the Cold War, reaching 55 in 1992, and then declined (see Figure 5.1). Of the total, 88 were classified as purely domestic and another nine as 'intra-state with foreign intervention'. The number of inter-state armed conflicts varied between four and zero per year during this period. Most inter-state conflicts have been at relatively low levels of violence, while many of the intra-state conflicts have been quite bloody, affecting the civilian population very severely [*de Soysa and Gleditsch, 1999: 14f*].

FIGURE 5.1
ARMED CONFLICTS BY SEVERITY AND YEAR, 1989–97

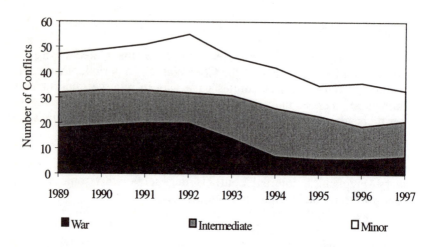

War is defined as an armed conflict with over 1,000 battle-deaths in a single year. Intermediate conflicts are those with over 1,000 battle-deaths in the course of the entire conflict, and minor conflicts are those with at least 25 battle-deaths in a single year, but less than 1,000. Both inter-state and domestic conflicts are included (Wallensteen and Sollenberg [*1998*], cited in de Soysa and Gleditsch [*1999: 14*]).

By 1997, armed conflicts had declined to 33 in 26 locations around the world. Of these, 21 were 'major conflicts', that is, wars and conflicts of intermediate intensity as defined in Figure 5.1 (see also Table 5.1). Despite a decline in the number of conflicts, the numbers of people affected are staggering: tens of millions of people were left at risk of hunger and malnutrition, including nearly 14 million refugees, 31 million internally displaced people, and an unknown number trapped within conflict zones. In contrast, in 1985, there were an estimated 11 million refugees and 10 million internally displaced persons [*Cohen and Pinstrup-Andersen, 1999: 1*].

TABLE 5.1
MAJOR CONFLICTS IN 1997

Country	Nature of conflict	Intensity of conflict
Israel	Internal – territorial	Intermediate
Turkey	Internal – governance	War
Afghanistan	Internal – governance	War
Cambodia	Internal – governance	Intermediate
India (Kashmir)	Internal – territorial	Intermediate
India (Assam)	Internal – territorial	Intermediate
India-Pakistan	Inter-state – territorial	Intermediate
Indonesia	Occupation of East Timor	Intermediate
Burma (Karen)	Internal – territorial	Intermediate
Burma (Shan)	Internal – territorial	Intermediate
Sri Lanka	Internal – territorial	War
Algeria	Internal – territorial	War
Burundi	Internal – governance	Intermediate
Congo (B)	Internal – governance	War
Congo (K)	Internal – governance	War
Senegal	Internal – territorial	Intermediate
Sierra Leone	Internal – governance	Intermediate
Sudan	Internal – territorial/governance	War
Uganda	Internal – governance	Intermediate
Colombia	Internal – governance	Intermediate
Peru	Internal – governance	Intermediate

Source: Sollenberg and Wallensteen [*1998*], as cited in Cohen and Pinstrup-Andersen [*1999*].

Part of the changing emergency environment is also the drastically changed humanitarian assistance regime or 'humanitarian space'. The predominant humanitarian actors of earlier times, namely, the International Committee of the Red Cross (ICRC) and the Red Cross and Red Crescent Movement as a whole, have been joined by a multitude of non-governmental organisations. They include long-established, responsible and experienced organisations, but also 'cowboys' [*Hampson, 1998: 68*], whose presence may attract media attention which puts pressure on other organisations to engage in high profile work to maintain donor support. In addition, many UN agencies are now engaged in humanitarian aid. Each of these actors is driven by its own specific mandate as well as different ethical and moral perspectives, and these compound the sheer logistical challenges of co-ordination and all too often result in poor quality of aid. 'Overproliferation' of humanitarian actors and low standards of humanitarian relief have become primary concerns among the major organisations of the aid community [*Leader, 1999*].

II. CONFLICTS AS A CAUSE OF FOOD INSECURITY

Over the past 20 years, armed conflicts have cost up to a million lives per year, and most of the casualties have been civilians, not combatants [*Messer et al., 1998: 13*]. Those who survive often risk severe food insecurity in both the short and longer term.

1. Short-Term Food Security Consequences of Conflicts

When armed conflict causes the civilian population to lose their normal food provisioning capacity, international humanitarian law – essentially the 1949 Geneva Conventions and their two 1977 Protocols – seeks to ensure their access to food by stipulating the free passage of relief supplies to civilians in need (both during the combat stage and in the immediate post-conflict period). But the enforcement of that law, which was basically conceived for traditional inter-state wars, has proved to be increasingly difficult in contemporary intra-state conflicts. In the reality of today's 'complex emergencies', substantial amounts of relief food are diverted to feed the combatants of the warring factions: they are the last to die from famine.

Beyond such diversion to meet the needs of combatants, food is also often used as an outright 'weapon' by cutting off civilians' access to it altogether, by destroying crops and by stripping the enemy population of its productive assets – all this in outright violation of international humanitarian law. In these circumstances, 'food as a weapon' is applied as a means of pressure for the achievement of military objectives. This is not, of course, a new phenomenon: sieges and starvation of the enemy population belong to the millennia-old armoury of warfare. The 'food weapon' is often accompanied by the destruction of health and education services, community leadership and social structures. Recent examples of such food and non-food tactics can be seen in Liberia, Mozambique, Sierra Leone, Somalia and Sudan [*Davis, 1998*].

In a broader sense, 'food as a weapon' is also an issue in political conflicts – in the form of economic sanctions, sometimes endorsed by the international community at the highest level, the UN Security Council, despite serious human rights concerns regarding their legitimacy. The international sanctions against Iraq and the US embargo against Cuba are cases in point [*Schroeder and Proescholdbell, 1998; Pellett, 1998*]. While the political effectiveness of such sanctions is questionable, their negative consequences for food security and the nutritional health of the civilian population, especially women and children, can be considerable – and not just in the short term, as these two countries witness.

2. Longer-Term Food Security Costs

In post-conflict situations, the prospects for food security often remain well below pre-conflict levels for long periods. Armed conflict destroys agriculture and its resource base – land, irrigation works, rural markets, means of transport and other infrastructure. In this way, it lays the foundations for long-term food insecurity lasting well beyond the conflict itself. Under the impact of armed conflict, existing agricultural production systems undergo deep and lasting changes. Seed multiplication systems and biodiversity are often severely damaged for years. Land mines impede access to agricultural land and restrict mobility in rural areas. Rural families lose not only their productive assets, but also their capacity to survive transitory food insecurity by means of traditional 'coping strategies'.

The effects of local conflicts on food production in sub-Saharan Africa have been the subject of a recent IFPRI-sponsored quantitative study [*Messer et al., 1998*]. The study seeks to compare actual and 'peace-adjusted' food production in individual countries and the region as a whole, and covers 14 countries (with 60 per cent of sub-Saharan Africa's population), which between 1970 and 1993 experienced one or more internal armed conflicts. It concludes that on average the 14 countries' per capita food production in wartime was 12.3 per cent below that of 'peace years'. Superficially, this average difference between 'war and peace' may seem of secondary importance. However, in view of the precarious food situation in the region, even seemingly modest average production shortfalls can have serious consequences for food security. The often dramatic effects of conflict on food production become evident from an examination of the study's country-specific results: in Angola, war-time food production per capita was 45 per cent below that in peace time; in Liberia 26 per cent; Somalia 23 per cent; Zimbabwe 20 per cent; and in Sudan 19 per cent.

Moreover, protracted armed conflicts destroy health and other social-sector systems, thus increasing the risk of health and nutrition problems and depriving the next generation of even an elementary education. They leave national economies in ruins, which makes the restoration of food security to at least pre-conflict levels even more difficult.

The costs can be staggering. In the case of Mozambique, the cumulative costs of the 1982–92 conflict with the Renamo rebels have been estimated at more than US$20 billion. In addition, the conflict entailed enormous military investments for neighbouring Tanzania and Zimbabwe, which sought to protect themselves from the spread of hostilities into their territories. These expenditures imposed high costs on their populations in terms of lost development, in particular of food security and health care [*Messer et al., 1998: 13*].

III. UNDERSTANDING THE NATURE OF CONFLICTS: FOOD INSECURITY AS A CAUSAL FACTOR?

While it is generally accepted that armed conflict causes food insecurity, the obverse of the relationship is less certain: does food insecurity cause conflicts? Far too little effort has been invested in analysing the complex origins of conflicts, compared with the importance of their role in today's reality. Generally speaking, food insecurity and conflicts in the Third World have their common roots in the legacies of colonialism and the Cold War, and in current policies which tend to marginalise and discriminate against certain population groups. Conflicts are of a political, economic and socio-cultural nature. They are generally multi-causal, and opinion is frequently divided as to the relative weight of specific causal factors. Table 5.2 presents an attempt at a summary of the causes and underlying factors of recent conflicts.

The table illustrates the multiplicity of causal and contributing factors, with a certain predominance of ethnic, religious and economic factors. As regards the latter, access to natural resources, especially land and water, is a dominant element. Food insecurity, in its extreme manifestation as famine, appears to have a 'conflict-trigger' function, but is hardly recognised as a causal factor. The overall picture to emerge from Table 5.2 merits some further discussion.

TABLE 5. 2

CAUSES OF RECENT AND PAST CONFLICTS IN AFRICA, ASIA AND LATIN AMERICA

Country	Causal and underlying factors of conflict
AFRICA/M. EAST Sudan	Since 1950, conflict was mostly triggered by inadequate government response to the outbreak of famine, but causes are of a *racial, ethnic and religious* nature (Arab-Islamic interests of the North against the Christian and animistic population in the South)
Ethiopia	Famine was an initial trigger of the multi-decade civil war that originated in the 1974 overthrow of the Haile Selassie regime, but the worst famine followed rather than precipitated the initial violence, with the forcible resettlement of ethnic populations and the subsequent denial of emergency food aid by the Dergue Junta. *Regional* and *ethnic* factors as well as foreign influences determined the civil war of the next 20 years. Extreme poverty and food insecurity were always associated with conflict, but *ethnic* and *political* factors were probably more influential on the particular form taken by the conflict
Rwanda, Burundi Senegal–Mauritania Israel–Palestine	*Ethnic-political* factors, *resource-scarcity* (see text) Border wars over *land and water* control, with *racial-ethnic* motivations *Land/water resource* factors anchored in *racial, religious and ideological-political* causes
CENTRAL AMERICA Guatemala, El Salvador, Nicaragua	'Revolutionary struggle' of *ethnic groups against ruling elite for resources (land)*, 'fair' wages, *human rights* protection; civil wars followed prolonged food crises and human rights violations (peace accords signed in Guatemala and El Salvador in 1996)
LATIN AMERICA Peru, Colombia	Similar to Central America (but linked to economic interests in drug trade)
ASIA Burma, Cambodia, Sri Lanka India (Kashmir) Indonesia	Mix of *economic, ethnic* and *ideological* factors Struggle over *land resources*, fanned by *ethnic-religious* motives (Tamil–Sinhalese) Struggle of the local population over *land* and *religious* autonomy *Political-economic* motives of the Indonesian government vis-à-vis East Timor
CENTRAL ASIA Azerbaijan, Chechnya, Georgia, Tajikistan	*Cultural-religious* and *political-economic* conflicts (territorial control, in some cases also oil interests)

Source: Based on Messer *et al.* [*1998: 10f*].

1. The Role of Ethnic Factors

The role of ethnic factors as a cause of conflict has become the subject of intense international debate. At a superficial level, most contemporary political emergencies are labelled as ethnic or religious conflicts. Events in Africa's Great Lakes region as well as in the former Yugoslavia and USSR seem to support this view. But the origins of most conflicts are too complex to be reduced to a single 'label'. In fact, there is a growing understanding that 'ethnic conflict is often a cover for a "conflict among the elites" for power, though eventually it acquires a life of its own', as the 1995 *Tokyo Statement of Principles for Peace and Development* by a group of experts on conflict puts it [*United Nations, 1995*].[2] The Netherlands National Advisory Council for Development Co-operation, in its report on Development Co-operation between War and Peace, expresses this view in an even more pointed way:

> Too often, the escalation of conflicts is attributed to ethnic factors. Ethnicity is a construct exploited by political leaders to whip up grass roots support. It is used to conceal the misuse of state authority and the abuse of power by those who wish to seize that authority. The deliberate perpetuation of inequalities between population groups makes those groups susceptible to appeals to their perceived ethnic identity [*NAR, 1996: 2*].

A prominent exponent of the 'complex emergencies scene', Rwanda's Vice President and Minister of Defence, Paul Kagame, confirmed precisely this position, when he said in a recent press interview: 'Every leadership elite can manipulate a population group in such a way that it assaults another one' [*Kagame, 1999: 131*].

This view is essentially corroborated by recent studies. For example, a 1997 WIDER study concluded that, contrary to many analysts who have emphasised 'ethnic conflict' as a major source of bloodshed, it is governments rather than spontaneous explosions of ethnic hatred that usually launch the violence. In a number of cases, political and ethnic killings had been planned and organised long before the humanitarian emergency began [*Holsti, 1997*]. Already in 1996 IFPRI emphasised in the context of events in Burundi and earlier in Rwanda that their root causes were to be found less in ethnic

---

2. *The Tokyo Statement of Principles for Peace and Development: Problems of Conflict in Africa* summarises the results of a symposium of 21 experts in the field of conflict prevention, management and resolution, organised by the Japanese government, the UN secretariat and the United Nations University.

strife between Hutus and Tutsis than in poverty, food insecurity and environmental degradation [*IFPRI, 1996a*]. And the UN Secretary General, in his 1998 report to the Security Council and General Assembly on 'The causes of conflict and the promotion of durable peace and sustainable development in Africa' pointed to the competition for scarce land and water resources in Rwanda and other densely populated regions of Central Africa as the cause of conflict [*United Nations, 1998*].

2. Socio-economic and Political Factors

Elaborating on the causes of conflict, an econometric WIDER study identifies six factors as the causes of conflicts [*Nafziger and Auvinen, 1997*]:

(i)   income stagnation and decline in developing countries;
(ii) high inequality of income distribution as a contribution to regional, ethnic and class differences;
(iii) inflation as a cause of increasing dissatisfaction, especially among lower income groups;
(iv) strategies of the political elites in response to the above problems;
(v)   the central role of the military;
(vi) history of violent conflict.

In the context of income stagnation and decline, the study also identifies *slow or declining growth of food production* as a possible causal factor, and concludes that failure in agricultural development can play a role in conflict causation. It also points to the *social conflicts* which are frequently triggered by economic stabilisation and structural adjustment programmes – the most prominent being 'food riots'.

Socio-economic factors thus appear to be a predominant explanation of the causes of conflict – with notable exceptions (possibly Kosovo and the current Ethiopian–Eritrean conflict). This view is confirmed by recent research at the International Peace Research Institute in Oslo (PRIO) [*de Soysa and Gleditsch, 1999*]. This study starts from the observation that conflicts are concentrated in countries where the economy is heavily dependent on agriculture – economies which are among the world's poorest. It identifies 'subsistence crises', loss of livelihoods and failure of development as well as the collapse of states as the origins of post-cold war humanitarian crises. The statement that the 'new internal wars ... are largely apolitical' (p.66) may appear surprising, even when interpreted as 'non-ideological' in the Cold War sense. It is certainly true of a number of internal conflicts of a predominantly 'gangland' nature (such as Somalia). But beyond these, the PRIO study itself provides ample examples of agriculture- and food security-related conflicts which are shaped by political and ideological factors.

3. Food-Security-Specific Factors

Within the socio-economic group of causal factors, conflicts linked specifically to agricultural and food-security issues have been tentatively classified into four categories: (i) land distribution conflicts, (ii) environmental conflicts, (iii) water conflicts, and (iv) food conflicts [*Wallensteen and Sollenberg, 1998*].

(*i*) *Land distribution conflicts*: The struggle for access to land is a widespread source of internal, and at times inter-state, conflict potential. It often has an ideological dimension directed at the fundamental reform of society. Examples include:

– Zimbabwe: Tensions and conflict potential, with African farmers claiming European settler land, and land reform measures having had only limited success;
– Brazil: conflict between the government and the 'movement of the landless' (Movimiento dos Sem-Terra – MST);
– Mexico/Chiapas: revolutionary movement based on demands for land distribution with broader socio-political reform objectives;
– Guatemala, El Salvador: similar to Mexico; since the 1996 peace accords, little progress has been made on the land reform front and concerning other socio-economic reforms, and conflict potential continues to be high;
– Philippines/Mindanao: armed conflict over land demands of the Islamic population.

(*ii*) *Environmental conflicts*: Environmental change can lead to conflict through exacerbation of resource scarcity or through man-made environmental destruction. Such conflict potential could increase in the future. Examples include:

– Mali and Niger: conflict between Tuaregs and the government, as a consequence of drought- and desertification-induced reduction in the Tuaregs' 'livelihood space'; additional factors are environmental destruction through uranium mining, rural settlement

schemes, and actual or perceived discrimination against the Tuaregs;
- Niger: similar conflict with Toubou nomads;
- Papua New Guinea/Bougainville – an example of man-made environmental destruction: separatist movement among the Bougainville island population in the wake of heavy environmental damage caused by Australian copper mining companies and the failure of the PNG central government to share the copper income 'fairly' with the island population;
- worldwide: the construction of large-scale dams is among typical examples of man-made environmental destruction with attendant conflict potential.

Nevertheless, the strength of the causal relationship between environmental factors and violent conflict remains a subject of intense debate. For example, a 1998 conference on 'Environmental Conflict and Preventive Action' organised by the Norwegian Institute of International Affairs (NUPI)[3] concluded that [*Rønnfeldt et al., 1999*]:

> Environmental factors are neither sufficient nor necessary causes of political conflicts, but they can be an underlying variable and are often used for violent behaviour ... Environmental crises may reflect a more general political and socio-economic failure. Conflict that arises from contending demands for land and related natural resources is equally environmental, as it is socio-economic ... What emerges overall is that the problems we are looking at in conflict causation are integrated with each other. Policy instruments must be capable of an equal degree of integration.

(iii) Water conflicts: The control of water resources constitutes one of the largest potentials for conflict, nationally as well as internationally, in the twenty-first century. The prospects are for a dramatic increase in water scarcity over the next 25–30 years. In view of the fact that currently some 340 million people experience temporary water shortage, this figure could rise to 3,000 million by 2025 [*Rosegrant, n.d.*]. Increasing water scarcity threatens future agricultural production and food security. Potential water conflicts have an important international dimension: more than 200 waterways are shared by two or more countries [*IFPRI, 1996b: 14*]. Among the more important conflict-potential areas are the Tigris-Euphrates region (Turkey, Syria, Iraq),

---

3.   In co-operation with the Centre for Environmental Studies and Resource Management (CESAR) and the International Peace Research Institute, Oslo (PRIO).

the Jordan region (Israel, Jordan, Syria), the Ganges-Brahmaputra region (Nepal, India, Bangladesh) and the Niger River region (Benin, Cameroon, Chad, Guinea, Côte d'Ivoire, Mali, Niger, Nigeria, Burkina Faso) [*Moss, 1998; Wolf, n.d.*].

(iv) Food conflicts: 'Food riots' are among the most spontaneous and visible manifestations of conflict, frequently triggered by economic policy changes such as the introduction of economic stabilisation and structural adjustment programmes. 'Food riots' have often accompanied such programmes; the events in Indonesia in 1998 are a recent example, and Zambia, Tunisia and Morocco are among classical examples. Rising prices and actual or perceived food scarcity are 'trigger factors', but the underlying causes are to be found in fundamental structural imbalances such as the aforementioned income inequalities. In the discussion of the causes of conflict, these structural factors are frequently also referred to as 'structural violence', which is defined as indirect violence or damage transmitted through the existing social system [*Kent, forthcoming*].

4. Governance and Human Rights

The various causal factors are closely intertwined with the way countries are governed. In its 1998 Yearbook, the Stockholm International Peace Research Institute (SIPRI) identified as 'a striking feature of the conflicts in Africa, and to some extent in Asia and South America, ... the link between armed conflict and a weak state' [*Sollenberg and Wallensteen, 1998: 23*] – a phenomenon which should come as no surprise. The importance of good governance and democratisation in preventing humanitarian emergencies is generally recognised today. In a truly democratic society where there is the rule of law, equal opportunity, accountability of power, and a leadership sensitive to social needs, primary group identities will be less appealing and discriminatory tendencies less pronounced. In such circumstances, humanitarian emergencies are less likely to occur [*Ake, 1997*].

Good governance, in turn, is closely linked to the realisation of human rights. Inherent in most of the factors identified as possible causes of conflict is the non-realisation or outright violation of human rights. And it is precisely the slow progress – and often regression – in the achievement of human rights, notably economic, social and cultural rights, and the outright violation, particularly of civil and political rights, which provide the breeding ground for conflict.

5. Development and Humanitarian Assistance

External assistance, if not conflict-sensitive, can easily become a contributing factor in the causation of conflict or can prolong existing conflicts. Development co-operation often tends to support ruling elites at the expense of marginalised population groups. In acute crises, humanitarian assistance, especially food aid, frequently ends up in the hands of the warring factions rather than the targeted civilian population and thus enables the former to continue hostilities. These issues, which will be discussed further below, underline the need for a conflict-sensitive approach to international co-operation which takes a holistic view of conflict prevention, relief and resolution, and post-conflict peace-building.

IV. CONFLICT PREVENTION, FOOD AND HUMANITARIAN AID AND CONFLICT RESOLUTION, AND POST-CONFLICT PEACE-BUILDING

The preceding analysis has sought to delineate the 'state of the art' of our current understanding of the relationship between conflict and food security as well as broader development parameters. In what follows, an attempt is made to apply this understanding, however deficient, to practical approaches to conflicts before, when and after they occur, and to identify critical gaps in our knowledge and ways of filling them.

1. Conflict Prevention

The record to date in predicting and preventing conflicts is no better than poor. To a significant extent, this is explained by the weak understanding of the nature of conflicts and the dynamics with which they develop. Significantly, many of the analyses of the causes of conflict have been undertaken only in recent years, suggesting a prolonged neglect of the problem. Where conflicts and disasters were predictable, such as the 1994 genocide in Rwanda, the response mechanisms failed to translate early warning into early preventive action.

(i) Does food security contribute to conflict prevention? The above assessment of the causes of conflict suggests that food insecurity is not a *primary cause* but an underlying factor which – in extreme cases – can become a 'trigger point'. While it is true that conflict causes hunger, the opposite – hunger causes conflict – does not hold equally true. Hunger and food insecurity are in themselves the result of

broader political and socio-economic failure. Thus, the primary causes of conflict are of a political and socio-economic nature, involving discrimination against certain population groups along racial, ethnic, religious and other lines. Such discrimination can involve factors specifically related to food security, such as access to land, water and other productive resources, which can become an *underlying cause* of conflict. Slow or declining agricultural development, in the context of unequal distribution, also needs to be carefully monitored as a potential causal factor.

To the extent that food-security policies and programmes contribute to the reduction of socio-economic inequalities and foster food production and availability, they also help to reduce conflict potential and to enhance conflict prevention. And where food security has been achieved, other aspects of socio-economic failure are also likely to have improved. In such circumstances, conflict is much less likely to occur.

(ii) Improving conflict understanding: While we have a general understanding of the causes of conflicts, more information is needed about the origins of violent conflict and the dynamics leading up to it in order to provide better predictions of impending hostilities or their escalation [*van Walraven, 1998: 163*]. This implies, *inter alia,* the development of improved methodological tools. In addition, more emphasis needs to be placed on human rights analysis, in view of the fact that at the heart of all conflicts is the violation or non-realisation of civil and political as well as economic, social and cultural rights [*Mackintosh, 1998*].

Improved analytical tools could be usefully complemented by case-studies which help to pinpoint the underlying causes and triggers of conflict. These studies could also analyse the reasons why conflict does not erupt in some resource-poor areas [*Cohen and Pinstrup-Andersen, 1998*].

(iii) Early warning information and response mechanisms: With regard to early warning information on conflicts and lower-intensity tensions and disturbances, there is an overwhelming amount of sources of information. Government diplomatic representations use their own (confidential) channels. The ICRC and other humanitarian NGOs have elaborate networks for intelligence gathering. Among the UN information systems are the Humanitarian Early Warning System (HEWS) and the regional/country networks of the Integrated Regional Information Network (IRIN). HEWS, which used to combine

statistical socio-economic data with qualitative information in such areas as human rights, military/arms, the political situation, is currently undergoing a complete overhaul. IRIN is largely based on qualitative information.[4] In addition, there are numerous academic and research institutions working with early warning methods.

There can be no general prescriptions for the 'ideal set' of early warning indicators. On the basis of the above assessment of causal and underlying factors, an indicative set of key indicators for complex emergencies might include the following:[5]

— trends in income/productive assets (land) distribution, income and employment security, according to socio-cultural groups (ethnic, religious, etc.);
— livelihood factors, including household food security and nutrition;
— environmental factors;
— human rights protection/violations;
— ethnic/religious tensions;
— ratio of military social expenditures as a proxy for the role of the military;
— state of preparedness of local, national and international institutions for crisis prevention;
— state of democratic institutions (government, parliament, elections, independent judiciary, free press, etc.).

An interesting, but fairly complex, example is the 'Eawarn project for ethnological monitoring' of the Centre for the Study and Management of Conflict at the Russian Academy of Sciences, which monitors ethnicity-related conflict potential in the former USSR. It uses a total of 46 indicator sets in seven categories; these are summarised in Box 5.1.[6] The value of this example lies in its illustration of the wide range of aspects to be taken into consideration, as well as the many 'intangibles' among the indicators and the complexity of the model. But it is precisely these aspects which make the Eawarn model, important as it is for the in-depth study of conflict causes, little conducive to application in regular monitoring at field level.

---

4. For a brief description of various systems see Kristensen [*forthcoming*].
5. See also UNDP [*1994*].
6. The author is indebted to Dr Valery Stepanov, Senior Researcher, Institute of Ethnology and Anthropology, Russian Academy of Sciences, for providing a detailed listing of the structure of the model.

Box 5.1
Summary of 'Eawarn Project' Indicators

Category 1. *Environment and Resources*
Five indicator sets, including water, land, mineral resources, environmental factors and ecological disasters.

Category 2. *Demography and Migration*
Four indicator sets, including population dynamics, ethnic composition, refugees, IDPs.

Category 3. *Power and Politics*
Eight indicator sets, including political systems, ethnic representation, centre–periphery relations, human rights.

Category 4. *Economy and Social Relations*
Eight indicator sets, including macroeconomic dynamics, income and employment, social mobility, crime and communal violence.

Category 5. *Culture, Education and Media*
Eight indicator sets, including religious tolerance, education, structure and control of media.

Category 6. *Contacts and Stereotypes*
Seven indicator sets, including group grievances, previous conflicts and group traumas, group ideologies, levels of tolerance.

Category 7. *External Conditions*
Six indicator sets, including stability of neighbouring countries, territorial claims and border disputes.

Source: Personal communication from Valery Stepanov, Institute of Ethnology and Anthropology, Russian Academy of Sciences, July 1999.

There is broad agreement that, while information is abundant, it is not necessarily of the right kind and quality. Specifically, it has been suggested that 'the quality of early warning information at the United

Nations should be improved' [*Rønnfeldt et al., 1999: 4*]. Such improvements will require not only improved understanding of the origins and causation of violent conflict, but also more knowledge of the decision-making processes in and among the various institutions involved in early warning and conflict prevention or containment. Such knowledge is necessary so as to ascertain how best to frame, and when to issue, warnings to political decision-makers [*van Walraven, 1998: 163*].

Even if the assessment of a particular conflict situation is correct and timely warnings have reached decision-makers, it is by no means certain that 'early action' will be taken.[7] Identification of the factors determining 'early action' is the subject of 'receptivity analysis', a relatively new tool in analyses of early warning and conflict prevention [*Wallensteen, 1998*].

In view of the linkages between peace/conflict and development, it has been proposed that development activities, especially those in conflict-prone environments, should be regularly assessed in terms of their impact on peace and conflict. An assessment methodology has been developed to this effect and needs to be tested [*Bush, 1998*].

The final value of improved information and analysis has to be measured against the quality of the response. The key issue in early warning and conflict prevention is not the signal as such, but the response it triggers. The adequacy of response mechanisms is only partly a matter of communication logistics; above all, it is a question of political decision. And that aspect is the most difficult one to address.

2. Food and Humanitarian Aid and Conflict Resolution

In conflict situations the provision of emergency food aid and other humanitarian assistance is governed by international humanitarian law – essentially the four 1949 Geneva Conventions and their two 1977 Additional Protocols. As already noted, the conventions were basically conceived for inter-state conflicts, but one article common to all four conventions (Article 3) contains the core of humanitarian principles applicable to inter- and intra-state situations alike. Moreover, the Second Additional Protocol is entirely devoted to 'non-international armed conflict'.[8] However, in the light of the changing conflict environment, questions are being raised about the continuing validity

---

7.   On the subject of the gap between early warning and conflict prevention see also Andersen [*forthcoming*].
8.   For a summary of international humanitarian law and its relation to human rights and refugee law, see Kracht [*1999a*].

of some of the ethical foundations of the principles enshrined in the Conventions. And with the greatly changed humanitarian assistance regime in the field, there is concern about maintaining the quality of the assistance provided.

(i) Humanitarian law and principles and conflict resolution – ethical and political concerns: International humanitarian law is built on the principle of the 'humanitarian imperative' which stipulates that humanitarian action is about saving lives and reducing suffering, and that 'no other consideration may override this principle' [*ICRC, 1998: 17*]. In this spirit, humanitarian assistance rests on the three 'ethical pillars' of *respect for human dignity, non-discrimination (impartiality)* and *neutrality* (not taking sides). Humanitarian action is understood to have two distinct functions: that of *protection* from violence as well as protection of basis human rights in acute crisis, and that of *assistance* in terms of humanitarian relief such as the provision of food, shelter and medical services to civilian victims of conflict.

The very principle of humanitarianism, as defined by the 'humanitarian imperative' with its exclusive focus on saving lives and reducing human suffering, irrespective of any other effects, has come under assault in recent years. Increasingly, scholars and aid workers are calling for the substitution of *solidarity* for *neutrality*. Many others are concerned that food aid and other assistance may undermine the protection function of humanitarian action as well as political efforts aimed at conflict resolution. This latter debate has revolved around three principal arguments:

(a) Humanitarian assistance risks being used as substitute for political action: In the opinion of ICRC President Sommaruga, 'one of the major challenges facing humanitarian organizations today is the tendency to use humanitarian assistance as a substitute for political action' [*Sommaruga, 1997: 180*]. This concern appears to be borne out by evidence from, for example, Rwanda where the *Joint Evaluation of Emergency Assistance to Rwanda* concludes that a key lesson is 'that humanitarian action cannot serve as a substitute for political, diplomatic and, where necessary, military action' [*United Nations, 1996, Vol. 3: 157*]. The argument runs that the provision of assistance is not only an inadequate response, but will remove the impetus to deal with the difficult causes of conflict by creating the impression that something is being done – thus postponing real solutions. This concern also underlies UNHCR's statement in its *Strategy Towards 2000* that 'UNHCR should resist becoming involved in protracted humanitarian operations which are not supported by broader peacemaking strategy or in which it is clearly not in a position to enlist respect for humanitarian principles' [*UNHCR, 1997: para. 67*]. However, the same strategy document also admits [*para. 50*] that the 'provision of assistance reinforces UNHCR's protection activities'.

(b) Humanitarian assistance undermines protection from violence and prolongs conflict: The provision of humanitarian assistance may prolong the conflict by sustaining the combatants themselves. All humanitarian actors have had to deal with the issue of the forced diversion of aid from civilians to combatants. Some have set informal limits for such diversion, beyond which they feel the positive effects of the assistance are outweighed by the negative effect of its diversion (some NGOs tend informally to accept diversions of up to one-third of food aid). In view of the fact that armies are always the last members of society to starve and that they will take food from civilians by force if necessary, some have even adopted the deliberate feeding of an army as a form of civilian protection, as some NGOs did in relation to assistance for Rwandan refugees in the camps in Zaire [*Mackintosh, 1998: 41*]. In fact, the purpose of humanitarian aid is sometimes stretched one step further, to use it as a bargaining tool to encourage respect for human rights and humanitarian law, as in the case of the Southern Sudan Ground Rules Agreement. On the other hand, there are situations where unplanned diversions take on such dimensions that the utility of the assistance is completely in question. As Oxfam Director David Bryer observed after the looting of 400 aid vehicles and millions of dollars worth of equipment and relief goods by Liberian warlords: 'I do think that more lives are likely to be saved by preventing such looting than by providing humanitarian aid' [*ibid.*].

(c) Humanitarian assistance undermines human rights protection: Humanitarian aid may directly affect the conflict in ways which undermine human rights. Assistance will tend to support the powers that be, either directly (by supplies, taxes, wages) or by relieving them of their obligation to provide for the civilians for whom they are responsible. The presence of international agencies may lend legitimacy to those in power. The regime may violate human rights; indeed, this may be at the root of the conflict. Increased awareness of these human rights implications has inspired a range of NGOs to adopt the principle of 'Do No Harm' in their humanitarian work. Save the Children (UK), for example, has suspended its operations in Afghanistan as a result of the acute gender discrimination and persecution of women there, in particular because this has made it impossible to recruit female staff and reach women beneficiaries [*Mackintosh, 1998: 42*].

The humanitarian community – practitioners and scholars alike – have wrestled with these issues and a long list of related 'ethical dilemmas'. While there is often a need to judge such issues in a particular situational context, there is equally a need to make such judgements against the background of fundamental principles and the commitment to basic standards of humanitarian action, irrespective of the specific situation. A significant number of humanitarian actors have recognised this and have made clear commitments to principles and standards in their work.

(ii) The quality of humanitarian aid – statements of principle and operational concerns: As noted earlier, the 'overproliferation' of humanitarian actors in the field has increasingly put the quality of humanitarian services in serious jeopardy. A number of scholars, practitioners and NGOs have responded by restating their fundamental positions and committing themselves to basic standards of operational achievement. Among early efforts in this direction are the Providence Principles and the Red Cross/Red Crescent and NGOs Code of Conduct.

The *Providence Principles of Humanitarian Action in Armed Conflict*, which were drawn up at a consultation organised in 1992 within the framework of Brown University's 'Humanitarianism and War' project, build on the spirit of the 'humanitarian imperative' and reflect the principles of humanity, neutrality and impartiality enshrined in humanitarian law (Box 5.2). Where they are at odds with humanitarian law is in the subordination of state sovereignty to humanitarian objectives (subsidiarity of sovereignty). At the same time, they go beyond the narrow, exclusive definition of the 'humanitarian imperative' by placing humanitarian aid within the broader context of conflicts, their causes and the link to human rights ('contextualisation').

Box 5.2
The Providence Principles of Humanitarian Action in Armed Conflicts

1. *Relieving Life-threatening Suffering:* Humanitarian action should be directed toward the relief of immediate, life-threatening suffering.

2. *Proportionality to Need:* Humanitarian action should correspond to the degree of suffering, wherever it occurs. It should affirm the view that life is as precious in one part of the globe as another.

3. *Nonpartisanship:* Humanitarian action responds to human suffering because people are in need, not to advance political, sectarian, or other extraneous agendas. It should not take sides in conflicts.

4. *Independence:* In order to fulfil their mission, humanitarian organisations should be free from home or host political authorities. Humanitarian space is essential for effective action.

5. *Accountability:* Humanitarian organisations should report fully on their activities to sponsors and beneficiaries. Humanitarianism should be transparent.

6. *Appropriateness:* Humanitarian action should be tailored to local circumstances and aim to enhance, not supplant, locally available resources.

7. *Contextualization:* Effective humanitarian action should encompass a comprehensive view of overall needs and of the impact of interventions. Encouraging respect for human rights and addressing the underlying causes of conflicts are essential elements.

8. *Subsidiarity of Sovereignty***:** Where humanitarianism and sovereignty clash, sovereignty should defer to the relief of life-threatening suffering.

Source: Minear and Weiss [*1993: 19*].

The *Code of Conduct for the International Red Cross and Red Cre-*
scent Movement and NGOs in Disaster Relief and its follow-up, the
Sphere Project, are dealt with in Chapter 13 in this volume. In the
fields of food aid and nutrition, UNHCR and the World Food Programme (WFP) have actually quantified technical standards by elaborating joint *guidelines and quantified standards for estimating food*
and nutritional needs in emergencies [UNHCR/WFP, 1997] and for
selective feeding programmes in emergency situations [UNHCR/
WFP, 1999]. These two sets of guidelines should be of value to all
humanitarian actors providing food aid.

A recurrent theme of the various statements concerns the *issue of*
accountability as an integral part of the quality of humanitarian aid.
For many humanitarian NGOs the 'accountability track' is complex, if
not 'bewildering' *[Leader, 1999: 2]*. Agencies are accountable to the
people they intend to serve. They are accountable to their donors.
They are also accountable to their own organisation's charter or mandate and to the legislation governing charitable organisations, both at
home and in the country of operation. And, in a sense, they are
accountable to international law, even though they are not parties to
the legal instruments. This is a grey but important area. Some agencies, in fact, challenge certain provisions in international humanitarian law, notably those concerning neutrality and impartiality.

An innovative initiative has been directed to the question of agency
accountability to their clients, i.e. the beneficiaries or claimants of
humanitarian assistance: that of establishing an *Ombudsman for*
Humanitarian Assistance [BRCS, 1999]. Based on ombudsman
schemes in other fields, the basic concept of the proposal is that a
Humanitarian Ombudsman (HO) would act as an impartial and independent voice for those people affected by disaster and conflict, and
that the establishment of the HO would be constituted as an international scheme of all international humanitarian organisations, with
an independent and neutral status. The original proposal was developed under the leadership of the British Red Cross Society (BRCS),
with the participation, in one way or another, of most UK humanitarian NGOs and funding from Oxfam and the UK government (DFID).
In its current phase, the project has embarked on a broad Northern-
and Southern-based consultation aimed at developing the proposal
further.

These few examples, which in fact represent the positions and commitments of a large number of humanitarian actors, confirm two
important aspects of humanitarian action in conflicts and other disasters: (i) the continuing validity and acceptance of the humanitarian

imperative as a guiding principle, although applied in a broader context of conflict causes and human rights as opposed to its narrow and exclusive 'life-saving' definition; and (ii) the commitment to maintaining professional standards in the provision of humanitarian services against the background of a proliferation of humanitarian actors with divers mandates, motivations and experience.

3. Post-Conflict Peace-building

Post-conflict peace-building – in developmental and political terms – has much in common with conflict prevention. After all, a main objective, once a conflict has been settled, is avoiding a recurrence of hostilities. How conflict prevention in pre- and post-conflict situations can best be achieved through country-specific strategies depends on a thorough understanding of the causal scenarios of conflicts and the driving forces behind them. Such understanding, in turn, requires the combined efforts of capable policy analysts, a sensitive staff in diplomatic missions, international agencies and NGOs in the country or region concerned, and supportive information systems.

Much has been said about the 'continuum from relief to development'. There appears to be a growing understanding, at least within the UN system, that the 'continuum concept' – because of its oversimplicity – 'has done more harm than good'. 'Complex emergencies cannot be neatly sequenced into various phases during which different actors of the UN system pass on the baton and then sit back to watch the rest of the race. Humanitarian assistance is not an effective instrument for response to complex crises when used in isolation. Emergency relief, peacekeeping, diplomacy, human rights and development activities must be carried out simultaneously and must be structured to be mutually reinforcing' [*Duggan, 1998: 134*].

V. TOWARDS A HOLISTIC APPROACH TO DEALING WITH CONFLICTS AND ITS IMPLICATIONS FOR INTERNATIONAL CO-OPERATION

Food security depends on protecting peace where conflict is imminent, achieving peace where conflict is active, and sustaining peace where conflict has ended [*Cohen and Pinstrup-Andersen, 1999*]. As conflicts are the result of multiple causes which act in an integrated manner, conflict prevention, relief and resolution, and post-conflict peace-building require integrated policy responses. This means a holistic approach to dealing with conflicts before, when and after they occur. At the international level, it implies, above all, an explicit 'conflict sensitivity' in all co-operation activities. Within the United

Nations family, UNICEF is the first agency to have decided to integrate emergency sensitivity and preparedness into its regular country programming process [*Csete, 1999*].

At the core of a holistic approach to dealing with conflicts is what the aforementioned *Tokyo Statement* calls 'preventive development' before conflict can develop. Preventive development consists of support for broadly-based economic growth; reduction of income and wealth inequalities; economic stabilisation and adjustment programmes mindful of the needs of lower income groups; good governance, democratic institutions and development processes, realisation of human rights – civil and political as well as economic, social and cultural; and policies which minimise elite polarisation and excessive state intervention [*Nafziger and Auvinen, 1997; Ake, 1997; Emizet, 1997*]. In short, this so-called 'preventive development' is development as it should be when human beings are placed at its centre. The proposal for applying peace/ conflict impact analyses to development activities deserves to be tested.

Food-security policies and programmes need to be increasingly integrated into this overall framework. This means, specifically, greater emphasis on land reform, access to water and other essential production factors, and sustainable rural development. As in the overall development framework, food-security measures must aim at reducing and eliminating discrimination along racial, ethnic, religious and other socio-cultural lines. These are, in general, extremely sensitive issues politically, requiring particular diplomatic efforts in the context of international co-operation.

At the international level, co-operation efforts should aim, in particular, at preventing potential inter-state water and environmental conflicts. International early warning systems should keep a watch on potential crisis regions.

Nationally and internationally, there is a need to develop better crisis preparedness and response capacity, which would include:

–   further development of analytical tools aimed at a better understanding of the causes and processes leading to conflicts;
–   improved early warning systems and 'early response' mechanisms;
–   improved emergency intervention capacity, including adequate logistical arrangements and commitment to adhering to fundamental humanitarian principles and acceptable quality standards for the delivery of humanitarian services;

– much greater efforts aimed at integrating emergency relief, peacekeeping and peace-building, diplomacy, human rights and development activities in mutually reinforcing ways.

VI. CONCLUSION

Since the end of the Cold War, man-made emergencies in the form of conflicts of varying intensity have overtaken natural calamities in creating humanitarian crises. Increasingly, these conflicts occur within states as opposed to the 'traditional' pattern of inter-state warfare, with important ramifications for relief and conflict-resolution efforts. Moreover, the overproliferation of humanitarian actors in recent years has made it difficult to maintain acceptable professional standards for the provision of humanitarian services.

Armed conflicts invariably cause food insecurity and hunger in the short term, often with long-term food-security consequences. In turn, food insecurity is increasingly often a contributing factor to the causes of conflict, within the broader context of political and socio-economic failure. In its extreme form, food insecurity can act as a trigger for conflict.

Current ways of dealing with conflict, which are of a predominantly ad hoc and reactive nature, need to shift towards a holistic approach to conflicts before, when and after they occur. This implies, above all, more conflict-sensitive and equitable development efforts, including food security programmes. It implies an understanding that, in the case of acute conflicts, emergency relief, peacekeeping, diplomacy, human rights and development activities must be pursued simultaneously and must be structured to be mutually reinforcing. More specifically, there is also an urgent need for improved understanding of the causes of conflict and the processes leading to it, and for more relevant early warning systems and more effective response mechanisms. Efforts by large numbers of humanitarian actors to maintain high professional standards in the provision of food and humanitarian aid through commitment to clearly stated humanitarian principles and appropriate operational standards are worthy of support.

REFERENCES

Ake, C., 1997, *Why Humanitarian Emergencies Occur: Insights from the Interface of State, Democracy and Civil Society*, UNU/WIDER Research for Action No. 31, Helsinki: World Institute for Development Economies Research.

Andersen, R., forthcoming, 'Bridging the Gap between Early Warning and Conflict Prevention: the Role of Information', The Fridtjof Nansen Institute, to be published in *Disasters, The Journal of Disaster Studies, Policy and Management*.

BRCS (British Red Cross Society), 1999, 'The Ombudsman for Humanitarian Assistance: An interagency initiative to establish a Humanitarian Ombudsman', Web site: www.oneworld.org/ombudsman/...

Bush, K., 1998, *A Measure of Peace: Peace and Conflict Impact Assessment (PCIA) of Development Projects in Conflict Zones*, Working Paper No. 1, Hull, Canada: The Peacebuilding and Reconstruction Program Initiative & The Evaluation Unit, IDRC.

Cohen, M.J. and P. Pinstrup-Andersen, 1999, 'Food Security and Conflict', *Social Research*, Vol. 66, No. 1, pp. 375–416.

Csete, J., 1999, 'Integrating Emergency Preparedness and Response into UNICEF Programming: Key Recommendations and Next Steps from the Martigny Consultation', Nairobi: UNICEF/ESARO (April).

Davis, A.P., 1998, 'Sudan – Food Atrocities as the Way of War', in Latham and Campbell, eds.

De Soysa, I. and N.P. Gleditsch, 1999, *To Cultivate Peace: Agriculture in a World of Conflict*, PRIO Report 1/99, Oslo: International Peace Research Institute and Washington DC: Future Harvest/CGIAR.

Duggan, C., 1998, 'UNDP's Role in Promoting and Protecting Human Rights in Crisis and Post-Crisis Countries', in DFID and University of Essex/Human Rights Centre, Proceedings of *Conference on the Promotion and Protection of Human Rights in Acute Crisis*, Human Rights Centre, Essex University, pp. 131–38.

Emizet, K.N.F., 1997, *Zaire after Mobutu: A Case of Humanitarian Emergency*, UNU/WIDER Research for Action No. 32, Helsinki: World Institute for Development Economies Research.

Hampson, F.J., 1998, 'International Humanitarian Law in Situations of Acute Crisis', in DFID and University of Essex/Human Rights Centre, Proceedings of *Conference on the Promotion and Protection of Human Rights in Acute Crisis*, Human Rights Centre, Essex University, pp. 61–71.

Holsti, K.J., 1997, *Political Sources of Humanitarian Emergencies*, UNU/WIDER Research for Action No. 36, Helsinki: World Institute for Development Economies Research.

ICRC (International Committee of the Red Cross), 1998, *Protection – Toward Professional Standards*, Report of the Workshop, 17–19 March, Geneva: ICRC.

IFPRI, 1996a, 'Food Insecurity Lies at the Root of Conflict', *News & Views – A 2020 Vision for Food, Agriculture, and the Environment*, Washington DC: International Food Policy Research Institute.

IFPRI, 1996b, *Feeding the World, Preventing Poverty, and Protecting the Earth: A 2020 Vision*, Washington DC: International Food Policy Research Institute.

Kagame, P., 1999, Interview with *Der Spiegel*, No. 28 (12 July).

Kent, G., forthcoming, *Structural Violence against Children*, Honolulu HI: University of Hawaii Press.

Kracht, U., 1999a, 'Towards a Global Policy Agenda: The World Food Summit in the Context of International Development Summitry in the 1990s', in U. Kracht and M. Schulz, eds., *Food Security and Nutrition – The Global Challenge*, Münster and New York: LIT Verlag and St. Martin's Press, pp. 631–64.

Kracht, U., 1999b, 'Human Rights and Humanitarian Law and Principles – An Overview of Concepts and Issues', paper prepared for UNICEF/ESARO, Nairobi.

Kristensen, A., forthcoming, *Early Warning as a Basis for Preventive Action: A Study of the Information Basis for Norwegian NGOs*, Oslo: Norwegian Institute of International Affairs.

Latham, M.C. and C.E. Campbell, eds., 1998, *Food as a Weapon of War or for Political Purposes*, WAHNAR Bulletin, No. 7 (Sept.).

Leader, N., 1999, *Codes of Conduct: Who Needs Them?* RRN Newsletter No. 13, London: Overseas Development Institute, Relief and Rehabilitation Network (March).

Mackintosh, K., 1998, 'International Responses to Acute Crisis: Supporting Human Rights through Protection and Assistance', in DFID and University of Essex/ Human Rights Centre, *Proceedings of Conference on the Promotion and Protection of Human Rights in Acute Crisis*, Human Rights Centre, Essex University.

Messer, E., M.J. Cohen and J. D'Costa, 1998, *Food from Peace: Breaking the Links between Conflict and Hunger*, Food, Agriculture and the Environment Discussion Paper 24, Washington DC: International Food Policy Research Institute.

Minear, L. and T. Weiss, 1993, *Humanitarian Action in Times of War. A Handbook for Practitioners*, Boulder, CO/London: Lynne Rienner Publishers.

Moss, R.H., 1998, 'Resource Scarcity and Environmental Security', in SIPRI, *Sipri Yearbook*.

Nafziger, W. and J. Auvinen, 1997, *War, Hunger, and Displacement: An Econometric Investigation into the Sources of Humanitarian Emergencies*, WIDER Working Papers No. 142, Helsinki: World Institute for Development Economies Research.

NAR, 1996, *Development Cooperation Between War and Peace*, 'In Brief' Information from the NAR No. 18, The Hague: National Advisory Council for Development Co-operation.

Pellett, P., 1998, 'Food, Nutrition and Health in Iraq', in Latham and Campbell, eds. .

Rønnfeldt, C.F., E. Barth Eide and D. Smith, eds., 1999, *Environmental Conflict and Preventive Action*, Proceedings of a Seminar organised by NUPI, CESAR and PRIO for the Norwegian Ministry of Foreign Affairs, Oslo-Lysebu, (23–24 Nov. 1998).

Rosegrant, M.W. (no date), *Water Resources in the Twenty-First Century: Challenges and Implications for Action.* Food, Agriculture and the Environment Discussion Paper No. 20, Washington DC: International Food Policy Research Institute.

SIPRI, 1998, *Sipri Yearbook 1998, Armaments, Disarmament and International Security*, Stockholm: International Peace Research Institute; Oxford: Oxford University Press.

Schroeder, D.G. and S.K. Proescholdbell, 1998, 'Food and the US Embargo against Cuba', in Latham and Campbell, eds.

Sollenberg, M. and P. Wallensteen, 1998, 'Security and Conflicts, 1997', in SIPRI, *Sipri Yearbook*.

Sommaruga, C., 1997, 'Humanitarian Action and Peacekeeping Operations', in ICRC, *International Review of the Red Cross*, No. 317 (March).

UNDP, 1994, *Human Development Report 1994*, New York: UNDP.

UNDP/DHA, 1996, *International Law of Disasters and Armed Conflict. Disaster Management Training Programme*, New York: UNDP/DHA.

UNHCR, 1997, *Strategy Towards 2000*, Geneva/New York: UNHCR.

UNHCR/WFP, 1997, *Guidelines for Estimating Food and Nutritional Needs in Emergencies*, Geneva/Rome (Dec.).

UNHCR/WFP, 1999, *Guidelines for Selective Feeding Programmes in Emergency Situations*, Geneva/Rome (Feb.).

United Nations, 1995, *The Tokyo Statement of Principles for Peace and Development: Problems of Conflict in Africa*, New York: United Nations.

United Nations, 1996, *Joint Evaluation of Emergency Assistance to Rwanda*, New York: United Nations.

United Nations, 1998, 'The Causes of Conflict and the Promotion of Durable Peace and Sustainable Development in Africa', Report of the Secretary-General, A/52/871–S/1998/318, New York: United Nations.

van Walraven, K., ed., 1998, *Early Warning and Conflict Prevention: Limitations and Possibilities*, The Hague: Netherlands Institute of International Relations 'Clingendael', Kluwer Law International.

Wallensteen, P. and M. Sollenberg, 1998, 'Armed Conflict and Regional Conflict Complexes, 1989–97', *Journal of Peace Research*, Vol. 35, No. 5, pp. 621–34.

Wallensteen, P., 1998, 'Acting Early: Detection, Receptivity, Prevention and Sustainability. Reflecting on the First Post-Cold War Period', in van Walraven, ed.

Weiss, T.G. and C. Collins, 1996, 'Evolution of the Humanitarian Idea', in *Humanitarian Challenges and Intervention*, Boulder CO: Westview Press.

Wolf, A.T. (no date), *Middle East Water Conflicts and Directions for Conflict Resolution*, Food, Agriculture and the Environment Discussion Paper No. 12, Washington DC: International Food Policy Research Institute.

World Conference on Religion and Peace, 1994, *The Mohonk Criteria for Humanitarian Assistance in Complex Emergencies*.

World Food Summit, 1996, *World Food Summit Plan of Action*, Rome: FAO.

6

Humanitarian Crisis and Conflict: Food Assistance and Nutritional Security Issues

JEREMY SHOHAM, FIONA O'REILLY AND JANE WALLACE

I. INTRODUCTION

This chapter sets out to give an overview of the recent performance of emergency food assistance in terms of its delivery and associated nutritional outcomes. Its main finding is that there is an association between persisting undernutrition and other nutritional disorders and the provision of emergency food assistance. In particular, food assistance continues to be provided at substantially lower levels than the agreed norms necessary to avoid undernutrition, and its composition is unlikely to avoid problems of malnutrition. The chapter then goes on to specify and categorise factors that may impede its effectiveness. Its context is recognised to have changed dramatically over the past decade, with the majority of emergency operations having been associated with situations of conflict and war. It is argued that emergency food assistance is less effective than it could be, with adverse nutritional consequences, and that these consequences could be mitigated to some degree if decision-making were better informed by field-level experience and current thinking on combating nutritional problems. The chapter concludes by identifying mechanisms and processes which can help to further clarify these impeding factors and improve the provision of aid at the institutional level where there may be room for manoeuvre.

II. FOOD ASSISTANCE PERFORMANCE

Three criteria are used to assess the nutritional effectiveness of emergency food assistance: Is enough food being provided? Does the food provide adequate amounts of micronutrients? Is the food appropriate in terms of palatability, acceptability, ease of preparation and spoilage?

Before examining some of the critical evidence, two caveats are appropriate. First, it is important to recognise the considerable progress that has been made in planning and delivering appropriate amounts of emergency food assistance, much of it since the ACC/SCN workshop on the Improvement of the Nutrition of Refugees and Displaced People held in Machakos, Kenya in 1994 [*ACC/SCN, 1996*]. Notable improvements have been the commitment to provide micronutrient fortified blended foods to populations dependent on food aid, the raising of the initial ration from 1,900 kcals/capita to 2,100, and the acceptance that refugees and internally displaced persons (IDPs) have a right to the same quantity and quality of food rations as are indicated in the WFP/UNHCR technical guidelines on minimum nutritional requirements [*WFP/UNHCR, 1997b*].

Second, it is also important to emphasise that the nutritional outcome of emergency programmes cannot solely be associated with the amounts and quality of food assistance provided. Nutritional status (usually measured in the under-fives) is determined primarily by three key variables – food intake, health status and caring practices – as identified by the UNICEF conceptual framework. The nutritional status of emergency-affected populations can therefore be markedly compromised by poor health status and health care as well as by inadequate emergency food assistance. Relatedly, the nutritional outcome may also be adversely affected by the failure to provide non-food items like fuel and cooking utensils, the inclusion of which in emergency programmes is often problematic.

1. Quantity of Emergency Rations

Until recently the minimum amount of calories per capita recommended for emergency-affected populations totally dependent on food assistance was set at 1,900 kcals/capita [*ACC/SCN, 1989*]. As noted above, this has now been revised to 2,100 kcals/capita [*WFP/UNHCR, 1997b*]. In contrast, information compiled by the Refugee Nutrition Information System (RNIS) indicates that general rations delivered to emergency-affected populations in sub-Saharan Africa have in the past often fallen far short of these figures (Figure 6.1). However, it should be recognised that in some cases, particularly in protracted relief operations (PROs), rations have been set at lower levels on the basis of populations being at least partly self-sufficient. Furthermore, actual amounts of food consumed rarely equate with the amounts delivered by humanitarian agencies. Even in the most closed and austere camp situations, those relying on the ration have often had access to other sources of food. For example, in Auschwitz, where rations were in the region of 1,600 kcals/capita, microeconomies set up within the camps and the immediate environment permitted the survival of many who would otherwise have perished on such a small ration.

In assessing performance the gap between intention and outcome needs to be recognised. In those cases where rations are deliberately reduced, actual deliveries have often fallen short of those planned. Recent examples were the Sudanese refugees in northern Uganda where shortage of general rations was never compensated for retrospectively, thus reducing the overall amount of food available for the refugees [*Payne, 1997*], or in the Somali refugee camps in south-east Ethiopia where emergency per capita rations have consistently been low over an eight-year period. Refugees in some of the more isolated or closed camps may be almost totally dependent on emergency rations. Furthermore, planning of emergency general rations only provides for the minimum per capita requirements. A small shortfall in caloric level can therefore have dramatic nutritional consequences.

Comprehensive analysis of the additional food sources available is often lacking among implementing agencies. There have been several examples recently of emergency general rations having been severely curtailed, leading to predictions of imminent starvation. The actual outcome was that the refugees survived perfectly well by having access to other sources of food and that their nutritional status remained stable. This was the case in the Goma camps for Rwandan refugees at the beginning of 1995, when for several months ration receipts were less than 800 kcals/capita and yet levels of wasting remained at between 2 and 4 per cent. Subsequent surveys showed that many refugees had access to employment on local farms [*ODI, 1996a*].

Yet, while there are many examples of ration energy content falling short of planned deliveries, there are also a number of recent successes. For example, the evaluation of the Great Lakes emergency programme concluded that, given the scale and speed of onset of the emergency, the delivery of emergency food assistance can be judged to have been highly successful [*ODI, 1996a*]. There have also been 'successes' in difficult security situations. For example, the WFP evaluation of the Liberia region emergency programme concluded that food aid deliveries were of a high standard and reached areas in need

under the most difficult physical and security conditions [*WFP,
1997*].

What are the consequences of under-provision? First, relatively
higher malnutrition levels and mortality are potentially associated
with an inadequate ration supply. The association between wasting
(below-norm weight for height in children) and increased mortality
has long been recognised, and is clearly seen when we examine
reports from refugee situations. Second, there may be micronutrient
deficiencies.

One of the main types of information included in the RNIS reports
is nutritional survey data on the prevalence of wasting. During 1995–
97, roughly half the reports showed levels of over 10 per cent and
almost one-fifth over 20 per cent (Figure 6.1). On the other hand,
some of the worst situations may be inaccessible to outside agencies
so that surveys are not possible. As expected, there is a strong association between wasting and crude mortality rates (see Figure 6.2).

FIGURE 6.1
WASTING LEVELS IN DIFFERENT EMERGENCY SITUATIONS FROM JANUARY 1995 TO JUNE 1997

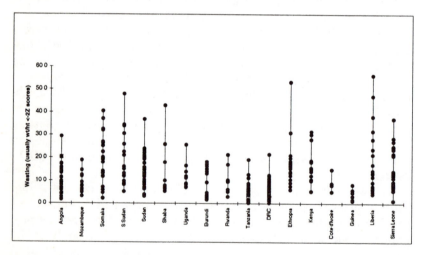

Source: RNIS.

FIGURE 6.2
WASTING AND CRUDE MORTALITY RATES (CMR) (LOG SCALE)

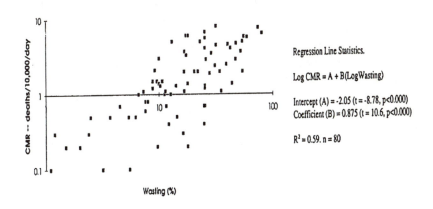

Regression Line Statistics.

Log CMR = A + B(LogWasting)

Intercept (A) = -2.05 (t = -8.78, p<0.000)
Coefficient (B) = 0.875 (t = 10.6, p<0.000)

$R^2 = 0.59$. n = 80

Source: ACC/SCN (1993/4), RNIS.

Rations providing over 2,000 kcals/person/day were associated with benchmark mortality rates (1death /10,000/day), whereas <1,500 kcals/ person/day were associated with mortality rates ranging from two to ten times higher [*ACC/SCN, 1994*]. However, these data must be treated with care. First, they do not correlate actual shortfalls in consumption with mortality levels; for instance, rations may be deliberately low because the beneficiaries are partly self-sufficient. Second, other factors may affect levels of wasting and the resulting mortality: for example, market stimulations/prices, freedom of movement and income-earning opportunities provided by humanitarian agencies. Furthermore, the health and caring environments may have a significant, or greater, impact. It could therefore be argued that there is no known reason for a strong correlation between the data on rations delivered and mortality, though intuitively it seems obvious. Unfortunately, systematic analysis has yet to be undertaken.

Cases of reductions in malnutrition associated with adequate supply of rations provide further qualitative evidence of the ration–malnutrition linkage. Despite many reports over recent years of high levels of wasting and micronutrient deficiency disease (MDD) associated with inadequate provision of general rations, there are also a number of notable successes. The Great Lakes evaluation involving the collation of information on the nutritional situation of refugees in Zaire,

Tanzania and Burundi and IDPs in Rwanda during the first year of the emergency, came to the conclusion that, within a short period of time, two to five months, the nutritional situation had been stabilised, largely due to the successful delivery of emergency food assistance. The most intractable nutritional problems during this programme were attributable to inequitable distribution systems at camp level rather than inadequate provision of emergency food aid [*ODI, 1996a*].

Indeed, a phenomenon frequently reported over the past few years has been the rapid reduction in levels of wasting once areas previously cut off because of conflict and insecurity have become accessible to humanitarian agencies. There have been many reports from Angola, Liberia and southern Sudan of catastrophic levels of wasting in areas isolated from outside assistance. However, following improved security or negotiated access and the establishment of emergency feeding programmes, these levels have been dramatically reduced [*Barrett, 1993; Berard, 1993; Borrel, 1994*]. Although much of this reduction has been attributed to the provision of emergency food aid, other factors like the re-establishment of markets, the resumption of agricultural activity and freedom of movement have also played a significant role.

2. Micro-nutrient Content of Emergency Rations

Diets based on cereals, legumes and oil – the standard emergency rations – typically do not supply sufficient micro-nutrients, and micro-nutrient deficient diseases (MDD), such as vitamin A deficiency (night blindness), scurvy, beri-beri and pellagra, result. However, it is extremely difficult to provide micro-nutrient-rich foods like vegetables and fruit for large numbers of refugees/IDPs in isolated camps. There is no single strategy which can cover all eventualities [*Toole, 1994*]. The provision of fortified blended foods has been considered central to any such strategy, and agencies such as the WFP and UNHCR now stipulate in their revised Memorandum of Understanding the provision of blended foods in the emergency general rations for totally dependent populations [*WFP/UNHCR, 1997a*]. While this approach is not ideal, there is probably no practical alternative at present. Meanwhile, other initiatives to address the micro-nutrient problem are afoot, such as the development and field testing of camp-level cereal milling and fortification equipment [*Field Exchange, No. 5*].

The advantage of blended foods is that micro-nutrient requirements can be incorporated via enrichment in the rations. Where this food is directly supplied by donors, this enrichment can be done at source in the food processing, as with the vitamin-enriched corn-soya blend (CSB) supplied by the United States. However, there are also many disadvantages in relying on fortified blended foods. First, the few grammes provided in the emergency general rations do not contain sufficient nutrients to bring the density in the diet to the recommended levels. Second, blended foods may not be consumed by the entire population, although recent research challenges this supposition [*Oxfam, 1998*]. Third, there are cheaper alternative vehicles for micro-nutrient fortification, for example cooking salt and sugar, which also have a strong taste and therefore reduce the risk of over-consumption of potentially toxic nutrients like vitamin A. Fourth, fortifying such alternative vehicles also has considerable logistical advantages; a specifically designed highly fortified food like salt should enable the use of a much smaller quantity of fortified food.

Finally, supplies of blended foods cannot always be guaranteed; in 1998, for example, it was predicted that the main supplier of CSB, the US, would not be able to supply much of this commodity. Problems of supply have been observed in many recent emergencies. For example, in the Dadaab camps for Somali refugees in Kenya supplies for the blanket supplementary feeding programme were difficult to sustain; a policy of supplying blended foods only during the dry season was introduced, even though the initial assessment indicated that they were needed all the year round. This contributed, some say predictably, to a rise in the prevalence of wasting and scurvy in the camps [*ACC/SCN, 1997*].

TABLE 6.1

REPORTED MDDS IN EMERGENCY CAMP SETTINGS, 1995–97

Deficiency	Location	Public Health Problem
Vitamin A	Camps for displaced, Khartoum, Sudan	yes
(seen as	Somalia (IDPs)	yes
night blindness)	Red Sea Hills, Sudan (IDPs and residents)	yes
	Ethiopia – IDPs in Gode (2)	yes
Vitamin C	Red Sea Hills, Sudan (displaced and resident)	mild
(seen as scurvy)	Somali refugee camps, Kenya	moderate, but seasonal
	Bhutanese refugee camps, Nepal (3)	mild
	Somali refugee camps, Kenya	moderate, but seasonal
	Ethiopia – IDPs in Gode	mild
	Ethiopia – IDPs in Gode	moderate
Vitamin B	Bhutanese refugee camps, Nepal	mild
(seen as beri-	Red Sea Hills, Sudan (displaced and resident)	mild
beri)	Bhutanese refugee camps, Nepal (2)	mild
Niacin	Mutarara district, Mozambique – returnees (2)	mild
(seen as pellagra)	Bhutanese refugee camps, Nepal	mild
	Camps for refugees from Rakhine State, Myanmar, in Bangladesh	mild

Source: RNIS Database.

In practice, the provision of blended foods has not always proved straightforward and questions have also been raised about its appropriateness as a strategy to prevent MDD. The fact that MDDs do not appear in all cases of inadequate provision of micro-nutrients reflects the fact that emergency-affected populations often manage to employ strategies which allow dietary diversification. Nevertheless, the RNIS database shows that cases of MDD still occur all too frequently, particularly in isolated or closed camp situations (Table 6.1).[1] In some instances these diseases are seasonal in nature. For example, seasonal outbreaks of scurvy have been reported in Somali refugee camps in Kenya, while a pellagra outbreak, possibly also seasonal in nature, occurred in Mozambique towards the end of 1995 [*Moren et al., 1990*]. In other cases MDDs appear after a long stay in a camp, as has been seen in Ethiopia and in some camps in Tanzania, where there was little opportunity for cultivation and/or trading, and the food aid diets were consistently unvaried and gradually deteriorated. A perplexing situation has also persisted in the Bhutanese refugee camps in Nepal where, despite a varied ration including fortified blended food and fresh vegetables, low levels of scurvy, beri-beri and vitamin B2 deficiency have been continually reported. Possible reasons may relate to the sale of general rations to purchase other essential household items, or intra-household food distribution patterns leading to inadequate consumption of micronutrients by some individuals [*ACC/SCN, 1997*].

3. Poor Quality of Rations

According to the most recent WFP/UNHCR guidelines [*WFP/ UNHCR, 1997b*], emergency general rations should be acceptable to the beneficiary population and should therefore conform as closely as possible to their normal foods. They should also be palatable for all demographic groups; for example, young children have small stomachs and therefore require energy-dense foods to obtain the appropriate amount of calories. Foods should be easily prepared in the given environment; for example, if they require a lot of cooking and there is a fuel shortage, then they are not appropriate. They should also be in good condition, that is, not spoiled.

Again, there is considerable evidence of a gap between concept and practice. The extent to which poor quality has resulted from inadequate ration planning or failing to make the best of the types of

---

1. It must be cautioned that all the outbreaks identified in Table 6.1 were not rigorously verified and some MDDs are notoriously easy to confuse with other unrelated conditions.

commodities available is unclear. The complex issues involved are shown in the cases of the Rwanda and Liberia operations. The Great Lakes evaluation found a number of examples of poor quality. For example, the maize-based ration was considered inappropriate for young children. During the evaluation it was discovered that young Rwandan children were used to consuming sorghum-based porridges and that this commodity could and should have been provided in the general ration. It was also established that Rwandans were not used to soaking beans so that the types of beans provided (which required an unusually long soaking time) were cooked without soaking. The WFP Liberia evaluation concluded that bulgar wheat would have been a far more appropriate and cheaper staple than rice to include in the general ration, yet the switch was made only after several years of the programme.

The consequences of poor planning can be quite various. In the Rwandan refugee camps in Tanzania the lengthy cooking time for beans had a considerable impact on the local environment which was already under strain from the large numbers of refugees seeking fuel for food preparation. Also, the unpopular maize was exchanged for other commodities that were relatively more expensive, with substantial loss of energy content [*Jaspars, 1994*]. Furthermore, locally purchased blended foods were often of poor quality and large amounts had to be thrown away. In Liberia more resources were allocated for a less appropriate food.

Fortified blended foods are commonly used in *supplementary feeding programmes* as a way of increasing the micro-intake of specific target groups. The product most often used is CSB with added oil and sugar, most of it supplied by major food aid donors. However, there have recently been moves to increase the use of locally produced blended foods like Unimix or Superunimix as a way of reducing the risk of supply problems, and cutting down the lead time in obtaining the product and transport and handling costs.

Their use is reported to be associated with a number of practical problems, however. NGOs are increasingly concerned about their poor quality. Extruded CSB is seen as inefficient in terms of promoting weight gain, because of its high phytate and fibre content and the number of 'anti-nutrients'. There are also problems of quality control, with poor labelling and lack of composition or enrichment specifications on the bag (ACF, personal communication); sometimes the contents have a different composition from that given on the bag. The need for reinforcing ongoing monitoring of local production facilities is constantly mentioned (Editorial, *Field Exchange*, No. 2 Aug. 1997).

III. FACTORS REDUCING THE EFFECTIVENESS OF EMERGENCY FOOD
ASSISTANCE

Despite the many successful adaptations of humanitarian programmes
to the changing nature of emergencies, substantial problems remain.
What follows is an attempt to identify some of the factors that may
impede the provision of adequate emergency food assistance. It is
based on the observations of a number of experienced headquarters
nutritionists working for relief agencies and academics/researchers, as
well as individuals operating in emergency food assistance branches
of government and UN agencies.

1. Conflict-Related Factors

Conflict-related factors are a major determinant of the success or failure of emergency food assistance programmes; their scale and speed
of onset have tested humanitarian response capacity to the full.
Whereas slow onset natural disasters such as drought or pest attack
can allow for preparedness [*ODI, 1993*], conflict-related emergencies
afford no such luxury. Several such crises in recent years have led to
the need for emergency operations in areas of high rainfall and normally productive agricultural systems rather than semi-arid areas. The
locations of SSA emergencies have therefore changed. Furthermore,
the nature of food insecurity has also changed in that it is not due to
crop failure *per se*, but often to an inability to farm for security reasons or because of a breakdown in the marketing system and population displacements.

A number of recent positive experiences in providing sufficient and
timely quantities of emergency food aid for large numbers of displaced people within an extremely short timeframe reflect an adapta-
bility in programming and establishing structures for rapid
mobilisation [*ODI, 1996a*]. For example, the practice of regionalising
emergency programme planning so that, as populations move between
countries in a region, it is administratively easier to reallocate resources at regional level, has greatly increased flexibility.

Conflict-related emergencies give rise to particularly politicised
environments. A number of factors may therefore need to be
considered with regard to the provision of emergency food aid and the
implementation of such programmes needs to be adjusted accordingly.

First, international law which attempts to make provision to protect
the rights of emergency-affected populations also protects national
sovereignty, and this may create tensions. For example, in many con-

flict situations those in power are often the perpetrators of human rights abuses and are unlikely to respect international legislation regarding the provision of humanitarian assistance. This often necessitates lengthy and complex negotiations to secure access to victims, a spin-off of the resulting accommodations often being a transfer of money and resources to forces maintaining the conflict. For example, during the civil war in Somalia in 1992, both warring factions made political and financial gains from keeping Mogadishu port open and functioning [*Operations Review Unit, 1994*].

Second, conflict-related emergencies routinely create problems of access, requiring elaborate logistical systems. Humanitarian food assistance is therefore obliged to rely on new mechanisms of delivery, for example, air transport and the creation of safe havens or convoys under military protection. Although these strategies have overcome obstacles of limited access, they have also proved highly expensive and inefficient as compared with other modes of food delivery. RNIS reports have frequently highlighted funding crises over expensive airlifts in southern Sudan and Burundi, for example [*ACC/SCN, 1994*]. Furthermore, during emergencies in the Somalia civil war, a great deal of food was leaked to unintended beneficiaries with the informal sanction of implementing agencies, in order to maintain security.

Third, in the Somalia emergency of 1991–93 and also in the more recent conflict around Kisangani, Zaire, it quickly became apparent that food had become the main form of currency and that certain types of food were highly prized and therefore extremely lootable. Feeding from on-site kitchens therefore became the main mechanism of delivery – a method considerably more expensive than a dry take-home general ration [*Jaspars, 1998*]. The WFP Liberia evaluation also established that in situations of conflict and insecurity beneficiary populations often preferred to receive emergency food assistance via selective feeding programmes and in a form that was not so highly prized, such as CSB, as this put them at much less risk.

Fourth, there can also be profound implications for allocation of resources. Food distribution systems often fall prey to vested interests, thus resulting in highly inequitable allocations of emergency food assistance, as in 1994 in the Goma camps in eastern Zaire and the IDPs camps in what was formerly called Zone Turquoise in Rwanda. The inequitable distributions resulted in high levels of wasting for the excluded households, with much of the food being given to the politically favoured. As the humanitarian agencies got to grips with the problem, the distribution was gradually reorganised to ensure greater accountability, transparency and equity, and the nutritional situation stabilised dramatically. In subsequent emergencies in the region, the distribution systems have been designed and established to ensure greater equity at the outset of the programme [*Mirghani and Bhatia, 1998*].

2. Inadequate Ration Planning

Ration planning means defining the quantity, type and proportion of the various commodities needed in a given situation to ensure adequate nutrition for all groups of the population. At the start of any emergency programme some form of initial assessment will be carried out. These assessments may take the form of a multi-donor/UN/NGO/host government assessment of food needs; such assessments are normally very high profile and occur over a two–three-week period [*WFP/UNHCR, 1986*]. At the other extreme, the assessment may be performed by a single NGO which then submits a unilateral request for emergency food assistance to a set of donors. Where displacement has occurred the assessment will usually find that a full general ration is needed. This is less likely to be the case where the people have not been displaced since some resources are still likely to be available to them. In the case of a WFP-led assessment a full general ration would now mean a minimum per capita daily ration of 2,100 kcals, while in the case of an ICRC-led assessment it would mean 2,400 kcals/capita per day.

An initial emergency assessment usually takes place within a short timeframe so that resource mobilisation can begin almost immediately, and normally takes the form of a rapid appraisal. It will vary, however, depending on a number of factors, including in-house agency guidelines, the type of staff available and their experience in-country, and security factors. As a rule, the recommendations made about caloric requirements/ration levels in these initial assessments are not prone to substantial error where populations have been displaced. If not available as primary data, the variables to be taken into account can be obtained from secondary sources, such as the demographic pattern of the population, the ambient temperature, the assumed level of physical activity, and the general level of health and nutritional status [*Schofield, 1994*].

Problematic aspects of planning emergency food aid: The single most important piece of information for ration planning is how many people need food. Without a reliable estimate of the numbers requiring assistance, refining estimates of per capita calorie requirements becomes superfluous. But obtaining this kind of information can be difficult in an emergency context – even in a closed camp situation. There are many reasons for this: insecurity, lack of trained staff, the desire of the affected population to inflate numbers, etc. In some situations a formal or accurate registration may simply not be possible. The 'science' of registration has advanced in recent years [*Stephenson et al., 1988*], as has thinking about alternative methods of estimating numbers should registration not be feasible or desirable. These include aerial photography, habitation density mapping and estimating population from information obtained through other means, for example vaccination surveys. However, inaccuracy in population estimates probably remains the single most important constraint in ration planning. Updating the numbers can also be problematic as new arrivals, births and deaths can rapidly make initial estimates redundant.

Inappropriate recommendations are sometimes made about the types of commodity to include in the food basket, reflecting a lack of attention or priority given to nutritional considerations in the assessment. For instance, in the Great Lakes emergency no nutritionist was involved in the initial assessment, which, furthermore, was not a multi-donor assessment [*ODI, 1996a*]. A typical constraint faced by UN agencies and governments at the outset of an emergency is difficulty in locating a nutritionist at short notice who can participate in a rapidly mounted assessment.

The greatest likelihood of misjudgement probably occurs in protracted emergency programmes when the beneficiary populations have established some degree of self-sufficiency and the donors and multilateral agencies want to reduce or modify the rations accordingly, so as to conserve resources, discourage dependency or ensure that markets and local production are not adversely affected by a glut of food. Two of the most recent external evaluations – the DHA's review of Operation Lifeline Sudan and the WFP's Liberia evaluation – found that modifications to rations were based on tenuous assumptions, leading to ultimately flawed recommendations [*DHA, 1997; WFP, 1997*]. In both cases it was concluded that there was a lack of information on which to base decisions about targeting and reducing rations. An important conclusion from the Liberia evaluation was that ways and means need to be found to improve the capacity of joint WFP/UNHCR/donor/NGO assessment missions to monitor the socioeconomic circumstances of beneficiary populations. Such conclusions are hardly new and readily trigger recollections of how planning decisions were made in earlier emergencies. During the Ethiopian refugee crisis in Somalia in the 1980s, for instance, refugee camps were divided into three categories of self-sufficiency based on helicopter reconnaissance and rations were reduced accordingly, often with disastrous consequences in terms of nutritional deterioration [*Hassan and Mursal, 1990*].

The standard and credibility of information on which programming decisions are based are often questioned. The need to improve assessment methodologies has been a constant plea from those responsible for implementing emergency programmes. An inter-agency meeting in Amsterdam at the end of 1997 highlighted many weaknesses in current approaches [*MSF Holland, 1997*].

Another factor that may affect the adequacy of ration planning is the danger that recommendations may be affected or constrained by assumptions about what is available at donor-government level. This phenomenon may have been more prevalent in the days when most emergency food aid was derived from surplus intervention stocks. With the increased substitution of finance for surplus food aid, it may now be less of a constraint; the WFP reports that at least half the emergency aid is now provided as cash. Nevertheless, so long as donor practices like the tying of food aid remain in place resource mobilisers in agencies such as WFP and the ICRC will inevitably make assumptions about the types of commodity likely to be made available. Multilateral agencies like WFP make requests to particular governments on the assumption that they prefer to provide certain commodities. This prior knowledge of donor preferences is seen as a useful institutional 'expertise' facilitating the process of resource mobilisation. There have certainly been examples of commodities identified in needs assessments having been removed from the final list of recommended commodities on the ground that they would not be readily available from, or resourced by, donor governments [*WFP/ UNHCR, 1988*]. In some of these cases nutritionists and food specialists have wondered whether agencies have 'pressed' donors hard enough. There is also a sense that in other situations inappropriate commodities have been introduced into the general ration simply because it was known that they were readily available. Those of us who have experienced refugee reactions to fish protein concentrate have little doubt that this has occurred.

Historically, fortified blended foods have their origin in the limited basket available from the major donors. For the US this basket has been determined by the Department of Agriculture's list of surplus commodities. Micro-nutrient-rich foods were frequently not available. The current UNHCR/WFP strategy of relying mainly on fortified blended foods to provide adequate micro-nutrients in ration planning has also been the subject of much debate and criticism. The inherent problems of overdependence on this one type of commodity were discussed in the previous section of this chapter. Other strategies have been suggested. Fortification of cereals is one such, and at least two studies [*Field Exchange, No.5; Oxfam, 1998*] have recently been undertaken to examine the feasibility of this approach. Others include promoting home garden production/micro-gardening, germinating pulses before consumption [*Riddoch et al., 1998*], adding plant ash to foods and encouraging the formation of markets at camp level.

Another aspect of planning to be criticised is the focus on what are called type 1 nutrients. Usually when wasting or stunting is identified, the response is to assume a need for more protein or energy and to provide a general ration of cereals, beans and oil or increase the existing ration. But this does not cover the need for type 2 nutrients, such as sodium, zinc, magnesium, potassium, phosphorus, etc., a deficiency of which can often lead to poor growth, stunting and wasting. In other words, having identified a nutritional problem the response is not in accordance with current nutritional thinking. Furthermore, the requirement for type 2 nutrients varies with age, gender and nutritional/health status. It is possible, therefore, to have a recognised *adequate* general ration but a continued need for selective feeding as type 2 nutrient deficiencies are not being met adequately, resulting in cases of severe marasmus and kwashiorkor and high levels of stunting [*Golden, 1995*].

A point frequently made about ration planning, and one that arises from some of the issues raised above, is that there is a need to tailor rations to specific target groups, thus reducing the need for selective feeding programmes. In one sense, the ICRC has always adopted this approach through its strategy of providing a minimum of 2,400 kcals/capita per day for wholly ration-dependent populations, the rationale being to provide a ration with an energy level surplus to requirements so that some of it can be sold or exchanged to provide a commodity that can be used at home for young undernourished children (a form of household-controlled dry supplementary feeding). This concept could be expanded to enable general ration planning to take more account of the specific needs of different target groups in terms of commodity palatability and acceptability and types of nutrient.

3. Availability of Resources and Factors Governing Their Provision

A lack of resources is frequently cited by agencies as a reason for inadequate emergency food assistance. The resources available for food aid have been reduced. At 7.5 million tonnes, global deliveries in 1996 were less than half the 16.8 million tonnes distributed just three years earlier and the smallest volume delivered in more than a decade. Levels fell in 1997 and increased only slightly in 1998. This reduction is a consequence of many factors [*IFPRI, 1997*]. Whether it is also a reflection of reduced need is unclear, however [*ODI, 1998*].

It is usually difficult to gauge whether it is a lack of resources or a lack of political commitment that ultimately leads to the identification of resource shortages. In some cases there is a lack of *appropriate* resources. For example, certain types of foodstuff may not be available for commercial purchase. During the Great Lakes emergency it was not possible to purchase roots and tubers, which were the preferred staple of the beneficiary population. Teff, the staple food of many Ethiopians, has also frequently not been available for purchase in emergency programmes.

The national and regional interests of donor governments can have a significant impact on the amount of food aid made available for a particular country. Policies and legislation (national and international) have been developed as a consequence of these interests, for the protection of the donor and its constituents [*Hanrahan, 1998*] and also for the protection of potential beneficiaries. Nutritionists and others working in the food and nutrition sector of emergency operations are usually ignorant of the national and international processes which govern the provision of emergency food aid and which have a marked impact on its nutritional adequacy. But there is very little empirically based evidence on the extent of this impact. Occasional statements in reports and evaluations indicate links between these processes and the final emergency ration allocated, but these linkages are never thoroughly explored in terms of whether the processes have any adverse effect or could be modified. What follows is an attempt to identify and categorise a number of procedural, legislative, institutional and political constraints which may impinge on the nutritional adequacy of emergency food assistance. Four types of factor are identified.

(i) National and international policies and regulations: Changes in agricultural policies in North America and the European Union, the implementation of the Uruguay Round trade agreements and changing geopolitical and domestic concerns within donor countries are affecting the availability of food.

The consequences of the changing policy regimes for emergency programmes have been to diminish interest and support for food aid among donors, especially the United States which reduced its food aid deliveries from over 10 million tonnes in 1993 to less than 4 million in 1996. An increasing proportion of the reduced food aid has also been channelled through targeted relief operations and development projects – 60 per cent in 1996 compared with 49 per cent in 1990 – rather than through untargeted country programmes. In 1990 only 28 per cent of the WFP expenditure was for relief; by 1994 this had risen to 63 per cent. New commitments in 1994 showed an even more marked difference, with relief accounting for 81 per cent in value terms. Thus, emergency assistance appears to have been protected or at least prioritised in a climate of diminishing resources. Individuals within WFP have indicated that up to now all resources required for food assistance programmes in the acute phase of emergencies have been forthcoming following the appropriate appeals. Others have supported this view (see Chapter 3).

Resource problems have arisen more in Protracted Relief Operations (PROs), with the WFP increasingly being required to provide donor governments with justification for continued assistance (personal communication). Within the WFP some of these resources appear to have had to come from development programmes. This strategy has been successful, with 93 per cent of PRO resource requirements being met in 1997. The WFP has also shifted to resourcing PROs by means of separate emergency appeals. In 1998 a new category of funding window was created – the Protracted Relief and Recovery Operation (PRRO) which covers both PROs and recovery situations – and consideration was being given to whether the PRRO should be opened up to development and emergency funding.

The decline in development project food aid has sometimes resulted in a longer lead-time for emergency provision. In the start-up phase the WFP often needs to resort to diverting project food aid in the region or country to an emergency programme. With the decline in the number of development projects there are fewer opportunities for this type of resource reallocation. Typically, it may take between four and six months to complete the cycle of resourcing and delivery of in-kind food contributions.

Some people, for instance Shaw and Singer [1996], have argued that maintaining food aid flows sufficient to respond to all potential requirements is likely to become more difficult in the future. Overall, it is unclear whether governments and the WFP will continue to be able to protect the provision of emergency resources. Views range from predictions that the humanitarian community will not be able to provide adequate assistance in the event of another substantial refugee crisis because of the large reduction in food aid resources, to those who see scope for protecting and enhancing emergency resource provision within existing institutional and policy frameworks.

A number of initiatives have already been taken or are being considered in the United States. In 1996, Congress replaced the wheat reserve by a Food Security Commodity Reserve (FSCR) of wheat, corn, sorghum and rice, to be used to meet unanticipated emergency needs in developing countries. A consortium of US PVOs (the Coalition for Food Aid), which is primarily concerned with the use of PL480, Title II, has made proposals for replenishing the reserve. Noting that the unallocated reserve set aside for emergency response under Title II proved insufficient in the mid-1990s and that food aid allocated to development projects was being diverted to meet emergency needs, its recommendations focus on altering FSCR operations to improve the US response to emergencies, while maintaining the capacity to use food aid for development projects [*Hanrahan, 1998*].

The Food Aid Convention which originated as a form of international burden-sharing for supporting food aid as part of the 1967 GATT negotiations, seeks to ensure a minimum availability of food aid, both to meet emergency requirements and to sustain developmental activities. The minimum commitments under the FAC are intended to provide a floor or safety net preventing large inter-year fluctuations in food aid (see Chapters 3 and 4). An important consequence of the FAC has been that a substantial amount of food aid is purchased in the market. However, as donors were obliged to increase the provision of financial resources when faced with reduced surplus stocks this has been linked to a substantial reduction in real resources from certain governments, and ultimately smaller amounts of food aid (WFP, personal communication). Although there is a considerable literature on the additionality of food aid [*Benson and Clay, 1998; also Chapter 10*], this analysis has not been applied specifically to the emergency context and to whether the existence of intervention stocks has led to additional emergency food aid allocations over and above those which would be committed in terms of financial resources.

It is also not clear whether the FAC has restricted the flexibility of emergency food assistance response in terms of commodity choice. FAC obligations were limited to cereals, with pulses allowed only since 1995, so that other foods may have to be funded by many donors from non-food aid budget lines. This inflexibility was identified as a constraint on commodity choice during the southern African drought of 1992–93, particularly with regard to the Mozambique programme when, for example, most UK food aid was required to be in the form of maize, wheat or rice [*Clay et al., 1998*]. Others, for example within ECHO, maintain that it is the budget which determines which commodities are purchased and that there is considerable flexibility and freedom of choice (personal communication). Similarly, CIDA officials have argued that the FAC is not 'much of a constraint'. Views within the WFP are that the FAC commitment is simply a 'floor' commitment which donors must fulfil, and it does not preclude them from putting in more resources.

The 1999 FAC has considerably broadened the range of commodities that can be provided as humanitarian assistance, to include vegetable oils and sugar. This suggests that some of those involved in the negotiation see the FAC as a constraint (see Chapter 4). However, the FAC has not been subjected to a transparent assessment in terms of its overall effects on emergency food aid provision from a nutritional perspective.

Many economists have argued that donor policies of tying food aid to their domestic markets increase costs and place additional strain on dwindling resources as well as limiting the flexibility of commodity choice [Clay et al., 1998]. The extent to which emergency food aid is tied varies enormously among governments, with virtually all US and 90 per cent of Canadian food aid coming from domestic sources. In contrast, cash contributions from ECHO are given to partners who are encouraged to purchase locally or regionally on the basis of encouraging development.

Apart from the resource implications, the practice of tying food aid to purchases from domestic markets is likely to restrict the flexibility of commodity choice, and in some instances this may not be optimal from a nutritional point of view. For example, with regard to *oil,* commercial importers may select lower-cost and vitamin A-rich palm oil, which nutritionists also prefer, rather than rape or soya bean oil which is often provided by donors in emergencies, as happened in Bangladesh following the 1992 cyclone. Fortification meets the nutritional concern but increases costs.

Tying to *yellow maize* (white maize is processed by most Africans) and *rice* typically involves very high transaction costs where European donors are providing grades and types that neither the recipient country nor the multilateral agency would have selected. Thai rice is much cheaper than European rice and probably acceptable (30 per cent broken) to most emergency-affected populations.

There are, however, arguments in favour of continuing the practice of tying food aid. For example, local purchases can push up the prices of local foods; even trivial increases in demand can lead to substantial price rises. Regional purchases can also produce a ring of price increases around the famine area. Some developing country markets are also poorly developed and fragmented, which can make local purchases far more expensive than buying in bulk from a developed country market. Clearly this subject would benefit from some form of review of the nutritional and financial consequences of tying emergency aid, which should focus on the appropriateness of commodity choice during a number of recent emergency programmes and whether alternative and more appropriate commodities might have been available from non-tied sources.

The changes in EU regulations in 1996–97 illustrate the unintended effects of changes in procedures. Although these regulations do not apply at present to ECHO, there is concern that they will make it more difficult to purchase from small producers in developing countries and to access commodities which would normally be obtained from such producers, such as seeds, pulses, groundnuts, etc.

There are also constraints on the use of EU intervention stocks for emergency food aid. The attempt in 1997 to utilise stocks of beef for the emergency in North Korea demonstrated how bureaucratic and institutional constraints can impede the use of surplus food as emergency aid which could have overall economic as well as humanitarian benefits. Following the BSE scare the EU introduced schemes for buying up beef in order to support the market price. Around 600,000 tonnes were stored, mostly in France and Germany. In 1997, a meat processors organisation suggested to the European Commission storing a small proportion of the beef in the form of tinned beef, which could then be used for emergencies like that in Korea. This would have reduced EU expenditure by $200 /t as storage was more expensive than de-frosting and canning the beef. However, the suggestion was not taken up, apparently because the food aid budget would have had to incur these costs and this would not have constituted an efficient use of its resources. There are precedents for this type of action in aid to the former Soviet Union between 1993 and 1994, but these were funded under the agricultural budget. It seems important to clarify what constraints and impediments exist regarding the use of intervention stocks, in order to determine whether they should be relaxed if similar problems arise in the future.

(ii) Donor and multilateral agency practices and procedures: The WFP repeatedly identifies lack of resources for the Immediate Response Account (IRA) and the International Emergency Food Reserve (IEFR) as a major constraint on its ability to mount effective emergency food assistance programmes, particularly in the early

stages of an emergency. The IRA is completely untied cash. In 1997 its target was US$35 million but, as in previous years, donors only partially met this target, providing only $20 m. The IEFR is a commodity-based facility with an annual replenishment target of 500,000 tonnes. There is an increasing tendency on the part of donors to insist on advance information on where resources given to the IEFR are to be used. Combined with under-pledging of the IRA, this means that the WFP has to go back to governments if it needs to reschedule a commodity. At the very least, this increases storage costs, and at worst can considerably delay emergency assistance. Not surprisingly, WFP staff are increasingly concerned about the time it takes for donors to provide resources once they have made a commitment.

Donors' reluctance to commit fully to WFP multilateral mechanisms may arise from a desire to exert greater political control over resources or the administrative requirement for more rigorous accounting or monitoring of effectiveness. ECHO has not contributed in the past to either the IRA or the IEFR, and insists on prior knowledge of where resources will be spent. CIDA officials have indicated informally that they would increase their commitments to the IRA if these programmes could be shown to have a nutritional or morbidity impact. Their fear is that IRA resources might be used as a stop-gap for politically unattractive situations (personal communication).

Both the WFP and the International Committee of the Red Cross report that donors' increasingly rigorous and complex administrative and accounting procedures substantially increase the lead-time of emergency food assistance delivery. This may be a function of the increased substitution of financial resources for surplus food stocks, since governments are required to be far more circumspect about how monies are spent than about how surplus food is used. Some donors have been reported as asking for a shopping list of information. For example, the ICRC has to set up files of prices on local purchases, especially as tenders on the world market are usually only valid for 24 hours.

Another apparent administrative bottleneck within the agencies themselves is the time it takes to approve appeals for emergency assistance, which can take from one day to three months. For consolidated appeals all the agencies involved need to agree, and even in the case of WFP Emergency Operations the WFP and FAO both need to sign.

The trend on the part of donors towards directing resources to specific operations rather than providing them as contributions to multilateral facilities increases the lead-time considerably and reduces the capacity of agencies like the WFP, and to a lesser extent the ICRC, to respond quickly, while also restricting commodity choice. In any event, almost all WFP resources are now directed, while less than 50 per cent were directed in the mid-1980s; in 1997 directed contributions to the relief categories amounted to 86 per cent for the IEFR and 56 per cent for PROs. It is unclear to what extent the increased tendency to direct aid is a consequence of more rigorous accountability procedures with aid budgets under pressure or is politically driven. The increase in conflict-related emergencies and their resulting politicisation may have increased the need for donors to direct resources in accordance with political aims and priorities.

The fiscal cycles of some donors, such as Japan, the US and the UK, do not coincide with those of the WFP and other UN agencies. This affects the timing of pledges and when funds can be made available, and consequently the agencies' ability to plan ahead and contract in advance. Another constraint may occur in relation to market prices. Commodity prices tend to be cheaper at certain times of the year, but the WFP may not be in a position to take advantage of this. However, knowledge of fiscal cycles can be exploited. Towards the end of fiscal years donors may rush to disburse funds. The WFP is aware of this and tries to take advantage of this tendency by timing its requests strategically.

The WFP's experience of problems in meeting the additional costs of providing emergency food aid led it to introduce a Full Cost Recovery policy (FCR) whereby donors must cover all the additional costs associated with getting foods to extended delivery points, including direct operational and support costs and indirect costs related to the tonnages of food provided and the overheads per programme category. These can be considerable; for example, in Cambodia the FCR requirement was $30 per tonne of food. The FCR policy may be leading to more directed aid as donors insist on the additional monies accounted for and spent in accordance with their wishes.

(iii) *Institutional thinking*: Institutional thinking is an imperfect way of describing the subtle assumptions, implicit *policies* and dogma which may influence decision-making with regard to emergency food aid provision at donor or multilateral agency level. Some forms of institutional thinking can have a significant impact on emergency programmes. The way in which institutional thinking affects decision-making will probably vary between and within governments over time as staff come and go. However, there is frequently a lack of clarity and explicit statement concerning certain issues, which makes it difficult to challenge the assumptions and reasoning behind such thinking. There is some evidence of thinking which may lead to decisions which adversely affect emergency-affected populations. Examples of agencies' predetermined views include the following: opposition to the sale of general ration commodities; insistence on the parity of the beneficiary population's nutritional status with that of the host population; intolerance of over-registration; expectations of increasing self-sufficiency; preference for separate distribution systems; and opposition to the retrospective provision of emergency rations.

Beneficiary populations often sell off some of their emergency rations. The reasons for doing this vary considerably. The commodities provided may be of high economic value so that a greater quantity and variety of food can be secured by selling them. The items may be considered inappropriate or culturally unacceptable and may have to be exchanged for a more habitually used food. Food may need to be exchanged for other essential non-food commodities. And, of course, rations may be sold because the population has too much food. It is this last reason which is often inferred by donors and agencies, and can result in the reduction of food rations to the overall population. Unfortunately, such assumptions may be inaccurate. For instance, large quantities of maize were sold in 1994 in the Rwandan refugee camps in Tanzania, partly to cover milling costs and partly to finance purchases of preferred commodities [*Jaspars, 1994*]. Many people have agreed that emergency food commodities should be regarded by donors not simply as food but as an income transfer, which beneficiaries can use in any way they see fit to maximise their nutritional and economic security, and that penalising them for doing so runs contrary to humanitarian principles.

Emergency needs assessments often contain in their terms of reference a requirement to compare the nutritional status of the displaced population with that of their hosts. Comparison of nutritional data with international or local standards is accepted assessment practice. However, such information has been used as an argument for reducing assistance to the emergency-affected population [*WFP/UNHCR, 1986*]. Two premises may underlie this approach. If the nutritional status of the affected population is better than that of the hosts this may create tensions between the two. Second, it may be difficult to promote a better nutritional status among the displaced group even if levels of malnutrition are high in the host population. This may be because of a combination of factors including high levels of endemic disease and poor food security, feeding and care practices.

Many people believe it is the duty of the humanitarian community to provide a minimum level of assistance commensurate with need, and that if this creates tensions with the local population, then the baseline standard should be set by the displaced and not the host population. The latter should receive additional support rather than withdrawing support from the emergency-affected population. This logic is certainly compelling. It seems counter-humanitarian to accept any level of beri-beri or vitamin A deficiency in a refugee population just because it exists in the surrounding population – especially when it would be an easy matter to eradicate the problem in a camp situation. There is also a conceptual flaw in basing ration adjustments on anthropometric data alone. Nutritional status can be confounded by many factors unrelated to food security. Decisions about changes in rations should therefore be based primarily on food security information.

Over-registration by refugees appears to be par for the course. It probably occurs for a number of reasons. Refugees will try to maximise their resources rather than satisfy minimum basic needs [*Relief and Rehabilitation Network, 1997*]. General rations aim to provide the minimum requirements with no surplus. At best, this provides an extremely bland diet, at worst an inadequate diet which, if consumed for long periods, will lead to nutritional decline.

Refugees regard food commodities as a potential income transfer, which can be used to purchase other essential goods such as soap, clothes, livestock, agricultural equipment, seeds, etc. Where these other needs are met by humanitarian agencies there is undoubtedly less need to cheat the system and over-register. The ability to do so will depend on many factors, such as the proximity of registration points to one other; the reproducibility of cards; the expertise of the registration team; and the degree to which refugees can organise themselves, etc. The consequences of over-registration include resource implications and opportunity costs; the ongoing need to revise planning figures and therefore food allocations; and inequitable distributions.

The response of donor agencies to over-registration is a major influence on food aid provision. As an almost knee-jerk reaction, rations may be cut. Agencies (such as the UNHCR) will be encouraged to re-register the population but this is not a straightforward task and there may be many impediments, as well as a lack of urgency. There are, however, many examples of ration reductions where over-registration has been noted by donors, perhaps the most notorious being the Somali refugee camps in south-east Ethiopia where an estimated 200,000 refugees held over 400,000 ration cards. Support for this population rapidly declined so that per capita rations of only 1,000 kcals were available for long periods, with an increase in wasting in this formerly well-to-do refugee population from 8 to over 26 per cent [*Shoham et al., 1989*]. One strategy suggested to overcome this problem is that ration reductions should be implemented much more cautiously and that safety nets, including monitoring and selective feeding programmes, should be in place.

Another widespread belief in donor circles is that, in long-term emergency programmes (PROs), beneficiaries should be encouraged to become more self-sufficient. Unfortunately, the assumption often appears to be made that self-sufficiency comes automatically with time.

The Operation Lifeline Sudan evaluation found that emergency food aid was reduced by decreasing the size of the ration, limiting the aid to certain times of the year and using more specific targeting. The perceived role of food assistance also changed from that of a life-saving measure to one which supported livelihoods or agricultural production. However, the OLS review team concluded that there was an increasing dependence on economically, socially, and environmentally unsustainable strategies, which often indicated extreme stress rather than increased self-reliance. Those displaced by war were often forced into exploitative labour relations, which supported the government's aim of transforming them into a cheap labour force [*DHA, 1997*].

While there is often inadequate information about who has become self-reliant and the degree of this self-reliance, there is also inadequate monitoring to detect any adverse effects from a reduction in food assistance. Without such close monitoring nutritional decline can occur rapidly and unnoticed. The strategy of switching assistance from general rations to food-for-work (FFW) programmes is often used in PROs in order to discourage dependence and promote rehabilitation. However, methodologies are poorly developed to determine when to switch from one type of intervention to another, which is hardly surprising, given the lack of socio-economic data collection during emergencies. Furthermore, the impact of FFW programmes on the community in an emergency context is little understood. For example, there may well be implications for caring practices if these programmes involve women or older children. This is an area which would benefit enormously from review and research. Without better information, decisions on the timing of the introduction of FFW programmes in the wake of an acute emergency may not always be appropriate.

The rationale for introducing an emergency supplementary feeding programme (SFP) is often complex and can be justified on many levels [*ODI, 1996b*]. The issue here is the extent to which emergency SFPs are automatically assumed to be the most appropriate way of redressing moderate malnutrition or preventing its emergence in young children during an emergency, rather than providing resources that may have an equivalent impact by means of emergency general rations. There has been a marked trend towards introducing what are called blanket emergency SFPs which were used successfully in the Great Lakes crises and in the Dadaab refugee camps in Kenya.

The explicit and implicit reasons for reliance on SFPs in emergencies are many. They ensure targeting the most vulnerable, the foods are more suited to young malnourished children, the programme resource use is more easily accounted for, and the interventions are visible. Nevertheless, many of the assumptions can be challenged [*ODI, 1996b*]. Furthermore, the costs of establishing separate food distribution systems can be enormous (ten times that of general ration distributions) and raise questions of efficiency at many levels. Separate distribution sites have to be set up, with high staffing and infrastructural requirements, transport is often duplicated, economies of scale are not properly exploited (SFPs involve the movement of far smaller quantities of food), separate procurement procedures are needed at donor level and there is multi-agency resourcing, that is, many NGOs will be drawing on the same donors.

The issue here is whether there is too inflexible a mind-set at donor level regarding the appropriateness of SFPs, particularly if one considers the way in which the retrospective provision of rations is perceived amongst donors and multilateral agencies. Lack of such provision is often justified on the basis that if malnutrition results from missing general rations then the effects will be catered for by selective emergency feeding programmes. Little consideration is given to the idea that the provision of rations retrospectively might obviate the need for an emergency SFP at all. Evaluation is required of the costs of establishing separate SFPs in a variety of situations and of the likely alternative costs of strengthening the general ration programme to ensure an equally targeted distribution of the same amounts and types of food. Such an assessment could lead to considerable savings of resources within the humanitarian community.

When there has been a break in the food aid pipeline or logistical or security problems have prevented general ration distribution, there will be no retrospective compensation for these rations. This is an implicit policy within the WFP [*Payne, 1997*], and possibly within some donor agencies. In situations where one or two items are missing from the food basket, however, guidelines do now exist for substituting fixed proportional quantities of available commodities for a period of one month. Nevertheless, where general rations have been inadequate for several months a policy of no compensation can have severe and lasting adverse consequences for the nutrition status of the affected population. The refugee population is also likely to employ some *coping* strategy to make up for the general ration shortfall. This may involve selling off assets or more drastic measures involving risk, such as prostitution or foraging for wild foods in unsafe areas [*Van Nieuwensuyse, 1997; Dirks, 1980*]. In the event that assets are sold off, this may undermine long-term viability/self-sufficiency. Given that in many protracted refugee situations donors, host governments and humanitarian agencies often have the objective of promoting long-term self-sufficiency, it seems contractually unfair and counter-productive to penalise beneficiaries and set back their efforts and achievements as a result of events beyond their control.

Clearly there is a lack of explicit policies within the UN and donor agencies regarding the above issues. Debate and logical development of policies on these subjects are long overdue, and in some cases (for example, increased general rations versus supplementary feeding) further research may well be needed.

(iv) Political factors: There is a widespread belief that emergency food aid allocations are largely driven by political pressures. Perhaps the most obvious sign of political preferences is the disparity in rations that is often seen between refugee populations. In most African emergencies the typical ration comprises cereals, pulses, oil and blended foods. Salt and sugar may also be provided. In contrast, in the Bosnia emergency there was a summer and a winter ration, and the size of the ration was far larger in terms of per capita calories than that usually allocated in Africa [*Watson and Filipovitch, 1998*]. Furthermore, during the 1990s there has been a large increase in the percentage of the relief budget spent in developed countries, with donations appearing to have been more generous. For example, WFP spending in sub-Saharan Africa was $1.80 per capita compared with $5.43 in Europe and the Newly Independent States in 1993. The increased flows of food aid to eastern Europe and the FSRs in the early 1990s were only partly additional and involved a substantial diversion of resources from developing countries. Some commentators have

asserted that 'there is a gap in the arrangements in monitoring donor performance that is perhaps of increasing importance in periods of severe budgetary pressures and rapidly changing policy priorities' [*Benson and Clay, 1998*].

Multilateralisation of food aid through agencies like the WFP and the UNHCR is intended to ensure apolitical resource allocation. However, an ODI study in the mid-1990s found that close on 50 per cent of pledges to the WFP were directed, and that it was this which created bottlenecks in the emergency aid process. Informal discussions with WFP staff now indicate that over 90 per cent of donor allocations are directed to an end country stipulated by the donor. Very few donors allocate multilaterally. The ICRC has also indicated that the biggest constraint on its efforts to mobilise food resources is the increasing earmarking of funds [*ACC/SCN, 1998*]. In Chechnya it had to stop its programme for this reason.

Humanitarian food assistance is used as a policy instrument, as illustrated by the following examples. The reduction in food aid to the Goma camps was seen by many as a knee-jerk response to the realisation that the aid was being used to sustain the position of those guilty of genocide and their capacity to mount incursions into neighbouring Rwanda. The reduction of food aid to camps like Tingi-Tingi in Zaire in 1996 was seen as an attempt to encourage the repatriation of refugees, as was the stipulation that food aid would be provided only for 30 days to refugees around Kisangani towards the end of the Mobutu regime. The UNHCR justified this use of food aid on the grounds that repatriation was essential as the refugees were at huge risk and could not be protected by the humanitarian agencies (Postscript in *Field Exchange*, No. 3, Jan. 1998). The reduction in rations to Somali refugees in Kenya at the end of 1996 was also seen as a strategy to encourage their repatriation; the outcome was a marked decline in nutritional status (*ibid.*, letters page).

These cases imply a potential conflict between immediate humanitarian and other policy objectives. Some in the humanitarian community consider it unacceptable to sanction the short-term denial of food, which may lead to starvation, in favour of other potential longer-term benefits, such as increased regional stabilisation and bringing an emergency to an end. Moral and ethical considerations are involved in such decisions. Other policy objectives are rarely spelt out or made explicit, and so the success of such policies can never be evaluated. These considerations have played a role in the move towards codes of humanitarian conduct discussed in Chapters 13 and 14.

The WFP has always had to fight against powerful lobbies in donor countries which have wanted their governments to purchase commodities like cheese or canned fruit, even dates, as part of the food aid package. Since an IFPRI evaluation in 1991 recommended maximising tonnages of cereals, pulses and vegetable oil to provide cheaper protein sources, the WFP has increasingly encouraged donors to provide more cash. Some governments, such as the Netherlands, now provide only cash instead of dairy products. Denmark used to supply canned meat, cheese and fish, while Norway supplied dried fish. The WFP has not accepted dried fish since 1996 but does still accept canned fish. Nevertheless, supplier pressures still affect the choice of commodities provided by donors. For example, EU supplies of vegetable oil have undoubtedly increased with the growth of internal surpluses of rape seed oil; Canada and Norway have historically provided fish, and there is still a powerful rice lobby in the US; and Japan encourages the use of rice, canned fish and HP biscuits.

Producers and processors obviously have a strong interest in seeing their products used. Furthermore, there is always the risk that when donor budgets cease to be tied to specific domestic produce the resources may be given to other non-food aid programmes. What is not clear, however, is whether these kinds of pressure, and the eventual way in which donor monies are spent, still lead to less cost-effective and nutritionally compromised food baskets in emergency situations.

IV. CONCLUSIONS AND RECOMMENDATIONS

This chapter has come to the conclusion that emergency food assistance is far from as effective as it could be and that this leads to adverse nutritional consequences. These problems of ineffectiveness are inextricably related to the decisions made at donor and multilateral agency level: the constraints on resources, the tying of aid, the decision procedures and institutional thinking on policy. The key question is 'What, if anything, can be done to address these factors so as to improve the performance of food assistance provision?'

Both methodological problems and limited evidence preclude a comprehensive answer. The evidence presented is also biased towards the perceptions of humanitarian field workers. Recommendations are therefore made with these considerations in mind. It is also recognised that much of the time food aid modalities and the rationales governing them are unclear to those outside the decision-making process but who are responsible for managing emergency food aid on the ground.

Three types of initiative are therefore suggested. They are more about process than short-term changes, they are not mutually exclusive and they could be undertaken concurrently.

1. Information Exchange

Fora could be established for dialogue between key decision-makers in donor and multilateral agencies and nutritionists and programme implementors in the food and nutrition sectors of emergency operations to address issues such as:

– What types of food aid procedure, policies, regulations and institutional mechanisms adversely affect the nutritional adequacy of emergency food assistance and what room for manoeuvre is there to alter these?
– What types of policy or institutional thinking adversely affect the nutritional adequacy of emergency food assistance and are they, and the strategies for adhering to them, appropriate or should they be modified?
– What aspects of emergency food aid planning, provision and programme implementation are based on insufficient information and what aspects require further review, evaluation and research?

2. Evaluation and Research

Retrospective and prospective reviews and evaluations of emergency programmes are needed to identify situations where emergency rations were or are nutritionally inadequate and the factors which contribute(d) to this inadequacy, such as food aid procedures, ration planning and policies or institutional thinking. This will help identify significant linkages between the process of emergency food assistance provision and the nutritional outcome, which can be fed into the dialogue discussed above.

Research is also needed on specific subject areas such as the impacts of food-for-work programmes on the community, and the extent of type 2 nutrient shortfalls in emergency general rations and the commodities which could be added to the food basket to redress this.

To achieve these objectives, donor agencies could establish a self-regulatory body to attempt to standardise and regulate intergovernmental mechanisms and processes and make these explicit to operational agencies.

REFERENCES

ACC/SCN, 1989, *Nutrition in Times of Disaster*, report of an International Conference held at the World Health Organisation Headquarters, Geneva, 27–30 Sept. 1988.

ACC/SCN, 1994, *Update on the Nutrition Situation*, Geneva: ACC/SCN.

ACC/SCN, 1996, *Report of the Workshop on the Improvement of Nutrition of Refugees and Displaced People in Africa*, Machakos, Kenya, 5–7 Dec. 1994, Geneva: ACC/SCN.

ACC/SCN, 1997, *The Nutrition of Refugees and Displaced Populations: Third Report on the World Nutrition Situation*, Geneva: ACC/SCN.

ACC/SCN, 1998, *Report on SCN Working Group Meeting on Refugees and Displaced Populations*, Oslo (March).

Barrett, G., 1993, *Nutrition Survey, Kismayo, Somalia*, Brussels: Médecins sans frontières.

Benson, C. and E.J. Clay, 1998, 'Additionality or Diversion? Food Aid to Eastern Europe and the Former Soviet Republics and the Implications for Developing Countries', *World Development*, Vol. 26, No. 1.

Berard, L., 1993, *Nutrition Survey, South Eastern Regional Liberia*, AICF.

Borrel, A., 1994, 'Report of Nutrition Survey and Morality Patterns for Malange', *Concern* (Feb.).

Clay, E.J., N. Pillai and C. Benson, 1998, *The Future of Food Aid Policy Review*, London: Overseas Development Institute (Jan.).

DHA, 1997, *A Review of Operation Lifeline Sudan*.

Dirks, R., 1980, 'Social Responses during Severe Food Shortages and Famine', *Anthropology*, Vol. 21, No. 1 (Feb.).

Field Exchange, No. 5 (in press).

Forde, K., 1998, 'Crisis in the DPRK', *Field Exchange*, No. 3 (Jan.).

Golden, M., 1995, 'Specific Deficiencies Versus Growth Failure; Type I and Type II Nutrients', *SCN News*, No. 12, Geneva: ACC/SCN.

Hanrahan, C.E., 1998, *The Food Security Commodity Reserve: The Replenishment Issue*, CRS Report for Congress, Congressional Research Service, Washington DC: Library of Congress (April).

Hassan, B. and H. Mursal, 1990, *Anaemia and Scurvy; RHU Experience*, Magadishi: MOH Refugee Health Unit.

IFPRI, 1997, *The World Food Situation: Recent Developments: Emerging Issues and Long-Term Prospects*, Washington DC: IFPRI (Dec.).

Jareg, P. and C. Marangwanda, 1993, *Drought in Zimbabwe 1991–92; Examining the Child Supplementary Feeding Programme with Special Reference to the Response of Redd Barna – Zimbabwe*.

Jaspars, J., 1998, 'Responding to the Crisis in Congo-Zaire; Emergency Feeding of Rwandan Refugees. May-July 1997', *Field Exchange*, No. 3.

Jaspars, S., 1994, *The Rwandan Refugee Crisis in Tanzania: Initial Successes and Failures in Food Assistance*, Relief and Rehabilitation Network, Paper 6, London: Overseas Development Institute.

Konandreas, P., R. Sharma and J. Greenfield, 1998, 'The Uruguay Round, the Marrakesh Decision and the Role of Food Aid', paper presented at ODI/NUPI workshop on Food and Human Security, Oslo (April).

Mirghani, Z. and R. Bhatia, 1998, 'The Role of Women in Food Management', *Field Exchange*, Vol. 3 (Jan.).

Moren, A., D. Lemoult and A. Brodel, 1990, 'Pellagra in Mozambican Refugees', *Lancet*, Vol. 385, pp. 1403–4.

MSF, Holland, 1997, *A Report on the Inter-Agency Meeting on Emergency Needs Assessment*, Amsterdam: Médecins sans frontières (Dec.).

ODI, 1993, 'Recent Changes in the International Relief System', *ODI Briefing Paper*, London: Overseas Development Institute (Jan.).

ODI, 1996a, *Multi-donor Evaluation of the Humanitarian Intervention in the Great Lakes Region during 1994*, London: Overseas Development Institute.

ODI, 1996b, *Supplementary Feeding Programmes*, RRN Good Practice Review, No. 2, London: Overseas Development Institute.

ODI, 1998, 'The State of the International Humanitarian System', *ODI Briefing Paper*, No. 1, London: Overseas Development Institute (March).

Operations Review Unit, 1994, *Humanitarian Aid to Somalia*, The Hague: Ministry of Foreign Affairs.

Oxfam, 1998, *The Use and Acceptability of Micronutrient Enriched Foods: A Study by Oxfam*, UNHCR and Micronutrient Initiative, Oxford: Oxfam.

Payne, L., 1997, 'Impact of Food Delays on Refugees', *Field Exchange*, Vol. 2 (Aug.).

Refugee Studies Programme, 1991, *Responding to the Nutrition Crisis Among Refugees; The Need for New Approaches*, report of the International Symposium, Oxford 17–20 March.

Relief and Rehabilitation Network, 1997, *Counting and Identification of Beneficiary Populations in Emergencies: Registration and its Alternatives*, RRN Working Paper, London: Overseas Development Institute.

Riddoch, C., C. Mills and G. Duthie, 1998, 'An Evaluation on Germinating Pulses and Beans as a Potential Source of Vitamin C in Refugee Foods', *Clinical Journal of Nutrition*, Vol. 52, No. 2.

Schofield, E., 1994, 'Evaluating Energy Adequacy of Rations Provided to Refugees and Displaced Persons', paper prepared for the Workshop on the Improvement of the Nutrition of Refugees and Displaced People in Africa, Machakos, Kenya, 5–7 Dec. ACC/SCN Geneva..

Shaw, D.J. and H.W. Singer, 1996, 'A future food aid regime: implications of the Final Act of the Uruguay Round', *Food Policy*, Vol. 21, No. 415.

Shoham, S., J. Rivers and P. Payne, 1989, *Hartisheik*, London: School of Hygiene and Tropical Medicine.

Stephenson, R. *et al.*, 1998, 'Issues of Distribution and Logistics as Constraints on Adequate Nutrition in Times of Disaster', Working Paper, No. 6 for the Conference on Nutrition in Times of Disaster, Geneva, 27–30 Sept.

Toole, M., 1994, 'Preventing Micronutrient Deficiency Diseases', paper for the Workshop on the Improvement of the Nutrition of Refugees and Displaced People in Africa, Machakos, Kenya, 5–7 Dec.

UNHCR/WFP, 1998, Joint Evaluation of Emergency Food Assistance to Returnees, Refugees, Displaced Persons and other War-Affected Populations in Bosnia and Herzegovina, Executive Board Second Regular Session, 12–15 May. Evaluation Reports, Agenda Item 3, Rome: WFP.

Van Nieuwensuyse, C., 1997, 'Improving the Quality of the WFP Emergency Operations', *Field Exchange*, No. 1 (May), pp. 11–12.

Watson, F. and A. Filipovitch, 1998, 'Reconstruction in Bosnia: Implications for Food Security and the Future Aid', *Field Exchange*, Vol. 3 (Jan.).

WFP, 1997, *Evaluation of Liberia Programme (1990–95)*, Rome: World Food Programme.

WFP/UNHCR, 1986, *Report on the Joint WFP/UNHCR Mission to Pakistan in July 1986 to Assess the 1987 Food Aid Requirement for Refugees*, Rome: World Food Programme.

WFP/UNHCR, 1988, *Report on the Joint WFP/UNHCR Mission to Malawi in May 1988 to Review the Implementation of the Feeding Operation for Mozambican Refugees and to Assess the 1989 Food Aid Requirement*, Rome: World Food Programme.

WFP/UNHCR, 1997a, *Revised Memorandum of Understanding*, Rome: World Food Programme.

WFP/UNHCR, 1997b, WFP/UNHCR Guidelines for Estimating Food and Nutritional Needs in Emergencies, Rome: World Food Programme.

7

Humanitarian Crises and Natural Disasters: A SADC Perspective

ROGER BUCKLAND, GRAHAM EELE
AND REGGIE MUGWARA

I. INTRODUCTION

In southern Africa, drought is the most important natural disaster in economic, social and environmental terms. The economies of the region are particularly susceptible because of their geographic position, the high proportion of people dependent on rain-fed agriculture for their livelihoods, and the strong links between agriculture and the rest of the economy. The traditional view of humanitarian crises caused by droughts has been that of sudden and widespread famine and starvation, requiring large inflows of food aid. This chapter argues that this view is no longer valid. The rapid and dramatic changes that have taken place in the region over the past ten years have, to a large extent, resulted in a much lower risk of famine, although it is important not to be complacent. However, the removal of the acute threat of mass starvation has not removed the humanitarian crisis, rather it has changed its nature. In place of the acute threat of famine, the countries and peoples of the region are now subject to a much more intractable chronic problem, that of widespread and increasing poverty. The change in the nature of the crisis requires a substantial change in the ways in which it is addressed. This chapter calls for a paradigm shift in the way food aid is used in southern Africa.

The most recent region-wide drought in the Southern African Development Community (SADC)[1] was the1991/92 drought which was closely followed by the less damaging 1994/95 drought. In the case of the 1991/92 drought, estimates put the total number of people

---

1. Currently the Community includes 14 countries, Angola, Botswana, Lesotho, Malawi, Mozambique, Namibia, South Africa, Swaziland, Tanzania, Zambia and Zimbabwe to which the analysis in this chapter refers plus the Democratic Republic of the Congo (formerly Zaire), Mauritius and the Seychelles.

affected at 86 million, 20 million of whom were considered to be at serious risk of starvation. Cereal output in SADC (excluding South Africa, not then part of the community) fell from an average of 11.3 million tonnes to 6.2 million tonnes. Import needs rose to 7 million tonnes, with a further 5.5 million tonnes for South Africa. In total, 11.4 million tonnes of cereals were imported.

In the regional appeal launched in 1992 in conjunction with the Department of Humanitarian Affairs (DHA) of the United Nations, 1.6 million tonnes of targeted food aid was requested, together with 2.5 million tonnes of programme food aid for commercial sale. A further US$173 million was requested for non-food assistance. Actual deliveries totalled 1.5 million tonnes of targeted food aid and 1.7 million tonnes of programme food aid; in addition, South Africa imported about 5.5 million tonnes of cereals. Of the 5.9 million tonnes imported into SADC, excluding South Africa, during the relief operation, 2.7 million tonnes were purchased commercially. As in previous droughts, the principal focus of both the internal and external response was on food shortages and the need to meet the threat of starvation. So, while droughts in southern Africa cause major shocks to the whole economy, they have been managed mainly by the massive mobilisation of food aid.

The agricultural sector is a major component of most SADC economies. In addition, large proportions of their populations are smallholders who rely predominantly on rain-fed agriculture for their livelihoods. When droughts have occurred in the past, it has been this sector that has suffered worst. Inevitably, the region will experience drought again. However, political changes, the cessation of hostilities in the region, and the adoption of more liberal economic policies now allow a different approach in reacting to such events. Furthermore, the growing conviction that food aid should contribute to longer-term objectives, coupled with a general decline in funds available from donor countries for such action, has prompted a re-examination of the role of food aid in the context of longer-term food security. New approaches to ensuring food security and offsetting the impacts of variability are being developed which put much greater emphasis on incomes. In this light, the role of food aid is increasingly being seen as a complement to other longer-term developmental actions rather than as an end in itself.

This chapter draws on the lessons learned from the widespread droughts of 1991/92 and 1994/95 to point to how food aid might now contribute to development and drought-proofing rather than simply mitigating drought impacts. The major theme is that food aid in

SADC should now be viewed increasingly as an instrument for promoting long-term development and poverty eradication rather than solely as providing relief from starvation. Of course, mitigating the impacts of droughts will still be important, especially in areas perennially affected. However, preparedness and development should now be the major focus, with aid being used to make individual sectors and economies as a whole more capable of managing the impacts of drought by themselves.

II. CHANGING FOCUS

Southern Africa is a drought-prone region and past droughts have had a substantial impact at the local, micro level, at the level of markets and institutions (termed the meso level by the World Bank) and at the national or macro level. Communities and whole countries are susceptible to the effects of drought, reflecting the economic structure of countries, the location of people, and high levels of poverty. Although the contribution of agriculture to Gross Domestic Product is declining in most of the SADC region (Mozambique is the major exception and this reflects the process of recovery after years of war), the majority of people are still dependent on some kind of agricultural activity for their livelihoods. Irrigation is very limited and most people are dependent on rain-fed crop production, predominantly cereals. Large numbers of rural families, whose main economic activity is cereal production, are directly affected when droughts occur. Furthermore, as a result of policy intervention over many years and of changes in tastes, maize (especially white maize) is the predominant crop in the smallholder sector. White maize, especially many hybrid varieties, is stressed if water availability is low for more than about a week at crucial stages of crop growth. The combination of increasing climate variability and the spread of maize to areas where agro-climatic conditions are not always favourable has meant that the impact of rainfall failure has been magnified.

The impacts of droughts on the manufacturing and services sectors are often severe and can sometimes be felt for several years. Furthermore, the costs of recovery are often high. Recent research [*Benson and Clay, 1998*] suggests that the impacts are not the same for all SADC economies. In particular, countries with large agricultural sectors, strong links between agriculture and the rest of the economy, a high dependence on hydroelectricity, and large water-consuming industries are most affected. Within SADC, Zimbabwe and to some extent South Africa are closest to this model. With the exception of

Botswana and Namibia, which have well-developed mineral sectors, the macro impact of drought is substantial and can affect economic management strategies in nearly all SADC countries.

In the past, droughts have tended to be seen primarily as food crises for two main reasons. One was that the people who were first affected and who were the most vulnerable were food producers. At the local level, the numbers of people affected have sometimes been a significant proportion of the population. The impact on local economies has therefore been severe and has necessitated the delivery of food relief. A tacit assumption among both governments and donor agencies has been that the rural people in southern Africa have been and should continue to be self-sufficient, subsistence food producers. If areas were affected by drought and food production fell, making the local population no longer self-sufficient, the usual reaction was that direct provision of food aid was required to prevent starvation. This view was reinforced by the dramatic and disastrous famines in the Sahel and the Horn of Africa in the 1970s and 1980s and by the fact that, until recently, marketing systems were poorly developed and were largely controlled by governments to extract surpluses for use in urban centres. The recognition that resources at household and community level are limited has meant that there has often been no alternative to humanitarian aid. In addition, the impact of war and civil conflict has limited the capacity to cope with droughts at both the individual and national levels.

The second reason for viewing droughts as food crises has been, at least until the early 1990s, the emphasis in SADC member states on national food self-sufficiency. One of the driving forces behind the establishment in 1980 of a regional food security programme in the then Southern African Development Co-ordination Conference (SADCC) was the need to reduce dependence on food imports from South Africa and to manage drought shocks. This view was held by both national governments and the main donor agencies and food aid was seen as the main way of responding to droughts, at the macro level to reduce apparent cereal deficits, given the limited foreign-exchange reserves and, at the local level, to prevent famine and starvation.

In many SADC countries, inappropriate policies and economic incentives adopted in the immediate post-colonial years militated against substantial development of agriculture, the main engine for growth in much of the region. Pan-territorial and pan-seasonal prices, subsidies to consumers, market regulation, and the involvement of inefficient parastatals all contributed to stagnation in agriculture and misallocation of resources. Poor marketing and trade links, even within countries, exacerbated this. Market and other information systems, physical transport and marketing infrastructure, and support institutions were all relatively weak or undeveloped. However, all the economic reform programmes that have been introduced embrace the central concept of market forces as the vehicle for allocating resources. For good or ill (and the short-term pain is certainly visible), these programmes appear irreversible. The question now is whether and how markets can cope with natural disasters which at the regional level, as has been argued above, are considered to be synonymous with droughts.

The understanding of food security issues and the analysis of droughts have changed in recent years. At the technical level, many researchers, managers and officials have been influenced by writers such as Sen [1981] who pointed to the importance of access to food rather than food availability as the basic cause of starvation. This has been reinforced by research carried out within the region and by an extensive advocacy campaign carried out by SADC's Food Security Technical and Administrative Unit and others. However, it is only the major political and economic changes in the region during the 1990s that seem to have brought this home to politicians. More generally, under the SADC Treaty of 1992 and the inclusion of South Africa within the Community, the focus of the region has changed to one of economic integration rather than of confrontation and inward-looking food self-sufficiency. The more outward-oriented approach accepts, at least in principle, the benefits of increased trade and greater regional co-operation.

The dramatic political change in South Africa and the complete reorientation of SADC have been paralleled by substantial changes in the structures of almost all the economies of the region. In part, these reflect pressure from outside, especially in the form of conditions imposed by the IMF and the World Bank. They are also part of a more fundamental process of internal reform including greater democratisation, greater emphasis on transparency and accountability and greater participation in decision-making. From the point of view of food security and the management of droughts, a key element of the reform process has been a fundamental change in the role of the state from being the principal food provider to one of facilitator. Other elements include the liberalisation of markets, especially produce markets; the removal of foreign-exchange controls and the freeing up of international trade; the closure, privatisation, or at least major restructuring, of grain marketing parastatals; and the removal of subsidies and other market distortions. Coupled with the end of external destabilisation, peace in Namibia and Mozambique and the potential for peace in Angola, this has resulted in a substantial change in the relationship between drought and humanitarian crises.

The need to cope with droughts at the same time as economic adjustment measures are straining national resources has also stimulated changes in policy-makers' views of how droughts and their impacts should be handled. The growing realisation that aid flows for development, as well as for humanitarian crises, are diminishing has added to this. International aid agencies are dependent on their constituencies for their resources and, however benign their intentions, these resources are more limited these days. There is therefore clearly a need to use whatever resources are available to create a situation in which a drought-prone region, such as southern Africa, its individual member states, and the communities within those states can withstand such shocks without resorting to external assistance to the degree they have had to in the past.

III. RECENT EXPERIENCE

In the past, droughts in southern Africa have been associated with the threat of famine. For example, once the rainfall failure in the 1991/92 agricultural season was identified, but before the drought had had much impact, the analysis of many commentators was almost apocalyptic (literally so in the case of Green [*1992*]). Coloured by their recent experiences in the Sahel and the Horn of Africa, many people feared the outbreak of famine and starvation. In the event, this did not happen and there was little or no increased mortality directly attributable to the drought [*FSG, 1994*].

This success cannot be directly ascribed to the efficiency and effectiveness of food aid. Although, as set out above, assistance from donors, especially in the provision of food aid, was substantial, the impact of food relief was much more limited. Detailed research and analysis from a number of countries and different communities indicates that the government and donor-sponsored distribution of relief had little direct effect on food consumption. Furthermore, such relief was frequently politicised and was often captured by key pressure groups that were neither needy nor particularly vulnerable.

For example, in Zimbabwe, 5.6 million people were registered for drought relief or food-for-work supplies in 1992. It was intended that most of the emergency food for them would be distributed through food-for-work schemes. However, due to management constraints, a large proportion was in practice distributed without a work requirement. Intended recipients repeatedly reported receiving less than the official ration, delays in distribution and poor targeting, with richer villagers receiving as much as, and sometimes more than, poorer villagers. For most people food aid had little impact on their food consumption; to a large extent they depended on purchases in local markets [Eldridge, 1997]. Another study finds that the quantities distributed appeared to be too small to make any significant contribution to households' income. Moreover, as much aid was transferred to the wealthy as to the poor [Christensen and Zindi, 1996]. These findings are in accord with those from Botswana [Gyeke, 1992] and Namibia [Devereux et al., 1995]. With growing realisation of the inefficiencies at a time of reduced national resources and market liberalisation, there is now a growing consensus that the role of food aid and the way in which it is delivered need re-examination.

In 1994/95, widespread drought again affected the region. However, this did not result in famine, even though the level of donor assistance was this time much lower. Once again, it seems that most people were able to secure food through purchases in markets, using a mixture of savings, credit and the liquidation of assets. The ways in which food markets work are therefore increasingly becoming the dominant factor in assuring food security in times of crisis. This is also happening in more normal times and the process is accelerating. Economic reform programmes are liberalising markets and reducing the extent of state intervention. Governments are no longer able to pursue social goals through direct control of markets. Rather, their options are limited to influencing the behaviour of key actors. What governments do still has an enormous impact and is still necessary in many cases. However, it is now much less clear to many policy-makers what policies they should adopt to influence food security. The links are now much more complex.

It is important to note that the potential welfare gains from an efficient and competitive food market in southern Africa will not necessarily be available to all players, especially the poor and vulnerable. Market failures are still widespread and most produce markets in southern Africa are not yet well developed or well integrated [Jones, 1996]. Reliable information is often not readily available and few actors have sufficient knowledge or experience to make rational expectations about future prices. In this kind of situation, there is potential for speculative and monopolistic behaviour. As has been demonstrated in South Asia, under these conditions food markets can be quite unstable [Ravallion, 1987] and, in the absence of external intervention, the food security of poor consumers can be seriously threatened.

Overall, the evidence of recent years suggests that the threat of sudden mass starvation and widespread famine in southern Africa has receded. This is not to be over-complacent nor to suggest that the threat could never reappear but, rather, to emphasise that the nature of humanitarian crises has been ameliorated by changes in national economic policies, by greater regional involvement in information and co-ordination, and by growing regional trade. Yet, while the acute threat of famines has receded, the underlying chronic problem of widespread poverty has become more apparent. The need now is to promote market-based solutions to increase and sustain incomes.

IV. THE NEED TO ADDRESS POVERTY

Poverty is not a new phenomenon in southern Africa and it is a problem which is becoming increasingly severe. However, the emphasis on acute food security problems associated with droughts has meant that the underlying chronic problem has tended to be ignored. Its extent is well documented and is evidenced, among other indicators, by a substantial proportion of the population living below the poverty line, high levels of child malnutrition, and high infant mortality rates [*World Bank, 1997; UNICEF, 1997*].

The growing number of people in poverty in the region and their vulnerability to exogenous shocks such as droughts pose serious problems for planners. The causality works both ways. Droughts contribute to the erosion of the social fabric, reduce economic activity, lower personal and public income, and put pressure on resource bases and the ecology in general. Because people are poor, they have few assets and are vulnerable to the effects of an external shock such as drought which reduces crop production as well as the opportunities for off-farm employment. Without savings or other types of coping strategy, a collapse in incomes or a sudden deterioration in terms of trade can have a major impact on poor households, resulting in inadequate food consumption, ill-health and the loss of productive assets. At the same time, exogenous shocks such as drought are also a cause of poverty. They result in reduced income, tend to reduce future investment because of the need to hold savings in a liquid form, and can result in a loss of assets.

Addressing poverty on a sustained basis is much more complex than dealing with the acute problem of starvation and the role of food aid in this context is more difficult to identify. Distributing food to someone who is starving makes sense and is an obvious thing to do. It is less obvious, however, that direct food hand-outs are an efficient and effective response to poverty. Indeed, there is a substantial literature on the potential negative impact of food aid, in creating dependency, in providing disincentives to productive activities and in masking market signals.

Understanding the link between poverty and drought in southern Africa and the potential role of food aid requires a detailed analysis of the nature of poverty in the region and how it is changing. While there is not space here to go into much detail, a number of points can be made. First, demographic changes are resulting in a changing poverty profile. Rapid rural-urban migration has resulted in dramatic growth in the proportion of people living in towns and cities. In 1998, almost 45 per cent of the population in southern Africa were living in urban areas, and this proportion will be greater than 50 per cent within the next ten years. Second, the reduction in subsidies and policy distortions in the agricultural sector, together with changes in the pricing of natural resources, especially land and water, have resulted in a change in comparative advantage. For many people living in the drier, southern part of the region, the use of expensive scarce resources to grow low value crops such as cereals no longer makes economic sense. Together, these two factors are changing the way people ensure their food security. More and more people are now dependent on the market to secure the food they eat. The idea of a self-provisioning rural population is already invalid and will become more and more unrealistic as time goes on. At the same time, as infrastructure improves, the locus of surplus production of maize and other cereals is likely to move towards the north. National food security for many countries will increasingly be determined by international trade [*van Rooyen, 1997*].

For many smallholders in drought-prone areas, this implies that rain-fed cereal production is never likely to generate sufficient income to lift them out of poverty. In many areas, the solution will be to move out of cereal production, either to other forms of agriculture or, more likely, to other activities in other locations. The major food security challenge of the next twenty years in the region will be how to assist this process of transition. How governments and other agencies respond to droughts, therefore, will be important. At the very least, there is a need for congruence between the objectives of safety-net type programmes and long-term development. The provision of continuous drought relief in the hope that at some time in the future people will become self-sufficient is neither an efficient nor an effective way of alleviating poverty.

These arguments support the view that assistance should now focus on developing macroeconomic marketing, and microeconomic policies to promote overall growth, together with trade development. However, it is not immediately clear how the role of the state can be changed from being the major guarantor and provider of goods and services to that of a facilitator. Apart from the loss of patronage and rent-seeking that this implies, the market systems are still weak and the mind-set of many of those in power precludes letting go of the reins of economic power. It may well be, therefore, that the SADC countries should not yet aim for wholesale reliance on market systems. Safety nets for the vulnerable, especially the aged and female-headed households, will be needed and they can only be provided by the state. In addition, the large-scale investments required for the informational infrastructure to support open market operations, let alone for improving roads and communications networks, suggest that there is considerable room for public involvement. Furthermore, the need to draw up market-friendly enabling legislation and harmonised regulations among SADC countries will mean that governments will still be major players in this area for some time to come.

V. A NEW PARADIGM FOR FOOD AID

Poor targeting, delays in deliveries (sometimes until the next harvest), the moral hazard associated with local distribution with little or no accountability, the loss of patronage and political gain, and the relative expense of getting food to recipients, all point to the need for more market-based relief and development measures. But for these to be successful, governments will need to be confident that welfare goals, let alone development goals, will be met if they withdraw. Policy debate and research will also be needed to ensure that the policies adopted to encourage alternative food flows are consistent and are likely to meet both food-security and developmental objectives.

As an adjunct to this, markets will not operate as well as they might if there is uncertainty about the intentions of governments in the context of providing relief. Traders need to know that a market exists and that it will not be undermined by free hand-outs when political pressures become too great. Transparency with respect to policy and adherence to decisions are therefore likely to be necessary preconditions for ensuring that the private sector will enter markets when the government withdraws. A policy environment that encourages intra-regional trade as a means of increasing aggregate food availability and reducing fluctuations in local supplies will also be necessary. The private sector has an obvious role to play and governments may wish to see a wide participation in such trade rather than relying on a few major transnational firms.

A further policy measure requiring transparency is the government's use of national stocks to stabilise prices. The rationale for using such stocks includes the potential for improving poor people's access to food at times of shortage, reducing opportunities to make excess profits, and offsetting any immediate impacts of exchange-rate fluctuations. For such measures to be successful in stabilising prices without crowding out private traders, the rules of the game must be open. Price boundaries need to be clearly stated and adhered to. The mechanism for release should also be clear and preferably be through open trade rather than through hand-outs. Associated with such measures is the possibility of using triangular deals to source supplies and then using market channels to distribute them. This process has always found favour with SADC because it helps promote output in those areas with natural advantage, while helping to keep private distribution channels open with all that that implies for employment and income generation.

As indicated earlier, the incidence of poverty in SADC has tended to increase in recent years reflecting population increases, the adverse effects of conflicts, droughts, and inappropriate policies. Aid that treats the symptoms and not the causes by providing relief at times of stress may certainly mitigate the impact of a short-term problem but does not provide the wherewithal to meet long-term problems. So there is a need to ensure that food aid is part of a poverty alleviation programme and that, when relief is necessary, it is provided as a component of a wider safety net and in conjunction with codified practices of targeting.

VI. SADC'S ROLE

In the years since its inception in 1980 (originally as the Southern African Development Co-ordination Conference), there have been considerable changes in the way SADC has approached the question of humanitarian crises. Regional activities to complement national action have become increasingly important, one of the more visible evidences being the progressively greater role the region has played in collecting, monitoring, analysing, and disseminating information on food availability. A Regional Early Warning System (REWS) is in place with increasing capability to monitor supplies and to provide detailed information, based on ground observations backed up by satellite imagery of rainfall and vegetation across the region. The REWS, in collaboration with climate scientists across the world, was instrumental in providing an early forecast of the 1997/98 season when a major El Niño event increased risk of drought. It continues to be a major source of information for all decision-makers. However, there is still a need to incorporate socio-economic indicators, especially at household level, and market prices, including local markets, in the range of information monitored and disseminated. Risk-mapping activities and the development of methods to identify groups at risk will also help to provide longer lead-times for agencies wishing to provide relief. Droughts are slow-onset phenomena and longer lead-times and inter-seasonal forecasts will therefore help reduce their impact. Some progress has already been made in the science of inter-seasonal predictions. However, the methods need to be refined and further research and support for initiatives such as the International Research Institute of the National Oceanic and Atmospheric Administration of the United States are needed.

Like all regional organisations, SADC's role in the context of humanitarian crises has been to co-ordinate the responses that are decided by its constituent member states. An increasingly sophisticated institutional capacity is required for this to work successfully and efficiently. During the 1991/92 drought, a regional drought task force was formed, bringing together representatives of Ministries of Agriculture and Transport, as well as of organisations associated with food distribution and water and health issues. This remains in place but is only activated when necessary. The food security co-ordinating unit acts as the secretariat for the task force and ensures that regional activities decided upon are implemented. It was the co-ordinating unit, for example, that was responsible for compiling the international appeals that were launched in 1992 and 1995. While this is an advance on the previous system under which each country was responsible for its own approach to the international community, and while it provided the international community with an opportunity to aggregate grain shipments and other forms of assistance, the responsibility for actually providing assistance to those in need was and remains the responsibility of individual governments. The benefits for the region and for donors in having one co-ordinated approach are clear and are likely to foster further reliance on regional institutions. Droughts, among other natural calamities, become humanitarian disasters in situations where information is suppressed. The SADC experience has been that member states have discharged their responsibility to inform more readily in a regional context.

A review of SADC's whole programme of action has highlighted the need for a single institution to co-ordinate and direct programmes in the food, agriculture and natural resources sector. The certainty that droughts will recur means that the function of co-ordinating the region's responses will probably remain with the co-ordinating unit. Clearly, the capacity to manage such emergencies will therefore have to be retained and enhanced.

The importance of ensuring that the notion of climate variability and the links to humanitarian and economic well-being are incorporated in economic and fiscal planning is obvious. It is especially so in the context of structural adjustment programmes. At the regional level, the clear need for much greater emphasis on policy research and debate in these areas has already been recognised. Setting up a Regional Policy Analysis Network to address such issues has already received official blessing. This network is expected to make significant contributions to the debate surrounding the development of smallholder enterprises, poverty, and comparative advantage as economic rather than political issues. Research into the interaction between macroeconomic, market, and welfare policies also needs much more analysis in the region. A more direct focus on poverty and the way communities and individuals are affected by swings in climate or in economic development could help move policy-making into a more development-friendly stance.

Region-wide research into drought-resistant grains will also be necessary to help widen the range of crops available to producers. This will need to be accompanied by programmes to encourage the expansion of small-scale trading and processing. This will help the process of crop diversification and could potentially increase smallholders' involvement in markets. Again, there is an underlying poverty-alleviation rationale for such work.

Considerable investment is required in human resources and in physical infrastructure throughout the region if food flows are to take place autonomously at times of shortage. Increasing training in managing economic issues is a major requirement. Promoting regional approaches to these issues is a regional task and is linked to the notion that regional trade and economic integration will help promote more rapid economic development, while stabilising prices and improving the allocation of resources to areas where they can be used most efficiently. It is critically important, therefore, that the SADC trade protocol of 1996 should be ratified and implemented. Considerable difficulties are foreseen in this regard, since economies such as that of South Africa are sometimes unwilling to relinquish the protection for their relatively high cost industries. Again, research and wide public debate are necessary. A mechanism for resolving regional trade conflicts could well be beneficial (and not just to the lawyers).

Associated with the legal framework for enhancing trade in the region are the issues of transport routes and charges, harmonised trade and customs documentation, and common standards in zoosanitary and phytosanitary regulations and their application. The last are critically important at times of crisis because of the potential for the introduction of exotic pests. Indeed, during the 1992 relief effort, imports into Zambia from Tanzania on behalf of one well respected relief agency were directly responsible for the introduction of the Larger Grain Borer into that country. It has since spread across the whole of Zambia and has been reported in Zimbabwe and in northern Botswana and Namibia. Not only must the regulations be in place to prevent such mishaps, the capacity to implement them must also exist.

This chapter has argued that the focus of humanitarian aid should be on the longer-term problem of poverty eradication, as that would markedly reduce the susceptibility of populations to the impacts of natural disasters. Yet there will always be a need for some short-term response to meet demands beyond the resources of individual countries. The SADC member states are mostly in a situation where immediately available resources to meet unbudgeted needs are severely restricted. Leaving part of the responsibility to meet such needs to the markets is a strategy that could well be applied in many countries even now. To ensure that this works well, some form of financing mechanism to support cereal trade in the region may be appropriate. Import/export guarantee schemes to allow governments quick access to imports, or finance for regional trading entities with little access to credit, perhaps through promoting some sort of regional banking consortium, could also merit examination. The resources required to back such a scheme are likely to be large, so some partnership with the international community in setting up such a mechanism is now envisaged.

The way in which SADC currently responds to humanitarian crises has changed substantially in recent years, both at the national and the regional level. In part, this reflects the improvements in information and increased understanding of the way the climate works. More important, however, is the increasing emphasis being given to promoting development, particularly in the smallholder sector, as a way of enhancing self-reliance. All countries have developed drought strategies. At the regional level, two major workshops have reviewed country positions and drawn up recommendations for action, many of which are reflected in the arguments advanced in this chapter. Preparedness is now given much greater prominence and the nexus between natural disasters and the capacity of economies, and hence of sections of the population, to cope with shocks has been moved into the arena of policy research and debate. It is comforting, therefore, that droughts are now being seen increasingly as a development problem rather than as isolated disasters that can be dealt with outside the framework of regional or national planning.

REFERENCES

Benson, C. and E.J. Clay, 1998, *The Impact of Drought on Sub-Saharan Africa*, Technical Paper No. 401, Washington DC: World Bank.

Christensen, G. and C. Zindi, 1996, *The Determinants of Household Food Security and Child Nutrition in Rural Zimbabwe: Implications for Public Policy*, Oxford: Food Studies Group.

Devereux, S., D. Lebeau and W. Pendleton, 1995, *The 1992–1993 Drought in Namibia*, Windhoek: Gamsberg Macmillan.

Eldridge, C., 1997, 'Drought in Zimbabwe: Effects and Responses at Household Level', Mbabane: Save the Children Fund (UK), Regional Office for Southern Africa.

Food Studies Group (FSG), 1994, *Final Report of the Drought Management Workshops in Southern Africa*, Oxford: Food Studies Group.

Green, R.H., 1992, 'Sound the Tocsin: The Third Horseman Rides', mimeo, Brighton: Institute of Development Studies.

Gyeke, G., 1992, 'Income and Employment Generation in Rural Botswana: A Preliminary Analysis of a Four Village Case Study', mimeo, Gaborone: University of Botswana.

Jones, S., 1996, *Food Markets in Developing Countries: What Do We Know?*, Working Paper No. 8, Oxford: Food Studies Group.

Ravallion, M., 1987, *Markets and Famines*, Oxford: Clarendon Press.

Sen, A. K., 1981, *Poverty and Famines: An Essay on Entitlement and Deprivation*, Oxford: Clarendon Press.

UNICEF, 1997, *The State of the World's Children*, Oxford: Oxford University Press.

Van Rooyen, J., 1997, 'Developing a Strategic Agenda for Food Security in Southern Africa: New Roles for the Agricultural Sector', paper presented at a conference to develop a new food security strategy for SADC Harare (March).

World Bank, 1997, *World Development Report*, New York: Oxford University Press.

8

Food Aid for Development?
A Review of the Evidence

NITA PILLAI

The volatility of food aid as a resource and its marginalisation within donor aid portfolios have been outlined elsewhere in this volume. This environment of uncertainty is leading donors to re-examine the evidence for food aid's effectiveness in achieving key developmental objectives. Increasingly donors are placing the goals of poverty alleviation, reduction and elimination at the centre of their development programming, and the role of food aid in helping to meet these priority objectives is again being questioned.

Two types of food aid transactions are utilised for development purposes – programme and project food aid (as defined above in Chapter 1, pp. 23–5). This chapter reviews the evidence on the developmental impacts of both these forms of assistance. It has its origins in a policy review commissioned by the Department for International Development (DFID) to examine the 'Future of Food Aid' [*Clay et al., 1998*] as part of a re-examination of the UK's own bilateral programme during Britain's presidency of the European Union. In reviewing the evidence, the chapter takes into account a number of evaluations of donor food aid operations carried out in recent years, including evaluations of Australian, Canadian and US programmes [*Australian Development Assistance Bureau, 1997; Freeman et al., 1997; McClelland, 1997*] as well as a study of EU Programme Food Aid operations [*Clay et al., 1996*]. It also considers the tripartite evaluation of the World Food Programme [*Chr. Michelsen Institute, 1993a*] as well as that agency's own recent stocktaking of its development activities [*WFP, 1999*]. A number of the other papers reviewed for this synthesis are themselves reviews of the literature, summarising the results of empirical research.

At the outset it may be useful to explain the methodological limitations of the evaluations themselves. It has been suggested that
evaluation of food assistance programmes is 'woefully incomplete,
excessively focused on univariate analysis and on individual case studies' [*Barrett, forthcoming*]. All the evaluations used a 'before' and
'after' approach to assessing the intervention rather than modelling a
counterfactual prediction of what might have happened without it.
Similarly, little attempt has been made to compare the impacts of food
aid interventions with what might have been achieved using alternative resources. The underlying assumption is that food aid is a constant (which may well be the case for some US-funded PVOs and
NGOs), so the tendency is to determine the most effective use for it
rather than to assess it 'on a level playing field' against other resources. Food aid evaluations also tend to assess projects against impact
and cost-effectiveness criteria rather than entering into any form of
cost-benefit analysis.

The chapter is organised in two sections: first, it examines the evidence for the use of food aid as a resource for poverty alleviation and
livelihood security; second, there is an exploration of its effectiveness
as a tool for improving the health and nutritional status of the poor.

I. POVERTY ALLEVIATION AND LIVELIHOOD SECURITY

1. Programme Food Aid

Programme Food Aid (PFA), as general support to economic development and growth, is by its very nature able to make an impact on poverty. Indeed, it has been suggested that the optimal use of PFA might
be as a way of reducing commercial food imports. This allows the
saved foreign exchange to be reallocated to finance other needed
imports, cover balance-of-payments deficits or repay external debts
which can all play an important role in supporting economic and
social development [*Colding and Pinstrup-Andersen, forthcoming*]. In
theory, PFA also has the potential to make a developmental impact,
either through the direct provision of food assistance or via the generation of counterpart funds (CPFs) from monetisation, channelled to
developmental purposes, on- or off-budget.

Case-study evidence accumulated during the Joint Evaluation of
EU PFA [*Clay et al., 1996*] indicated that this form of intervention is
ineffective in enhancing the household food security of the poorest
through the support of direct food distribution programmes. Indeed,
the evaluation found that many public ration and subsidy systems dis-

criminate against the poor, with the majority of benefits accessible mainly to urban, public and formal sector employees, the military, the civil service and similar groups. USAID PFA distributions were concluded to have reached only those consumers with purchasing power, and thus obviously not the poorest [*McClelland, 1997*].

On occasion, the use of so-called self-targeting commodities – those disproportionately consumed by the poor, for example, soft wheat in Bangladesh and wholemeal bread in Egypt – has had progressive effects as an income transfer to poorer consumers. But the subsidised distribution of such commodities is limited by the fact that they are sometimes purchased for use as animal feed. Self-targeting commodities represent a blunt and inefficient way of achieving an income transfer to food-insecure households.

The impact of monetised PFA on poverty and food insecurity depends on how the CPFs are distributed. Generally the proceeds from the sale of PFA are used as public budget revenue, so the developmental benefits depend on the public expenditure priorities of the recipient government. Consequently PFA will only have an indirect effect on the food security of the poor [*Colding and Pinstrup-Andersen, forthcoming*]. Because of this the directed use of CPFs has been viewed as a way of targeting PFA to projects aimed specifically at increasing the food security of vulnerable households. Over the years donors have sought to become increasingly specific about the targeting of CPFs, regardless of how they are budgeted. It is difficult, however, to ascertain the developmental impact of on-budget CPFs because of the fungibility of food aid. In cases where resources are provided off-budget, it is also not always possible to conclude that there has been additionality, as they may have triggered a reallocation of budgetary resources away from the sector to which the CPFs were allocated. Also, in many instances, agreements guiding the disbursement of CPFs have been too nebulous to ensure that donor conditionalities are met. It is difficult, for example, to determine whether any CPF-associated agricultural development projects funded by EU Community Action and the member states have actually succeeded in prioritising food-insecure regions or groups. Problems in management and accounting of CPFs also mean that improvements in food security for the poorest are very difficult to achieve.

Policy reform initiatives leveraged by PFA can theoretically benefit the poor if they effect change on issues critical to food security and poverty. But only the US has seen itself as having sufficient weight, in terms of food aid shipments, to engage in bilateral policy dialogue to influence recipient countries' sectoral and macroeconomic policy

[*USAID, 1989*]. Donors working in tandem have had only limited success in dialogue with recipient governments on policy issues. Historically PFA has proved to be a blunt instrument for levering policy change and indeed can sometimes act as a disincentive to sustainable development, by allowing governments to postpone implementation of suitable policies.

It appears that there is no evidence to suggest that PFA is more pro-poor in its impacts than other forms of programme aid. Such conclusions have led most donors to shift their food aid allocations increasingly to alternative methods of distribution which can, in theory, focus more effectively upon particular beneficiary groups.

2. Project Aid

The justification for project food aid as an appropriate developmental tool rests on the assumption that it can be used discriminatingly and so be effectively targeted at the neediest, with sustainable results. Proponents of project food aid argue that it can achieve various development goals including infrastructural development and employment generation through labour-intensive public works, improved nutritional and health awareness mediated by mother and child health initiatives (MCH), and increased attendance and improved educational performance through school feeding programmes (SFPs). These sectoral uses of food aid are considered in more detail below.

(i) Labour-intensive public works

The single most important resource that most poor people have is their own labour and it has long been argued that this resource can be utilised effectively to address the problems of poverty and hunger, mediated by labour-intensive public works [*Burki et al., 1976*]. The nature of these labour-intensive works can vary greatly, ranging from relief works offering temporary wage employment in crisis situations to long-term employment programmes designed to provide secure livelihoods for the most vulnerable [*Clay, 1986*]. Payment has generally been made in the form of either cash or food (Food-For-Work – FFW).

Three questions need to be considered when judging the appropriateness of labour-intensive works in the context of this review. First, what impact have these activities had upon poverty and livelihood security objectives? Second, how effective is food as a wage for this type of activity? And third, if food-for-work is indeed an appropriate and effective developmental intervention, what role does food aid have in supporting it?

(a) Livelihood security: The impacts of these public works programmes on food and livelihood security appear to be highly dependent
upon the circumstances in which they are implemented. In Asia some
works programmes originating in emergency programmes have been
successfully expanded to provide employment and income transfers
during subsequent periods of food insecurity. For example, the State-
run Employment Generation Schemes (EGS) in India which guarantee
unskilled labourers cash-wage employment on rural infrastructure
works (for example, road and soil conservation, afforestation and irrigation) have played an important role in combating seasonal malnutrition and insecurity by providing year-round employment [*Drèze and
Sen, 1989*]. Furthermore, they have been found to improve livelihood
security by reducing the income variability of labourers by 50 per cent
in comparison with those employed in non-EGS villages [*Dev, 1995*].
The Bangladesh FFW programme has been similarly successful in
providing slack season employment for landless and marginal farmers
when demand for agricultural labour is low [*Ahmed et al., 1995*]. It
has been argued, however, that the success of labour-intensive public
works in South Asia has limited relevance to the less densely populated regions of Africa [*Clay, 1986*].

Others dispute this and contend that local population densities in
Africa can reach high levels, making these works a viable strategy for
poverty alleviation in this continent also [*von Braun et al., 1991*].
There are notable examples where FFW projects have been expanded
during short-term food shortages, preventing the need for distress
migration [*CIDA, 1998*]. An analysis of the household food economy
of the Tezeke Lowlands in north-east Ethiopia [*SCF, 1997*] indicates
that relief works during poor crop years have allowed the poorest
households in the region to meet their food needs without migration to
Gonder, with its inevitable damage to communities and families as
well as future livelihoods. Indeed, the relief distribution in this
instance has enabled some of the poorest households to increase their
asset base by freeing them from the usually overriding preoccupation
of meeting their daily food needs. Others cite the experience of successful schemes in Niger and Zimbabwe [*Webb, 1995; Webb and
Moyo, 1992*]. However, the apparent success of such schemes is also
disputed, especially in a crisis context [*Devereux et al., 1995;
Eldridge, 1997*].

Problems with the effectiveness of these projects have largely been
encountered where rural works, with the short-term goal of providing
food to the hungry, have also been intended to have long-term sustainable impact [*CIDA, 1998*]. Public works projects cannot effectively

achieve both goals simultaneously and should generally have one or other as their primary objective.

(b) Asset creation and sustainability: A recurrent theme in the literature is the appropriateness or quality of investment undertaken through labour-intensive rural works where income generation by means of employment creation is the primary objective. The sustainability of assets created through these works, and thus the ability to have an impact on longer-term food security and poverty reduction goals, has provoked considerable controversy. A review of the Canadian government's multi-year programme in Ethiopia [*Rempel, 1997*] found it impossible to determine whether its goal of increasing long-term, sustainable household food security had been achieved. Little attempt had been made by NGOs to measure the assets' contribution to increased sustainable food production, nor indeed their potential contribution when matured.

Sometimes the assets created are of questionable quality and have frequently been left to deteriorate. WFP-funded agro-forestry projects in Ethiopia, for example, which created physical conservation structures and tree plantations, have been lost due to a lack of maintenance. Similar problems elsewhere raise the issue of the degree to which the assets created reflect the technical and administrative capacity of the implementing agency rather than the needs and interests of participants and the wider community. The involvement of communities and beneficiaries in the planning stages of projects is unfortunately all too rare, and this risks a perception of a lack of ownership on the part of the community towards the assets being translated into lapses in maintenance and upkeep. In its recent policy review, the WFP committed itself to ensuring that participants are more systematically involved in the selection and design of assets [*WFP, 1999*].

The long-term success of all works projects ultimately depends on the rights of beneficiaries to the use of the assets they have created and are expected to maintain. Clear tenure and usufructuary rights are rarely established beforehand and, as the evaluation of WFP programmes elucidated [*Chr. Michelsen Institute, 1993a*], the long-term benefits of the infrastructure created are often appropriated by the better-off members of the community. Even the redistributive taxation measures implemented in the EGS in India have failed to redress this imbalance [*Hirway and Terhal, 1994*].

Operational and technical problems have also hampered the developmental effectiveness of FFW projects. For example, small-scale CIDA-funded projects implemented in Malawi, which included the construction of communal tree plantations, primary schools and seed gardens, were frustrated by a lack of critical non-food inputs and irregular food delivery [*Vandenberg, 1997*]. The tripartite evaluation of WFP development activities also noted that the mobilisation of non-food items was not always successful or timely, and was a key aspect of project failure.

(c) Targeting the poorest: The performance of public works in successfully targeting the poorest is mixed for both cash- and food-based employment schemes. The EGS in Maharashtra State, India, has over 90 per cent participation by the poor, an increasing proportion of them women. The Rural Maintenance Programme (RMP) in Bangladesh, which employs destitute women for a cash wage in farm-to-market rural road maintenance, also has a 95 per cent success rate according to the strict targeting criteria used [*Guest, 1997*]. Furthermore, the wider Bangladesh FFW programme which pays wages in wheat reported effective targeting of the project to the poor, with a large female participation rate [*Ahmed et al., 1995*].

However, a review of targeting in Ethiopian FFW interventions [*Sharp, 1997*] found that, for a number of projects, less vulnerable members of the community were benefiting disproportionately. A recent follow-up to this study by Daniel Clay and colleagues [*1999*] also found that there were high levels of inclusion errors, with the most food-secure and most food-deficit households receiving the same levels of food aid. Evaluation of WFP-supported projects also found that the benefits, in terms of food as a wage, often accrued to the less vulnerable. Government employees in Ghana were part-paid with food aid for work on agro-forestry projects [*Chr. Michelsen Institute, 1993b*], and landowners were comparatively greater beneficiaries of rural development projects in Pakistan [*Chr. Michelsen Institute, 1993c*]. There are a number of possible explanations; it may be that less vulnerable households are more likely to have surplus labour and so be able to access FFW opportunities without sacrificing other sources of income; non-competitive payment rates may preclude participation by the neediest as they provide inadequate income to support the poorest households; it may also be that the targeting system is open to manipulation by those in power for moral or political reasons.[1] Often, the unintentional effects of targeting practices

---

1. Sharp [*1997*] has suggested that in Ethiopia targeting may have proved unsuccessful because local authorities resist the principle of prioritising the needy when many in the community are viewed as equally deserving or that the distribution was manipulated for electioneering purposes.

may actually be to discriminate against the very people the project is designed to reach.

As female-headed households are typically more labour-constrained and thus less able to participate in such projects without harming on-farm production and future livelihoods, these works may in practice also discriminate against them. Rural development works in the North West Frontier Province in Pakistan earmarked a proportion of workdays for women, none of which were utilised in the first three years of the project. In the same region training programmes in support of rural women reached only 20 per cent of the target, and it was felt that food aid was proving to be an insufficient incentive to participation. Similarly, agricultural projects in Malawi specifically aimed at increasing the food security of female-headed households were, in practice, supporting a number of male-headed households. Moreover, the leadership of village-level farmers' groups assembled by the project was predominantly male [*Chr. Michelsen Institute, 1993c*].

A recent Ethiopian study [*Clay et al., 1999*], however, suggests that the practice of targeting women and the elderly can result in the overrepresentation of these groups among beneficiaries, irrespective of food needs. To be successful, targeting systems need to use truly needs-based criteria rather than falling back on preconceived notions about who the food-insecure are.

Attempts to target food-insecure areas geographically and concentrate resources on them have also proved problematic. In the case of Ethiopia, Clay and colleagues [*1999*] found that households in Tigray, a historically deficit area, were more likely to receive food aid regardless of need than in any other area. In addition, households were more likely to receive food aid in the current year if they had been recipients in past years. The relationship became stronger and more significant as the number of past years of food aid increased. This indicates the inflexibility of the food aid system and its inability to reach communities outside of the 'normally deficit' areas. Years of food aid receipt reflect the institutional capacity that has built up in the delivery system, including personnel, equipment and local knowledge. This then creates a powerful reason for continuing with 'business as usual' and distributing to the same areas. It has been suggested that use of geographic targeting may induce migration of beneficiaries but there is little empirical evidence that this is the case [*Moffitt, 1992*].

(d) Cash or food wages? The literature suggests that the mode of payment should be governed largely by local conditions including the market situation, the specifics of likely household food consumption

behaviour and the indirect effects on non-participating vulnerable groups. In circumstances of food scarcity, payment in kind has the obvious advantage of providing food to the hungry whilst simultaneously augmenting local supplies. If food supply is highly inelastic in the short term, then cash payments without a complementary injection of food would raise prices for excluded groups [*Basu, 1996*]. In circumstances of high inflation, payment in food is also probably the more appropriate means as it maintains the real value of wages to the beneficiary. There is also some evidence that the use of food as a wage can lead to increased calorie consumption at the household level, although in itself this does not constitute a sufficient reason for payment in kind (the nutritional impacts of food aid are discussed later in this chapter). Some of the more successful continuing rural works programmes, ranging from the vast scale of provincial programmes in China [*Zhu and Jiang, 1995*] and State Employment Guarantee Schemes in India [*Hirway and Terhal, 1994*] to small island programmes in Cape Verde [*Ferreira Duarte and Metz, 1996*], combine cash wages with complementary market interventions to ensure food availability and stable, often subsidised, prices for consumers.

An oft-proclaimed strength of food, compared with cash-wage employment, is that this resource provides an effective means of reaching specific beneficiary groups. This assertion is based on assumptions about the self-targeting nature of food wages, which contend that only the poorest will work for self-targeting commodities, at wages set below the market rate, or will engage in the strenuous labour typically required in FFW activities. The problems of effective targeting have already been highlighted. In addition, some potentially vulnerable groups, such as the elderly and the disabled, as well as those living in areas too distant to allow regular travel to worksites, may be excluded.

Delays in the provision and distribution of food commodities have also disrupted works programmes. Indeed, a recent examination of the Ethiopian Employment Guarantee Schemes suggests that delays have been as long as six months [*Middlebrook, 1999*]. It is no surprise, then, that the targeted beneficiaries often choose not to participate since they are unable to defer payment until commodities become available [*Sharp, 1997*]. In circumstances where the timely provision of food commodities cannot be guaranteed, payment in cash is likely to be preferable. There has been concern about the possible disincentive effects of food wages upon beneficiary agricultural production. But it appears that there is little empirical evidence of reduced involvement in farming by participants of major FFW programmes in Ethiopia [*Maxwell, 1991*] or Bangladesh [*Ahmed et al., 1996*].

Cost-efficiency is obviously a crucial issue. A cash wage appears to be more efficient than food payments where handling and transportation costs are high. In Bangladesh it is estimated that cash rather than food wages could reduce programme costs by 25 per cent, by avoiding commodity-related transaction costs [*Ahmed et al., 1995*]. Cash payment also obviates the need for beneficiaries to sell a portion of their food wage, when it constitutes a large proportion of household income, in order to meet other needs. This involves further transaction costs which are often ignored in cost-effectiveness calculations.

To sum up, the choice of mode of payment should be largely determined by the functioning of the market, especially when a crisis event has occurred, and targeting considerations. When markets are functioning relatively efficiently, cash payment may be a better option since it can be more easily monitored; it also creates demand for local food production and is easier to handle. Where markets are poorly integrated and there are serious imperfections or there is high inflation, payment in kind may be the best option in the short term. A 'mixed' food and cash wage may sometimes be the preferable option as it provides greater flexibility for both implementing agencies and beneficiaries. A further consideration is the indirect impact of the intervention on those excluded from the programme. The appropriate choice of payment in a rural works programme should also take account of other complementary interventions. The accumulated evidence about mode of payment underlines the need for decisions to be made on the basis of a careful consideration of local conditions.

(e) The role of food aid: Food aid can support labour-intensive public works in three ways: through the provision of commodities for payment in kind, through public distribution systems which can then be drawn upon for wage payments, or through the generation of local currency to finance these works. The first option has predominated, to the extent that food aid and FFW have become almost synonymous in much of the literature.

The issue of cost-efficiency, already mentioned briefly, is fundamental to the question of whether food aid is the most suitable way of supporting FFW projects. Transaction costs including international and local transportation and storage and handling costs can be prohibitively high, raising questions about the efficiency of the direct use of food aid commodities. Another factor is the choice of commodity with which to make payment. If the commodity selected is determined by the existence of exportable surpluses and poses problems of acceptability to the consumer, there is little basis for building public works programmes around food aid. These two problems are being addressed to a certain extent by the trend of increased purchase of commodities in developing countries. However, cost-efficiency remains an important consideration.

The sustainability of programmes supported by food aid is also a crucial issue. In the short term, fluctuations in local food supply can make it sometimes inappropriate to import food. But switching between food and cash and between imports and local acquisition to take account of these fluctuations is technically difficult. In the longer term there may be funding problems, especially for relatively large rural works programmes, such as the Bangladesh and Ethiopian FFW programmes. These rely on the willingness of donors to sustain them, as it is unlikely that host governments will be in a position to substitute locally produced commodities owing to budgetary constraints. With market liberalisation, cash-wage-based rural works may also be more suitable than FFW. Monetisation and the use of sales proceeds to fund cash for work could then have a transitional role in assistance.

In summary, the empirical evidence on the role of labour-intensive public works in achieving poverty reduction and long-term livelihood security is mixed. The record of sustainable asset creation is poor, but there have been many positive impacts on short-term food insecurity in situations of acute food shortage and also in providing a safety net for the chronically poor. This mixed record is partly the result of overambitious project designs which combine incompatible short- and long-term goals, and partly because it reflects the implementation of works in regions or countries to which they are not well suited.

The role of food aid as a support for effective and efficient FFW programmes appears to be limited to situations of market dysfunction and food scarcity, conditions which are more likely to be found in crisis and post-crisis rehabilitation situations. Under these circumstances, food aid distributed as payment in kind can be crucial in maintaining household consumption at adequate levels, providing that appropriate and effective targeting is undertaken to reach the poorest. There is also a challenge in ensuring a timely transition to cash-based schemes or other activities where there is continuing need for poverty-alleviating, safety-net programmes.

(ii) School feeding programmes (SFPs)
This type of intervention typically involves the distribution of a food supplement to primary school children, although programmes have

also been undertaken in secondary schools, universities and colleges [*Barrett, forthcoming*]. Project objectives, besides improving nutritional status, are concerned with human resource development, and include improving enrolment and attendance, often of girl children specifically, reducing drop-out rates and enhancing cognitive development and academic performance.

During the 1980s, a series of negative evaluations led to a decrease in the importance accorded to SFPs among donor priorities. It appears, however, that some agencies and governments have recently been revisiting SFPs as a means of promoting sustainable development, largely for two reasons. The immediate impact of structural adjustment programmes on the poor has been so regressive in many instances that the role of SFPs in mitigating these negative impacts is being recognised. Also, the greater emphasis on human development as characterised by the UNDP Human Development Index [*UNDP, 1996*] has refocused attention on the role that food aid has to play in reaching the poorest and most vulnerable, particularly children. A reassessment of the role of food aid-supported SFPs is therefore timely.

(a) Developmental impact: Evaluations of WFP-supported projects have noted how difficult it is to establish with any degree of certainty how far school feeding goes in improving cognitive function and academic performance [*Chr. Michelsen Institute, 1993a*]. The only area where some positive effect could be ascribed was in the concentration shown by those children who travelled long distances to school. The review of similar USAID-supported interventions was more positive in its conclusions. Programmes in Honduras, Burkina Faso and Bangladesh were all credited with improving enrolment and attendance rates, and some anecdotal evidence was provided of improved attention spans, learning abilities and academic performance as a consequence of supplementation [*McClelland, 1997*]. The Honduran Bonos Mujer Jefe de Familia (BMFS) programme essentially acts as an income-transfer programme rather than a traditional feeding intervention by providing children in primary schools in areas of severe malnutrition and poverty with coupons which can then be used to buy food and other goods or converted into cash. NGOs have also reported positive effects of more conventional supplementary school feeding in post-drought Zimbabwe. They observed reduced levels of school drop-out and also fainting during the intervention period and reported a 20 per cent average weight gain of the children participating [*Christian Aid, 1997*].

(b) Targeting the poorest: Targeting of SFPs to the poorest and most insecure families has proved problematic. Past research has indicated that those attending primary school are more likely to come from less vulnerable backgrounds, suggesting that SFPs may even discriminate against the neediest. Levels of enrolment and attendance and whether SFPs can in fact influence these appear crucial. The Jamaican 'Nutri-bun' programme, implemented in 1986, has successfully distributed daily milk and fortified buns to its targeted beneficiaries as a consequence of the almost universal enrolment rates of primary school children in that country [*World Bank, 1989*].

The general assumption that SFPs increase the number of girls attending school also appears to be more a matter of belief than consistently established fact, although a successful pilot programme in Bangladesh indicates that it can be achieved. The Bangladesh project targets vulnerable households which have difficulty in sending children to school because of the high value placed on their labour, by compensating them with wheat for the loss of child earnings [*McClelland, 1997*]. It has been particularly effective in reaching girl children, because of the requirement that *all* the children must attend school for the household to be eligible for participation. Such experiences highlight the importance of considering the local socio-economic conditions when determining the most appropriate form of intervention.

The use of food aid as an effective and cost-efficient tool for supporting SFPs appears to be debatable. Evidence of positive developmental impacts is limited, often to pilot schemes where the constraints can be more easily addressed. SFPs appear to have had greater success when they have been implemented as income-transfer programmes to the poorest families rather than as direct feeding interventions for poor children. The logistical and financial problems in providing and maintaining food supplies and complementary non-food inputs are clear and undermine the cost-effectiveness of this form of intervention. Moreover, even if project objectives are successfully achieved, their long-term sustainability will still be in doubt because of the high proportion of recurrent costs. The tripartite evaluation of the WFP suggested that it was unlikely for most programmes that host governments would continue funding to the same level, if at all, were aid to be withdrawn [*Chr. Michelson Institute, 1993a*].

In choosing how to allocate local funds, alternatives involving lower transaction costs, such as reducing or waiving school fees, may be a more effective way of increasing enrolment of poor children [*Jackson, 1982*]. Only if there is convincing evidence that SFPs also improve nutritional status and performance might they be preferable as an incentive to attendance. In areas with pre-existing high enrolment levels of poor children, or where these can reasonably be achieved, food aid distributions might also be a suitable means of making an income transfer to the neediest families. Where these conditions cannot be guaranteed, benefits are likely to accrue disproportionately to the better-off.

(iii) Supplementary feeding programmes

This term is a wide-ranging one and can be used to describe interventions including Mother and Child Health programmes (MCH), Vulnerable Group Feeding (VGF) and Therapeutic Feeding Programmes (TFPs). Besides improving the nutritional status of poor mothers and babies, MCH programme objectives include improved health and nutritional knowledge and practices, and the generation of supplemental income through small enterprises and gardening. VGF programmes encompass MCH-style interventions as well as the provision of food to hospitals, orphanages and other institutions. They attempt to go beyond simply dealing with malnutrition to include health education, functional literacy and other forms of training. TFPs target individuals severely malnourished as a result of some emergency event, be it drought, war or flood, and aim to rehabilitate them and promote weight gain through the use of food rations in conjunction with medical care and supervision.

In common with school feeding programmes, MCH and VGF-type interventions received less attention in the 1980s because of inconclusive evidence as to their direct health and nutritional effects and sustainable developmental impact. But they are now also being re-examined with the increased prioritisation of human development and security, in particular of women and children. The poverty, nutritional and health aspects of these interventions are complex and difficult to separate, both conceptually and practically, and are discussed further in Section II.

(a) *Effectiveness*: Experience of these projects as long-term developmental interventions has been mixed. Problems have been encountered in linking the direct intervention – the provision of a food supplement – with the overall objectives of the projects. A VGF project undertaken in the Yemen Arab Republic, for example, failed to relate the feeding component to any complementary programme for nutritional or health education.

In contrast, the large VGF programme in Bangladesh, initiated in the wake of the famine in 1975, which targets poor, distressed women, was concluded to have positively affected their status within the community, and increased their own and their children's food consumption and calorie intake, as well as having a positive impact on their economic position [*Guest, 1997*]. The crucial difference between this and less successful projects is the provision of an effective development support package including literacy, numeracy, health and nutrition education and training in income-earning skills. In general, VGF programmes do not address the root causes of malnutrition and food insecurity and as such are ill-equipped to act as a tool for sustainable development. They act simply as direct food distribution interventions that provide an income transfer [*Chr. Michelsen Institute, 1993a*]. The question remains as to whether a food intervention, supported by food aid, is the most cost-efficient and practical way of achieving objectives even for those projects that did prove successful.

The educational components of some MCH projects funded by USAID were judged to have had some beneficial outcomes, with evidence of improved breast-feeding, weaning and other health practices, but it is likely that comparable impacts could have been achieved without costly food interventions. The positive non-nutritional impacts of these programmes may also only be attained hand-in-hand with non-nutritional costs, for example the creation of dependence on short-term unsustainable handouts at the expense of self-reliance and sustainable development.

Many projects, however, have their origins in, or are considerably expanded as, crisis response measures, assisting displaced and refugee populations or resident populations affected by conflict and acute food insecurity. MCH and VGF interventions, under these circumstances, provide a way of simultaneously addressing a potentially acute nutritional situation and making a targeted income transfer to affected or vulnerable households. There is considerable evidence that such actions are often the only project option available and are 'supplementary to nothing' [*Shoham, 1994*]. Consequently there *is* an argument for sustaining them as part of a crisis-management system, especially where food markets are thin and likely to break down in crisis and where alternative institutional arrangements for intervention are not possible.

To sum up, under the crisis circumstances in which these programmes are sometimes implemented, the combination of severely malnourished individuals and acute food shortages means that food aid, mediated by MCH and VGF-style interventions, is a crucial input for saving lives and responding to immediate nutritional needs. The role of such interventions in a more stable situation of endemic poverty and chronic hunger is more contentious and raises the question of alternative ways of providing safety nets, supporting health education and promoting development in a sustainable way.

II. IMPROVING NUTRITIONAL AND HEALTH STATUS

There is a widespread belief that nutritional status is determined solely by the amount and nutritional value of food consumed [*Shoham, 1994*]. Thus the nutritional impact of food aid interventions, on the rare occasions it is even considered, is assumed to be a positive one. In fact, an individual's health status, itself affected by a host of environmental variables, is as important a determinant of their nutritional status as access to food. This is even more apparent in developing countries where the health environment is often poor and adequate health facilities and services are lacking. For children, adequate maternal and child health care are also recognised as complementary factors [*Haddad et al., 1996*]. Indeed, a study in Ethiopia found that differences in food availability and access had a limited effect upon the differences observed in child nutritional status [*Pelletier et al., 1995*].

Even mild and moderately malnourished individuals are at increased risk of disease because of the debilitating effects on the immune system. Disease, in turn, can be a significant cause of malnutrition because of the reduction in intake and retention and/or absorption of nutrients. Increases in calorie intake do not automatically translate into improved child health and nutrition, unless the accompanying high rates of diarrhoeal disease are simultaneously addressed [*Alderman and Garcia, 1993*]. The cyclical relationship between health and nutrition is such that it is increasingly recognised that adequate health and environmental inputs must be provided alongside food interventions for the latter to have any effect on nutritional status. The disease burden of the environment must be minimised through immunisation, water, sanitation and health education programmes, and the scale and quality of health services accessible to the vulnerable must also be improved. Indeed, systematic reviews of food-based interventions alone indicate little measurable impact on nutritional status, morbidity or mortality levels except in crisis situations [*Clay, 1997*].

Growing emphasis is being placed on the role of micronutrients as a determinant of nutritional status. The interaction between micronutrient deficiencies and morbidity/mortality, particularly in young children, is increasingly recognised. Vitamin A supplementation, for example, results in an average reduction of 23 per cent in mortality rates of children under five years of age. The role of food aid commodities in supporting programmes with more refined micronutrient objectives is unclear, although it has been suggested that the proceeds of food aid monetisation could support such initiatives.

Evidence to evaluate the nutritional impact of food aid interventions is limited, in part because of the cost and complexity of obtaining accurate and reliable anthropometric data (weight-for-height and height-for-age) and also because of the methodological difficulties in disentangling the effect of food from the host of other variables impacting upon nutritional status.

1. Programme Food Aid

Recent evaluations of both the US [*McClelland, 1997*] and Canadian [*CIDA, 1998*] governments' programmes noted that PFA has seldom made a significant contribution to the alleviation of hunger and food insecurity. PFA has often replaced commercial imports that would otherwise have been brought in and so has generally not added to the available food supply. Even if it had resulted in increased aggregate food availability, this is still only a necessary but not sufficient factor in improving access for the most vulnerable.

These findings largely concur with those of the Joint Evaluation of EU Programme Food Aid [*Clay et al., 1996*], which was basically 'non-negative' in its conclusions on the relationship between food imports, food aid and nutritional status, the exception being circumstances of acute food shortage, where large-scale food aid imports are additional and supplement local supplies, and thus are crucial in preventing widespread starvation. This report also highlighted the inadequacy of using the bulk supply of food for sale as a means of supporting interventions concerned with the micronutrient composition of beneficiaries' diets.

2. Project Food Aid

The historical evidence on food-based nutritional interventions indicates little measurable impact on nutritional status, morbidity or mortality levels among targeted groups. Beaton and Ghassemi [*1982*], in their comprehensive and widely cited survey of supplementary feeding programmes, found that anthropometric improvements were surprisingly small and that programmes were expensive for measured benefits. The evidence of project food aid's impact on nutritional status from the recent round of evaluations has been similarly equivocal.

Although the USAID review of food aid states [*McClelland, 1997: 38*] that 'American food aid has its greatest social and nutritional impacts through ... direct food distribution programmes', the evidence presented is inconclusive, and this tends to be true of the other evaluations reviewed. Project food aid, where it has been successful, has typically acted as a safety net, increasing consumption in the short term rather than effecting longer-term nutritional improvements.

(i) Labour-intensive public works
The controversial use of food-for-work as a developmental tool has already been discussed. Assessment of its role as a means of raising the nutritional status of poor and vulnerable individuals has proved equally inconclusive. It has been strongly argued that providing food rather than cash as a wage results in increased household consumption, particularly if the wage is controlled by women. But, as already noted, increased consumption does not automatically translate into improved nutritional status.

A recent review of Employment Generation Scheme targeting practices in Ethiopia [*Sharp, 1997*] highlighted the phenomenon, by no means restricted to Ethiopia, of 'thin-blanket syndrome', in which rations are distributed so widely that the neediest receive too little for there to be any significant effect on their situation, nutritional or otherwise. Reasons for this over-distribution are, in part, attributable to a cultural aversion to the concept of selecting beneficiaries. Work entitlements are often too thinly shared, either by the rotation of beneficiaries or the severe limitation of the number of work days allowed per household. Frequently beneficiaries are selected and food distributed to them in accordance with project guidelines, only for the rations to be redistributed later, sometimes involuntarily, amongst the whole community. As Sharp states, this problem is a difficult one to combat and undermines the value of labour-intensive works as a nutritional guarantee. It has also been hypothesised that the heavy workload in some works projects may offset, in energy terms, the effect of the food wage and so minimise the impact on nutritional status, although at this stage there is little empirical evidence to support this theory [*Webb, 1995*].

A recent assessment of FFW in Bangladesh shows some positive impacts on the calorie consumption of participating households, but anthropometric impacts are not established [*Ahmed et al. , 1996*]. This is a problem common to many studies which focus on 'food expenditure' or *apparent* calorie intake data taken from food expenditure and consumption surveys, but which do not provide sufficient evidence to infer nutritional improvement.

Female-controlled income is usually associated with higher household food expenditure and nutrient intake than income controlled by men. So, the argument goes, by targeting FFW programmes at women, a valuable and empowering resource is placed in the hands of the family member most responsible for household food security. In his study of intra-household resource allocation in Brazil, Thomas [*1997*] found that the share of the household budget devoted to human capital, for example household services and health, increased when income was controlled by women. Specifically he found that nutrient intakes rose more quickly as women's income increased and that maternal income had a significantly greater effect than paternal income on child anthropometric indicators. Evidence from a number of studies in different geographical locations supports this assertion [*Hoddinot and Haddad, 1991*; *Engle, 1993*]. But the erratic success of FFW programmes in reaching women, as detailed in Section I, precludes there being a consistently positive impact on the nutritional status of the household.

The implications of maternal work outside the home for child care and thus child nutrition should also be considered. The evidence so far is mixed [*Engle et al., 1997*]. Some studies have demonstrated significant negative effects between maternal work and the nutritional status of children. For example, an evaluation of 2000 rural mothers in India found that the children of mothers engaged in agricultural labour were likely to be significantly malnourished [*Abbi et al., 1991*]. In contrast, other studies have found no negative effect [*Wandel and Holmboe-Ottesen, 1992*] or indeed some positive effects [*De Groote et al., 1994; Brown et al., 1994*]. Further research is obviously required to clarify the effects of maternal time availability and workload upon child health and nutritional status.

(ii) School feeding programmes
The available evidence does not provide compelling support for the use of SFPs as a means of improving child nutritional status. There is no proof that this form of intervention consistently reaches the neediest children. Furthermore, operational difficulties, including irregular food delivery and distribution and the lack of complementary financial and technical support, have continually undermined project effectiveness, and thus nutritional impact.

The WFP's distribution of food supplements to primary school children has seldom demonstrated measurable improvements in nutritional status [*Chr. Michelsen Institute, 1993a*]. Evaluation of USAID-supported interventions produced mixed findings. An evaluation of the USAID programme in Burkina Faso concluded that this 35-year school lunch project was responsible for reduced rates of malnutrition amongst the beneficiaries [*ISTI, 1981*]. But reviews of the Honduran and Ghanaian school feeding programmes reported that the average daily amount of calories provided was probably not sufficient to effect a measurable improvement in child growth or nutritional status [*Rogers et al., 1995; McClelland, 1997*].

(iii) Supplementary feeding programmes
The improved nutritional status of poor mothers and babies is generally only one objective of these programmes. As previously noted, nutrition and health education and small-scale income-generation activities are also aspects of this form of intervention. The US has evaluated its support to MCH interventions in five countries, finding mixed results. In all the programmes, food supplementation alone showed little, if any, direct or sustainable impact upon the nutrition of under-fives suffering from moderate or mild malnutrition. One possible reason is the widespread evidence of ration sharing amongst all family members. This begs the question of whether nutritional improvement is a truly appropriate objective for MCH programmes, or whether it best serves as an income transfer to poorer households [*Mora et al., 1990*]. The USAID-supported Honduran programme was judged to have had some success in raising nutritional status [*Philips et al., 1995*]. But simultaneous improvements in overall health conditions made it difficult to disentangle the effects of the food intervention from the other activities taking place, such as vaccinations and improvements in water supply/sanitation. Given the evidence of other programmes, it seems safe to assume that the nutritional impact of the MCH programme alone was minimal.

The tripartite evaluation of the WFP concluded that VGF programmes had negligible nutritional impact [*Chr. Michelsen Institute, 1993a*]. They were judged not to address the root causes of malnutrition and food insecurity and so to be ill-equipped to act as more than simply feeding interventions. Too often, they acted in isolation from the other determinants of improved nutritional status: nutrition education; income generation; potable water supply, to name but a few. Feeding projects need to be integrated within a more holistic approach to malnutrition and related diseases to maximise their nutritional impact. The inability of these interventions to link maternal nutrition and health education, immunisation and oral rehydration to the food supplement, as well as the absence of complementary environmental interventions, has so far restricted their nutritional impact.

III. A DEVELOPMENTAL ROLE IN DOUBT

Despite the methodological problems and incompleteness of the literature, the considerable number of evaluations and analyses has narrowed, if not entirely settled, the controversy surrounding the usefulness of food aid as an input for sustainable development. As the 1993 evaluation of the WFP pointed out, food for development is frequently a cumbersome resource, demanding specialist expertise and organisation [*Chr. Michelsen Institute, 1993a*]. There are also inherent institutional and community-level problems. It is frequently argued that developmental food aid projects act merely as palliatives, without addressing the root causes of poverty and food insecurity. But supporters contend that food aid provides a unique means of targeting the poorest and most vulnerable, whilst assisting long-term development. Indeed, the WFP recently reiterated its conviction that food aid is an enabling tool with 'its own niche and distinctive role' [*WFP, 1999: 3*]

Programme food aid has rarely focused on the poor and seldom had an impact on poverty alleviation efforts. A sequence of evaluations has found that PFA is an ineffective method by which to increase the income and consumption of the poorest and may even have negative short-term effects on this group through its consequences for local production. As a result, donors have reached a near-consensus that this form of food aid has a role to play only in response to acute emergencies, when there is a temporary food or foreign-exchange gap.

Project food aid takes many forms and there is a wide body of literature to draw on when judging its effectiveness. From this, the rationale for food aid-supported projects appears to be clear and strong in only a limited set of circumstances, namely, situations of food scarcity and/or market breakdown. Project food aid has proved effective when acting as a safety net for livelihoods and food security in circumstances of short-term food shortage or high inflation; as an income transfer to needier families through SFPs where enrolment levels of poorer children are high; as an input in MCH programmes in crisis and rehabilitation situations. It has not been demonstrated to have significant impacts on sustainable developmental objectives

216

either through the creation of assets or in linkages with educational and health interventions.

Food aid's ability to reach the poorest, especially women, is not consistently demonstrated by the evidence, although many projects did indeed succeed in reaching their intended beneficiaries. WFP-supported projects, for example, have provided minimal information as to positive impacts on women through their access to the food distributed, the income generated, or the assets created. This lack of empirical evidence after 30 years' experience seriously weakens claims that food is a more effective resource than cash for supporting poorer women at the household level. It is crucial that truly effective and needs-based targeting criteria and practices are defined and implemented in development programming. In their absence, the use of food aid as a developmental input is difficult to justify. It could be argued that if food aid is reaching the poor, if not the poorest, it still has some value. But supporters of food aid argue that its great advantage over other forms of aid lies in its unique ability to reach the most needy. If this is not the case, what is food aid's comparative advantage? The theme of the comparative strength of food aid for development is taken up by Jens Schulthes in Chapter 10 of this volume.

The evidence indicates that food aid interventions have rarely had a demonstrable positive impact on the nutritional status of beneficiaries, except in circumstances of acute food shortage. Under these conditions, food aid has been critical in ensuring adequate food availability to the most needy. The health environment in which many emergency distributions are undertaken is extremely hazardous, however, and this negatively affects the 'size' of the nutritional improvement that can be achieved through supplementation. Indeed, the prevalence of diseases such as diarrhoea, TB and measles in these situations can accelerate so rapidly that nutritional crises occur despite the adequate provision of food.

Chronic malnutrition has clear socio-economic dimensions in terms of poverty and social exclusion. Unless these aspects, which include access to health services, water and sanitation improvement, and economic development, are simultaneously addressed, improved nutritional status is unlikely to be realised through food supplementation alone.

REFERENCES

Abbi, R. *et al.*, 1991, 'The Impact of Maternal Work Status on the Nutrition and Health Status of Children', *Food and Nutrition Bulletin*, Vol. 13, No. 1.

Ahmed, A.U., D. Puetz, S. Zohir and N. Hassan, 1996, *Bangladesh: An Extended Study*, London: Overseas Development Institute.

Ahmed, A.U., S. Zohir, S.K. Kumar and O.H. Chowdhury, 1995, 'Bangladesh's Food-for-work Program and Alternatives to improve Food Security', in von Braun, ed.

Alderman, H. and M. Garcia, 1993, *Poverty, Household Food Security, and Nutrition in Rural Pakistan*, Research Report No. 96, Washington DC: International Food Policy Research Institute.

Australian Development Assistance Bureau, 1997, *Report of the Committee of Review on the Australian Overseas Aid Program* (The Simons Report), Canberra: AusAid.

Barrett, C.B., forthcoming, 'Food Security and Food Assistance Programmes', in B.L. Gardner and G.C. Rausser, eds., *Handbook of Agricultural Economics*, Amsterdam: Elsevier Science.

Basu, K., 1996, 'Relief Programs: When It May Be Better to Give Food Instead of Cash', *World Development*, Vol. 24, No. 1.

Beaton, G.H. and H. Ghassemi, 1982, 'Supplementary Feeding Programs for Young Children in Developing Countries', *American Journal of Clinical Nutrition*, Vol. 35, No. 4.

Brown, L.R. *et al.*, 1994, 'Rural Labor-intensive Public Works: Impacts of Participation on Preschooler Nutrition. Evidence from Niger', *American Journal of Agricultural Economics*, Vol. 76, No. 5.

Burki, S. J., D.G. Davies, R.H. Hook and J.W. Thomas, 1976, *Public Works Programs in Developing Countries: A Comparative Analysis*, World Bank Staff Paper 224, Washington DC: World Bank.

Christian Aid, 1997, 'School Supplementary Feeding Programme in Manicaland and Masvingo: Impact Indicators', London: Christian Aid (unpublished note).

Christian Michelsen Institute, 1993a, *Evaluation of the World Food Programme: Final Report*, Bergen: CMI.

Christian Michelsen Institute, 1993b, *Evaluation of the World Food Programme: Case Study – Ghana*, Working Paper, Bergen: CMI.

Christian Michelsen Institute, 1993c, *Evaluation of the World Food Programme: Case Study – Pakistan*, Working Paper, Bergen: CMI.

CIDA, 1998, *Performance Review Report: Food Aid*, Ottawa: Canadian International Development Agency, Performance Review Branch.

Clay, D.C., D. Molla and D. Habtewold, 1999, 'Food aid targeting in Ethiopia: A study of who needs it and who gets it', *Food Policy*, Vol. 24, No. 4.

Clay, E.J., 1986, 'Rural Public Works and Food-for-work: A Survey', *World Development*, Vol. 14, Nos. 10/11.

Clay, E.J., 1997, 'Food Security: A Status Review of the Literature (with special reference to the human and social dimensions of food security since the mid-1980s)' (ESCOR, No. R5911), London: Overseas Development Institute.

Clay, E. J., S. Dhiri and C. Benson, 1996, *Joint Evaluation of European Union Programme Food Aid. Synthesis Report*, London: Overseas Development Institute.

Clay, E.J., N. Pillai and C. Benson, 1998, *The Future of Food Aid: A Policy Review*, London: Overseas Development Institute.

Clay, E. J. and O. Stokke, eds., 1991, *Food Aid Reconsidered*, London: Frank Cass.

Colding, B. and P. Pinstrup-Andersen, forthcoming, 'Food Aid as a Development Assistance Instrument: Past, Present and Future', in F. Tarp, ed., *Foreign Aid and Development: Lessons Learnt and Decisions for the Future*, London: Routledge.

De Groote, H. *et al.*, 1994, 'Credit with Education for Women in Mali: Impacts on Income, Food Security, and Nutrition' (mimeo), Report to USAID, Washington DC: International Food Policy Research Institute.

Dev, S. M., 1995, 'India's (Maharashtra) Employment Guarantee Scheme: Lessons from Long Experience', in von Braun, ed.

Devereux, S., D. Lebeau and W. Pendleton, 1995, *The 1992–1993 Drought in Namibia*, Windhoek: Gainsberg Macmillan.

Drèze, J. and A. Sen, 1989, *Hunger and Public Action*, Oxford: Clarendon Press.

Eldridge, C., 1997, 'Drought in Zimbabwe: Effects and Responses at Household Level', Mbabane: Save the Children Fund (UK), Regional Office for Southern Africa.

Engle, P. L., 1993, 'Influences of Mother's and Father's Income on Children's Nutritional Status in Guatemala', *Social Science and Medicine*, Vol. 37, No. 11.

Engle, P.L., P. Menon and L. Haddad, 1997, *Care And Nutrition. Concepts and Measurement*, Washington DC: International Food Policy Research Institute.

Ferreira Duarte, R. and M. Metz, 1996, *Cape Verde: An Extended Study*, London: Overseas Development Institute.

Freeman, T., R. Vandenberg and B. Vincent, 1997, 'Principal Observations from CIDA's Food Aid Performance Review', Ottawa: Canadian International Development Agency, Performance Review Division.

Guest, B., 1997, 'Evaluation of the Multi Year Food Aid Program to Bangladesh', Ottawa: Canadian International Development Agency, Performance Review Division.

Haddad, L. *et al.*, 1996, *Managing Interactions Between Household Food Security and Preschooler Health*, Discussion Paper 16, Washington DC: International Food Policy Research Institute.

Hirway, I. and P. Terhal, 1994, *Towards Employment Guarantee in India*, New Delhi: Sage.

Hoddinott, J. and L. Haddad, 1991, *Household Expenditures, Child Anthropometric Status, and the Intrahousehold Division of Income: Evidence from Côte d'Ivoire*, Research Program in Development Studies, Discussion Paper No. 155, Princeton, NJ: Woodrow Wilson School of Public and International Affairs, Princeton University.

International Science and Technology Institute (ISTI), 1981, 'Upper Volta Food for Peace/Title II Evaluation Final Report', Washington DC: USAID.

Jackson, T. with D. Eade, 1982, *Against the Grain: the Dilemma of Project Food Aid*, Oxford: Oxfam.

Maxwell, S., 1991, 'The Disincentive Effect of Food Aid: A Pragmatic Approach', in Clay and Stokke, eds.

McClelland, D.G., 1997, 'Food Aid and Sustainable Development – Forty Years of Experience', Center for Development Information and Evaluation, Washington DC: USAID.

Middlebrook, P., 1999, 'The Road Ahead: New Directions for Employment Generation Schemes in Ethiopia?', paper presented at the WFP Workshop on Employment Generation Schemes, Addis Ababa (Feb.).

Moffitt, R., 1992, 'Incentive Effects of the US Welfare System: A Review', *Journal of Economic Literature*, Vol. 30, No. 1.

Mora, J., J. King and C. Teller, 1990, 'The Effectiveness of Maternal and Child Health Supplementary Feeding Programmes', Logical Technical Services.

Pelletier, D.L. *et al.*, 1995, 'The food-first bias and nutrition policy: Lessons from Ethiopia', *Food Policy*, Vol. 20, No. 4.

Philips, M. *et al.*, 1995, 'The Costs and Cost-Effectiveness of School Feeding and School Bonos Programmes in Honduras', Tegucigalpa: USAID/Honduras.

Rempel, E., 1997, 'NGO Multi-Year Food For Work Program Review', Niverville: Canadian International Development Agency, Performance Review Division.

Rogers, B. *et al.*, 1995, 'Food and Income Subsidies and Primary Schooling in Rural Honduras: An Evaluation of the Impact of the Bonos and PL 480 Title II School Feeding Programmes', Washington DC: USAID.

Save the Children Fund (SCF), 1997, 'Tekeze Lowlands, North East Ethiopia: Household Food Economy Analysis', London: SCF.

Sharp, K., 1997, *Targeting Food Aid in Ethiopia*, Addis Ababa: Save the Children Fund (UK).

Shoham, J., 1994, *Emergency Supplementary Feeding Programmes*, Good Practice Review No. 2, London: Overseas Development Institute.

Thomas, D., 1997, 'Incomes, Expenditures, and Health Outcomes: Evidence on Intrahousehold Resource Allocation', in L. Haddad, ed., *Intrahousehold Resource Allocation in Developing Countries. Models, Methods and Policy*, Baltimore, MD: Johns Hopkins University Press.

USAID, 1989, 'The Development Impact of US Program Food Assistance: Evidence from the A.I.D. Evaluation Literature', Washington DC: Bureau for Food for Peace and Voluntary Assistance.

UNDP, 1996, *Human Development Report*, Oxford: Oxford University Press.

Vandenburg, R., 1997, 'Lessons from Evaluations of CIDA Bilateral Food Aid', Ottawa: Canadian International Development Agency, Performance Review Division.

von Braun, J., T. Teklu and P. Webb, 1991, *Labor-Intensive Public Works for Food Security: Experience in Africa*, Working Papers on Food Subsidies No. 6, Washington DC: International Food Policy Research Institute (July).

von Braun, J., ed., 1995, *Employment for Poverty Reduction and Food Security*, Washington DC: International Food Policy Research Institute.

Wandel, M. and G. Holmboe-Ottesen, 1992, 'Maternal Work, Child Feeding, and Nutrition in Rural Tanzania', *Food and Nutrition Bulletin*, Vol. 14, No. 1.

Webb, P., 1995, 'Employment Programs for Food Security in Rural and Urban Africa: Experiences in Niger and Zimbabwe', in von Braun, ed.

Webb, P. and S. Moyo, 1992, 'Food Security through Employment in Southern Africa: Labor-Intensive Programmes in Zimbabwe', Report for GTZ, Washington DC: International Food Policy Research Institute.

World Bank, 1989, 'Jamaica: Adjustment under Changing Economic Conditions', Washington DC: World Bank, Country Department III, Latin America and the Caribbean Regional Office.

WFP, 1999, *Enabling Development*, Rome: World Food Programme.

Zhu Ling and Jiang Zhongyi, 1995, 'Yigong-Daizhen, China: A New Experience with Labor-Intensive Public Works in Poor Areas', in von Braun, ed.

9

The World Food Programme (WFP) and International Food Aid

JUST FAALAND, DIANA MCLEAN
AND OLE DAVID KOHT NORBYE

I. THE ORIGIN AND DEVELOPMENT OF THE WORLD FOOD PROGRAMME

By the early 1960s food aid had become an important part of bilateral development assistance. Food surpluses were produced, notably in North America, and were made available as food aid, mostly in the form of bilateral programme aid to food-deficit countries. The food thus supplied was sold on the domestic market and the sales proceeds – the counterpart funds – were made available for development expenditure. At the time, such food aid was clearly additional to other development assistance, and this helped to ease the macro-economic problems of the recipient developing countries. The impact of this kind of food transfer on the nutritional conditions of the very poor, however, was at best indirect. Yet it was recognised that, if differently organised, food aid could also be used more *directly* to feed undernourished people, most urgently under emergency conditions and also in areas and situations of recurrent or permanent food shortage and undernourishment.

In 1961 this led the United Nations General Assembly and the Food and Agriculture Organisation (FAO) Conference to approve the formation of a World Food Programme as a joint subsidiary body, on a three-year experimental basis. The rationale was that 'the effective utilization of available surplus food stuffs ... provided an important transitional means of relieving the hunger and malnutrition of food-deficient peoples, particularly in the less developed countries, and for assisting these countries in their economic development' [*UN, 1961; FAO, 1961*]. In 1965 the WFP was put on a regular footing and its life extended 'for as long as multilateral food aid is found feasible and desirable'. As the need for food aid in emergencies became more frequent, and following a recommendation of the 1974 World Food Conference, an International Emergency Food Reserve (IEFR) was established in 1976 'as an emergency reserve to strengthen the capacity of the Programme to deal with crisis situations in developing countries'.

Throughout its life of almost four decades the *raison d'être* and functioning of the WFP have evolved, and in the 1990s the Programme was subjected to a much needed further evaluation, review and reform. This chapter deals mainly with the analysis, findings, recommendations and follow-up of the so-called Tripartite Evaluation of 1992–93, described in section II below. The world in which the WFP operates has greatly changed and further change is foreseen, notably in four respects: first, market surpluses of food production in developed countries are dwindling, as are government-held food stocks; second, prices of major food grains are expected to rise; third, international aid flows generally are on the decline or at best have levelled out; and fourth, the need for food aid in emergencies has increased significantly in the recent past and is expected to remain, or at least recur, at a new, higher level.

Moreover, the challenge to the WFP has always been to demonstrate – initially on an experimental basis – that surplus food, when provided as aid, could be effectively used both to alleviate the hunger and malnutrition of the poor in developing countries and to underpin and accelerate the rate of their overall development. As the record shows, the WFP has proved itself a most useful instrument of support for food security during emergencies and crises, but has not been able to show convincingly that its food-based development projects are generally successful and efficient in support of development. When, as in the past, food aid could be considered as largely additional to other development assistance, the requirement to show the cost-effectiveness of the WFP development efforts was often readily met; even so, questions were sometimes raised about the role of the WFP as a development agency. In recent years, in the new environment of increasing market dominance and decreasing aid, the debate has intensified.

Thus, there is not much controversy about the potential usefulness of food aid in emergency cases, although financial aid could also be used to procure the food supplies needed in such situations. But the usefulness of food aid to support development, either as balance of payments *cum* budget support (programme aid) or as a resource for development projects, is subject to considerable controversy. In this chapter that deals with the role of the World Food Programme, we shall mostly concentrate on its function as a development agency.

In 1993, when the Tripartite Evaluation was conducted, total food aid reached a peak of nearly 17 million tonnes. Three years later, in 1996, this total had shrunk to less than half, mainly as a result of a drop of two-thirds in programme aid and one-half in relief. Project aid, however, has fluctuated between two and three million tonnes a year in the 1990s [WFP, 1997c: Tables 9 and 14]. The share of the WFP in total food aid shipments was around one-sixth in the late 1980s, but rose sharply to around one-quarter in the 1990s, primarily as a consequence of its enhanced role in handling relief shipments, for which it took on little more than one-fifth in the late 1980s and well over one-half in 1996.

In the 1990s, the WFP's share of food aid for development activities fluctuated considerably: it reached a peak of over one-half in 1992; it was little more than one-third in 1996 [ibid: 31; WFP, 1997d: Tables 4–7]. Between those years the volume of food channelled through the WFP for its development projects was halved to 670,000 tonnes. The WFP itself expects no reversal of this decline; it assumes that five years hence there will have been a further 10 per cent decline [WFP, 1997a: 36].

II. THE TRIPARTITE EVALUATION OF THE WORLD FOOD PROGRAMME

During 1992/93 the development aid authorities of Canada, the Netherlands and Norway collaborated in sponsoring a comprehensive evaluation of the World Food Programme. It was performed by independent experts[1] working in close co-operation with the WFP both at its headquarters in Rome and at its country offices in nine developing countries in Africa, Asia and Latin America. The report[2] was published early in 1994 after the final draft had been discussed with representatives of the three governments and senior officials of the World Food Programme. The analysis, findings and recommendations of the report are presented, albeit summarily, in this section.

---

1. The three authors of this chapter were all members of the evaluation team.
2. Governments of Canada, the Netherlands and Norway, *Evaluation of the World Food Programme: Main Report 1994*. Canada — Canadian International Development Agency. Netherlands — Ministry of Foreign Affairs. Norway — Royal Ministry of Foreign Affairs. Ottawa, 1994. In addition, a short summary was also published as well as nine country studies of Bangladesh, Bolivia, Ethiopia, Ghana, Guatemala, Malawi, Morocco, Pakistan and Vietnam.

1. The Global Market

In the developed world, the relentless advance of technology since 1950 and the widespread practice of basing income support to farmers on production, have together driven farm output to levels exceeding domestic requirements and trading opportunities. In the developing countries, production has also increased – in some cases most impressively – but in many Least Developed Countries and in particular in sub-Saharan Africa this has not been enough to prevent a decline in per capita output in the past decade. These countries are severely constrained in mobilising foreign exchange to finance food and other imports needed. Moreover, given the extent of undernutrition in many developing countries, as well as the extent of food insecurity at household level, the case for food aid remains strong.

In the opinion of the evaluation team food aid has two major advantages: first, to some, though today rather limited, extent it may be additional to other development aid, and, second, food can be a particularly valuable resource in some circumstances, provided that it is composed of food items of the right kind, that it arrives at the right moment, and that in fact it reaches the intended beneficiaries.

If, as expected, ongoing policy changes in the EU and other developed countries lead to increases in world prices of food, they will also raise the opportunity cost of food aid as seen by the donors. This, in turn, will require a review of the efficiency of food aid in support of development projects compared with financial aid, not only for aid through the WFP, but for food aid in general.

The inherent cost inefficiency of food aid in kind in food-for-work development projects is sometimes aggravated by a shortage of complementary non-food items, including both material and human support. Yet, even when food-for-work activities have only a marginal impact, they may be effective in meeting critical needs of combating hunger and malnutrition, albeit only transitorily. The feeding element of food aid-assisted projects is an important objective in itself, which might or might not (according to country circumstances) be pursued as well or better with the more flexible aid resource of money rather than food products.

When food is used directly as a resource in development projects, it is not only the food supplies themselves which are important, but also the quality and experience of the people who design and implement the projects. Bilateral aid agencies, NGOs and the WFP have acquired valuable expertise in project activities in which the feeding of poor and vulnerable people is the major objective.

The evaluation team recommended that donor countries without market surpluses of food products, where food aid is financed within the development aid budget, should consider providing their contribution in cash, not tied to food items, whether through the WFP or through other agencies. Also, for emergency assistance to meet the food requirements of the affected populations, the evaluation team urged that resources be mobilised by the donors as much as possible in cash rather than kind. Where appropriate, this would permit food to be purchased either in surplus areas in the stricken country or nearby, and would avoid the long lead-time required for the mobilisation and transport of food from donor countries.

2. Mandate, Governance and Working Relationships

The evaluation found that the mandate of the WFP and its operational mode will call for further consideration as global food supply and trading conditions unfold, as the food aid policies of the major donors change, and as the perceptions for appropriate development modes evolve. Yet, at the time, the judgement of the evaluation team was that a major mandate review would be premature.

The evaluation team suggested that the risk of being saddled with weak projects could be reduced by changes in the way in which the Committee on Food Aid Policies and Programmes (CFA) approached the WFP's development role. The CFA and management had not gone far enough, it was found, to focus the WFP's work at country level, and in moving towards a programme as distinct from a project approach. Changes in these respects, it was suggested, would enable the CFA's Subcommittee on Projects (SCP) to have a greater impact; they would also permit greater delegation of authority for project approval by the Executive Director. A more active role by the CFA in monitoring the quality of WFP programmes at country level was urged.

As seen by the evaluation team, the CFA fell short of being an effective body for handling international food aid policies. It was suggested that the debate on policy questions be much more clearly separated in the CFA from WFP housekeeping matters, and that governments be encouraged to send to CFA meetings representatives chosen according to the precise nature of the issues to be discussed.

Moreover, a clearer policy was needed regarding country eligibility for WFP development food aid, replacing objective criteria for *ad hoc* decisions. The overall thrust should be to reduce the number of countries in which the WFP operates.

The WFP should seek a clearer understanding with each recipient country on how the WFP's development aid would best support government policies and priorities, through a policy dialogue with which the WFP should seek to associate other food aid donors and funding agencies.

Arrangements should be made for recipient governments to be more closely and systematically associated with the development of Project Ideas. Particularly in the final stages of the Project Cycle, WFP Headquarters should refrain from introducing changes without consulting its Country Office and/or the recipient government.

One way for the WFP of reducing the risk of failure in project implementation is to build closer relationships with the implementing agencies and thus ensure that WFP projects receive the attention they require for effective operation. Since shortage of staff is likely to be a constraint, generous arrangements for training would have to be included in the project.

The WFP is required by its General Regulations to co-operate with other UN agencies. This co-operation may be extended and assume a more integrated form in the future, going far beyond present arrangements, if UN resolutions to those ends are fully implemented. The evaluation team strongly recommended that the WFP explore more actively with other specialised development agencies the acceptability and practicability of channelling more of its food aid resources through joint projects, as it has done in several cases with IFAD and also the World Bank.

3. Resources

WFP resources are made available through a series of 'windows'. Regular resources are used mainly for development projects and the administrative budget. At the time of the evaluation, the proportion of resources provided in cash, needed for transport and administrative costs, had been rising; however, it still fell short of the agreed target of one-third. A separate window had been established in 1989 for Protracted Refugee or Displaced Person Operations (PROs). Commodity pledges under this window were to be accompanied by whatever cash was needed for their transport. The International Emergency Food Reserve (IEFR) funded all WFP emergency operations. Pledges to the IEFR can be made in advance or may be made *ad hoc* for particular emergencies; they may be untied or restricted to a specific purpose. In practice, the IEFR has been difficult to manage because of the relatively small proportion of untied advance pledges. The Immediate Response Account (IRA) has a cash window to get emergency

operations off to a quick start by purchasing foodstuffs in the neigh-
bourhood of the stricken area. Its target for 1993 was US$30 million,
but contributions and pledges by mid-year amounted to only US$17
million. Contributions for Special Emergency Operations cover airlifts or other major logistic expenditure for relief. Contributions for
non-food items (NFI) are made available on a limited scale both for
development projects and for PROs. Finally, on a direct cost coverage
basis, the WFP provides bilateral services to donors – working in
effect as their agent – in the fields of food purchase, transport and
monitoring.

As a result of the very high costs of relief operations, just over half
of all WFP expenditure in 1992 was in cash rather than commodities.
One-third of these cash contributions were used by the WFP for the
purchase of commodities; in fact, slightly more than one-quarter (by
value) of all commodities handled by the WFP in that year were purchased. A further major item of cash expenditure was charges for the
internal transport, storage and handling (ITSH) of commodities which
may be paid by the WFP (rather than the recipient government) in
Least Developed Countries and those in similar conditions.

The evaluation team reviewed WFP practice in commodity purchases, commodity swaps and the monetisation of commodities (*inter
alia* to pay for cash expenditure on ITSH) and found that all these
devices were helpful in increasing the flexibility and efficiency of
operations. The WFP's food basket, as augmented and adjusted
through swaps and purchases, appeared to be generally appropriately
balanced.

The evaluation team was not convinced that it was useful to have
an arbitrary limit of 15 per cent on the proportion of commodities that
could be monetised; on balance, the technique of monetisation had
probably been under-utilised by the WFP. A more flexible approach
to monetisation was therefore advocated, under which the WFP would
have some liberty to monetise resources in particular circumstances
and for pre-defined purposes.

Four sets of problems were highlighted for future review of funding
arrangements. First, as the funding structure was rather complicated,
simplification in the form of a smaller number of resource windows
seemed desirable. Donors should be encouraged to make multi-year
contributions so as to reduce the inherent problem of, on the one
hand, the WFP having to make food aid commitments for many of its
projects of up to five years or more, while, on the other hand, resources available to it were typically pledged for only up to two years. In
order to reconcile short-term pledging with longer-term project

227

commitments the WFP should develop a more sophisticated model for projecting the total resource requirements of approved projects in future biannual pledging periods.

Second, in the interest of more flexibility generally and given the need for a smooth transition from relief through rehabilitation to development, there appeared to be a case for a less absolute division between resources for emergencies and resources for development.

Third, the IRA should be fully funded as a priority for special donor contributions for as long as the WFP has a serious cash problem and cannot afford to use unrestricted cash pledges to kick-start emergency operations. The IRA could be dispensed with as a special window if and when there was ample cash within the regular resources.

Fourth, the IEFR in its present form bore only limited resemblance to what was envisaged by the World Food Conference. Indeed it was little more than a label attached to WFP emergency operations. As such, it might inhibit the flexible use of resources for either relief or development. However, the IEFR would be a really useful facility if there were a major increase in advance and untied pledges and at the same time donors found a way to allow it to carry over unutilised resources from one financial period to another. In this way it would be possible to build up, in periods of low activity, a genuine reserve that could be drawn upon in years when relief needs were unexpectedly high.

4. Organisation and Management

Many of the issues raised in the Tripartite Evaluation related to strictly administrative and managerial problems, but in this review only matters which have a direct bearing on the way food aid is utilised are included.

At the time of the evaluation major changes in the organisational structure had been implemented. The five Regional Bureaux at WFP Headquarters (HQ) had been made responsible for all phases of emergency operations and PROs, including assessment. The former Disaster Relief Service had become the Emergency Division with responsibility for managing emergency activities carried out by the Regional Bureaux and forming an emergency support service. The Emergency Division was placed at the same level as the Development Division in an effort to bring relief and development closer together. In fact, the WFP had coped with the requirements to build up relief operations by mobilising its development staff to carry out emergency operations. As seen by the evaluation team, a number of ambiguities remained in the new arrangement, including the degree of control that the Director of Emergencies was able to exercise over the Regional Bureaux Managers.

Following the shift of responsibility to the Regional Bureaux, staff members who had been recruited for development were now also handling all phases of emergency operations. The evaluation team recommended that a thorough performance review of all staff involved be undertaken, to relieve from such duties those who did not appear to possess the necessary aptitude for relief work by reassigning them so as to allow them to concentrate exclusively on development.

The team urged the WFP to go ahead with the formation of a Rapid Response Team. Besides selecting a core of permanent staff, the unit should establish and draw on a roster of individuals who could be made available immediately when required; it might also consider the recruitment of a small number of international staff especially for service in areas of conflict. The question of special conditions of service for staff exposed to physical danger is of concern to all humanitarian organisations of the UN system, and certainly for the WFP.

In January 1993 the WFP maintained 87 staffed Country Offices, many of them in areas of the world where basic infrastructure, facilities and communications are poor. In the present era of UN reforms and donor constraints, it was unlikely that the WFP would be able significantly to solve staffing issues with additional people; it seemed more realistic for it to consider closing some Country Offices, consolidating its diverse portfolio, relying more on national staff in Country Offices, more fully joining forces with other UN agencies, international finance institutions and other donors, etc. so as to better match WFP activities and responsibilities with existing staff.

On the issue of food management, the evaluation noted that, while the commodities available from year to year were still strongly correlated with surpluses in the WFP's major donor countries, the WFP had obtained a reputation for relatively efficient resourcing of commodities. Its outstanding reputation was strengthened by an evaluation carried out for the European Communities which pointed to the WFP as generally the most effective agency. The 1990 Nordic Study of the UN 'recommended that the World Food Programme be formally designated as the UN agency with primary responsibility for matters relating to logistics and transport for both food and non-food items, including assistance to countries in developing their own transport arrangements' [Nordic UN Project, 1991].

As regards the WFP's internal decision-making structure, the Tripartite Evaluation found the in-house Project Committee to be a major point of weakness, and was particularly critical of its functioning and apparent lack of control over the quality of development projects. In respect of staff capability the most visible weakness was the relative absence of specialists available for support in design and implementation of development projects. The country case studies provided further evidence that limits of competence in project planning and management were so clearly exceeded that drastic reductions in the number, scope and complexity of projects were called for.

At the time of the evaluation in 1993, the Executive Director had expressed her determination to decentralise decision-making to the extent possible. The evaluation team generally supported placing more responsibilities on those closest to field operations and again stressed that the concentration of available staff in fewer Country Offices was the most effective solution in a situation of staff constraint.

5. Relief Operations

Up to the end of the 1980s relief operations represented in most years less than half of the WFP's distribution of food. In the early 1990s this changed: WFP shipments for emergency operations and PROs in 1992 were about two-thirds higher than for development projects. In 1993 the WFP handled more than half of all international food for relief.

The first important stage of a relief operation is the assessment of needs, for which there is no uniform 'best practice'. Thus, for instance, needs arising from crop failures must be assessed differently from those of refugees or displaced persons. In the former case, based on a macro-level assessment of the immediate food situation and its outlook, an estimate of food aid needs is normally prepared jointly by FAO and the WFP in consultation with the government concerned. In the latter case of refugees or displaced persons, the key question is the number of people to be fed. The evaluators found that there was a need for a more sophisticated approach to providing answers to this question and urged the WFP to work with the UNHCR to develop a firmer basis for the determination of the numbers of refugees or displaced persons in need. The evaluation report also recommended that overall needs assessment be combined with a further developed micro-assessment, so as to ensure greater effectiveness in WFP emergency operations.

Given the experience gained within the WFP in relief operations, the WFP should be in a position to make itself available at short notice and in answer to a government request to assist in relief planning. To this end, and generally to be able to respond quickly in emergency situations, the WFP was advised to establish a specially recruited and directed Rapid Response Team. The evaluators found that there was quite some way to go to ensure improved planning and targeting of relief; adapting operations to local coping systems and maintaining the resilience of communities; taking into account the role of the commercial sector and the local trading system; and ensuring, wherever possible, that the aid provided helped to deal with the root causes of the emergency and to reinforce long-term development objectives.

The country studies indicated that the interfacing of relief and development was difficult to achieve, since in many situations the requisite capacity was not available in the national and local administrations concerned. It is helpful to distinguish between attempting to reach developmental goals through relief operations and gearing development projects to disaster prevention. The evaluation reviewed WFP documents available at the time, which included reports of successful examples in both categories, and briefly examined aspects of vulnerability mapping, early warning systems, post-emergency rehabilitation, and the use of food security stocks for disaster preparedness.

Since its inception, the WFP has been wrestling with the long delivery-cycle for food coming from distant donors to meet emergency needs as and where they arise. Borrowing from in-country stocks, purchasing food from surplus areas in the country affected or nearby, and diverting shipments already on the high seas are some of the basic techniques used to get operations off to a quick start. The evaluators found that, in general, such arrangements and actions had been successful; in fact, none of the country studies reported major difficulties in this respect. However, as borrowing and diversion of shipments can create secondary problems, the authority, funds and capacity to kick-start operations with purchases, locally and in the region, are particularly important for WFP effectiveness; donors were therefore urged to ensure the full funding of the Immediate Response Account.

The evaluation addressed the issue of monetising food aid for relief purposes. Here the major worry is whether this increases the risk that aid may reach those who can afford to buy food and exclude those who are destitute. After a review of WFP experience, the evaluation concluded that the WFP should continue to experiment cautiously with monetisation in emergency situations, but also in every case conduct a full *ex-post* assessment of the pros and cons.

The evaluation brought out clearly the need to monitor the WFP's operations systematically, including, where possible, economic, social and nutritional indicators. Specifically, the resumption of formal evaluation of relief operations was advocated, as well as a critical review of evaluation methodologies.

The ultimate observation of the evaluation on this subject was that donors have three main options: to provide emergency assistance bilaterally; to work through NGOs; or to use the World Food Programme. There was no other polyvalent international organisation in a position to provide the services offered by the WFP.

6. Development Project Portfolio

The WFP's development portfolio was examined in the Tripartite Evaluation with a view to determining whether there was any discernible pattern of project effectiveness which might suggest that some types of development activity were meeting with greater success than others. The analysis of a detailed classification of the WFP's development portfolio raised the question whether the WFP ought to concentrate on a much more limited range of activities in the interest of greater efficiency. Each type of activity requires its own specialist expertise to design, implement and evaluate and makes its own special demands on government capacity in recipient countries. The evaluation concluded that such concentration was necessary to enable the WFP to perform at acceptable levels of efficiency and effectiveness.

Each major type of project showed mixed performance. Key problems noted in the case of agricultural projects included lengthy payback periods for investments by farmers, lack of integration of project activities into local production and marketing systems and very limited success in achieving agricultural development objectives in the wider context of rural development. Evaluations of forestry projects also showed varied performance; projects carried out in China appeared to have been very successful, while in a number of other countries considerable difficulties had been encountered.

As regards food-for-work projects in general, the review showed that there had been considerable problems in the design of projects, often reflecting unrealistic assumptions about the implementation capacities of governments, as well as insufficient provision of technical assistance. There was a general lack of evaluation of the impact of food-for-work projects on the poor, and inadequate attention was given to targeting in general, and to community participation in particular.

Similarly, supplementary feeding projects, that cover school feeding and vulnerable groups' development, had met with difficulties in targeting, and in some cases resulted in the emergence of dependence. Here again, there was a general lack of evaluation of the impact of the projects.

The evidence as evaluated demonstrated no clear case for the WFP to favour or eliminate projects in agriculture, forestry, vulnerable group development or school feeding. Success was highly dependent on local conditions, on the strengths of the key counterpart agencies, as well as on the WFP's capacity to ensure adequate project design, implementation and evaluation. The evaluation did bring out, however, a marked need to integrate food aid with technical and financial assistance, such as can be provided from the UNDP, the World Bank, IFAD and others.

On a more technical point, but one of great importance for WFP deployment of its resources, attention was drawn to the fact that the WFP continued to draw the line between the Low Income Food Deficit (LIFD) countries of priority concern for the WFP and those better-off at a very much higher level than that used by the World Bank and others for identification of countries to benefit from particularly generous treatment. The WFP and the CFA were advised to reconsider the criteria for classifying a country as LIFD.

7. *Process and Performance*

In the Tripartite Evaluation the process of planning, approval, implementation, monitoring and evaluation of WFP-assisted development projects was reviewed with a view to assessing performance and elaborating recommendations and suggestions for improvements.

The evaluation stressed that the WFP's activities must be integrated more fully into the national development strategies of the countries with which it works. The preparation of a Country Strategy Outline is one device to assist with this. However, as seen in the evaluation, it was unrealistic to expect most Country Offices to be able to develop such strategic documents on their own. In fact, the WFP at country level was seen as rather passive in the debate on how best to use food efficiently and effectively in support of development.

The WFP has laid down a series of six steps to be followed in project preparation. Yet an evaluation of Project Summaries (which describe the basis of the projects) concluded that project preparation was often analytically and operationally weak; also, at times, important issues raised by technical experts had been ignored or only superficially considered. More quality control over proposed development projects, assisted as needed by specialist staff, was called for, with a view to avoiding the many design deficiencies noted in the field. The country studies questioned the WFP's *capacity*, not its willingness and good intentions to ensure a reasonable level of design quality for the projects it supports with food aid.

One of the key weaknesses noted in the country studies was the excessively optimistic assumption made about the administrative and programming capacity of counterpart agencies. At the same time – and partly as a consequence of this lack of realism – measures to secure technical assistance when required were generally inadequate. Another issue was that projects requiring complementary non-food items were sometimes approved without any assurance that such inputs could be provided, with serious consequences for project implementation.

By contrast, the WFP appeared to be fully capable of dealing effectively with commodity exchanges and almost all Country Offices visited were also able to manage food movements successfully and support the logistics involved. Also, the types of commodities made available by the WFP were generally well accepted by the recipient; in fact, at times, rations provided in food-for-work projects had a higher value than local wages, with the result that better-off farmers and labourers were attracted to the projects, thus impairing the self-targeting nature of food aid to the poorest.

Monitoring of projects is an important major function of the WFP. The evaluators were favourably impressed by the quality of management reviews and of interim and thematic evaluations, but noted the lack of information about impact. The WFP's capacity to monitor development projects was stretched beyond reasonable limits. There was hardly any assessment of data on the effectiveness of projects and almost no information on their impacts. The quality of monitoring and reporting suffered from a lack of agreed and relevant indicators of achievement, particularly at the level of immediate objectives; moreover, there was little systematic monitoring of the fulfilment of project preconditions, even those upon which WFP involvement was expressly conditioned. A number of important specific evaluation problems were identified: there was a lack of baseline data and of qualitative information on beneficiaries; targeting was seldom considered in depth in project design and evaluation; very little was known about how WFP food was used by households; and economic analyses of projects were seldom undertaken. A major recommendation of the Tripartite Evaluation, therefore, was that the WFP move towards fewer, perhaps larger, projects with less complex objectives and lower expectations, more focused sector approaches and fewer country programmes.

The WFP was strongly urged to move more decisively towards a country programme approach and to adhere more rigorously to programming objectives when approving projects. There was a clear need for it to assess more realistically the capacity of implementing agencies, and to be more active and consistent in providing institutional support, including relevant training and systems for effective project management. Moreover, targeting of projects could be improved to ensure that benefits reach more effectively the most food-deficit regions, the poorest and most food-insecure members of the community, and that women participate more fully. More effective community-level participation in the identification of project activities would help to ensure a community sense of ownership and responsibility for maintenance of the assets created.

In order to upgrade the technical capacity in project design, the evaluation recommended a stronger complement of technical specialist staff at HQ; more flexible and innovative arrangements for using outside consultants, including those from other UN agencies; and an expanded use of national consultants by Country Offices.

The evaluation noted that many of the most successful WFP projects were those in which other development organisations had taken the lead, with the WFP supplying food as the input. Greater efforts were urged, therefore, by the WFP in particular but also the international system generally, to integrate WFP food aid into projects formulated and implemented by other UN agencies, the international financial institutions, and other agencies with stronger technical expertise.

Finally, as a development agency the WFP needs to be much more active in ensuring that its assistance, with its inevitable tendency to create budgetary dependence for key ministries, is accompanied by an explicit programme of action for phasing out that assistance, and for budgetary and institutional sustainability. The team emphasised, however, that there are situations where it is fully justified to keep a food-aided project going for many years, even decades.

8. The Future

At the end of the intensive Tripartite Evaluation exercise a view of a possible future evolution of the WFP was elaborated, reflecting shared judgements.

While adjustments were identified as needed in the way the WFP goes about its business as a relief agency, these were generally of a marginal and incremental nature. The firm judgement of the evaluation, therefore, was that the WFP would remain in the future a critically important and effective channel of food relief operations, well deserving of donor support.

As regards its work as a development agency, the analysis had pointed to some successes, but had also identified a disturbing number of weaknesses in its development projects. In essence, the WFP performs well in the physical movement of food but has been much less successful in coping with the strictly development aspects of its projects. For it to remain in the business of implementing food aid projects for development is therefore open to question. In forming a judgement on this issue, the Tripartite Evaluation placed special emphasis on the argument of equity. It noted that even some of the richest nations have domestic food programmes for the benefit of people living below the poverty line. If a development programme targeted at the poorest people in the poorest countries, organised by the United Nations system, based on bringing food to the hungry and aiming at long-term impact as well as short-term benefits, could be run effectively and efficiently, it would continue to deserve the support of its donors. Therefore, the conclusion was formulated: 'we should be thinking of improving effectiveness and efficiency, not about winding up the programme.'

When forming a judgement of the WFP's performance, it must be borne in mind that food is a less flexible – and in some ways more difficult – resource to handle than financial and technical aid. Furthermore, concentrating its efforts, as it should, on the least developed and other low-income countries, where implementation capacity is weakest, the WFP faces challenges of extraordinary difficulty. However, even making allowance for these inherent difficulties, it was concluded that the WFP could have done a better job. The evaluation indicated that the WFP had made two strategic errors: it had gone in too much for stand-alone WFP projects and it had offered too broad a range of project types. Nevertheless, more positively, the WFP had built up over the years a very considerable and potentially valuable capacity for handling poverty- and hunger-related projects, and a wide experience of what works and does not work in particular countries.

The team put forward three options for the future:

– to reduce the number of countries in which the WFP operates, concentrating on those with the lowest incomes, especially those which are disaster-prone,

- to keep the present spread of countries, but limit activities to a much narrower band of project types in which food aid functions well, or
- to phase out development projects except for relief-related development activities (disaster preparedness, rehabilitation, PROs, settlement of repatriated refugees).

9. A Final Comment

The Tripartite Evaluation did not have as its principal objective to evaluate food aid as such, but to review the way in which the WFP handled the food aid that is channelled through it. The bulk of the evaluation, therefore, dealt with the WFP as a development and relief agency, and many of the problems covered by the evaluation are common to all development and relief agencies, regardless of whether they are multilateral or bilateral, have large or small financial resources, are governmental or NGOs. In fact, the numerous evaluations which have been made of other aid agencies, or of individual activities or projects, reveal most of the same problems as those exposed by the Tripartite Evaluation of the WFP.

The evaluation underlined the difference between food aid as a *resource* and food aid as a *tool* or *input* to be used directly. As a direct input food aid has limited uses, and a main lesson from the evaluation is that more circumspection is called for to ensure that food aid is used as a tool only when it is clearly appropriate. The evaluation also stressed that, even when it is efficient to use food products directly, it is not necessary that donors provide their support in kind. On the contrary, financial assistance can be used to buy food, the right kind of food, from the most convenient suppliers. There is clearly a strong need to supply hungry people with food, but food aid in kind is not a necessary condition for achieving this objective.

III. FOLLOW-UP OF RECOMMENDATIONS: POLICY ISSUES

Evaluations often – too often – take the form of a quick review by a group of outsiders who then express their views on how a project should have been designed and implemented or an organisation ought to have been managed; this can usually be of only limited value. The Tripartite Evaluation was organised and financed so as to be based on thorough studies of the available documentation and lengthy discussions with those involved in the operations, giving the evaluators the opportunity to become familiar with the various aspects of the WFP and to draw on the views of the many insiders who themselves had their own ideas on desirable changes in the way in which their institution could be operated. As a consequence, the evaluation was taken seriously by the WFP: it has not gathered dust on bookshelves during the years that have passed since it was completed.[3]

The Chair of the CFA extracted a list of 94 suggestions and recommendations found in the evaluation report, and developed a management section grid from them, indicating responsible parties and target dates for completion. Many of these actions were for the donor community and the governing body, and were broadly classified as policy issues and management issues, but with some overlap. In this section and the next we deal with these policy and management issues respectively.

The WFP has reported periodically on the progress made in implementing the recommendations, the last review of such progress being dated June 1997. The WFP has acted or initiated action on nearly every suggestion and recommendation made in the Tripartite Evaluation. In some cases it has taken even bolder actions than were suggested. Here we shall not attempt to describe all the changes made – routinely reported to each Executive Board as 'Reform and Revitalisation Measures in the WFP' – but will highlight some of the most important policy issues for donors and the WFP management.

One of the important overarching policy changes which has occurred since 1994 is the revision of the WFP's Financial Regulations and General Regulations, permitting it to be more autonomous from FAO administrative control and allowing the WFP governing board and its management more flexibility than in the past. This has contributed to the development of four-year Strategic and Financial Plans on a two-year rolling basis, and of Resource Policies and Long-Term Financing principles, and the adoption of policies on Country Programme Resource Levels.

We first deal with *the reactions of donors*. As observed in the report, implementation of WFP development projects had frequently been frustrated by shortage of cash to provide the necessary goods and services for a more efficient execution of projects, which then could produce more sustainable results for the beneficiaries. Donors were, in principle, required to provide in cash one-third of their total regular contributions (which finance development projects and the administrative costs of the WFP), but that cash proportion had not been achieved. By contrast, food aid for emergencies and PROs (financed by *ad hoc* contributions) was in fact accompanied by the

---

3. In 1997, one of the authors of the present essay reviewed some elements of the follow-up to the Tripartite Evaluation; see CIDA [*1997a, 1997b*].

cash needed for the operations themselves, albeit arguably with inadequate support for the additional administrative burden on the WFP.

Since the Tripartite Evaluation was carried out, new Resource Policies and Long-Term Financing principles have been introduced requiring donor contributions to individual activities, including development projects, 'to cover all costs: direct operational; direct support; indirect support'. Unfortunately, this requirement has not been fully met by all donors. Moreover, although 'the policies were intended to provide greater flexibility in the allocation of resources, there has actually been a decrease in flexibility as donors have increasingly directed their contributions, particularly in the development category' [WFP, 1997b: 30]. Since a larger proportion of resources, therefore, can now be used only for specific projects in given countries, the WFP's ability to determine its own priorities is constrained, and its multilateral character is eroded.

A related observation in the evaluation report is that the contributions of most donors are not based on food surpluses, and therefore these countries could provide their entire contributions in cash and leave it to the WFP to procure food or otherwise use the cash efficiently for the support of their operations. The WFP itself refers to the new financing policies as a response to this observation, but the latest available statistics show that only five countries (including only two large donors) commit one-third or more of their regular pledges in untied cash. However, some countries provide significant contributions in cash-in-lieu-of-commodities (CLC), which can only be used for WFP purchases of food. Of the total regular pledges for 1996 of US$399 million, US$218 million were in commodities; US$55 million in CLC; and US$122 million in cash [WFP, 1997d: 66].

As regards contributions for emergencies the evaluation urged donors to increase untied advance pledges to the International Emergency Food Reserve and also to accept the carry-over of funds from one financial period to another, but no such reaction has occurred, even though the WFP, as it reports, continues to raise this matter with the donors. Similarly the evaluation recommended that donors should contribute in full the agreed target sum of US$30 million in cash to the Emergency Response Account, but in 1996 less than two-thirds of the target was committed, only slightly more than three years earlier. The purpose of these recommendations was to enhance the WFP's ability to react quickly in emergency situations, not only for the obvious reason that the need was urgent, but also to reduce the danger that food supplies would finally arrive so late that they created marketing problems in the recipient countries and became a disincentive to domestic food production.

As far as we are informed, there has been no relaxation of the rule that the WFP cannot 'monetise' more than 15 per cent of its food resources in support of individual projects. As the provision of food is a major objective also in development projects, there are reasons why food should not be sold but, as the evaluation found in some cases, greater flexibility would have enhanced the longer-term effectiveness and sustainability of some projects, particularly for non-food items. However, if the new financial principles function properly, further monetisation will not be required.

Turning next to the *reactions of the WFP* to the evaluation, it should be borne in mind that major policy decisions by the Executive Director have to be approved by the Executive Board (formerly by the CFA), where both donors and food aid recipients are represented. The most basic recommendations of the evaluation were, first, that the WFP should reduce the number of recipient countries and, second, should concentrate on fewer activities, with less complex objectives and lower expectations, more focused in sectors.

The first of these recommendations would necessarily meet with some resistance in the governing body, as it is somehow in conflict with the universal character of the WFP. Nevertheless, by the end of 1997 the WFP was due to have reduced by 20 the number of countries in which it has development activities. (As development activities stretch over a number of years, this is not yet reflected clearly in the statistics: of the 83 countries in which the WFP had operational development expenditure in 1992, such expenditure was incurred in 75 of them in 1996 [*WFP, 1997d: 16–19*].)

The WFP aims at using 50 per cent of the development resources in the Least Developed Countries (LDCs); in 1996 57 per cent of the value of *new* commitments was for LDCs, which then accounted for 42 per cent of the *total* allocated to ongoing and new development projects. A parallel target is to allocate 90 per cent of development resources to Low-Income-Food-Deficit (LIFD) countries, and this target has not yet been reached. The evaluation report noted that the WFP used the FAO definition for LIFD countries and recommended that it consider moving to a definition more consistent with the World Bank's eligibility criterion for IDA credits. So far, however, the discrepancy is still present – and it is large: for 1994 FAO and the WFP applied a GDP per capita figure of US$1,395 while, for 1995, the World Bank limit was US$905.[4] The result is that the WFP list of LIFD countries includes a dozen countries which are not eligible for IDA funds. The WFP maintains that it indirectly addresses the issue of priority for the poorer countries by the Executive Board's decision to allocate WFP resources based on relative needs.

This may indeed be a more rational approach, since the needs for food aid for poor people may well be independent of whether they live in a food-deficit country or not. One example of this is Bangladesh, where two major WFP-supported programmes reach a very large number of poor people who would need such assistance even in years when the country may have an overall food surplus. The basic objective of the projects is to reduce undernourishment, not primarily or necessarily to bring extra food into the country. The programmes were started when Bangladesh had not yet achieved food self-sufficiency and extra supplies were channelled through these programmes. But food entitlements will fall short of needs amongst the landless and very poor farmers even in years when national domestic grain production may exceed the market demand for food. Many other countries are in a similar situation. Neither at the time of the evaluation nor for the immediate future does there seem to be a case for maintaining any specific target for the proportion of WFP resources to reach the LIFD countries. Allocations are better made on the basis of relative needs, as stated by the Executive Board, taking into account, of course, the capability to implement well-targeted projects that will reach the people who are most in need of extra food.

The second recommendation, to concentrate on fewer activities of a less complicated character, was not controversial, and the indications are that this recommendation has been followed. During the years 1994–96 the WFP approved 47 development projects, 21 of which were expansions of ongoing activities. Judging by the titles of the projects, with few exceptions these were activities for which food appears to be an appropriate tool of support,[5] and in relation to which the WFP has experience in supervising their implementation.

A further recommendation, to bring about improvements in the preparation of projects as well as their implementation, was that the WFP should as far as possible make its food aid resources available through specialised development organisations, notably IFAD and the World

---

4.   The FAO number, used by the WFP, is quoted in WFP [*1997b: xiii*]; the World Bank number in World Bank [*1997: 234, fn.c*]; exceptionally a very few countries with GNP above that operational cut-off are also eligible for IDA loans.
5.   The titles alone give no clear indication of the degree of complexity of the projects.

Bank. The Tripartite Evaluation had found that such co-operation had proved successful in the past, but no updated information is available to show whether the WFP has been successful in this respect – or even whether real effort has been made.[6]

In order to focus WFP assistance on development projects which respond to high priority needs in the recipient countries, the evaluation suggested that projects should be approved within the framework of a Country Programme; a step in this direction had already been taken through the preparation of some Country Strategy Outlines (CSO). Considerable progress appears to have been made in this direction: the principle of country programmes has been approved, efforts are being made to produce more and better CSOs (in total 33 CSOs at the end of 1997), and the first Country Programmes have been prepared (three in 1996; six more were planned for 1997). On the basis of the Country Programmes the WFP can establish an overall resource framework by country, as a basis for the approval of individual projects. When such a resource framework is in place, the focus of attention in decision-making may shift to the selection of activities in which food *per se* is a crucial and appropriate tool. Even then, of course, the problem of marshalling resources other than the food items needed will remain.

The country programming exercise is designed so as to involve closely governments, other United Nations agencies and other aid organisations generally. WFP personnel will operate as part of the UN country team, under the leadership of the Resident Co-ordinator, to support governments in preparing Country Strategy Notes. Such a role for the United Nations has been advocated for decades. If now successful, the major shortcoming in WFP projects stemming from weakness in implementation may be better addressed. Yet, with the increased concentration of the WFP's development activities in LDCs and other LIFD countries where needs are most pressing, shortages of qualified counterpart personnel to plan and implement projects will be even more serious. Political will on the part of the government to implement projects effectively is necessary, but it may not be

---

6. One of the authors of this essay had the opportunity at WFP headquarters to conduct a quick review of Project Summaries that were approved by the governing body or the Executive Director during 1994–97. It was not possible to assess the extent and type of cooperation with other aid agencies in detail. However, the impression was that there is practical cooperation with other agencies in a slightly higher proportion of the *new* projects, than in the older projects that have been modified and extended in time ('expansion'). In both categories less than half of the projects include some kind of cooperation with other aid agencies, governmental or NGOs. But in far fewer cases does the WFP provide the food to projects executed by another international agency.

sufficient if the required experience and capacity are not also available. Also for projects of high priority in Country Programmes (or in the UN Country Strategy Notes), the WFP must realistically assess the capacity of the implementing agencies. The extensive training programme of counterparts undertaken by the WFP (5,000 participants per year) is an important step in the right direction, but short-term training cannot compensate for shortages of experienced specialised staff. Where this situation exists, the WFP will have to identify and select for support those projects that are relatively uncomplicated to implement and have achievable objectives.

It was pointed out in the evaluation that fairly frequently substantive changes were made by the WFP headquarters in the preparation of the final product document, the Project Summary, without consulting the Country Office in the country concerned, and hence not the recipient government either. This further reduced the feeling of ownership of projects on the part of those who were due to implement them. The WFP maintains that the country programming approach and further delegation of authority to the field offices will bring recipient governments into closer contact with the decision procedures.

The evaluation team observed that the targeting of project activities on the poor and poorest beneficiaries, and in particular on women, in many cases did not have the intended effects. The WFP claims that there are ongoing efforts to overcome this deficiency. Thus, the targeting of the poorest and particularly women is specifically addressed by means of vulnerability mapping and the WFP's general commitment to women; a major study on participatory approaches is completed and draft guidelines issued. The solution of the targeting problem might be a concentration on activities which guarantee a stringent selection of beneficiaries. However, this might exclude activities with a potentially significant development impact, such as food-for-work projects. Experience has shown that when workers have been offered an adequate daily ration for their labour, the self-selection effect has frequently failed to function because less poor farmer households have found it advantageous to offer their services, thus reducing job and income opportunities for the very poorest, many of whom are women. This is a dilemma that cannot be wished away; it is a problem which faces not only the WFP but also other aid agencies, multilateral as well as bilateral, that seek to address their support directly to the poor. For the WFP it remains a challenge which demands continued vigilance, imagination and persistence.

One of the problems which preoccupied the evaluators and has been taken seriously within the WFP is the possibility of following up emergency and rehabilitation assistance with development activities. For man-made emergencies which in most cases involve large numbers of displaced persons within a country and/or refugees in other countries, repatriation is the only sustainable solution. Sometimes displaced persons may be assisted in establishing economic activities in their temporary place of residence, but this is exceptional as a general solution. The established, pre-existing population may well also need support to prevent a deterioration of their environment resulting from the inflow of a large number of people from outside. In recent years the WFP has approved three development projects which deal with problems created by man-made emergencies: in Guatemala, postwar assistance to returnees, displaced persons and needy population; also in Guatemala, construction of infrastructure in depressed areas previously affected by internal conflict; and in Mozambique, reconstruction and rehabilitation in rural areas. In addition, there is an ongoing PRO project (extended in 1995) that deals with environmental rehabilitation in refugee-impacted areas in Pakistan.

In areas hit by natural calamities many relief projects contain an element of rehabilitation, such as the provision of seeds, tools, domestic animals, etc. to people who have lost or exhausted their belongings in droughts, floods or other catastrophes. Many of the WFP's development activities take place in particularly vulnerable areas, and have in some cases been accelerated when crop failures have resulted in emergency situations. Moreover, where successful, WFP activities in such areas may effectively reduce the danger of future emergencies. A concentration of WFP activities in vulnerable countries, and in particularly fragile regions within them, may be a feasible way of bridging relief and development.

In sum, the reaction of the WFP to the recommendations in the Tripartite Evaluation has undoubtedly been very positive, and in some areas significant changes have been made. As regards many specific recommendations, the WFP is making efforts to respond positively, but its ability to do so is clearly constrained in many ways, including in some cases by its own scarce technical competence, in other cases by hesitation on the part of other aid agencies to enter into co-operation with the WFP in using food as an input in development projects [WFP, 1997b: 19].[7] Amongst the United Nations organisations the

---

7. It is worthy of note that the WFP collaborates with more than 1,000 national and international NGOs, and by the end of 1996 in addition had concluded memoranda of understanding with eight NGOs, 'establishing a clear division of responsibility based on the comparative advantages of each organization, thus maximizing the efficiency of operations'.

WFP has a unique experience in channelling food to poor people, but it needs to co-operate with others in order to ensure that its efforts in the development area lead to sustainable, significant benefits for the intended beneficiaries.

IV. FOLLOW-UP OF RECOMMENDATIONS: MANAGEMENT ISSUES

Amongst the 94 observations, suggestions and explicit recommendations in the Tripartite Evaluation which the WFP has monitored, there are many which deal with very specific management issues that clearly influence the WFP's ability to fulfil its mission. Here we concentrate on the follow-up of recommendations directed to the effective use of food as a tool in development activities.

The evaluation found that the then Committee on Food Aid Policies and Programmes (CFA) had been ineffective in ensuring that development projects were well planned and implemented, and had achieved little as a body for handling international food aid policies. It should be noted, however, that in 1994 the CFA undertook a major review of the WFP's policies, objectives and strategies which resulted in the approval of a WFP Mission Statement at the end of that year. The transformation of the CFA into a smaller and more efficient Executive Board in 1996, in line with the broader United Nations General Assembly resolution 48/162 adopted in December 1993, promises more effective action in the future.

The introduction of the country programming approach should make it easier for the Executive Board to assess the suitability of projects submitted for approval. It remains an open question, however, whether this Board will provide the supervisory and decision-making functions more effectively than the CFA's Sub-Committee on Projects did in the past, particularly since its function appears to be oriented more towards country strategies than to individual projects. In any case, it will still be a long time before most of the WFP project portfolio will have been selected in reference to the framework of Country Programmes.

The most important change in the organisational structure in recent years has been the transfer of authority to field offices. At the beginning of 1997 the WFP operated development projects in only 61 country offices against 76 in 1992. In 1992 the Country Directors (CDs) were mostly senior professionals (P4 and P5); only a few had the higher rank of director or the lower rank of P3. Very few of the Country Offices (COs) had specialised staff with prior experience or the competence to analyse food policies in their respective countries and to engage in forward planning. Thus, most COs were unable to produce Country Strategy Outlines on their own. By contrast, they generally performed very well in the management of food aid supplies and transport to the final destinations, in several cases in extremely difficult circumstances. This competence has been heavily drawn on in the mobilisation of food aid in many emergency situations.

Further reorganisation was needed to allow more of the planning and decision-making to take place locally in field offices and not only at WFP headquarters. The Organisation Change Initiative that was begun in 1996 was due to be fully in effect by the start of 1998 when nine out of 11 regional 'cluster' offices would have been created to place decision-making authority closer to the beneficiaries and implementing partners. In addition, there were to be six stand-alone Country Offices. Regional Managers in cluster offices and Country Directors would thus have wide authority to make strategic and operational decisions, with the role of the WFP headquarters' service divisions being to control less and support more. As a part of this reorganisation staff were to be moved out of Rome into the field. Combined with the reduction in the number of countries in which the WFP will continue development activities, this should lead to stronger links with governments and other partners in the recipient countries, and a more realistic choice of activities to be supported by the WFP's resources.

As regards staffing of the country offices, the evaluation recommended more use of national, locally recruited staff. This has taken place as the number of national officers increased from 98 to 113 between 1994 and 1996. It is reported that 30 national officers have replaced ten international positions. The total number of professional staff in the COs increased from 505 to 587 during the same period.

Traditionally there was an 'us–them' culture between headquarters and field office staff, but this is reported to have been much improved, *inter alia* as more HQ staff are being posted in the field. Another problem was that staff both at headquarters and in the field mainly had experience in handling development activities, while to an increasing extent they were entrusted with the management of emergencies. These and other human resource problems now appear to have been seriously addressed by the WFP through changes in its personnel policies, performance standards and appraisal as well as by better communication. The organisational dichotomy between emergency and development activities is also being removed, in particular by moving more of the responsibility for both types of activity to the field offices. The extent to which these efforts will lead to improved performance remains an open question, as it ultimately depends on the competence of the field staff. From 1994 to 1997 the WFP had not recruited additional 'permanent' (unified) staff, but hired talented individuals with emergency management and development skills on a fixed-term basis.

Concern was expressed in the Tripartite Evaluation about the small number of sectoral experts who were available to review project proposals. It was suggested that the recommended reduction in the number of Country Offices could save staff and thus give room for the appointment of more specialist staff. Like other development agencies, the WFP depends on external consultants to assist in the preparation of projects, but in-house specialists who can communicate with outside experts are also needed. As of 1997, the Technical Support Service does not appear to have been significantly strengthened and there are no in-house specialists in natural resources management, forestry, agriculture, the environment, health and education. Currently, the WFP only has a specialist staff of five, two in gender, two in nutrition, and one in monitoring and evaluation plus one grant manager for some special support activities.

The evaluation also recommended that WFP policies and practices regarding the use of outside consultants, including people from other UN agencies, should be reviewed and that more flexible and innovative arrangements for the use of such consultants should be found. The WFP has taken several steps to make the use of outside expertise more cost-effective and to ensure more rigorous technical support.

For emergencies the evaluation strongly supported the idea of a Rapid Response Team and a roster of outside emergency managers who could be called in to help deal with sudden emergencies. The Rapid Response Team could also bolster the capacity, albeit temporarily, in the relevant Country Offices when necessary. The WFP has instituted these changes.

For the important task of correctly assessing the real needs in emergencies the evaluation recommended that practical micro-assessment methodologies should be developed, which would also take into account local coping systems that should not be undermined by excessive outside assistance. This recommendation went beyond the established practice of WFP staff participating in assessment missions together with the UNHCR and FAO. The WFP has started experimenting with better assessments in collaboration with non-governmental organisations. This is very important because one of the most serious criticisms against the use of food aid has been that it may create lasting dependence amongst the beneficiaries. Improved methodologies for needs assessment would also help ensure better targeting during emergency operations.

Similarly for WFP development projects, better targeting would be possible with enhanced assessment of the poverty situation in the geographical regions in which development activities are operated. This, in turn, would also provide a basis for later evaluation of the impact of development projects.

One fundamental aspect of targeting in the WFP is to reach the most vulnerable, who in most cases are women and children. The WFP is clearly committed to ensuring that women take part in the planning and implementation of development activities, and thus in benefiting from the results. 'Specific targets are being introduced into Country Programmes to invest 60 per cent of resources in women and girls. For example, in the Bangladesh Country Programme, specific targets were introduced within the Rural Development Programme to reach more women beneficiaries and to meet the required investment level of overall resources in women and girls' [WFP, 1997b].

The WFP has for a long time had detailed guidelines for the preparation and implementation of food-aided development activities. These guidelines are constantly reviewed and improved, and the evaluation team recognised that the WFP puts strong emphasis on the quality of its development activities. Yet, the evaluation found that the results did not correspond to the intentions. It was observed that one reason was the WFP's inability to control the quality of what was done at the different stages in the preparation of development projects. One weak element was the review of the project documents in the internal Project Committee. The WFP now maintains that the system has been strengthened by a change in the mandate of the new Programme Review Committee, and that the new Regional Offices will have strengthened specialist capacity. It remains an open question whether these organisational changes will suffice to bring about the much needed improvement in practice. One clear weakness of the former Project Committee was that its members had many other assignments, were often on travel outside headquarters and hence hardly had the extra capacity to review projects in sufficient detail and ask the relevant questions. This problem will remain, unless more staff resources are allocated to project preparation.

The evaluation found that the quality of Management Reviews and evaluations was generally good, but there was almost nothing to be found on the impact of the development activities reviewed. This was not primarily due to weaknesses in the presentations of targets and objectives, but to the lack of baseline surveys as well as studies of the consequences of project activities. This underlines the need for micro-assessments both before a project is started and during and after its implementation.

In the new organisational structure introduced since 1994, the evaluation service has become linked directly to the Executive Director which highlights its importance. Evaluation is an expensive operation and its quality depends on the resources that are available for it. Moreover, as stressed above, it depends also on the material that is available on which evaluations can be based. So far there is no evidence of better impact evaluation.

The performance of institutions using food for development activities depends crucially on the availability of resources. The Tripartite Evaluation found that the many resource 'windows' created problems for the WFP. Even though some simplification has taken place in recent years, resources are still kept in somewhat watertight compartments. In the evaluation it was pointed out that shortage of the so-called non-food items, that is, goods and services that were needed for efficient project operations and which the national implementing agency did not have the resources to provide, weakened the performance of projects. It remains to be seen if the new financing arrangements that have been agreed will allow sufficient funds for such non-food items. This will also depend on the WFP's own ability to persuade the donors that such costs are not overhead expenditures, but part of the direct project activities.

In 1996 there was a serious shortage of resources in relation to WFP commitments for development activities: the Annual Report for 1996 states that there was a shortfall of 207,000 tonnes, representing 20 per cent of overall project commitments. The introduction of strategic and financial plans for a four-year period, revised every second year, will help the WFP to anticipate large variations in its resource base. But past WFP commitments were also based on assessments of future supplies of food aid, and there is no guarantee that there will not be unexpected deep cuts in donors' allocation of food aid to the WFP's development activities.

There is no doubt that, in recent years, the WFP has taken steps to make better use of the resources at its disposal. This augurs well for the future and warrants a wait-and-see attitude to assess how well ongoing improvements affect programming. Yet, the viability of the WFP as a development agency ultimately depends on the ability and willingness of donors to keep up the volume of food aid available for development. In this respect the outlook is not very favourable.

V. THE FUTURE ROLE OF FOOD AID AND OF THE WFP

The origin of food aid is in one respect comparable to that of private contributions to help people in an emergency. Appeals for clothing etc. were, and still are, met by donations of used items which can readily be spared; the only effort required is to sort out the items and take them to a collection point. When food aid became an important part of the richer countries' assistance to poorer countries, the major donor governments had stocks of surplus food, which were already paid for; thus, the cost of the assistance was mainly to transport the foodstuffs to their destination. Such food aid out of surpluses has undoubtedly been of great value to the recipients, even though, as many observers have pointed out, it may have had some perverse effects as well in certain situations.

In connection with the establishment of the World Trade Organisation to replace the GATT, agreement was reached gradually to apply the rules for international trade in other goods to agricultural commodities as well. If carried through fully, this would mean that in the longer run production volumes and prices of farm products would move so as to result in a balance between market supply and demand. Of course, crop and market fluctuations would occur, but there would be no long-term 'structural' surpluses. Even though it is unlikely that governments will refrain entirely from interference in the market, say when farmers are threatened with ruin due to bumper crops larger than the market can absorb without a major collapse in prices, there are already signs that the agreed policy reform measures have drastically reduced surpluses in the USA and the European Union. The stricter application of international trade rules to farm commodities has a mixed impact on developing countries. Those which are self-sufficient or even exporters of some farm products, will benefit from higher prices which are not undermined by subsidised exports from other countries. However, food-deficit countries will be harmed by higher prices on imported farm commodities. In addition, with smaller surpluses in richer countries, and much less of the stocks being held by governments, food-deficit developing countries are bound to find that their access to food aid is greatly diminished as well.

As already pointed out in the first section of this chapter, global food aid declined by more than half from 1993 to 1996. In an effort to assess the future of the WFP, too much should not be read into such a drop, one reason for which was the reduction by more than one-third in the volume of relief food aid,[8] another the reduction by two-thirds in the flow of programme aid which had been particularly high in 1993, and in which the WFP has (practically) no role. Yet, the reduction of project aid was undoubtedly also a result of donor countries' waning commitment to the supply of such aid.

There is no reason to question the WFP's role as a relief agency; its reputation in this area is strong and well deserved. It is quite possible that the WFP will be able to mobilise the food needed for its future emergency operations, but there is no reason for excessive optimism either: if indeed the overall supply of food aid continues to shrink it will clearly also be more difficult to mobilise such aid for people in dire need of food. However, the World Food Programme can perform its role as supplier of food to people in distress by buying food, and countries which are willing to assist in emergencies can do so by providing the cash with which the WFP can buy the food. This is already done to a large extent. In 1996 the WFP itself purchased one million tonnes of food, two-thirds of which was bought in developing countries [WFP, 1997b: 21]. Hence the ability of the WFP to provide relief is no longer dependent on the availability of surplus food in some rich countries, but on the willingness of donors to finance relief operations through its operations.

As regards the WFP as a development agency, its *raison d'être* is clearly less compelling: The WFP was originally established to use surplus food for the benefit of undernourished people through development activities. If, as seems likely, there are no surpluses available above what will be deployed for relief and programme aid, a UN agency to handle food aid for development purposes would appear to be redundant, particularly since the WFP has not convincingly proved to be outstandingly successful in its support of efficient and effective development activities. There are, however, also arguments for the WFP continuing as an institution for development.

First, there is a practical argument. A main reason why the WFP has been successful in handling relief operations is that it has developed strong competence in receiving, procuring and transporting food to the final users; also, it has been able to intervene to meet emergencies in different parts of the world where it was already present. While experience from interventions in, for example, nations of the former Soviet Union and in North Korea shows that the WFP can effectively operate also in uncharted waters, it has undoubtedly been

---

8.   It is true, of course, that there was a shortage of food also for relief operations in 1996 so that the fall was not exclusively due to a fall in demand. See WFP [*1997c: 31, Table 9*].

easier to channel resources for relief into places where the WFP was already operating. Even though it is now restricting its development activities to fewer countries, they are selected on the basis of their dire need for food aid; these are also often countries which are most vulnerable to emergencies of a nature that warrants international food aid operations. If the WFP remains active as a development agency, therefore, its effectiveness in many, if not most, emergencies in the future will be strengthened by the fact that the organisation already has a presence in the country.

Second, the World Food Programme is the only UN organisation which has a special mandate to combat undernourishment directly by bringing food to people in hunger. By now, it has gained considerable experience in doing so. The WFP has rightly been praised not only for its ability to handle emergencies, it has also convincingly demonstrated its competence in the more general handling of sea transport and other logistics, not only technically but also by reducing the costs of the operations. While the Tripartite Evaluation found that the ability of the WFP to achieve the objectives of its development activities was less than impressive, that evaluation did not include any comparison of the WFP's achievements with those of other development agencies. The message of the evaluation was that the WFP ought to do a better job and that it should be able to do so.[9]

With surpluses of food for aid declining, as must be expected, the question arises whether food aid, as we know it, remains an efficient instrument for international efforts to help alleviate hunger and malnutrition in poor countries, both in emergencies and, even more, in development projects. It is likely that some food aid, even in the future, will be available as a net addition to other international aid. Food aid from some countries' surplus stocks may continue to be directly additional, and there may also be some indirect additionality as electorates are shown that domestic food producers participate in making poor people less hungry. In fact, it may be possible to provide such food aid in a far more flexible manner than is mostly still the case: the WFP, NGOs and other agencies could receive food aid in the

---

9. One of the authors of the present essay undertook two assignments which involved examinations of a large number of evaluations and other reviews of development activities. One covered around 100 projects assisted by the Norwegian Agency for Development Cooperation, NORAD, and the other was a brief enquiry into the experiences of about a dozen multilateral and bilateral development agencies in Bangladesh. In both cases the same kinds of problems, difficulties and weaknesses were found as we had uncovered in the WFP's development activities: weaknesses in planning, over-ambitious objectives, vaguely defined goals, insufficient attention to the capacity of the recipient countries to implement projects. See Norbye [*1994*] and Norbye and Ofstad [*1996*].

form of 'vouchers' from the respective donors, which the agencies could use whenever appropriate. It is unfortunate that donors to the WFP seem to have moved in the opposite direction by tying their contributions even more than before to specific projects in specific countries. It would be more effective and efficient if the WFP were placed in a position to use its resources without constraints of this nature.

There is much talk in the international community about reducing the huge number of under-nourished people by half by some point at the beginning of the twenty-first century; 2015 is chosen as the target year. This can only happen if bilateral and multilateral aid agencies are given more resources to increase the 'food entitlements' of the poor and hungry. In 1996 the WFP provided supplementary food, and in many cases all the food, to 45 million out of the estimated 800 million people who are now suffering from hunger. Although general economic development may make its contribution, it has a long way to go to reach an estimated 400 million people! The world will need a strong WFP also in the future. Its mandate may have to be revised by eliminating the reference to it as an agency for using food aid, and instead emphasising its role in the alleviation of hunger. Food aid has been controversial because it can interfere with production and marketing in both deficit and surplus countries. Resources in the hands of agencies that directly combat poverty and hunger will stimulate food production, first of all in recipient countries but also in exporting countries, including many developing countries which are efficient food producers and have surpluses to sell on the world market. It is certainly early to say good-bye to food aid, but change is needed within and beyond the WFP. The World Food Programme could still remain the foremost United Nations agency that gives security to poor people who suffer from hunger and malnutrition.

VI. EPILOGUE (MAY 1999)

The world has moved on since this essay was written at the end of 1997, with new emergencies arising. The overall situation facing the WFP remains as before. Relief dominates its operations and efforts continue to be made to improve its performance as a development agency. In October 1998, the WFP called a consultative meeting to discuss a set of 19 different documents, written by WFP staff members and consultants; the above essay was also included. Subsequently two strategy and policy documents, prepared by the WFP, were discussed in a series of meetings with member government officials in

February and April 1999. The essential parts of these documents, as adopted in the light of these consultations, were presented in an Executive Board paper at its meeting in May 1999 [*WFP, 1999*].

In the course of the last five or six years the WFP's focusing on specific geographic areas and fields of action has been considerably strengthened. The guiding principles are, first, that WFP food aid should be used only in projects in which the feeding of undernourished people is a primary and direct objective. This will require intensified action to ensure effective targeting of WFP food aid. Second, the WFP will take special care to select its projects so that they will also contribute to the building of the resource base of its beneficiaries, thus helping to avoid food aid dependence in the future. This is not really new, of course; it has long been a central objective of the use of food aid for development. Yet, in the past, many projects have not contributed to the creation of assets within the control of the target group (for example a food-for-work project on road construction or on a plantation development in a state forest). In the future, therefore, the WFP will seek to identify and support food-for-work projects that will give lasting benefit to those who work on the project (for example planting of fruit trees or rehabilitation of fishponds as part of the local village economy). This is clearly a very ambitious objective.

In its reorientation the WFP will also include prominently investment in human resources through programmes for school and preschool feeding, food aid to expecting and lactating mothers, etc. Indeed, if successful, such programmes will bring lasting improvements in the knowledge, health and working capacity of the initial beneficiaries. Another priority field of action for the WFP in the future is the protection of a fragile environment.

As a result of the reorientation in WFP development activities, food aid will be concentrated in the poorest countries, and, within them, in the most marginalised and environmentally fragile areas of the country. However, the Programme also aims at expanding activities in poor urban areas where the numbers of undernourished and malnourished people are on the increase.

This reorientation of activities and the accompanying concentration on poor countries and regions are appropriate objectives. But the implementation of such a policy will create a heavy burden for the agencies that plan and implement the activities. For example, better targeting to reach the poorest, including women and children, and the use of an effective participatory approach are time-consuming and require well-trained personnel. Similarly, the implementation of projects in marginalised areas is always difficult, sometimes well beyond the capacity of executing agencies (not only of the WFP itself, whose primary role is to provide resources). The WFP recognises this as a problem, but maintains that the necessary steps will be taken to meet the challenge. Even so, the new approach must be facilitated by a firm shift in the project portfolio towards projects which are by themselves relatively easy to plan and implement.

As we found five years ago, the world needs a strong WFP. Without the WFP or with only a weak WFP in the future, the solemn international promise of reducing the number of over 800 million undernourished people by half by the year 2015 certainly cannot be met. To do so, stronger national and international efforts must be made to bring food to tens or even hundreds of millions of people. For the rich nations such stronger efforts will no longer be based on available food surpluses, but on their willingness to provide resources to buy food for distribution to hungry people or, in other ways, to raise the level of food entitlements of the poor.

REFERENCES

CIDA, 1997a, *World Food Programme: Since the 1994 Tripartite Evaluation*, evaluation report prepared by Diana McLean for the Performance Review Branch, Ottawa: Canadian International Development Agency (Aug.).

CIDA, 1997b, *Lessons Learned from the Implementation of Food Aid,* Performance Review Branch, Ottawa: Canadian International Development Agency (June).

FAO, 1961, *Conference Resolution 1/61*, Rome: FAO.

Governments of Canada, the Netherlands and Norway, 1994, *Evaluation of the World Food Programme: Main Report*, Ottawa: Canadian International Development Agency; Netherlands: Ministry of Foreign Affairs; Royal Norwegian Ministry of Foreign Affairs. (Referred elsewhere as Chr. Michelsen Institute, 1993.)

Norbye, O.D.K., 1994, *Development Cooperation Experiences in Bangladesh* (commissioned by the Royal Norwegian Ministry of Foreign Affairs), Bergen: Chr. Michelsen Institute (May).

Norbye, O.D.K. and A. Ofstad, eds., 1996, *Norwegian Development Aid Experiences. A Review of Evaluation Studies 1986–92.* Evaluation report 2: 96, Oslo: Royal Norwegian Ministry of Foreign Affairs.

Nordic UN Project, 1991, *The United Nations in Development. Reform Issues in the Economic and Social Fields. A Nordic Perspective. Final Report*, Stockholm: Almqvist & Wiksell International (distributors).

United Nations, 1961, *General Assembly Resolution 1714*, United Nations, New York (19 Dec.).

World Bank, 1997, *Annual Report 1996*, Washington DC: World Bank.

WFP, 1997a, *Strategic and Financial Plan 1998–2001*. WFP/EB.A/97/4-A, Rome: World Food Programme (17 April).

WFP, 1997b, *Annual Report of the Executive Director, 1996*, WFP/EB.A/97/3-A/Add 1, Rome: World Food Programme (28 April).

WFP, 1997c, *1996 Food Aid Flow. The Food Aid Monitor*, Special Issue, INTERFAIS, Rome: World Food Programme (May).

WFP, 1997d, *WFP in Statistics*, Rome: World Food Programme (May).

WFP, 1999, *Enabling Development*, Executive Board Annual Session, 17–20 May, Policy Issues, Agenda Item 4, WFP/EB.A/99/4-A, Rome: World Food Programme (4 May).

10

Is There a Future for the WFP as a Development Agency? Or Does Food Aid Still Have a Comparative Advantage?

JENS H. SCHULTHES

The two questions are one and the same: only if they can be shown that, even after the disappearance of burdensome surpluses, food aid can still have a comparative advantage as a development resource, will donors be ready to continue their support to the WFP and thereby assure its future. Yet, the debate between the two key partners[1] – the WFP donors and the WFP Secretariat – has so far lacked focus. The WFP Secretariat has concentrated its efforts on providing a broad and non-specific audience with arguments for the *need* for food, without noticing that its only real counterparts, namely, a handful of senior officials of the key donors, first expect a clear demonstration of the *comparative advantage* of food.

The purpose of this chapter is to concentrate the discussion on this issue of comparative advantage. To provide a step-by-step guide for such a discussion, it has been structured in a series of logically sequenced theses. These are drafted with the intention of stimulating the debate, to help readers to identify the exact points at which they agree or disagree, and so to articulate more clearly their own position.

The chapter is addressed only to that aspect of international food aid which in one way or another, through projects or programmes,

---

1. It is one of the WFP's inherent weaknesses that the third partner – recipient countries – is much less interested. What counts for them is the net resource transfer in whatever form or through whatever channel. If they had a free choice, all recipient countries would prefer financial aid to food aid. Yet, the debate does, of course, touch on certain issues of genuine concern to recipient countries, and these will be taken up throughout the chapter.

directly or indirectly, monetised or in kind, aims at poor food-insecure beneficiaries. It does not deal with the traditional 'bulk programme aid' (in any case much reduced today), which, without conditionality, and in particular without any attempt at targeting, serves purely as budgetary support to governments.

The debate can be confined to the developmental function of the WFP. In respect of its emergency function, there is no need for a similarly critical examination. During recent years, the WFP has developed into an exceptionally effective organisation precisely for what the donors need most: the logistical servicing of their large, bilateral food relief programmes, from the initial stage of procurement through international and national transport up to the delivery to the distribution authority. There are a few issues pending mostly concerning the borderlines of the WFP mandate: the responsibility for needs assessment (which needs to be much improved) at one end of the spectrum, and the responsibility for distribution to the final beneficiaries, at the other. However, these are issues more of UN inter-agency turf (the WFP contending with FAO in the former case and with UNHCR in the latter), than of substance. On the whole, the function of the WFP as a provider of emergency food logistics is so logical and coherent, and its performance so satisfactory, that if WFP did not exist, an organisation would have to be set up, and it would probably not look very different from the current WFP Logistics Division.

The question is: can the same be said about the WFP in development?

Thesis No. 1: *The answer cannot be expected only from the WFP Secretariat. The key donors must articulate their own thinking on the WFP more clearly and then guide the Secretariat more firmly than they have done in the past. For this, they must seek a minimum of consensus among themselves.*

On this count, criticism of the donors should not come as a surprise to them. That the WFP is searching for a renewed identity has been evident for a number of years, but the donors have so far done little to guide the Secretariat in that search (other than expressing frustration and reducing their contributions). Yet, donor guidance is essential for the WFP.

Although the WFP has been in the past, and indeed still is, the depository of a huge volume of resources, in respect of their use, it is more dependent on donor policy than most other UN programmes. The main reason for this is the volatile and unpredictable nature of its resource base. Longer-term food aid commitments are risky, and this has led to the historical reluctance on the part of donors to encourage, indeed to allow, the WFP to develop into a UN agency which formulates its own doctrine and, based on that, its own original claim for funding. In a nutshell: 'The WFP is not the originator, but the user of doctrine' (Richard Cashin, former Head of the WFP's Operations Department).

To be sure, consensus among donors on food aid doctrine will always be limited. Donors have different traditions of food aid, different levels and sources of commodity availability, different budgeting regimes, and, not least, different constituencies at home and abroad. However, they are today united at least in a common critique and suspicion: that the WFP Secretariat has too little evidence on the practical, down-to-earth quality of its work, namely its cost-effectiveness, the optimal allocation of resources to recipients, the selection of the most suitable projects, the most effective modes of implementation, in short, on 'what works and what does not work'. In all donor countries, the food aid debate will at times take on a more philosophical (or political) appearance, but the key question is that of 'comparative advantage'. Within all donor aid administrations, the budget authorities keep putting this question to the food security programmers, and there is a common frustration among the latter that the WFP Secretariat is providing them with so little ammunition to make their case.

Can the case be made?

Thesis No. 2: *Food aid for development makes sense only when it has at least an element of additionality. If ever the point were to be reached when food aid resources had to be drawn from fully fungible development aid budgets, development food aid would no longer have a comparative advantage. For the WFP this would mean that its development function should be terminated.*

This thesis will be contested (and it is anathema to the WFP, which has recently been making special efforts to demonstrate that food can indeed be 'better than cash' in combating hunger and malnutrition), but it is important here and worth an unemotional examination.

The thesis is that there is no developmental constraint of any kind that cannot be overcome more effectively with cash than with food. Obviously, *end* beneficiaries of development assistance will often benefit more from food than from cash – for instance undernourished children who cannot eat cash. However, the fact that the end beneficiaries of a project require food in kind, does not necessarily mean that, at the *outset* of that project, cash would not be a more effective source of funding. This is true even for projects whose ultimate purpose is wholly nutritional. But it is evidently much more true for those projects, like most food-for-work projects, in which food has at least partly an income transfer function as well. Unfortunately, it is even true where food has a direct nutritional function like in school feeding, but where an equivalent educational effect, although by a different 'route', could be obtained through an equivalent in cash assistance, for instance for increased remuneration of teachers. No Ministry of Education would ever opt for a school feeding programme if it were free to use the same amount of assistance to increase its budget for teachers' training or salaries.

The same is true for all other categories of WFP development projects. All of these are today making the effort to demonstrate a clear relation to 'food security', yet in all of them this purpose could be achieved more effectively if, at the outset of a programme, the planners were to handle cash instead of food. It follows that if ever the point were to be reached at which those development aid resources, which are today tied to food, were truly fungible in the sense that programmers on the donor as well as the recipient side could choose freely between food and cash, cash would prevail. If the WFP did not yet exist, nobody would set it up for the purpose of development. Since it does exist, a certain inertia would maintain it for a while, but support would dwindle and soon fall below the threshold of relevance. Unless it could find a new role for itself (which, this writer believes, is extremely unlikely, given over thirty years of 'path dependence' exclusively on project food aid), the WFP would – and indeed should – become something like the UN arm for food logistics. In the context of rationalising and cost-cutting in the UN system, such a move would not be unreasonable.

But are the assumptions realistic? Are food aid budgets fungible? Has food aid lost all of its former additionality?

Thesis No. 3: *Food aid budgets are, by their nature, not completely fungible. Food will remain available as a development resource because donors will continue to provide it for that purpose.*

The gloomy scenario of the previous thesis was based on a specific assumption: that future food aid would have lost all of its previous additionality and would have to compete fully for fungible cash. However, such an assumption is unrealistic because it ignores two intrinsic characteristics of food aid: *'political additionality'*, and *'second-best advantage'*.

1. The 'Political Additionality' of Food Aid

The term was proposed by Shlomo Reutlinger and sums up the many different reasons, interests and motives which today still lead, and will in future continue to lead, a few key donors to make a certain share of their international aid available in food, or in cash tied to the purchase of food [*Reutlinger, 1999*]. This is evidently not the place to re-enter the traditional debate over 'food aid needs and availabilities', that is, basically the projection of needs versus production. Whatever may be the 'needs' of developing countries for cheap food, massive surplus production in developed countries is a phenomenon of the past. But donors should examine a little more scrupulously why it is that they do not stop allocating some of their aid budgets to food – and not just to 'food security' but to feeding people. Indeed, they should honestly ask themselves why they continue to allocate resources to the WFP, in spite of their profound distrust of the Programme's effectiveness. Most donors would still today like to see a more effective WFP rather than none. There are many reasons, and they vary with each donor's individual 'aid-regime' [*Hopkins, 1987*]: strong food aid traditions; an established national expertise; firm budget lines and self-serving bureaucracies; the powerful appeal that 'hunger' has in attracting public funding; but probably most of all agricultural interests.

For most of the major donors, the production *potential* is very large, but their ability to fine-tune that production is limited. Faced with an attentive farm lobby, food aid continues to be a conveninent outlet for these donors for some of the eventual residual production. Compared with the overall volume of production, the volume of the residual may be small and irregular, but in good harvest years it is still much larger than the volume of food that can reasonably be absorbed by a carefully controlled food aid agency. And provided that agency is kept small, even in bad years its claim will not be large enough to cause serious problems. Contrary to earlier expectations, the GATT Agreement has not so far had a noticeable effect on food aid availability, and no prediction can be made for the future, except perhaps that the former grey area of concessional food sales should eventually shrink, while straightforward grant food aid should become the only acceptable channel. In short, at a time when aid is politically sensitive, and the allocation of resources jealously watched, the inclusion of some food in a donor's overall development aid basket is quite natural, and probably easier and politically less controversial than its systematic exclusion. Obviously, this is not equally true for all donors: food aid is a much more natural aid resource for those who *have* surplus food than for those who have to *buy* it (that is why the current WFP campaign to enlist 'non-traditional' donors is probably unrealistic). In any event, the available volume of development food aid will in future be small and irregular, but it will not be insignificant[2] – and it will be additional.

2. The 'Second-best Advantage' of Food Aid

'Political additionality' is one argument for continued food aid, but on its own it would not be very satisfactory. Even additional resources have to be put to good use, and much of the current uneasiness over food aid is less concerned with 'availability' than with 'good use'. Donors are no longer convinced that the kinds of projects that the WFP proposes for using food, are really successful, or sustainable, or cost-effective, or of high priority; or that they are the 'right' projects for food aid. There is a vague but strong feeling among donors that 'something better' could be done with their food aid.

To anticipate the outcome of the chapter: this feeling is not unjustified. The 'right' projects for food aid (as well as the 'wrong' ones) can be defined with greater precision than has so far been done, and the remaining sections of the chapter will attempt to do so. However, one general characteristic of food aid, its greatest 'natural strength', should be more clearly recognised at the outset. While almost never the best approach in theory, food aid is often in practice the only assistance possible. Other interventions might be more desirable and in the longer term more effective – technical assistance, training, institution building, investment – but their planning and implementation would require levels of administrative and managerial quality that would simply be impossible to achieve in the time allowed. One of the biggest problems in development aid is the limited absorptive capacity for it, even where it is clearly needed. Slow disbursement of their aid commitments is a constant issue between donors and recipients, and more recognition should be given to the fact that food aid usually does not pose that problem: It is almost always quick-disbursing (slow disbursement begins to occur when the technical complexity of projects becomes too great, see further below). Food aid has the enormous advantage that it offers donors the means for alleviating the worst consequences of poverty in an effective and visible way, when

---

2. These issues of the availability of food aid are discussed in Chapters 1, 3 and 4.

they are unable to take more permanent measures against the roots of that poverty. In short, food aid can be the quick and fairly large-scale answer to problems when there is no immediate better answer. This is a great comparative advantage of food aid which donors will certainly not wish to give up.

For all these reasons, food aid is likely to remain a sizeable, additional manoeuvreable mass for development, although available 'only' in the form of food, not cash. This means that its use cannot be judged as if it was cash, because, by definition, food aid is used only for purposes for which cash is not available. However, this does not, of course, mean that all purposes for which food can be used, are equally good. Where does food aid fit best? Where should it be avoided? What works and what doesn't?

The following sections will propose answers to these questions in the form of a few 'rules of thumb'. There will, of course, always be exceptions to these rules. Even if integrated into the most coherent framework of government plans or 'WFP Country Programmes', food aid will always be disbursed via projects, and projects are highly individual affairs, thoroughly dependent on local conditions, good will between the various partners and – most important of all and too little recognised – the capacities and attitudes of individual people. The right people can make almost any project work. However, there are only very few of the right people, and general strategies cannot count on them. For 'normal' agency and government staff, development projects can quickly become too complex and difficult, and the WFP (prompted over three decades by more detailed and project-focused supervision than most other UN agencies have received from their governing bodies) has probably become too ambitious in respect of the level of complexity that it takes upon itself to understand and manage. There is now clearly a need for simplification, and the following 'rules of thumb' reflect that need. The argument moves from the least suitable to the most suitable use of food aid.

Thesis No. 4: *Food aid is – as a rule – not a very effective resource for investment.*

This may be controversial, because 'immediately productive food-for-work projects' have traditionally been, and for many donors still are, the ideal for the WFP: they help produce more food and thereby 'work WFP out of a job'. The technical quality of this type of project and its rate of return have therefore been, and still are, important criteria for its selection and support by the governing body. Yet, it should make one stop and think that, over three decades and in spite of the WFP's never-ending search for 'co-operation' and 'partnering', neither the World Bank, nor any other development financial institution, nor bilateral donors, nor NGOs have shown any serious interest in using food-for-work for the funding of the unskilled labour components of their often large rural infrastructure or other investment projects. The fact is that the more 'bankable' a project is, the less suitable it is for food aid, even where the unskilled labour force is sufficiently food-insecure to accept food as wages. Funding investment with food aid goes 'against the grain'. Bankable rural infrastructure projects tend to be so complex, and their technical and managerial cost component so high, that, if the complexity can be mastered and the costs covered, the remaining unskilled labour component, because of the cheap labour available in rural areas, does not pose a funding problem serious enough to justify the extra complications involved in using food aid.

The WFP has tried to escape this dilemma by seeking out the less bankable, more social welfare-oriented public works programmes. Here, the record has been mixed, but, on the whole, not encouraging. Even the most basic rural public works schemes require more technical and managerial support than can usually be found, at least for the size of projects that the WFP would like to assist with food. A simple calculation demonstrates this: 1,000 tons of food per year is, for the WFP, a very small project, probably the threshold below which a project becomes uneconomical; yet 1,000 tons per year provides the wages for a huge workforce: 200,000 man-days or 2,000 workers (and their families) for 100 workdays per year. A workforce of this size, if it is to be used with at least a trace of efficiency, requires a volume of technical and managerial support (engineers, overseers, skilled workers, materials, vehicles, offices, telephones, etc.), which goes far beyond what governments, even with the help of donors, NGOs, etc., can normally mobilise for this type of project. As a general conclusion, too many of the traditional food-for-work projects have been technically too poorly supported to allow this approach to serve as an example for the future [*CMI, 1993*].

Admittedly, there are a few cases in the WFP's experience in which a government has been so highly committed to a public works programme that it has made the required cash support available from its own budget, or agreed to earmark other aid resources. Some of these are examples of the past, which today, under changed cost structures, would perhaps not be repeated in the same labour-intensive way. Yet, strong 'government commitment', particularly in respect of the social component of public works projects, that is their food-security or 'safety-net' function, can be a powerful driving force even in otherwise unfavourable conditions. This theme will be taken up in more detail below.

Thesis No. 5: *Food aid is – as a rule – more efficiently used for rehabilitation and maintenance of existing structures than for the creation of new ones.*

Again, this is not the common opinion of most donors, who have traditionally preferred to assist developing countries with one-time investments, expecting them to fund the recurrent costs of rehabilitation and maintenance from their own regular budgets. Indeed, one of the key conditions for judging the eligibility of rural infrastructure projects is usually the 'assurance' of future government maintenance. Yet, it is common knowledge that, in all developing countries, rehabilitation and maintenance budgets are critically insufficient, and it is indeed the WFP's experience that governments are invariably much more interested in using food aid for this purpose than for new construction. And food-for-work is evidently more suitable for maintenance than for new construction: The share of unskilled labour is higher and, in particular, communal maintenance works are more easily open to the poor; the requirements of materials and tools are lower; works can be more easily decentralised and supervised locally; the scope for people's participation is higher; work seasons for regular maintenance are longer than the often very short construction seasons; and as a general rule, maintenance works are more accessible to women than the more prestigious and semi-skilled employment opportunities offered by new constructions.

Admittedly, aid (not only food aid) to maintenance raises the issue of 'open-endedness', but significant assistance programmes in this area could well be the vehicle for encouraging gradual burden-sharing policies of recipient governments. To the extent that food-for-work has a future, this is probably among the most promising approaches. However, the scope will never again be as large as it has been in the past: food-for-work is becoming an anachronism.

Thesis No. 6: *Food aid is – as a rule – used more efficiently and with less friction for social development than for economic development. More specifically: food aid can support social entitlements more efficiently than it can support developmental activities.*

Sometimes it would help in the debate over the best use of food aid if donors would pause a moment to ask themselves how they would use it *in their own countries*. Would they ever put it to the test of economic rate of return? Would they even try to use it in 'poverty-alleviating' public works programmes? Is it so difficult to see – if the knowledge of one's own developed economy were for a moment allowed to serve as guide – what an enormous demand the traditional WFP food-for-work projects can make on the fragile capacity of developing countries for planning and management? Too little attention has in the past been given to the 'bureaucratic feasibility' of using food. All WFP experience points to a conclusion which developed countries would immediately draw for their own bureaucracies, namely, that food aid has a much more natural place in social development than in economic development. Economic development projects are complex, integrated, and cash-oriented. They depend on achievements that are not easily rewarded with food – initiative, choice, negotiation, mobility, competition, markets, risks, profits – not only for the big entrepreneur, but on a modest level also for the poor Bangladeshi woman who has 'graduated' from food aid to a BRAC micro-credit.[3] In short, once the capacity has been created for development activities, 'food rations' are usually no longer an efficient form of support. This is true for the managers of these activities, for whom the handling of food becomes an unwanted complication, but it tends also to be true for the participants who, even though poor and food-insecure, will increasingly have access to cash and who will consider food wages as no longer adequate. Some governments will of course be quite willing to use donated food for wages but, in these cases, food aid often acts as straightforward budget support.

Food assistance, whether funded by governments or donated through international aid, is by its very nature ('second-best advantage') most efficiently used in a direct transfer to those among the poor who not only lack the means for producing or purchasing food, but whom governments are not able to reach through developmental activities that would enable them to produce or buy food (the Bangladeshi woman above during her two pre-BRAC years). In developed countries, this would be 'social welfare' – a network of entitlements designed not just to provide 'humanitarian' relief, but to ensure that minimum of social security (health, education, nutrition, food security) which alone can enable poor people to even start fending for

---

3. Bangladesh Rural Advancement Committee (BRAC) is an NGO involved in the WFP-supported Vulnerable Group Development Programmes and other associated poverty-focused activities.

themselves and eventually 'graduate' to a higher stage of development. In developed countries, social welfare absorbs a huge share of public expenditure, with no one questioning its basic legitimacy. In developing countries, the need for social welfare is also huge, although donors do not like to get involved in it. Yet, the potential of food aid as a resource for social welfare entitlements is obvious: they require, as a rule, less complex planning and management, less 'bureaucratic integration' of different partners, and less proof of sustainable impact than do developmental activities. Social entitlements are therefore, for a weak and inexperienced administration, far easier to handle than are developmental activities. Moreover, in a poor food-insecure environment, food will remain an attractive good for entitlements even after it has ceased to be an acceptable wage good. If, theoretically, 'social welfare' were recognised as a legitimate, even prioritarian purpose of development aid, then there would not be any doubt that social welfare entitlements would be an excellent area for funding by food aid. The problem lies in the traditionally bad name of 'social welfare' as non-productive and non-sustainable, in short, an illegitimate objective of development aid.

The question, therefore, is: are there sectors of social welfare that are legitimate areas for aid? And if so, which of them should food aid take on, and under what conditions?

Thesis No. 7: *Food aid's greatest strength is that it can fund what donors do not – as a rule – fund with cash: The recurrent costs of food 'safety-net' policies.*

A second look at the issue of 'social welfare' makes it clear that there are many areas, typically in nutrition, health and education, in which the donor community has traditionally been quite willing to support *investment* components: studies, structures, equipment, training, management systems. More recently, the establishment of 'social safety nets', in particular the assurance of a minimum access to food, has become a legitimate objective of aid with considerable investments even by the World Bank. Donors are today ready to support countries in the identification, design and adoption of 'food security ("safety-net") policies'. However, they are not ready, and the available aid resources are believed to be quite insufficient, to support the recurrent costs of such policies. The consequence is that, except for those developing countries that have reached the stage where they can finance them from their own budgets, food safety-net policies remain all but illusory. It is here that food aid can have a legitimate place.

To be sure, the available volume of food aid is today far too small, and is likely to remain so, to cover 'food safety-net programmes' in any general way. There will be great need for selectivity. Where, then, are – for food aid – the highest priorities and the highest 'returns'?

Thesis No. 8: *What makes a food safety-net programme eligible for outside assistance for its recurrent costs is, more than anything else, the government commitment to that programme and its mainstream policy support.*

This statement may sound banal, because, in the theory of project design, 'government commitment' is routinely required for every kind of development project. In practice, however, no project requirement is more loosely interpreted, indeed more readily satisfied with hope rather than certainty, than is 'government commitment'. This is so particularly in the social sector in the poorest countries, and there is an added danger in the case of food aid: poor governments tend to view it more as relief than as a development resource. Very understandably, poor governments are often tempted to view food aid not as an integral component of, but as an alternative to, a government policy.

'Government commitment' is not equally essential for all types of projects. The closer a development project is located to the market, and the more directly it aims at an economic outcome, the more will there be measurable economic indicators to guide and motivate the participants, even if a weak or indifferent government stays on the side. Social welfare programmes, on the other hand, because they are not supported by market forces or commercial interests, require experience and skills of public administration, but beyond that a particular support and back-up by other public forces: popular consent and solidarity, a willingness to share, enforcement of a minimum of civic morale, in short: a clear political decision and mainstream legitimacy. To avoid misunderstanding: 'government' in this context does not necessarily mean central government or even provincial government. 'Government' can be local and informal. But it must be a public authority, and the welfare of the target beneficiaries must be a public concern. Once the concern exists, outside aid can do much to respond to it. But where it does not exist, aid cannot create it, 'Social progress is necessarily autochthonous' (James Ingram, former Executive Director, WFP).

Thesis No. 9: *NGOs cannot substitute for government.*

The potential role of NGOs as the future movers of social progress has received much advance praise in recent years, but this has so far not been confirmed by actual performance. There seem to be few examples of major food safety-net programmes operated by NGOs without at least strong policy support from government. National NGOs like BRAC (see footnote 3) or the Grameen Bank in Bangladesh are highly exceptional. NGOs tend to be small, dependent on individualist leaders with their own agendas (on which 'funding' often ranks high), and therefore sometimes short-lived, in sum: parochial rather than national. This is probably even true for most of the church organisations. Given this structure, NGOs are probably more effective as recognised partners of, than alternatives to, government line ministries. Being closer to the ultimate beneficiaries than line ministries, NGOs can be effective in motivating target beneficiaries towards 'participation' in a public health, or education, or food security programme, and they can effectively promote local institution-building. However, the outcome will be solid and sustainable only to the extent that programmes are ultimately anchored in firm public policy.

Thesis No. 10: *Government commitment and mainstream policy support can – as a rule – be found most easily for women and children; combating 'early malnutrition' is among the most developmental forms of social welfare.*

Broad safety-net programmes tend to be economically and politically controversial and, therefore, do not always have a robust mainstream position in a country's social policy. Or, if they do, that position is not likely to survive a change of the political regime. The situation tends to be better for those safety-net programmes which are targeted on population groups for whom food security is high on the priority lists of all political regimes: that is, expectant/nursing mothers, infants and small children through primary school age. At the same time, combating 'early malnutrition' is among the most developmental objectives for donors who want to be active in the broad field of food security. Even here, programmes are more complex than is often thought. Selective and often politically sensitive targeting, efficient, but also accurate, handling of commodities through several stages, reliable distribution by services basically charged with technical functions, the constant struggle in satisfying the recording/reporting/monitoring/

evaluation/audit requirements (and whims) of a multitude of donors – all these tasks, quite apart from their costs, add a new dimension of demands on already fragile government administrations where they are weakest: in policy awareness, interdepartmentmental planning and co-ordination, and in particular middle-level management. Food assistance to combat 'early malnutrition', in principle such an obvious use of food aid, requires a level of government commitment which is, in practice, quite rare.

Thesis No. 11: *Education, in particular pre-school and primary school education, is perhaps the most empowering approach to the sustainable alleviation of food insecurity. Donors should, therefore, review their position on pre-school and primary school feeding.*

From the inception of the WFP, donors have never quite overcome their weariness of school feeding, which they have suspected of being more humanitarian than developmental. The WFP Secretariat, on the other hand, has continued to submit school feeding projects, not so much out of conviction and on the basis of an articulate conceptual counter-argument, but by force of circumstances. Given their robust simplicity and social self-evidence, school feeding projects are for many governments among the most manageable and therefore most attractive forms of project food aid. For some governments, particularly in Africa, they are practically the only manageable form of WFP development assistance. If school feeding was excluded, the absorptive capacity of African countries for WFP assistance would fall to even lower levels.

To be sure, ease of management is not in itself a justification for aid. Nor is the importance of education, as such, the issue. That education, and in particular primary education, is among the most powerful means of sustainable poverty alleviation, is a commonplace. Even in poor subsistence farming, the level of productivity has been shown to be a function of primary education; functional literacy strengthens the mobility and bargaining power of unskilled labour, and it is clearly a precondition for skilled labour employment. Equally clearly established is the importance of literacy for the empowerment of women, including its correlation with effective family planning. All this is not in question. The question is whether food aid can make a cost-effective contribution to education.

That school feeding can have some impact on educational outcome, cannot reasonably be questioned: as an incentive for enrolment and attendance; by improving learning capacity through alleviation of short-term hunger; as a vehicle for nutrition and health services; and as a means to create a minimum of social equality – between the poor and the not so poor – where that equality counts most, namely in public primary schools. The problem is almost entirely quantitative. By their nature – promoting basic equality – school feeding programmes cannot be very narrowly targeted. They, therefore, necessarily reach a large number of children – perhaps the majority – who may welcome the food, but whose educational performance will not depend on it. The key question in each school feeding programme is, therefore: How large is the 'core' target group of poor and food-dependent school children or households, and does their share justify the necessarily broader coverage of that programme?

It is here that relatively simple research would provide much needed clarity. The economic value of completed primary education could be estimated for a given developing country per head of its population and related to the costs of a specific school feeding programme. There could be other approaches. In any event, the developmental potential of school feeding is such that it is surprising how little effort has been made so far to underpin it with a little economic research (the nutritional research has been done, but again has not dealt with the quantitative issue raised here).

Thesis No. 12: *Postwar, or post-disaster, rehabilitation programmes can have such an inherent 'social logic' and provide such favourable operational environments that food assistance can be effective even without strong government support.*

Ever since the WFP, in the early 1970s, channelled several hundred thousand tons of food aid to the post-war reconstruction programme in Biafra/Nigeria, it has been evident that, once a war has ended and a general reconstruction effort has begun, food aid can be immensely effective in supporting that effort. There are several factors that make food a particularly suitable resource: the visibility and obviousness of the problem, not only in terms of need as well as developmental potential, but also the expectation of its relatively short duration, which together make a good case for donors; the initial absence, not only of income but of functioning markets, which makes food a precious good for the recipients; the relative ease and flexibility of planning and the legitimacy of improvisation, together with a relatively high level of technical knowledge and easy availability of all sorts of skills which give a certain assurance for the technical quality of the reconstruction works; the concentrated presence of NGOs able to provide all sorts of support; and most of all, the broad consensus among all parties, ideally even between former enemies, about the need literally to join hands and do the job. The period during which conditions are in this sense favourable for food aid, are normally short, not longer than a year or two, and many mistakes have been made in the past by prolonging food aid programmes beyond their optimal duration, that is, beyond that short period of a commonly shared reconstruction effort. However, while they are in full swing, national reconstruction programmes offer probably the largest ground and the greatest comparative advantage for massive food security-cum-development food aid. The limitation of these programmes for donors lies in the fact that they occur irregularly, but may then be very large. For this reason, they tend to be funded more from emergency than from development budgets and cannot, therefore, provide a sound basis for the forward planning of developmental food aid.

CONCLUSIONS

The argument has moved from the 'least feasible' to the 'most feasible', which has meant – not surprisingly – a move along a 'continuum from development to emergency'. This does not mean that the use of food aid is limited to emergencies. Food aid has a large potential as a development resource, but in the absence of that power of 'self-management' which emergency environments can provide, governments must take on a larger responsibility than has traditionally been demanded of them. The twelve theses summarised above need not be recapitulated here. The most important among them will also be the most controversial: that development food aid has a place only where it constitutes an integral component of a firm, mainstream government policy of food security. In retrospect, one recognises the wisdom of the founders who saw WFP assistance much more in a supportive role to government programmes than they did in respect of most other UN agencies.

This chapter did not address other issues which have fuelled the discussion over previous years, such as open-endedness, cash support costs, monetisation, the establishment of country priorities and systems of allocation, to name but a few. The present writer believes that, if a stronger consensus were reached on 'where food aid fits', these issues and many others would become less difficult. Moreover, some of these issues, like monetisation or country allocations, are probably areas in which donors have divergent views and agendas which the WFP would be quite able to accommodate.

On one essential issue, however, donors must agree: what kind of development to expect from their food aid, and what – realistically – not to expect. The WFP's current uncertainty about its own identity has its roots also in the overambitious and unrealistic expectations on the part of donors. This was the main thesis of this chapter. Food aid does not, as a rule, enjoy a comparative advantage in anything that is 'bankable', and the outcome of food aid projects should not be measured as if they were 'bankable'. The comparative advantage of food aid lies elsewhere: in being able to meet the – equally developmental – needs that do not attract cash, foremost among them the recurrent costs of a certain category of 'social welfare', that is, food safety-net programmes.

Applying the above thoughts to the WFP will not cause a revolution. Many of its traditional development activities fit well into the context of 'government-supported mainstream social development' outlined here. Others would not stand this test , and those would be phased out and their repetition avoided. WFP programming documents would look a little different, containing more thorough assessments of government social policies, in particular, than they now do. Most important: WFP's current allocation 'system' with its emphasis on a semi-automatic, because statistically perfect, spread of small allotments of food over a large number of countries would give way to a more straightforward concentration on larger programmes in those – obviously fewer – countries which are capable of integrating food aid into their social policy. The traditional expectation for the WFP to be represented in all regions and in as many countries as possible, and the pressure on it actually to promote the absorptive capacity for food aid in the poorest countries, would give way to a greater initiative on the part of developing countries themselves to obtain WFP support for their social programmes.

This would also, on a number of fronts, reduce the direct and indirect cash support costs for WFP development projects. The more policy support a food aid programme has the lower could be the WFP contribution for planning, administration, technical support, monitoring, and so on, and the more the WFP could concentrate on larger programmes in fewer countries and also the more it could concentrate its currently far-flung field presence. Over recent years, direct and indirect support requirements in cash have been allowed to grow unreasonably high. Among the comparative advantages of food aid is the fact that, after all, it can be done with food, and not cash.

REFERENCES

Chr. Michelsen Institute, 1993, *Evaluation of the World Food Programme: Final Report*, Bergen: Chr. Michelsen Institute.

Hopkins, R., 1987, 'Aid for Development: What Motivates the Donors?', in E. Clay and J. Shaw, eds., *Poverty, Development and Food. Essays in Honour of H.W. Singer on his 75th Birthday*, London: Macmillan.

Reutlinger, S., 1999, 'From "food aid" to "aid for food": into the 21st century', *Food Policy*, Vol. 24, No. 1.

11

EU Food Aid and NGOs

MARIE-CÉCILE THIRION

I. NGOS AND FOOD AID

1. The Role of NGOs in Food Aid

There are three main categories of NGOs that manage food aid. First, there are the big international networks with more or less independent national and regional offices such as CARE, Caritas and the Red Cross. Secondly, there are national NGOs that rely mainly on national or European aid resources (for example, Oxfam-UK, Catholic Relief Services (CRS), SOS Sahel). Thirdly, there are NGO consortia, notably EuronAid which involves many NGOs from the second group (Box 11.1). NGOs managed around 19 per cent of global food aid between 1990 and 1997, with a general tendency towards increased share (Figure 11.1). This marked rise is largely due to the expansion of humanitarian aid, in which NGOs play a major part, and the decline in programme food aid (see Chapters 1 and 5).

EuronAid, a consortium of European NGOs, was until 1995 by far the main NGO provider of food aid as at that time it managed more than 20 per cent of NGO food aid (Box 11.1). Then came the major American private voluntary agencies (PVOs) or NGOs such as CARE-US and the Catholic Relief Services (each accounting for around 19 per cent of food aid managed by NGOs), Adra-US and World Vision-USA. Caritas, which is a network of Catholic NGOs, managed only 2 per cent of NGO food aid (bearing in mind that national Caritas offices can also manage their own volumes of food aid directly), while its nearest Protestant counterpart, the Lutheran World Federation, managed only 1 per cent.

This chapter is based essentially on summary reports by the author and colleagues at Solagral based on interviews with different European NGOs, and on interviews and documents provided by EuronAid, the NGO Liaison Committee Food Security Group and the European Commission [*Solagral, 1995a, 1995b, 1996; Volontari del Mondo, 1996; Euronaid, 1998, 1999*]. From French to English: Ros Schwartz.

FIGURE 11.1
NGOs' SHARE OF GLOBAL FOOD AID
(% OF TOTAL FOOD AID, CEREALS EQUIVALENT)

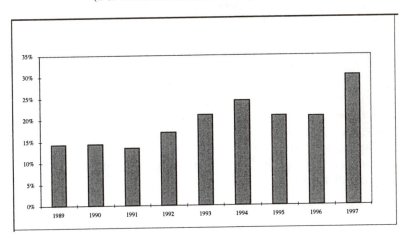

Source: World Food Programme Interfais.

No standardised data have been available internationally since 1995. However, as discussed below, the EU Community Action budget allocated to food aid managed by European NGOs plummeted in 1996 and 1997. Therefore, since US legislation assures minimum tonnages under PL 480 Title II (see Chapter 1, Box 1.3) it is likely that American NGOs are now the main providers of food aid for development. Furthermore, NGOs' access to EU food aid no longer automatically goes through EuronAid, and this has led to a major reduction in the consortium's activities.

2. NGO Food Aid Actions

It is difficult to distinguish between European NGO actions and those based in other countries. It can be said, however, that European NGOs have often been highly innovative in the use of food aid [*Euronaid, 1995; Solagral, 1995b*]. In addition to food aid distributed free in emergency situations or as food for work, there is a wide range of types of projects, including cereal banks, urban supply centres and support for the integration of vulnerable sectors of the population such as the disabled. Above all, most European NGOs have sought to treat food aid as an economic tool either to pump-prime development actions aimed at certain marginalised sections of the population, or to assist the transition in a period of crisis. Some have even helped initiate early warning systems making it possible to manage this aid for prevention purposes rather than as an emergency response.

While most NGOs tend to work at the micro level, developing projects in partnership with local associations and populations, the withdrawal of national governments has prompted some to involve themselves further and to participate in, and even take over, whole areas of social policy in some countries. For example, this has taken the form of taking over targeted social programmes involving labour-intensive work (food-for-work) which are often the only safety nets for vulnerable groups. But the problem of food aid in kind is that it requires the development of specific skills (logistics, storage, etc.) and heavy investments that can lead to specialisation and hamper the development of other actions.

3. The Specific Nature of European NGOs

The European NGO scene is highy varied, and this is reflected among NGOs implementing food aid actions. They vary in size, from large NGOs receiving extensive private donations and benefiting in many cases from government funding to, at the other end of the spectrum, small NGOs targeting assistance at a specific crisis-affected population such as in Bosnia or Kosovo. There is also variety in the type of NGO activity, ranging from those agencies specialising in emergency aid, often with a large food aid component, to others carrying out diverse development support activities that occasionally include food aid. And there is variety in the forms of implementation, with NGOs that work directly in the field, and others acting more as intermediaries between the partners in developing countries seeking funding, or to exchange experiences.

Despite, or rather thanks to, this diversity, European NGOs have often prompted reflection on food aid actions and embarked on innovative actions in the field of food security. The anti-food aid campaigns waged since the 1970s have been widely fuelled by the findings of NGOs working in the field, since they are well placed to report on the negative effects of badly managed food aid. NGOs are also behind the questioning of emergency aid that has been going on since the early 1990s, both its role in perpetuating some conflicts, and the need to launch development actions rapidly in an emergency so as to pave the way for rehabilitation and avoid the establishment of a situation of dependency. In the face of these developments, NGOs have sought to diversify their sources of funding by tailoring their resource requests to the degree of openness and the constraints of each donor.

However, it is true to say that not all NGOs are at the same point in their thinking. This means that, although it is possible to find complementarities in some cases, there are also contradictions when it comes to actions in the field, sometimes even between actions with the same sources of funding.

II. THE EUROPEAN UNION AND NGOS

1. A Major Donor of Food Aid

European NGOs have adapted to the demands of official donors, often the major source of funding. This is especially true with regard to food aid to developing countries which is expensive (purchasing products, transport, handling, storage, identification of recipients, distribution). The major source within the EU is Community Action.[1] Within a short space of time, the European Union through Community Action became a major supplier of food aid in kind (19 per cent of global food aid between 1990 and 1998 compared with 7 per cent between 1971 and 1977), surpassing bilateral aid from EU member states.

Within the framework of the Food Aid Convention, there is a collective commitment to the delivery of food aid by the entire European Union (see Chapter 4). This is then split between EU Community Action and National Actions by member countries. EU action directly fulfils a major part of the commitment through its involvement in the Common Agricultural Policy and its responsibility for the management of European stocks of food products.

This link with agricultural output has long been built into the system for managing EU food aid, which was initially managed by the Directorate-General for Agriculture (DG Agriculture). The Directorate-General for Development (DG Development) was responsible for food aid policy and allocating food aid to recipient countries and indirectly through NGOs and international agencies. It was only in

---

1. The European Union (EU) was known before the Maastricht Treaty as the European Community (EC). This earlier name is reflected in phrases such as 'Community Action' food aid and the European Community Humanitarian Office (ECHO). For simplicity in this chapter reference is made only to the European Union (EU), and European Aid and Community Action refer to aid funded under EU budget lines and administered by the European Commission. Member state food aid is collectively described as 'National Actions' or as the bilateral aid of the member state in question.

1986 that a specialist division was set up within DG Development to manage food aid.[2] Its budget then represented up to more than a quarter of total Community aid at the end of the 1980s, but there has been a marked decline in its importance chiefly due to a sharp increase in aid for overall development. The annual budget tends to fluctuate, as some years it benefits from special programmes.[3] For example, in 1998, the 'food aid/food security' budget was ecus 579 million, made up of an annual grant of ecus 530 m. and reallocations, for example in response to the crises in Central America (Hurricane Mitch) and Bangladesh (floods).[4] To this should be added emergency food aid managed by the European Community Humanitarian Office (ECHO). Factors that have contributed to the recent development of European humanitarian aid, and therefore emergency food aid, include the scale of the crises, the level of media coverage they attract and the coverage given to the humanitarian actions, as well as the need for the European Commission to have visibility in this area.

Given the size of the budgets traditionally dedicated to food aid by the European Commission, many NGOs got into the habit of making their requests for food aid in kind to the European Commission, while seeking support for food security actions from more flexible public or private donations. The widespread availability of this form of aid made the application and access procedures easier than for other forms of aid. Thus, unlike the co-funding procedures, NGOs were not asked to fund part of the project from other sources. This availability of food aid even prompted European NGOs to enter into discussions about the 'monetisation' of food aid, following the example of their American counterparts. It is also partly at the root of discussions on the choice between 'food or money for work'.

Although the regulations in force before 1996 were orientated towards the provision of direct food aid from Europe, the European Commission sought to diversify its actions. It developed local and triangular purchasing, albeit to a lesser extent than some EU member states (see Chapter 1, Table 1.4). These purchases involved products that were unavailable in Europe and/or were available at substantially lower cost than direct aid. The European Commission also funded projects for distributing seeds, tools and other inputs, and livestock

2.   Since June 1998, DG Development has been reorganised. The unit dealing with food security is now also responsible for rural development and the environment.
3.   These special programmes are implemented when there are major crises (for example, dismantling of the Eastern bloc, the Rwandan crisis).
4. The ecu based on a weighting of all EU member state currencies was replaced on 1 January 1999 on a one-for-one basis by the euro which does not currently include Danish, Greek, Swedish and UK currencies.

replenishment, but these projects were chosen on a case-by-case basis and remained exceptions. All the same, even though limited, these conditions were sometimes more flexible than those offered by some donors such as the United States government, and several American NGOs opened offices in Europe to have access to this source of funding.

Box 11.1 EuronAid: an NGO network

The role of food aid within European development aid and the wish of the European Community to extend its collaboration with NGOs led to the establishment, in 1980, of a consortium of NGOs: EuronAid. It currently includes some 30 NGOs but serves more than 100. A service organisation, EuronAid is open to all NGOs even if they are not members. It primarily offers a logistics service for NGOs that are eligible for European Union food aid, centralising applications to the European Commission. This leads to more flexibility in the programming of projects, and provides technical support for the formulation of projects, a purchasing and logistics department, the organisation of triangular and local purchases, and training.

The diversification of actions that can be funded from the 'food aid and food security' budget has not enabled EuronAid to extend its activities to supporting NGOs in setting up and implementing food security projects. Currently, it confines its support role to aid in kind (food products but also seeds, tools, livestock, etc.), but it remains a key negotiator with the European Commission, since NGOs are still major providers of food aid in kind and EuronAid is one of the few representative bodies in the NGO community specialised in this area.

A small survey carried out in 1994 by Solagral [*Solagral, 1995b*] among various European NGOs identified the main NGO criticisms of the European Commission's administration of food aid as follows:

- Aid in kind was not linked to other European development programmes, hence major difficulties in setting up development projects with a food component.
- Procedures were ill-suited to NGOs' specific requirements: the grouping of NGO applications in three tranches, major delays in supplies, cumbersome bureaucracy, poor organisation of ship-

ments with congestion of ports and other supply points, sporadic arrival of food products.

- Procedures for local purchases and triangular operations were ill-suited to the situation encountered in the field (calls for tender, demands for guarantees, reports, certificates for seeds, etc.) which increased the cost of operations.
- There were grey areas in the responsibilities of different EU structures involved in food aid. The problem arose chiefly in distinguishing between what should be emergency food aid financed by ECHO, and food aid coming within the remit of DG Development.

During the process of formulating its 1996 regulations, the Commission organised a number of consultations with European NGOs and some of the above criticisms were taken into account in the proposed changes [*Solagral, 1997*].

2. The 1996 Food Security and Food Aid Regulations

The regulations governing European food aid adopted in June 1996 concern only food aid used within the framework of development actions [*European Council, 1996*]. They do not therefore concern emergency food aid provided as humanitarian relief, which continues to be managed by ECHO.[5] As regards food aid for development, they confirm the willingness of the European Union to adapt its aid to the diversity of situations on the ground and to strengthen the link between food aid and food security. This had already been established in the Council of Ministers' resolution on food security adopted in November 1994.

The 1996 regulations on food aid and food security include a number of innovations in the policy and procedures for the use of food aid budget lines:

- Programme food aid is perceived essentially as budgetary aid, and the counterpart funds derived from the sale of the aid are in future to be allocated to the recipient's overall national budget. It must carry with it a conditionality regarding the definition of food security policies and the establishment of food security priorities.
- Within the framework of programme aid, permitting recourse to financial aid to fund imports makes it possible to strengthen the import capacity of operators, both private and public.

---

5. ECHO was incorporated into DG Development in 1999.

- The scope of project aid, which is particularly relevant to NGOs, is broadened to include the funding of tools, seeds, livestock, credit and training. This makes it possible to instigate projects that are better suited to the different stages of rehabilitation and development than aid in the form of food products. Local NGOs can submit their applications directly to the European Commission.[6] The setting up of storage projects and information systems comes within the framework of prevention and crisis management programmes.
- The EU earlier preference for acquiring products within the Single Market is offset partly by the introduction of forms of aid other than food products, and partly by the Commission abandoning an internally agreed limit on local and triangular purchases, provided they are financially competitive.
- Allocations are now concentrated on the least developed countries with a food deficit, according to a new profile of priority countries [*European Council, 1996*].

And so it appears that European food aid is increasingly breaking its links with the Common Agricultural Policy and is relatively independent of the commercial strategies of the large private European operators. The proportion of former food aid budget lines used for commodity aid in kind can be expected to fall substantially, especially if there are no large-scale food crises. This was in fact what happened in 1997 (Chapter 1, Figure 1.1, Table 1.5).

3. The Impact of the 1996 Regulations on NGOs

First, the *slowness in implementing the regulations* and in formulating the legal framework (regulations for mobilisation, general terms and conditions, etc.) should be emphasised. Implementation was and still is severely disrupted by major revisions of procedures and modalities for the management of European funds, a number of internal restructurings, and finally the impact of the scandals that rocked the European Commission in 1998/99, leading to a tightening up of monitoring procedures and a slowing down of the decision-making process. As a result, the real impact of the regulations on collaboration between NGOs and the European Commission is only slowly becoming apparent.

In 1996 and 1997, funding granted to NGOs by the European Commission declined significantly from around one-third in 1995 to about

---

6. Previously, NGOs from developing countries submitted their applications through European NGOs.

18 per cent of EU food aid (see Figure 11.2). The rise to 22 per cent of the budget in 1998 can largely be attributed to emergency actions following the floods in Bangladesh and the devastation caused by Hurricane Mitch in Central America. So there is indeed a drop in European Commission support for aid to reinforce food security via NGOs, following extensive investment at the beginning of the 1990s.

In practice, many organisations ramain critical of the imprecise application conditions, delays of up to several months in processing requests, and cumbersome procedures. It remains to be seen whether these difficulties are to do with the immediate financial effects and linked to the adjustment of the 1996 regulations and their instruments to conditions in recipient countries, or whether they are structural in character and reveal an incompatibility between the limitations of the NGOs and those of the European Commission. To this must be added the necessary time for the NGOs to adapt to the new constraints and to exploit the new opportunities.

The NGOs' view of the 1996 regulations has therefore been initially very mixed. Several positive points have been highlighted. First, the wide range of *fundable actions* and extending funding to cover all project costs potentially relieve NGOs of the need to find complementary funding sources or to use monetisation to meet non-food costs. Secondly, the *role of EU delegations in-country has been strengthened*. They are now closely involved in the examination of applications from NGOs and in monitoring project implementation. This is further supported by the sending of food security experts to priority countries identified by the European Union. The problem remains for countries that have not yet benefited from this expertise. Thirdly, this closer involvement of in-country delegations has the further advantage of *strengthening the links between different food security actions* financed by the European Commission, whether direct aid, WFP aid or NGO projects. There is also a major advantage in building *direct partnerships with developing country NGOs*, even though the procedures and conditions attached to the funding make such partnerships hard to envisage.

FIGURE 11.2
SHARE OF EU FOOD AID BUDGET MANAGED BY NGOs, 1985–98

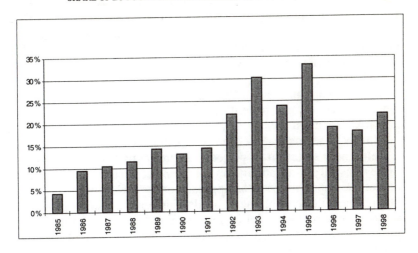

Source: European Commission, Activity reports 1986 to 1999.

However, there are still a number of difficulties impeding collaboration between NGOs and the European Commission. Below is a non-exhaustive list giving an indication of the practical difficulties facing NGOs in working within the 1996 regulations:

First, there is the problem of adapting the new regulations on mobilisation to the working conditions of the NGOs. Several inconsistencies have been identified. For example, the conditions attached to local and triangular purchases are hard to fulfil for small quantities bought from local traders, since they rarely satisfy EU standards. As regards the purchase of equipment, a distinction is made between goods for the recipients and equipment for the project, which must be subject to a call for tender. In actual fact, the distinction is often very hazy. Another example is the regulations regarding local purchases, which are only applicable if the product concerned is produced entirely locally, whereas, in the case of equipment, there can be some imported elements and it is not always easy to obtain this information at the pricing stage. Lastly, the container still remains the basic unit for the delivery of food aid in kind from Europe, but this does not always fit in with local needs and leads to a staggering of deliveries by type of product. If the European Commission wishes to develop its partnership with NGOs, it is essential for it to introduce more flexible procedures.

Secondly, the Commission goes in for a cumbersome bureaucracy. The extension of the types of food security projects that can be submitted and the attempt to ensure coherence between the different actions make the processing of each application more lengthy and complex. NGO projects cover a range of fields as varied as hydraulics, cereal banks, the distribution of seeds and tools and the vaccination of livestock. They require appropriate technical expertise and are more complex than the distribution of food aid in kind. Furthermore, these projects do not benefit from the technical support offered by EuronAid for aid in kind.

Thirdly, it seems that the European Commission is moving towards a preliminary selection of projects according to size. While this may make sense from an administrative point of view, it is to a certain degree incompatible with the approach of the NGOs, which is to operate in line with their partners' needs. Furthermore, small projects are often innovative. One solution remains the formation of consortia and joint NGO initiatives that would make it possible to combine a number of different projects. But, while this development is desirable in many cases, it is not suitable for all environments. It is bound to raise scheduling problems and, above all, it cannot be done quickly.

Fourthly, the Commission has introduced increasingly restrictive access conditions. A new *Vade Mecum* was issued at the end of 1998, setting conditions for subsidies to associations and increasing the number of administrative restrictions which already weigh heavily on these organisations [*European Commission, 1998*]. Out of a concern for transparency and the minimisation of risks, the Commission requires bank guarantees, increased follow-up and monitoring of projects, and the minimisation of management costs. These conditions, when applied uniformly and rigidly, are in practice restrictive not only for European NGOs, but also for NGOs in developing countries. The fact is that few NGOs in these countries are in a position to supply the guarantee in the form required, especially in countries where the movement is in its infancy, such as in sub-Saharan Africa and Eastern Europe.

Fifthly, there is lack of a clear division of responsibilities between the various European Commission bodies. The Commission has tried to clarify the roles of the various departments involved with food aid and food security and which work with NGOs. Therefore the unit responsible for co-funding NGO development projects should no longer, in theory, fund food security projects. However, it is clear that the boundary between development and support for food security is relatively hazy. To what extent is an irrigation project rural development support or food security support? The same question can be asked of production credit and marketing support projects and those aimed at combating poverty: the difference may only lie in the way the context is presented and in the declared aim.

The problem of unclear division of responsibility within the Commission also arises with regard to the definition of humanitarian aid. This type of aid should come within the remit of ECHO. But it is difficult to establish hard and fast boundaries between development aid and humanitarian aid, particularly since food aid in ongoing emergency situations or for refugees comes within the remit of the Directorate-General for Development, and knowledge of the field is required for the division of responsibilities between the different units. Also, in contrast to development aid, humanitarian aid can be envisaged for a country even if there is political disagreement between the host government and the European Union. In addition, there are the modalities for selecting projects and the different application conditions. By way of example, ECHO works on the basis of committing three months' funding followed by a halt for six weeks, which is a handicap for most ongoing crisis situations. On the other hand, ECHO's conditions applied to purchases are less restrictive, and its processing of applications is speedier than the DG Development service responsible for development food aid.

Co-ordination between the different European Commission bodies has been reinforced to avoid malfunctions as far as possible. Nevertheless, delays in processing some applications cannot be entirely ruled out, as they are passed from one department to another and the stated criteria disguise very different realities in the field.

III. WHAT ROLE FOR NGOS?

Even if the implementation of the new regulations has been slow, NGOs still regard them as a definite step forward in the attempt to improve the integration of food aid into support for food security, which is a priority aim for these organisations. Most NGOs have been campaigning for a long time for food aid to remain an emergency and transitional tool, and they have often proved innovative in this area. They should therefore continue to be partners of the European Commission, provided that modalities for working together can be found that are acceptable to both parties.

1. Macro–Micro Complementarity

After the adoption of the 1996 regulations, the European Commission placed the emphasis on the development of food security policies in the priority countries. In a number of countries, this process has begun, but its implementation remains to be completed. NGOs need actively to follow up the host government's formal commitment to the chosen strategy and ensure that pledges are fulfilled. This can range from monitoring the impact of policy measures on the food security of specific targeted and vulnerable populations to the concrete implementation of actions funded by these policies, or ensuring the participation of beneficiary populations in the identification of priorities and programmes.

In addition to monitoring and participating in national governmental policies, NGOs need to maintain their role in supporting food security for the most disadvantaged populations, who are not always taken into consideration by governments or are excluded from policy-making. They must be capable of drawing attention to the needs of these populations, entering into political discussions to obtain recognition for these needs and ensuring that they are taken into account in policy decisions for the longer term. This task is all the more complex in that it has to go hand in hand with actions that will improve the food security of these populations in the short term. It is perhaps on this transitional role of aid that the dialogue between NGOs and the European Commission is most fraught and remains to be clarified.

It is clear that, unless local actions are accompanied by an attempt at political coherence, they are often doomed to fail in the long term. NGOs, both local and international, must therefore be involved in discussions on the drawing up of national food security strategies. This dialogue is clearly a difficult process involving as it does many parties and diverse levels of thinking and capacity. It requires both an effort on the part of the European Commission to open up discussions with a certain transparency regarding the political choices and the criteria for aid allocation, and a complementary effort on the part of the NGOs which need to organise themselves so as to make this dialogue possible and effective.

2. Building the Capacity of Developing Country NGOs

This greater coherence between levels of food security action will only be possible if the NGO sector is well structured locally, possesses the necessary expertise to analyse the food situation, make proposals and monitor policy, and if it is informed of policy decisions at national and European level.

European NGOs certainly have a part to play in this area, especially if it is intended to confine food aid to short-term situations. It is therefore important to support developing country NGOs during these periods when food aid is provided, while also helping them to avoid specialising and thus acquiring a vested interest in the management of food aid in kind. As has been emphasised previously, European NGOs have different levels of partnership with local associations. Strengthening local capacities can therefore take various forms, including information, training and technical support for specific projects.

A few years ago EuronAid started providing training for NGOs in developing countries having recourse to European food aid. But we should envisage developing other levels of information and training. Whatever the form of partnership, it is clear that this effort will be all the more effective if there is a certain degree of NGO co-ordination in the area of food security.

3. Promoting Innovative Actions and Co-ordination

Co-ordination among NGOs is crucial to improving dialogue and collaboration with the European Commission, and to reaffirming the essential part NGOs have to play in the process of enhancing food security. This must take place at different levels, both with regard to the countries, so that they can act as a voice on national food security and empower developing country NGOs, and with regard to actions, so that they can put forward coherent projects of a certain size to the European Commission.

This co-ordination is also essential for the dissemination of ideas and information on innovative NGO projects. It is a task that has already been partially accomplished by the European groupings that make up EuronAid and the NGO Liaison Committees. However, the information disseminated by these groupings is often very much focused on relations between NGOs and the European Commission and does not sufficiently promote improved action by their members. Furthermore, it remains primarily aimed at European NGOs, while the dissemination of information among developing country NGOs relies on specific partnership relations.

4. Raising Awareness in Europe

The incorporation of food aid in a food security framework has been widely advocated by NGOs working in the developing countries. However, in most European countries, there is little public appreciation of these recommendations and why they are being made. In the face of crisis situations covered by the media, the initial reaction is often still to give food aid (for example, the Kosovo crisis).

Improving public understanding is an important task for NGOs not only because it can modify perceptions of developing countries and the most effective forms of aid, but also because it can help to counterbalance the powerful lobbies that could reverse the advances made by the European Commission in delinking food aid from the Common Agricultural Policy. It is important to stress that, in this area, levels of public awareness vary considerably from one European country to another.

REFERENCES

EU NGO Liaison Committee, 1997, 'De l'aide à la sécurité alimentaire', discussion of the French platform of the NGO Liaison Committee, Paris, 16 Dec.

EuronAid, 1995, *Food Aid as an Instrument for Combating Poverty*, Report of EuronAid Forum, Brussels, 13 Dec., The Hague: EuronAid.

EuronAid, 1998, *Summary of the European Commission Report to the European Parliament on the Implementation of the Food Aid/Food Security Regulations*, The Hague: EuronAid, 20 March.

EuronAid, 1999, *Annual Report for 1998*, The Hague: EuronAid.

European Commission, 1996, *Programme communautaire de sécurité et d'aide alimentaire*, Brussels: Directorate General for Development, Food Security and Food Aid Unit.

European Commission, 1998, 'A *vade-mecum* on Grant Management for Applicants and Beneficiaries', Brussels: Directorate-General for Development (DG Development).

European Council, 1996, 'Council Regulation (EC) No. 1292/96 of 27 June 1996 on Food Aid Policy and Food Aid Management and Special Operations in Support of Food Security', *OJL*, 166, Brussels, 5 July.

Solagral, 1995a, *L'aide alimentaire, un outil pour la sécurité alimentaire?* Report of a seminar, Brussels, 25–26 Jan., Paris: Solagral.

Solagral, 1995b, *Aide alimentaire et sécurité alimentaire: points de vue de quelques ONG européennes*, Paris: Solagral, Jan.

Solagral, 1996, *Aide alimentaire indirect: les ONG*, Paris: Solagral, Nov.

Solagral, 1997, *De l'aide à la sécurité alimentaire*, Conférence-débat de la plate-forme française du CLONG/UE, Paris: Solagral, Dec.

Volontari del Mondo, 1996, *The New Framework for Partnership between NGOs and the Commission with Regard to Food Security*, Report of a working seminar, Rome, 5–7 July, Rome: Volontari del Mondo.

12

Developing Codes of Conduct for Food Aid: Experience from the Sahel

ROBIN JACKSON

I. INTRODUCTION

The Food Aid Charter for the Sahel is a joint declaration by a group of donors and recipient countries aimed at improving the efficiency and effectiveness of food aid. The Charter was adopted in 1990 by the Sahelian Heads of State and six donors, with the broad objective of ensuring the integration of food aid into a long-term food security perspective. It is unique for two reasons. First, it is the only declaration of its kind that has been signed by both donors and recipients, and, second, the mechanisms which have been put into place to ensure adherence to it do not exist for other similar codes.

Since 1994–95 there have been a number of efforts to establish codes or charters of good conduct concerning food aid and food security. One such initiative at the regional level is an attempt to establish a code of conduct for the 'Greater Horn of Africa' or IGAD region (Intergovernmental Authority for Development) [*USAID, 1997*].[1] Another is a European Commission initiative to establish a code of good conduct at a global level, which at the time of writing had been incorporated in part into the 1999 Food Aid Convention (see Chapter 4). NGO initiatives include the Euronaid Code of Conduct on Food Aid and Food Security adopted in 1995 [*Euronaid, 1995*] and the Humanitarian Charter and Minimum Standards in Disaster Response, the so-called SPHERE project, which is multi-sectoral in its approach, with food assistance being one of several topics covered [*SPHERE, 1998*].

---

1. The 'Greater Horn' region as defined by the US government includes the IGAD states, Djibouti, Ethiopia, Kenya, Uganda and Sudan, and also non-IGAD Rwanda and Burundi.

These more recent codes are of two types. The first, and most relevant to this discussion, has food aid and related food security issues as its central focus. The second type includes codes in which food aid is examined within a broader development and humanitarian framework (see Chapter 13). These codes are usually public statements of principles or standards of performance to which organisations such as NGOs and donor agencies sign up on a voluntary basis, and against which organisations say they are willing to be judged.

The Food Aid Charter for the Sahel is particularly interesting because it illustrates the elements necessary for codes to have an impact on both donor and recipient behaviour. The evolution of the Sahel Charter demonstrates that codes of conduct or food aid charters cannot be simply stand-alone documents if they are to be more than statements of principle for which there is little accountability. Instead, the Sahelian experience suggests that, for the codes to have an effect, they need to be part of a process in which the concerns of different stakeholders are expressed. Thus they must contain a common view of the issues at stake concerning food aid and food security and must relate these issues to the country or regional context. In this sense, their actual content and their specific articles are not as important as the context within which they originate and the mechanisms put in place to insure that they are implemented. These compliance mechanisms are part of the process that upholds, validates and reinforces the very issues the codes are designed to address.

This chapter examines: the context within which the Food Aid Charter for the Sahel evolved; the process by which it was adopted; the mechanisms put in place to support the use of and adherence to the Charter; and the factors which contributed to its success. Although the origins and context of the Sahel Charter are very different from those of more recent initiatives, its evolution provides important lessons to subsequent codes if they are to have relevance and meaning for both donors and recipients.

II. CONTEXT: DROUGHT AND CONCERNS ABOUT FOOD AID

1. Food Aid Debates in the Sahel

Throughout the 1980s food aid was the subject of numerous studies and wide debate. In the Sahelian context it was heavily criticised, most notably for changing food habits, creating dependence on food distributions and disrupting local trade channels. Because of free distributions as well as generous subsidies on basic foodstuffs, food aid competed with products in local markets, driving prices down and discouraging agricultural production.

As early as 1981 the issue of whether food aid could be integrated into a well-planned strategy to improve cereal production was already being discussed in forums organised by the Club du Sahel and the CILSS (Comité Inter-Etats de Lutte contre la Sécheresse dans le Sahel).[2] Such integration of food aid into a much broader policy context was seen as a means of deterring its possible negative effects. This was the precursor to viewing food aid as part of a variety of measures to support food security, a concept which came to fruition nearly a decade later. These regional discussions also paralleled developments at country level, most notably in Mali.[3]

2. The 1984 Drought

The 1984 drought in the Sahel sent shock waves throughout the international community, prompting a spontaneous mobilisation of humanitarian assistance to cover food shortages in the region. Lives were saved and for the most part severe suffering avoided. Subsequent analysis of these events revealed major shortcomings and a serious lack of co-ordination both within the Sahel region and among the donor community.

Four major issues were highlighted by donors as requiring attention:

– the assessment of food aid needs was unreliable;
– although some local surpluses existed, they were not being marketed and the distribution of imported food aid threatened to further curtail the functioning of markets;
– triangular transactions planned by donors were extremely limited and often ran into difficulties; and
– co-ordination was recognised as critical to both relief and development food aid operations.

In 1985, the Club du Sahel and CILSS secretariats convened experts and development agencies to discuss how to cope better with future crises and deal effectively with major food needs in the region. The

---

2. The Club du Sahel is part of the Organisation for Economic Co-operation and Development (OECD) in Paris and is a donors' club working very closely with the regional institution, CILSS. The nine member states of the CILSS include Burkina Faso, Cape Verde, Chad, Gambia, Guinea Bissau, Mali, Mauritania, Niger and Senegal.
3. The Mali experiment in food sector reform has been widely reviewed. See, for example, Coelo [1994] and Lanser and Delefosse [1995a].

Network for Prevention of Food Crises in the Sahel was created, with the Club du Sahel donors and the CILSS executive secretariat making up the membership.[4]

The Network originated from a perceived need to deal with the recurring situation of supply deficits in the region, but in 1985/86 the Sahel had a bumper crop. Due to late deliveries of a significant amount of food aid from the previous year, the region found itself in a situation where local markets risked being disrupted by imported cereals with prices for local grains (millet, maize, and sorghum) declining due to the influx of imported cereals at harvest time. Moreover, the recipient countries were experiencing difficulties in transporting and storing both local and imported cereals.

The allocation of food aid during the years that followed failed to take account of the continuing surplus harvests in the region. In 1985/86, more than 600,000 tonnes of food aid were delivered to the Sahel, 200,000 tonnes over what had been requested by the Sahelian governments. At the end of the 1980s, deliveries continued to be substantial, ranging between 400,000 and 450,000 tonnes from 1986/87 to 1989/90 [*Jost et al., 1997*]. The negative impacts of this situation on agricultural markets and production began to worry policy-makers. Concern was expressed at the very small amount of food aid purchased locally in the region (under 10 per cent) during these years, despite surpluses in many of the countries. It was also clear that reliable information on agricultural production, particularly in zones at risk, was insufficient. Greater co-ordination was needed, especially concerning the modalities of food aid distribution and its utilisation, if potential negative impacts were to be avoided.

3. The Food Aid Charter

By the late 1980s it was recognised that food aid needed to be better integrated into national food security strategies and that a long-term approach was essential if policy-makers in both northern capitals and the Sahel were serious about promoting agricultural growth and poverty alleviation. The idea of an international code of good conduct came earlier, however, and was first suggested at the Club du Sahel–CILSS Mindelo conference on 'Cereals Policies in the Sahelian Countries' in December 1986 and was included in the conference's recommendations [*Club du Sahel, 1987*]. In 1988, the Club du Sahel and the French Ministry of Co-operation officially proposed that a

---

4. The Network is more usually known by its French title, Réseau du Prévention des Crises Alimentaires dans le Sahel, as its working language and that of the Club du Sahel and CILSS is French.

code of good conduct be established for the Sahel in order to use this form of assistance more effectively and to combine developmental and humanitarian objectives with the goal of improved food security.

The original proposal drafted by the French consisted of guidelines covering: reliable and co-ordinated needs assessments; co-ordinated management of regional aid; co-ordinated monitoring of food aid shipments and deliveries; the use of NGOs in food aid distributions and in the management of counterpart funds; the management of substitution in the multi-annual programmes so as to avoid competition between aid imports and local production when harvests are good; and the inclusion of food aid in broader development policies. These guidelines followed the policy direction previously adopted by the French government during the reorganisation of its own food aid programme, and also reflected recent thinking about food aid by many international donors.

The Food Aid Charter, as it was to be called, was drawn up by a committee of donors and the CILSS executive secretariat. As indicated in the text given in the Appendix to this chapter, it was formally approved by the CILSS Heads of State at their summit meeting in February 1990 and adopted by six donors: Canada, the European Community, Germany, France, the Netherlands, and the United States. It is thus a joint declaration of both donor and recipient countries in an effort to maximise the impact of food aid on food security in the region. The Charter is not legally binding, but is an 'agreement' between donors and members of CILSS announcing a shared vision of good practice in the domain of food aid. Moreover, signing the Charter is not obligatory for donors to the Sahel. This approach not only saved time in terms of getting the Charter accepted. It was also considered that a more formal document would be unlikely to be any better observed by some of the more reluctant signatories.[5]

III. PRINCIPLES OF THE CHARTER

The Charter was seen as a means of formalising much of the thinking that had been going on in the 1980s concerning food aid and ways to make it 'an active component of overall development aid efforts'. It introduced a new form of discipline and awareness concerning food

---

5. The Charter was 'noted', for example, by the European Community Council of Ministers in 1989, but never formally accepted as a statement of EC food aid or food security policy more widely. However, the European Commission, in its role of managing European Community Action food aid, accepted the Charter as the basis for its relationship with CILSS countries.

aid in the region. Throughout the 1980s the food situation in the Sahel was governed by substantial but uncontrolled and often unrecorded uses of food aid. The Charter heralded the start of a new approach based upon building up mutual trust and co-operation between donors and recipient governments. Instead of systematically supplying food-stuffs, decisions concerning food aid interventions were to be based on better quality information about local agricultural production trends, populations in zones at risk and market prices.

Moreover, attention was focused on how the food aid was to be supplied. Strong emphasis was put on local purchases and triangular transactions when surpluses were available locally, rather than always relying on importing food from outside the region. Within this broader framework food aid was no longer to be programmed inde-pendently, but to be integrated into national agricultural and rural development policies and co-ordinated with other aid.

The basic idea of the Charter is quite simple. Instead of using food aid as a stop-gap measure, the objective is to maintain food supply at a relatively stable per capita level, through local or regional trade, while guaranteeing supplies to high-risk or underprivileged groups.

The Charter is based on three principles. First, rather than guessing at food requirements, which are often exaggerated, more reliable information is fundamental to establishing appropriate levels of need. The information sought embraces local agricultural production and prices, consumption norms and population levels, as well as physical indicators such as rainfall and groundcover. Second, there is a strong emphasis on co-ordination, which is designed to be carried out not only between donors and recipients but also among donors. Moreover, there is a focus on encouraging co-ordination both within the indivi-dual Sahelian governments concerning their own food security systems and among the countries of the region. Third, the Charter foc-uses on aid modalities and the implementation of interventions. Ana-lysing the different lines of defence in order to respond to crises and manage food supplies is crucial. Responding first with local, and then with regional supplies, and using imported food only as a last resort in severe emergency conditions is the basis for encouraging local pur-chases and triangular operations whenever possible.

In order to meet the basic principles outlined in the Charter, close co-ordination between donors and recipients is seen as essential in the following areas:

- joint discussions of cereal balances to obtain better information for the current year and to ensure that the situation in previous

years is taken into account when estimating the current year's food needs;
- sharing of information on the types and amounts of food aid needed and agreement on these numbers early in the pre-harvest season; and
- co-ordination of food aid distribution so that optimum use can be made of logistical resources and commercial or co-operative networks, in conjunction with private traders and NGOs.

IV. MAKING THE CHARTER WORK

1. Underpinnings of the Charter

It is not enough to decide that better information and overall co-ordination are necessary, for them to be guaranteed. Methodical action is required to find the best discussion forums and to build trust among all the stakeholders. Donors, in the form of the Club du Sahel, together with the CILSS have supported three mechanisms which underpin the application of the Charter by providing and assessing information about the regional food security situation and consultation about appropriate responses. These essential mechanisms for implementing the Charter were already basically in place. Application of the Charter was, in effect, a way of making existing institutional arrangements function together more effectively.

First, as a measure to increase the *quality* and *quantity* of information, DIAPER[6] helps information systems in all nine CILSS countries carry out production surveys (pre-harvest estimates and preparing final harvest production assessments) and cereal balance sheets at a national level. DIAPER is a CILSS project supported by funding from the European Union. Other donors are also involved in improving the reliability of data for the region. For example, every October/November, the FAO's Global Information Warning System (GIEWS), in collaboration with CILSS/DIAPER, conducts annual crop assessments in each country of the region to evaluate the next harvest. The involvement of both an international and a regional agency implies a concerted effort to make a balanced assessment of the production situation in each country. National cereal balance sheets include food aid as well as commercial imports in their calculations, giving an indication of the evolution of the national food supply from one year to the next.

---

6. The Permanent Regional Project for Diagnosis of Food Security in the Sahel.

Second, the AGRHYMET Centre[7] in Niamey, established in 1974, is now part of the group of specialised CILSS institutions that provide essential early warning information. It houses the most important array of modern agrometeorological equipment in West Africa, including equipment for interpreting remote sensing from the main civil land observation satellites. Its objective is to provide timely and reliable climatological and vegetation cover data on the region. It has also embarked recently on analysis to identify populations and zones at risk. Its data and greening maps provide rapidly available information on the progress of the rainy season, planting, pasturage growth, and so forth.

The third mechanism underpinning the Charter is the Network for the Prevention of Food Crises which meets every November at the end of the Sahelian cropping season. The Network provides a forum for regular discussion which is informal, and has broad participation from Club du Sahel members, specialised international agencies such as FAO and WFP, representatives from the CILSS and its agencies, and from some NGOs, and technical experts. The main purpose of the annual meeting is to review the information presented by both DIAPER and AGRHYMET in order to agree on the food security situation for the forthcoming season.

Certain topics are discussed at every yearly meeting, namely the previous year's food balances, the current year's food balance forecasts, food aid operations during the previous year, as well as food aid requirements in the light of the current year's pre-harvest estimates. Other issues such as methodological problems in harvest estimations, the calculation of consumption norms, and the construction of early warning and market information systems are also discussed. In addition, current concerns in the region such as rising cereal prices, difficulties with local purchases and the status of various national security stocks are often brought up during the meetings.

The Network is a flexible instrument for analysing and identifying the best methods of responding to needs and pockets of deficit, even in good years. It is an established forum where information from regional sources as well as data from international organisations are presented and discussed. Donors are thus able to examine issues of current concern and make proposals in close association with Sahelian and other experts in the field. The Network ensures that a regular exchange of information and co-ordination among donors are encouraged and supported in a transparent, concrete and informal manner.

---

7. The Regional Centre for Training and Operational Application of Agrometeorology and Hydrology Information and Analysis.

2. Evaluation

The existence of a charter does not ensure its systematic application. Monitoring and surveillance are needed to see whether the institutions and agencies involved adhere in practice to the major principles or if, on the contrary, their operations fail to respect them. It is not enough to identify practices in contradiction of the Charter; the situation giving rise to these contradictions needs to be analysed and the reasons for variance from the principles understood. It is with this in mind that evaluations provided for in the Charter are carried out every year jointly by the Club du Sahel and the CILSS. Their results are presented and discussed at the annual meeting of the Network and included in its widely circulated reports.

These evaluations offer a way for donors to improve their performance and become aware of other donors' interventions in a given country. They also serve as an input in the co-ordinating process. They describe the current national information systems and their capabilities. All food aid interventions are also examined and information is provided on the different types of interventions, their geographical location, tonnage, objectives, difficulties encountered, etc. The evaluations thus serve not only to put pressure on donors to adhere to the Charter, but also to inform them of other interventions in the same country. Finally, the evaluation process also helps make the Charter and its framework better known not only in the donor community but also throughout the region.

3. Impact of the Charter

It is difficult to establish conclusively what impact the code has had on donor behaviour concerning food aid allocations and uses. There is the difficulty of developing a counterfactual scenario. For example, there is a widespread consensus that those donors who respect the Charter's principles would have carried out their food aid operations in the same manner even had there not been a code. There is the further difficulty of isolating the input of the Charter from that of the other regional mechanisms for supporting food security. However, the annual evaluations suggest that the code has acted as a brake on inconsistent behaviour by donors who would otherwise be inclined to disregard certain key aspects of good practice in food aid in the choice of modalities of food aid distribution. For example, the Charter and its compliance mechanisms helped to limit the monetisation of imported food provided by certain donors in the early 1990s and also increased the level of local purchases during surplus years. It is important to note that some of the donors who have officially adopted the Sahel Charter, as well as other agencies which distribute food aid, adhere to its principles in their activities in other parts of the world.

297

The Charter has had an impact on the CILSS member states as well. It has encouraged Sahelian responsibility for food security issues in the region. And it has supported Sahelian partnerships in addressing contentious regional issues concerning food aid, such as overcoming barriers to triangular transactions or determining appropriate levels of assistance. The existence of the Charter and the supporting regional mechanisms ensures both reliable information and co-ordination which have acted to reinforce donor–recipient dialogue. It has also provided many of the Sahelian governments with the context and the necessary tools to make appropriate appeals for food aid in conjunction with the donor community. This is not to say that there are no problems in the Sahel concerning the use of food aid, or concerning differing opinions on the severity of problems or the appropriate responses. Food aid is still considered as a source of revenue and a political tool by some governments in the region.[8] However, the Charter and its supporting structures constitute a solid basis for Sahelians to assume greater ownership of the process of assuring food security in the region.

A specific weakness of the Charter which has limited its impact is the fact that knowledge of its provisions and process is limited largely to those directly involved. Despite the annual evaluations and meetings of the Network for the Prevention of Food Crises, the Charter is familiar to only a relatively small circle of officials at headquarters. In addition, there have been new food aid donors to countries in the region which are unaware of the regional process. The Club and the CILSS are trying to address this issue. The constant turnover of both recipient government and donor staff in country offices makes this difficult, however.

It is impossible to isolate the influence the Charter has had on food aid deliveries during the 1990s in terms of tonnage and modalities. Figure 12.1 shows trends in food aid deliveries to the region from 1985/86 to 1997/98. Total food aid flows to the Sahel have decreased from a peak of 675,625 tonnes in 1985/86 to an average of 254,000 tonnes since 1993/94. Moreover, while project aid deliveries have remained fairly constant during this period, programme aid deliveries have plummeted. Emergency aid fluctuated from year to year reflecting production variations, with relatively small emergency needs since 1993/94. This downward trend is more consistent than for global food aid (cf. Chapter 1).

---

8. See, for example, the Evaluation of EU Programme Food Aid case-studies for the region in Cape Verde [*Ferreira Duarte and Metz, 1996*], Mali [*Lanser and Delefosse, 1995a*] and Mauritania [*Lanser and Delefosse, 1995b*].

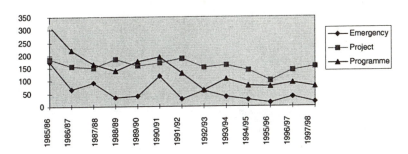

FIGURE 12.1
BREAKDOWN OF FOOD AID DELIVERIES TO CILSS
MEMBER COUNTRIES BY TYPE FOR MARKETING
YEARS 1985/86 TO 1997/98
(IN '000 t)

Source: WWW.FP.org/monit 99.

A major factor in the decline in the volume of food aid delivered to the region during this period has been the relatively better agricultural performance in recipient countries. This improvement has for the most part been linked to more favourable rainfall in the region halting or even possibly reversing the downward trend in total rainfall of the 1950s to 1980s. Another factor has been the reduced availability of programme food aid during the 1990s. In some cases, such as Cape Verde, this has involved a shift to commercial imports, whilst other recipients such as Mali have simply become more self-sufficient in cereals. The reduced availability of food aid is also linked to competition with other regions such as the Great Lakes, coupled with the emergence of new regions in need of large amounts of food aid, such as the Balkans. This has meant lower food aid deliveries to regions such as the Sahel.

Direct transfers still exceed local purchases and triangular transactions within the region (Figure 12.2). However, there has been a marked change since 1992/93. Local purchases, which are commonly part of food security projects, increased and on average made up almost 19 per cent of total deliveries from 1992/93 to 1997/98, while the average of the previous seven years was only 8 per cent. Triangular transactions show no clear trend. Consequently, with declining direct transfer levels, the acquisition of food within the region now provides a substantial share approaching one-third of the total.

FIGURE 12.2

BREAKDOWN OF DELIVERIES TO CILSS MEMBER COUNTRIES BY SUPPLY
TRANSACTION FOR MARKETING YEARS 1985/86 TO 1996/97
(IN '000 t)

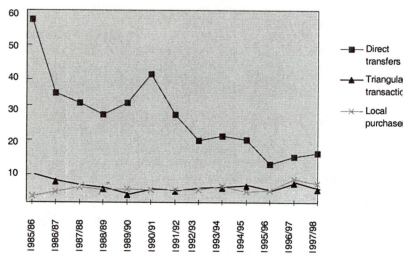

Source: WWW.FP.org/monit 99.

Although a direct correlation between the Charter and certain shifts in
the quantities and modalities of food aid to the region cannot be
made, the existence of the Charter marks an awareness among key
stakeholders of the importance of using food aid within a more coherent, longer-term development perspective. For the Sahel this perspective means a sharper focus on food security, including disaster
preparedness and prevention. The relative stability of triangular and
local purchases within the region is directly associated with projects
designed to use food from within the region, for example those
funded by Germany. The Charter underlines the importance of the
quality of interventions, not the quantity.

Since the mid-1980s, regional and even national food security
arrangements have not been put to the test of a drought-driven regional crisis. The mechanisms put in place thus far to provide reliable
and timely information and support co-ordinated interventions have
yet to be tested in a large-scale emergency. This in and of itself does
not invalidate the progress made to date with regard to the code and
its influence on donors' practices and co-ordination. However, it does

mean that the Charter's influence in a non-typical year or series of years needs to be examined to see whether this framework can still function effectively under disaster conditions. There is doubt, in certain quarters, as to whether either the international community or the Sahelians are truly prepared, and whether the co-ordinating mechanisms reinforced through the Charter would prove adequate in the event of another major drought in the region.

The increasing improvement in the national information systems as well as the growing competence of regional centres such as AGRHYMET mean that some of the preparedness mechanisms for a large-scale disaster are in place. The Network is also a well-established forum for discussing forthcoming problems, and particularly those to do with increasingly severe food insecurity. However, only the performance of recipients and donors in a major crisis will test the robustness and effectiveness of the arrangements that have been developed to support food security.

It is important to emphasise that, although the Charter aims to improve the effectiveness of food aid both in a normal year and in a crisis situation, its text is a statement of general principles and there is little detail to guide the various stakeholders in the face of a serious food shortfall in the region. However, in a severe emergency, it is not the articles of the Charter as such but the framework within which it exists, and the strength of those mechanisms which since 1990 have encouraged improvements in food aid practices in the region, that would be put to the test.

4. Factors Contributing to the Charter's 'Success'

The political and environmental situation in the Sahel lends itself to this kind of common agreement to manage food aid interventions. The Sahel is a region which is relatively stable politically, and where the most serious threat is climatic. Seven of the countries in the region share common agro-ecological features,[9] and the majority also share common cultural norms and economic structures. In particular, the five most important food producers, Burkina Faso, Chad, Mali, Niger, and Senegal, are part of the CFA Franc zone which has guaranteed monetary stability and facilitates trade (both official and unrecorded). These two characteristics contribute significantly to effective co-ordination and achieving a common vision of how to improve food aid interventions. Climatic disaster is easier to predict and prepare for

9.   Nine of the countries are at least partly in the semi-arid Sahel climatic zone. The exceptions are the Cape Verde Islands,which are largely arid and Guinea Bissau, which is a humid tropical coastal state.

than a complex conflict-related emergency. The region's common agro-ecological characteristics also mean that it is easier to identify problems and consider possible solutions on a regional basis. These are advantages which are not negligible when comparing the Sahel with other regions in Africa.

Moreover, commercial or political considerations are relatively less important in the region than elsewhere, and donors' interests in development and the food security debate have therefore been less muddied by other considerations. This has helped to focus the discussion between partners on agricultural and environmental issues and to identify problems and solutions in a more transparent and coherent manner.

Another factor contributing to the Charter's relative success is the existence of both a regional institution, the CILSS, and a parallel and voluntary donor-based institution, the Club du Sahel. Without the support of these two institutions, the focus on improved food aid practices in the region would not have been sustained once the drought-related crisis had passed. Moreover, one element of the Club's mandate is to improve donor–Sahelian co-ordination, co-operation and dialogue on a range of issues. Thus the North–South partnership embodied in the Charter has firm institutional backing.

V. WHAT CAN BE LEARNED FROM THE SAHEL EXPERIENCE?

The idea of using codes of good conduct or a charter to improve donor practice and establish minimum standards for humanitarian aid including food aid has been explored, partly in emulation of the Sahel Charter and as a response to widespread evidence of unacceptable practice in some major humanitarian operations [*Leader, 1999*]. This examination of the Charter and its performance since 1990 indicates some of the conditions necessary for success and what is realistically achievable in setting standards for aid practice.

First, the Food Aid Charter for the Sahel cannot be separated from the other mechanisms in place, which contribute to both its usefulness and the process of co-ordination as a whole. The Charter originated from shared concerns and a common perception of the problems associated with inappropriate food aid operations. It was a means of giving expression to these concerns, but importantly it was never seen as a stand-alone tool, but as part of a process to encourage co-operation with the aim of achieving long-term food security. The support and strengthening of the different information systems and the establishment of the Network for the Prevention of Food Crises provided the technical environment for the Charter to be implemented, discussed and evaluated. The fact that the Charter reflected the concerns of the day, and that the problems of different stakeholders were analysed within it meant that there was an interest not only in signing the Charter but also in adhering to it.

Second, the history of the Sahel Charter is not about establishing guidelines for good practice. The Charter is one tool among several, which is supported by both donors and Sahelians. The process of strengthening information systems, sharing and discussing information, and adopting common positions concerning the use of food aid is much more important than the Charter itself. The common view of the necessity to reinforce measures not only to predict but also to prevent food crises in the region is as important as the document itself.

Third, the Charter and certainly the continued success of the meetings held by the Network signal a mutual confidence on the part of the various stakeholders in the process in which they are engaging. The existence of a ready forum for consultation and informal discussions has facilitated the use of the Charter, and was essential to the way it has been implemented. The fact that the necessity of evaluating the application of the Charter was foreseen, and that these evaluations could be undertaken by regional institutions ensured the Charter's place in the overall debates about food aid and food security in the region.

A further question arising from the current interest in codes and charters is whether such statements or declarations are likely to be more effective if adopted at a regional or a global level. Judging from the Sahel Charter, it is evident that, in order for the principles to have real validity, there is a need for a shared understanding of the issues at stake – the problems faced by both the donors and the recipient countries.

> Any 'real' code needs wide participation in its development and opt-in so that it depends on a constituency with shared values and objectives. With a shared set of values and objectives, vagueness in a code can be acceptable; without it vagueness is a weakness and leads to confusion [*Leader, 1999*].

At a regional level, when most of the countries share common characteristics and they and the limited group of donor and multilateral agency stakeholders are in broad agreement about not only the problems but also the appropriate solutions, then a formal joint statement such as a code of conduct is more likely to be a useful device in co-operation, and with a better chance of success.

It is interesting to note that, although the Charter originated from concerns about too much food aid in the region, its principles still hold true, despite dramatic reductions in food aid flows. This is most likely due to the fact that the Charter is not the centrepiece of ensuring food security in the region, but rather the expression of a common view of the importance of co-ordinated action to prevent food crises and ensure food security for the region's population. Initiatives to create principles of good conduct or codes concerning food aid practices should look carefully at the Sahelian example, since it underscores the importance of process in assuring co-ordination and common approaches and highlights the uselessness of words on a page unaccompanied by support mechanisms.

REFERENCES

Club du Sahel, 1987, *Cereals Policies in Sahel Countries, Acts of the Mindelo Conference*, Paris.
Club du Sahel, 1990, *Official Text of the Food Aid Charter*, Paris: Club du Sahel and CILSS.
Coleo, S., 1994, 'Politique céréalière. Capitalisation de l'expérience des trois premières phases du PRMC au Mali', Report for the European Commission, Paris: Club du Sahel.
Egg, J. and J.J. Gabas, eds., 1997, *Preventing Food Crises in the Sahel*, Paris: OECD.
Euronaid, 1995, *Code of Conduct on Food Aid and Food Security*, Brussels: Euronaid and Liaison Committee of Development NGOs of the European Union.
Gabas, J.J., 1997, 'The Food Aid Charter in the Sahel', in Egg and Gabas, eds.
Jost, S., G. Simon and F. Trine, 1997, 'Ten Years of Food Aid in CILSS Member States', in Egg and Gabas, eds.
Ferreira Duarte, R. and M. Metz, 1996, *Cape Verde: An Extended Study* (Evaluation of EU Programme Food Aid), London: Overseas Development Institute.
Lanser, P. and O. Delefosse, 1995a, *République du Mali: évaluation rapide* (Evaluation of EU Programme Food Aid), London: Overseas Development Institute.
Lanser, P. and O. Delefosse, 1995b, *République Islamique du Mauritanie: evaluation rapide* (Evaluation of EU Programme Food Aid), London: Overseas Development Institute.
Leader, Nick, 1999, 'Codes of Conduct: Who Needs Them?' *RNN Newsletter*, No. 13, London: Overseas Development Institute.
SPHERE,1998, 'The SPHERE Project: Humanitarian Charter and Minimum Standards in Disaster Response' (A Programme for Humanitarian Response and Inter Action with Voice, ICRC, ICVA), Geneva.
USAID, 1997, 'A Code of Good Conduct for Food Aid within the Context of Food Security for the Greater Horn of Africa', Washington DC: USAID.

APPENDIX

Official Text of the Food Aid Charter

This document has been unanimously adopted by CILSS member nations and Club du Sahel donor countries (Canada, European Economic Community, Germany, France, Netherlands, United States). It was formally approved by CILSS heads of state at their summit meeting in Guinea Bissau on 10 February 1990.

The concerned parties
1- Recognizing the importance of food aid in the struggle against hunger and malnutrition;
2- Recognizing a pressing need for food aid to be treated as an active component of overall development aid efforts aiming to create an ability to provide adequate food supplies, either through production or commercial imports;
3- Recognizing that both donors and beneficiaries have expressed the wish that the food aid system be improved by drawing on past experience and by applying the recommendations made in this respect;
4- Recognizing the need to adapt, to the extent possible, food aid to the qualitative and quantitative requirements of target populations in such a way as to avoid significant falls in the market prices of food products, as well as resulting marketing constraints;
5- Recognizing the importance of supporting swift, flexible procedures allowing at minimal expense a reliable supply of food aid by sea, land, or, as a last resort, air;
6- Recognizing the need to avoid promoting a greater dependence on imports through actions liable to foster long-term changes in consumption patterns away from locally produced cereals;
7- Recognizing that food surpluses as well as food deficits can have a destabilizing effect upon prices, revenues, and food availability, and the need to integrate food aid into regional trade prices so that the market can better absorb local fluctuations in food supply;
8- Recognizing that there can be no real solution to the problems posed by food aid unless donors reach a consensus among themselves in agreement with the beneficiaries to coordinate efforts and actions.

Adhere to the following:

I. Definition of the objectives of food aid

The general objective of food aid is to help support food security by addressing, in a timely and appropriate manner, problems arising from food shortages or deficits, whether they are caused by structural deficiencies, or crisis situations calling for emergency actions.

The long-term objective is to prevent crises and to correct structural deficiencies by supporting overall development and taking actions aimed directly at vulnerable groups. In this context, food aid plays a positive role, whether it is supplied as foodstuffs, or through the use of counterpart funds generated through local sales.

II. Evaluation of the food situation

II.1. The concerned donor governments, multilateral aid organizations, and governments of beneficiary countries, in collaboration with all involved partners, undertake to cooperate on the evaluation of the food situation in Sahelian countries, to help base decisions on reliable information and realistic forecasts, particularly on deficits and surpluses. Similarly, when the situation calls for emergency aid, the parties agree to share immediately information at their disposal to facilitate appropriate decisions and actions. The parties undertake to continue in their efforts to improve the quality of national and regional data.

II.2. The concerned parties also undertake to improve and harmonize their own appraisal criteria, based upon:
– proper analysis of each country's food requirements and food availability: domestic production and consumption, movements of stocks, all types of imports and exports;
– indicators of the food situation, involving nutritional status and the purchasing power of the population groups concerned, prices on the different markets, and availability of food products in production and consumption areas;
– food aid absorptive capacity of each country, and availability of additional financial and technical resources needed to make effective use of food aid.

III. Evaluation of food aid requirements

Beneficiary governments and bilateral or multilateral donors undertake to hold discussions at least once a year in order to evaluate food needs on the basis of jointly derived food balance data, with a view toward defining:
– he objectives of food aid in its different forms;
– types, quantities, and qualities of aid to be supplied;
– the areas and population groups concerned;
– logistical constraints;
– periods when delivery is desirable, and periods when delivery would become inappropriate.
These components will determine the provisional supply schedule which food aid donors and national authorities will agree to implement. This schedule can then be used as the incremental framework for all subsequent action to be taken by the different partners. In countries where no coordination mechanism exists, action shall be taken to fill this gap.

IV. Practical implementation of food aid activities

IV.1. The donors undertake to harmonize their decisions, and agree to coordinate their actions. In order to ensure optimum satisfaction of requirements, and to make the best use of logistic resources, donors will work with each Sahelian country to jointly define:
- quantitative distribution of food aid shipments;
- the choice of products;
- the origin of food aid (local purchases, triangular operations, imports);
- beneficiaries.

The donors will keep each other informed on:
- the expected time lag between the assessment of needs and the supply of aid;
- means of food aid distribution and utilization;
- basic logistical organization.

IV.2. The concerned parties recognize the need to integrate food aid into agricultural and rural development policies, to coordinate it with other types of aid, trade policies and macro-economic policies, and to integrate food aid into long-term development plans. As is possible, multi-annual programs should remain sufficiently flexible to allow for the provision of financial or technical assistance in lieu of foodstuffs, provided the food supply situation warrants it. The donors therefore undertake:
- to indicate the quantities and types of annual or multi-annual aid they plan to allocate, so that beneficiary countries may take this into account when formulating their development policies;
- to adjust their aid to avoid, to the extent possible, harmful effects on local production and marketing, i.e., reduction of market share, lower producer prices, disruption of distribution channels, or saturation of storage facilities;
- to minimize actions directly promoting lasting changes in food consumption patterns to the detriment of local production.

IV.3. The donors and the beneficiary countries undertake:
- not to distribute food aid freely except in the case of emergency aid or to help vulnerable groups;
- to sell food aid without prejudice to domestic free market prices;
- to use counterpart funds proceeds to support development activities, particularly those aimed at food security.

IV.4. The donors and the beneficiary countries undertake:
- to promote cereal flows between surplus and deficit countries through economically viable triangular operations and the stimulation of regional cereals trade.

V. Food balance sheets and prospects

V.1. The annual meeting of the Network for the Prevention of Food Crises in the Sahel, jointly organized by the CILSS and the Club du Sahel, will provide an opportunity to make retrospect evaluations of:
- trends in the nutritional status of beneficiary populations;
- the impact of aid on the national economies of the beneficiary countries, in particular on trade and rural development;
- the contribution of donors and beneficiaries to overall food security.

V.2. The concerned parties undertake to examine possible improvements in this area in particular:
- monitoring of the food situation;
- coordination of evaluations;
- the distribution of tasks and responsibilities among donors and beneficiaries;
- the procurement of transport and other logistical means for the delivery of food aid;
- more generally, the overall mechanism promoting better coordination and closer cooperation among all parties.

Source: Club du Sahel [*1990*].

13

Follow-up of the Code of Conduct of the International Red Cross and Red Crescent Movement

ALAIN MOUREY

I. INTRODUCTION

The International Red Cross and Red Crescent Movement consists of the International Committee of the Red Cross (ICRC), the International Federation of Red Cross and Red Crescent Societies (IFRC) and the National Red Cross and Red Crescent Societies. The ICRC is the founding body of the Red Cross and acts as a neutral intermediary in armed conflicts and disturbances. The ICRC attempts, either on its own initiative or basing its action on the Geneva Conventions, to provide protection and assistance to the victims of international and civil wars and of internal disturbances and tension. The role of the IFRC is to contribute to the development of the humanitarian activities of the National Societies and to co-ordinate their relief operations for victims of disasters not caused by armed conflict situations. The IFRC is also involved in relief operations for refugees outside the areas of conflict.

The Movement's mandate is by no means centred on food aid. However, food aid may well be a substantial part of its disaster relief programmes. In 1993, the Movement adopted a Code of Conduct for disaster relief, in order to safeguard its standards in terms of independence, effectiveness and impact of disaster response. Hence the Code is specific not to food aid but to disaster response in general, but it obviously guides food aid activities as well. This chapter describes the Code and the subsequent steps taken by the Red Cross Movement and the wider NGO community to implement it.

II. THE CODE OF CONDUCT

In 1991, the Council of Delegates[1] adopted Resolution No. 17 as follows:

> The Council of Delegates,
> *concerned* for the respect for the Fundamental Principles of the International Red Cross and Red Crescent Movement, proclaimed by the 20th Conference and revised by the 25th Conference, [and] *aware* of the essential role of the International Red Cross and Red Crescent Movement in international humanitarian activities and related codification,
>
> (i) *asks* the International Federation of Red Cross and Red Crescent Societies, in consultation with the main relief organisations, to set up a group of experts to study the possibility of elaborating a Code of Conduct relative to humanitarian aid in situations of natural and technological disasters;
> (ii) *requests* the Federation, after consultation with the main relief organisations, to report on the outcome of that study to the next Council of Delegates.

Seven major NGO groups or alliances (the IFRC, Caritas Internationalis, the Catholic Relief Services, the International Save the Children Alliance, the World Lutheran Federation, Oxfam and the World Council of Churches) then set up a Steering Committee for Humanitarian Response (SCHR) to work out the terms of the Code. The following year, the ICRC also became involved, and the Code was revised to cover situations of armed conflict as well. The Code was therefore to be interpreted and applied in conformity with international humanitarian law. The version submitted to the Council of Delegates in October 1993 was approved by the Council in Resolution No. 6, in which the Council urged that steps be taken to promote the Code of Conduct by its dissemination amongst disaster response agencies, and that it be brought to the attention of governments by all appropriate means.

The Code is not concerned with operational details. It is a voluntary Code, implemented by the consent of the organisations which accept it, to maintain the standards it lays down. It consists of ten

---

1. This council constitutes the assembly of the Red Cross 'family', its members being representatives of the ICRC and the IFRC, as well as delegates from all the recognised National Societies. It meets every two years and, *inter alia*, is called on to give an opinion on questions of policy or on any other subject of common interest to the Movement.

succinct Principles together with three Annexes of recommendations directed respectively to: (a) the governments of the disaster-affected countries, (b) the donor governments and (c) the intergovernmental organisations, plus a registration form. The ten Principles are as follows:

1. The humanitarian imperative comes first.
2. Aid is given regardless of the race, creed or nationality of the recipients and without adverse distinction of any kind. Aid priorities are calculated on the basis of need alone.
3. Aid will not be used to further a particular political or religious standpoint.
4. We shall endeavour not to act as instruments of government foreign policy.
5. We shall respect culture and customs.
6. We shall attempt to build disaster response on local capacities.
7. Ways shall be found to involve programme beneficiaries in the management of relief aid.
8. Relief aid must strive to reduce future vulnerabilities to disaster as well as meeting basic needs.
9. We hold ourselves accountable to both those we seek to assist and those from whom we accept resources.
10. In our information, publicity and advertising activities, we shall recognise disaster victims as dignified human beings, not objects of pity.

As can be seen, the Code is very general and simply aims at outlining a broad ethic for humanitarian intervention. Its objective is to heighten the awareness of relief organisations in reference to the common principles in their work, which may also trigger better co-operation and co-ordination among these organisations. The fact that the Code is not legally binding is a positive factor in the sense that it is not so much intended to correct systematic mistakes which may have occurred in the past as to build up a culture of humanitarian intervention based on the good will and interest of the main relief organisations. Furthermore, in today's political, social and economic environment, a binding instrument might well scare off organisations rather than attract them. In the event, in view of the tremendous difficulties there are in obtaining compliance with existing binding instruments, it seems better to obtain adherence to a Code of Conduct because people are convinced of the cultural advantages of complying with it, rather than because it carries the threat of sanctions if it is not respected.

III. FOLLOW-UP TO THE CODE

1. Dissemination

After the adoption of the Code by the Council of Delegates in 1993, the Federation, acting on its own behalf as well as representing the SCHR, took steps towards disseminating the Code together with the ICRC. First, the Code was translated from English into French, Spanish and Arabic. Promotion of the Code was directed towards the programmes and agencies of the United Nations; the European NGOs via the Federation and the Liaison Office of the NGOs of the European Union in Brussels; and the American NGOs via the American Red Cross Society in collaboration with InterAction (American Council for Voluntary International Action) which encourages collective action within the activities of most important NGOs in the United States. The Code was also distributed to the Permanent Missions in New York, the Red Cross and Red Crescent National Societies, the offices and delegations of both the Federation and the ICRC, and the international donor community. The NGOs were invited to apply the Code on a voluntary basis but once they had adopted its Principles, they were regarded as committed to abide by them.

In 1995, the 26th International Conference of the Red Cross and Red Crescent issued the following Resolution 4E concerning the Code:

> *With regard to the Code of Conduct for the International Red Cross and Red Crescent Movement and Non Governmental Organisations (NGOs) in Disaster Relief, [the Conference]:*
> 1. *takes note of and welcomes* the Code of Conduct for the International Red Cross and Red Crescent Movement and Non Governmental Organisations (NGOs) in Disaster Relief. ... and further,
> 2. *invites* all States and National Societies to encourage NGOs to both abide by the principles and spirit of the Code and consider registering their support for the Code with the International Federation.

The important point about support for the Code by the International Conference was that it signified that the governments signatory to the Geneva Conventions and their additional Protocols also supported the Code, since the resolutions of the Conference are issued jointly by both the governments and the Red Cross and Red Crescent Movement.

These promotion efforts have resulted in 145 organisations having registered their support as well as about 175 National Societies. Also, some donors as well as the World Food Programme make registration of support for the Code a precondition for their funding of NGOs or for the application of NGOs to be their implementing agencies.

2. *The Sphere Project*

In 1995, following the Council of Delegates and the 26th International Conference of the Red Cross and Red Crescent, a mandate was given to the IFRC and the ICRC to work on setting up technical standards, as a follow-up to the Code. This stems from the fact that the Code belongs to the ethical side of humanitarian behaviour, and that the ethic needs eventually to be translated into practical humanitarian action. The Federation began to elaborate technical standards for its assistance, but the ICRC found difficulty in establishing universal minimal criteria owing to the diversity of situations, resources and local capacities with which it was faced. Eventually, the SCHR together with InterAction shouldered the responsibility of the project which is now called the 'Sphere Project', whilst the ICRC, together with VOICE, a European consortium of voluntary agencies working in emergencies, has the status of an observer. The UN agencies, including UNHCR, DHA, UNICEF and WFP, have declared their support for the Project and are also participating in the dialogue.

After a number of revisions, the Sphere Project eventually materialised in 1998. It consists of:

(i) A Humanitarian Charter outlining the philosophy under which humanitarian assistance operations are to be launched and carried out. This is based on existing international laws and practices and affirms the rights to which victims of disasters are entitled and which must be promoted and supported. The Charter is founded on the following principles and commitments:

- The affected people are to meet their basic needs first through their own efforts, whilst it is the primary role and responsibility of the state to provide assistance when people's own coping capacity is exceeded.
- The role and responsibilities of the humanitarian agencies reflect the reality that those with primary responsibility are not always able or willing to perform this role themselves.
- The signatories to the Charter reaffirm their belief in the humanitarian imperative and its primacy; in other words, they base

their intervention on the principle of humanity which means taking all possible steps to prevent or alleviate human suffering and affirming that affected civilians have a right to protection and assistance.

In particular, the following principles are of fundamental importance: the right to life with dignity; the principle of non-combatant immunity; and the principle of non-refoulement.

- There is also recognition of and support for the protection and assistance mandate of the ICRC and the UNHCR.
- In the event, the relief agencies should attempt to minimise as much as possible the adverse effects that assistance operations may have on the victims, especially in relation to the behaviour of warring parties.
- The aid agencies commit themselves to achieving the Minimum Standards of Humanitarian Response and to making every effort to ensure that disaster-affected people have access to at least their minimum requirements. They also hope to be held accountable to these commitments and are developing systems for accountability within their respective agencies.

The Charter is an introduction to the Minimum Standards of Humanitarian Response.

(ii) These Minimum Standards provide the basic technical guidelines for disaster response in the following fields: Water Supply and Sanitation; Nutrition; Food Aid; Shelter and Site Planning; and Health Services.
(iii) The Code of Conduct as described above.
(iv) A Code of best practice in the management and support of aid personnel, produced by People In Aid.[2]

---

2. People In Aid is a project which started in 1994, in order to make a survey into the working experience of expatriate field staff and managers working for British- and Irish-based agencies. The survey concluded that there was room for improvement. In response, a group of 11 organisations (Action Health, British Red Cross, International Health Exchange, Medical Foundation, Overseas Development Administration (DFID), Oxfam, RedR, Relief and Rehabilitation Network of the ODI, Returned Volunteer Action, Save the Children, Tear Fund) worked to produce the Code Of Best Practice In The Management And Support Of Aid Personnel.

These constituents of the Sphere Project have been widely circulated and are easily available in the humanitarian community. The participant agencies have been asked to investigate how the Project can be implemented in practice. In 1999, they provided valuable feedback for its final updating.

3. Institutional Follow-up

To achieve its objectives, the Sphere Project (which now includes the Code), needs to be followed up by actual implementation by the relevant organisations. Within the ICRC, it is discussed at every course concerning assistance. It is also the task of the Health and Relief Division, which is in charge of assistance, together with the Chief Medical Officer of the ICRC, to investigate the application and implementation of the Project and to formulate policies for its translation into practical operational programmes, projects and activities. It is important to stress, however, that the ICRC, as well as many other humanitarian organisations, have not waited for the Sphere Project to produce guidelines to ensure professionalism in their operations. For instance, in 1986, the Red Cross Movement adopted a Nutrition, Relief and Food Aid policy. Nevertheless, the Project is a valuable reminder of the basic principles in the main fields of humanitarian intervention.

IV. PROBLEMS WITH IMPLEMENTATION OF THE SPHERE PROJECT

Implementation of the Sphere Project faces difficulties for the same reasons as the implementation of international humanitarian law. First, there are too many stakeholders and too many different situations making it difficult to reach agreement. Not all actors have been directly involved in the elaboration of the Project, nor do they have the same interest in it. Where it is extremely positive that humanitarian organisations should reach a global agreement on how they ought to operate, this has little value when the authorities, governments, warring parties or economic actors see it either as a threat to their own affairs or as a source of their own profit and react accordingly. This is likely to lead relief organisations either to reduce their standards of working below the minimum set out in the Sphere Project, or to compromise in terms of actual behaviour. Also, the sometimes fierce competition within the 'humanitarian market' may cause the Sphere Project to be forgotten when it is not deliberately ignored.

The Code is also too vague when it comes to activities at field level. Phrases such as 'Aid priorities are to be calculated on the basis of needs alone', 'The Red Cross will respect culture and customs', 'Relief aid must strive to reduce future vulnerability to disaster as well as meeting basic needs' are easy to understand as broad statements of principle, and aid workers obviously agree with them. The problems start with their practical implementation, namely: How are needs to be assessed? What are to be the criteria for determining that there is actually a need for foreign assistance? What does it mean to respect culture and customs, how are they to be approached so that they can be understood as a prerequisite to being respected? How is vulnerability to be identified? What must be done to reduce vulnerability? etc.

Fewer valid guidelines exist about these practical issues, whilst many relief workers in the field, without in-depth knowledge of assistance or of people and culture, rely on their feelings and past experience and adopt a reactive approach, which quite often proves to be oversimplified and far from appropriate. An example of how preconceived ideas and untested concepts may turn assistance response in the wrong direction for years or decades, is the very question which arises today about the utility of food aid as a tool for development, whereas it has for a long time been taken for granted that it was in fact a very good tool.

The Sphere Project was supposed in part to resolve this problem of vagueness about how to implement the Code at the field level. However, while it provides basic guidelines about the main components of aid programmes, it does not give enough clues about the decision-making process and does not explain sufficiently how to do things. And these are the issues which matter when it comes to alleviating and preventing human suffering and reducing vulnerability. Hence, for those who already have experience and knowledge, the Minimum Standards are no more than extended check-lists, whilst for those with insufficient experience and knowledge, such check-lists will definitely not be enough to help them actually carry out an intervention. Also, having one chapter on nutrition and another on food aid does not make sense and can be quite misleading. In the event, the Project does indeed represent a step towards further professionalism in humanitarian intervention, but it still needs to be backed up by technical guidelines and manuals to link principles, concepts and practice.

Thirdly, follow-up to the Project (including the Code) by the signatory organisations is by no means straightforward. If these documents are an important reference, there is in fact very little precise information on how they are to be utilised. It would rather appear that agencies do not resort to them much in practice. Indeed, I personally have never heard any reference made to them when it comes to actually setting up an operation and co-ordinating activities. In the heat of action, the principles are assumed to be known, which means that they are quite simply forgotten; and when one is reminded of them, they may well be ignored since the notion of emergency is invoked every time one needs an excuse to sidestep them. It is also quite certain that many a worker at HQ or in the field does not actually know how to use the Sphere Project for better co-ordination, or does not remember or even know of its existence. In this respect, the rapid turnover of humanitarian staff does not help. In the event, it has to be acknowledged that for many people, the Code as well as the Minimum Standards are things it is 'nice to have' but that there is not much will to abide by them and certainly no such culture. This latter point stems partly from the fact that, as already noted, the documents are too vague and list things which at first glance appear so obvious that one can quickly be induced to forget about their existence. However, when looking at some current humanitarian operations, it is also obvious that even the most basic principles are not always applied for the first of the reasons given above. Hence reminders are necessary and efforts have to be made to implement them.

Another important aspect is that some of the relief actions carried out by the signatory organisations are motivated by such a competitive spirit that one is permitted to wonder about the actual utility of such an instrument. This sends us back again to the point about discussing the different stakeholders. In principle the signatory organisations should be seen as a common group of stakeholders, whereas in fact they are quite often stakeholders in their own interest. For instance, the SCHR recently received a written complaint about the behaviour of an NGO which was using its relief action as a pretext for active proselytism.

The precondition of registering with the Code to obtain funds for relief operations is easy to meet. However, donors have no way yet of evaluating whether the agencies actually comply with their commitments. Furthermore, the principles of the Code are general enough to allow for plenty of room for manoeuvre around them.Thus, if bad practice is deliberately undertaken, it will be easy to argue about it, whilst proof of bad practice will first have to be produced. And there is no control mechanism or entity with due authorisation to find out, demonstrate and argue that bad practice was actually deliberately carried out. Hence it will not be easy for donors to apply sanctions nor will it be easy for agencies signatory to the Code to bring pressure to bear on defaulters which could be considered objective sanctions in the context of the competition which exists today between the relief agencies.

V. CONCLUSIONS

At the level of the principle, the Code of Conduct is currently generating a quite universal dynamic of adhesion and wide acceptance, whilst the Sphere Project is now subject to still wider dissemination and support. With its last revision in line with feedback from its practical implementation, there will soon be a broad set of guidelines, ranging from the ethical aspects of disaster relief to its planning and, to a lesser extent, its implementation. This is without doubt a positive development in the humanitarian community. The Code and the Sphere Project represent two initiatives to bring coherence and accountability to the humanitarian response to disasters. The wide support for these documents reinforces their importance by confirming a general desire to improve disaster relief.

However, at the practical level, both the Code and the Sphere Project essentially emanate from the NGOs to guide their work and are of no help against the bad practices of governments, local authorities and warring parties, bad practices which eventually create many disasters. Since binding instruments such as international humanitarian laws are already very poorly complied with, NGOs are highly likely to face difficulties in persuading key actors in disasters to allow them to implement their relief activities according to the Project. These difficulties will exist essentially because of the absence of implementation mechanisms agreed upon by all the actors in disasters. The next step therefore is to design such mechanisms between the aid agencies and their partners in order to develop a common view of relief operations, and also to develop an inbuilt evaluation system in order to be able to improve and modify the humanitarian response in collaboration with all the actors involved.

As for the implementation mechanisms, a pilot project is currently being led by the British Red Cross to investigate the concept of an Ombudsman for humanitarian assistance. The idea is that the Humanitarian Ombudsman would monitor NGO misconduct and malpractice. This is an interesting initiative which needs to be undertaken carefully since it could have potentially positive and even negative consequences. The Ombudsman project is one amongst many possible ways of improving humanitarian assistance, and it is limited by being mostly directed at the voluntary sector humanitarian organisations. This means that other approaches have to be explored which would actually involve all the key actors concerned in the humanitarian response to disasters.

The Sphere Project, 1998, *Humanitarian Charter and Minimum Standards in Disaster Response* (A programme of The Steering Committee for Humanitarian Response & InterAction with VOICE, ICRC, ICVA). The Sphere Project, PO Box 372, 17 Chemin des Crêts, CH-1211 Geneva 19, Switzerland. First edition 1998. Geneva.

APPENDIX

Code of Conduct for the International Red Cross and Red Crescent Movement and Non-governmental Organisations (NGOs) in Disaster Relief

Sponsored by Caritas Internationalis, Catholic Relief Services, the International Federation of Red Cross and Red Crescent Societies, the International Save the Children Alliance, the Lutheran World Federation, Oxfam, and the World Council of Churches (members of the Steering Committee for Humanitarian Response), together with the International Committee of the Red Cross (ICRC).

Purpose

This Code of Conduct seeks to guard our standards of behaviour. It is not about operational details, such as how one should calculate food rations or set up a refugee camp. Rather, it seeks to maintain the high standards of independence, effectiveness and impact to which disaster response NGOs and the International Red Cross and Red Crescent Movement aspires. It is a voluntary code, enforced by the will of organisations accepting it to maintain the standards laid down in the Code.

In the event of armed conflict, the present Code of Conduct will be interpreted and applied in conformity with international humanitarian law.

The Code of Conduct is presented first. Attached to it are three annexes, describing the working environment that we would like to see created by Host Governments, Donor Governments and Intergovernmental Organisations in order to facilitate the effective delivery of humanitarian assistance.

Definitions

NGOs: NGOs (Non-Governmental Organisations) refers here to organisations, both national and international, which are constituted separate from the government of the country in which they are founded.

NGHAs: For the purposes of this text, the term Non-Governmental Humanitarian Agencies (NGHAs) has been coined to encompass the components of the International Red Cross and Red Crescent Movement – the International Committee of the Red Cross, The International Federation of Red Cross and

Red Crescent Societies and its member National Societies – and the NGOs as defined above. This code refers specifically to those NGHAs which are involved in disaster response.

IGOs: IGOs (Intergovernmental Organisations) refers to organisations constituted by two or more governments. It thus includes all United Nations agencies and regional organisations.

Disasters: A disaster is a calamitous event resulting in loss of life, great human suffering and distress, and large-scale material damage.

The Code of Conduct

Principles of Conduct for the International Red Cross and Red Crescent Movement and NGOs in Disaster Response Programmes

1: The humanitarian imperative comes first

The right to receive humanitarian assistance, and to offer it, is a fundamental humanitarian principle which should be enjoyed by all citizens of all countries. As members of the international community, we recognise our obligation to provide humanitarian assistance wherever it is needed. Hence the need for unimpeded access to affected populations, which is of fundamental importance in exercising that responsibility.

The prime motivation of our response to disaster is to alleviate human suffering amongst those least able to withstand the stress caused by disaster.

When we give humanitarian aid it is not a partisan or political act and should not be viewed as such.

2: Aid is given regardless of the race, creed or nationality of the recipients and without adverse distinction of any kind. Aid priorities are calculated on the basis of need alone

Wherever possible, we will base the provision of relief aid upon a thorough assessment of the needs of the disaster victims and the local capacities already in place to meet those needs.

Within the entirety of our programmes, we will reflect considerations of proportionality. Human suffering must be alleviated whenever it is found; life is as precious in one part of a country as another. Thus, our provision of aid will reflect the degree of suffering it seeks to alleviate.

In implementing this approach, we recognise the crucial role played by women in disaster-prone communities and will ensure that this role is supported, not diminished, by our aid programmes.

The implementation of such a universal, impartial and independent policy can only be effective if we and our partners have access to the necessary resources to provide for such equitable relief, and have equal access to all disaster victims.

3: *Aid will not be used to further a particular political or religious standpoint*

Humanitarian aid will be given according to the need of individuals, families and communities. Notwithstanding the right of NGHAs to espouse particular political or religious opinions, we affirm that assistance will not be dependent on the adherence of the recipients to those opinions.

We will not tie the promise, delivery or distribution of assistance to the embracing or acceptance of a particular political or religious creed.

4: *We shall endeavour not to act as instruments of government foreign policy*

NGHAs are agencies which act independently from governments. We therefore formulate our own policies and implementation strategies and do not seek to implement the policy of any government, except in so far as it coincides with our own independent policy.

We will never knowingly – or through negligence – allow ourselves, or our employees, to be used to gather information of a political, military or economically sensitive nature for governments or other bodies that may serve purposes other than those which are strictly humanitarian, nor will we act as instruments of foreign policy of donor governments.

We will use the assistance we receive to respond to needs and this assistance should not be driven by the need to dispose of donor commodity surpluses, nor by the political interest of any particular donor.

We value and promote the voluntary giving of labour and finances by concerned individuals to support our work and recognise the independence of action promoted by such voluntary motivation. In order to protect our independence we will seek to avoid dependence upon a single funding source.

5: *We shall respect culture and custom*

We will endeavour to respect the culture, structures and customs of the communities and countries we are working in.

6: *We shall attempt to build disaster response on local capacities*

All people and communities – even in disaster – possess capacities as well as vulnerabilities. Where possible, we will strengthen these capacities by employing local staff, purchasing local materials and trading with local companies. Where possible, we will work through local NGHAs as partners in planning and implementation, and co-operate with local government structures where appropriate.

We will place a high priority on the proper co-ordination of our emergency responses. This is best done within the countries concerned by those most directly involved in the relief operations, and should include representatives of the relevant UN bodies.

7: Ways shall be found to involve programme beneficiaries in the management of relief aid

Disaster response assistance should never be imposed upon the beneficiaries. Effective relief and lasting rehabilitation can best be achieved where the intended beneficiaries are involved in the design, management and implementation of the assistance programme. We will strive to achieve full community participation in our relief and rehabilitation programmes.

8: Relief aid must strive to reduce future vulnerabilities to disaster as well as meeting basic needs

All relief actions affect the prospects for long-term development, either in a positive or a negative fashion. Recognising this, we will strive to implement relief programmes which actively reduce the beneficiaries' vulnerability to future disasters and help create sustainable lifestyles. We will pay particular attention to environmental concerns in the design and management of relief programmes. We will also endeavour to minimise the negative impact of humanitarian assistance, seeking to avoid long-term beneficiary dependence upon external aid.

9: We hold ourselves accountable to both those we seek to assist and those from whom we accept resources

We often act as an institutional link in the partnership between those who wish to assist and those who need assistance during disasters. We therefore hold ourselves accountable to both constituencies.

All our dealings with donors and beneficiaries shall reflect an attitude of openness and transparency.

We recognise the need to report on our activities, from both a financial perspective and the perspective of effectiveness.

We recognise the obligation to ensure appropriate monitoring of aid distributions and to carry out regular assessments of the impact of disaster assistance.

We will also seek to report, in an open fashion, upon the impact of our work, and the factors limiting or enhancing that impact.

Our programmes will be based upon high standards of professionalism and expertise in order to minimise the wasting of valuable resources.

10: In our information, publicity and advertising activities, we shall recognise disaster victims as dignified human beings, not objects of pity

Respect for the disaster victim as an equal partner in action should never be lost. In our public information we shall portray an objective image of the disaster situation where the capacities and aspirations of disaster victims are highlighted, and not just their vulnerabilities and fears.

While we will co-operate with the media in order to enhance public response, we will not allow external or internal demands for publicity to take precedence over the principle of maximising overall relief assistance.

We will avoid competing with other disaster response agencies for media coverage in situations where such coverage may be to the detriment of the service provided to the beneficiaries or to the security of our staff or the beneficiaries.

The Working Environment

Having agreed unilaterally to strive to abide by the Code laid out above, we present below some indicative guidelines which describe the working environment we would like to see created by donor governments, host governments and the intergovernmental organisations – principally the agencies of the United Nations – in order to facilitate the effective participation of NGHAs in disaster response.

These guidelines are presented for guidance. They are not legally binding, nor do we expect governments and IGOs to indicate their acceptance of the guidelines through the signature of any document, although this may be a goal to work towards in the future. They are presented in a spirit of openness and co-operation so that our partners will become aware of the ideal relationship we would seek with them.

Annex I: Recommendations to the governments of disaster-affected countries

1: Governments should recognise and respect the independent, humanitarian and impartial actions of NGHAs

NGHAs are independent bodies. This independence and impartiality should be respected by host governments.

2: Host governments should facilitate rapid access to disaster victims for NGHAs

If NGHAs are to act in full compliance with their humanitarian principles, they should be granted rapid and impartial access to disaster victims, for the purpose of delivering humanitarian assistance. It is the duty of the host government, as part of the exercising of sovereign responsibility, not to block such assistance, and to accept the impartial and apolitical action of NGHAs.

Host governments should facilitate the rapid entry of relief staff, particularly by waiving requirements for transit, entry and exit visas, or arranging for these to be rapidly granted.

Governments should grant over-flight permission and landing rights for aircraft transporting international relief supplies and personnel, for the duration of the emergency relief phase.

3: Governments should facilitate the timely flow of relief goods and information during disasters

Relief supplies and equipment are brought into a country solely for the purpose of alleviating human suffering, not for commercial benefit or gain. Such supplies should normally be allowed free and unrestricted passage and should not be subject to requirements for consular certificates of origin or invoices, import and/or export licences or other restrictions, or to import taxes, landing fees or port charges.

The temporary importation of necessary relief equipment, including vehicles, light aircraft and telecommunications equipment, should be facilitated by the receiving host government through the temporary waiving of licensing or registration requirements. Equally, governments should not restrict the re-exportation of relief equipment at the end of a relief operation.

To facilitate disaster communications, host governments are encouraged to designate certain radio frequencies, which relief organisations may use in-country and for international communications for the purpose of disaster communications, and to make such frequencies known to the disaster response community prior to the disaster. They should authorise relief personnel to utilise all means of communication required for their relief operations.

4: Governments should seek to provide a co-ordinated disaster information and planning service

The overall planning and co-ordination of relief efforts is ultimately the responsibility of the host government. Planning and co-ordination can be greatly enhanced if NGHAs are provided with information on relief needs and government systems for planning and implementing relief efforts as well as information on potential security risks they may encounter. Governments are urged to provide such information to NGHAs.

To facilitate effective co-ordination and the efficient utilisation of relief efforts, host governments are urged to designate, prior to disaster, a single point of contact for incoming NGHAs to liaise with the national authorities.

5: Disaster relief in the event of armed conflict

In the event of armed conflict, relief actions are governed by the relevant provisions of international humanitarian law.

Annex II: Recommendations to donor governments

1: Donor governments should recognise and respect the independent, humanitarian and impartial actions of NGHAs

NGHAs are independent bodies whose independence and impartiality should be respected by donor governments. Donor governments should not use NGHAs to further any political or ideological aim.

2: Donor governments should provide funding with a guarantee of operational in dependence

NGHAs accept funding and material assistance from donor governments in the same spirit as they render it to disaster victims: a spirit of humanity and independence of action. The implementation of relief actions is ultimately the responsibility of the NGHA and will be carried out according to the policies of that NGHA.

3: Donor governments should use their good offices to assist NGHAs in obtaining access to disaster victims

Donor governments should recognise the importance of accepting a degree of responsibility for the security and freedom of access of NGHA staff to disaster sites. They should be prepared to exercise diplomacy with host governments on such issues if necessary.

Annex III: Recommendations to intergovernmental organisations

1: IGOs should recognise NGHAs, local and foreign, as valuable partners

NGHAs are willing to work with UN and other intergovernmental agencies to effect better disaster response. They do so in a spirit of partnership which respects the integrity and independence of all partners. Intergovernmental agencies must respect the independence and impartiality of the NGHAs. NGHAs should be consulted by UN agencies in the preparation of relief plans.

2: IGOs should assist host governments in providing an overall co-ordinating framework for international and local disaster relief

NGHAs do not usually have the mandate to provide the overall co-ordinating framework for disasters which require an international response. This responsibility falls to the host government and the relevant United Nations authorities. They are urged to provide this service in a timely and effective manner to serve the affected State and the national and international disaster response community. In any case, NGHAs should make every effort to ensure the effective co-ordination of their own services.

3: IGOs should extend security protection provided for UN agencies to NGHAs

Where security services are provided for intergovernmental organisations, this service should be extended to their operational NGHA partners on request.

4: IGOs should provide NGHAs with the same access to relevant information as is granted to UN agencies

IGOs are urged to share all information pertinent to the implementation of effective disaster response with their operational NGHA partners.

14

The Promotion of a Human Rights Perspective on Food Security: Highlights of an Evolving Process

WENCHE BARTH EIDE

I. INTRODUCTION: A CURRENT INTERPRETATION OF THE HUMAN RIGHT TO ADEQUATE FOOD

Human rights have received increased recognition and attention in recent years. This chapter focuses on the right to food as one of the internationally adopted human rights. It highlights the development of a human rights perspective on issues related to the alleviation of hunger and the promotion of access to adequate food and good nutrition over the last two decades – in academic debate and among human rights and development agencies and activists. It considers some of the factors that triggered the right to food among a group of food and nutrition policy analysts in the early 1980s, how the issue came to be put on the human rights agenda in the latter part of that decade, how it found its way on to the political development agenda only well into the 1990s – and, not least, how the concept matured in an interactive process. The discussion is limited to the development of a rights perspective on food and nutrition as derived from the normative framework under international human rights law, and does not enter into issues of humanitarian law.[1] Special emphasis is laid on relevant processes within the UN system in view of its role in standard-setting and in giving direction to, as well as monitoring, innovations and performance by states that are parties to binding conventions relevant to the right to food.

---

1. The distinction is made clear at the outset to avoid confusion with other chapters in this book dealing with charters and codes of conduct for humanitarian relief programmes and food aid (Chapters 12 and 13). The right to food as a *human right* is wider in scope, although the normative framework for the right to adequate food can and should accommodate state obligations during emergencies.

The meaning and scope of the right to food have been the subject of analysis and discussion for quite some time. A major breakthrough occurred with the adoption, on 11 May 1999, of a 'General Comment' on the right to adequate food by the Committee on Economic, Social and Cultural Rights (ESCR) of the United Nations.[2] This statement constitutes the first authoritative interpretation of that right since its expression in Article 11 of the International Covenant on Economic, Social and Cultural Rights (ICESCR), adopted by the General Assembly 33 years earlier, in 1966. At the same time it serves as a contribution to the fulfilment of the mandate given to the UN High Commissioner for Human Rights by the World Food Summit in Rome in 1996, to co-ordinate the work of UN institutions in partnership with governments and civil society 'to better define the content of the right to food and the steps needed to realise it'.[3] While the Committee on Economic, Social and Cultural Rights is an independent committee of experts appointed by ECOSOC, its mandate to monitor the implementation of the Covenant by State Parties[4] falls under the overall responsibility of the High Commissioner for Human Rights, on behalf of the United Nations, to protect and promote human rights, and considerable weight will be attached to its interpretation of the right to food. The General Comment on the right to food therefore constitutes a useful starting point for a retrospective summary of some of the events leading up to this milestone.

At the outset of the General Comment, the Committee on ESCR affirms the linkages between the right to food and other rights and development concerns, in that the right to food is

> ... indivisibly linked to the inherent dignity of the human person and is indispensable for the fulfilment of other human rights enshrined in the International Bill of Human Rights. It is also inseparable from social justice, requiring the adoption of appropriate economic, environmental and social policies, at both the

---

2. General Comment No. 12 of the Committee on ESCR: 'The Right to Adequate Food', E/C.12/1999/5.
3. World Food Summit, Plan of Action, Commitment 7.4 [*FAO, 1996*].
4. A country becomes State Party to a convention or covenant once it has *ratified* it. It is then binding for the state, which means that the state is obliged to take legislative and other steps to incorporate its content in domestic law and administration, and to report periodically on the realisation of the rights contained in it, to the United Nations' body(ies) specially set up for monitoring States Parties' compliance; in contrast, a *signature* by the incumbent government at the point of first adoption of the instrument by the UN is *not* binding for that state. The convention *enters into force* when a sufficient number of states have ratified it (for the CESCR this was set at 30, which happened in 1976).

national and international level, oriented to the eradication of poverty and the fulfilment of human rights for all (*para. 4*).

However, the Committee recognises that

> ... despite the fact that the international community has frequently reaffirmed the importance of full respect for the right to adequate food, a disturbing gap still exists between the standards set in article 11 of the Covenant and the situation prevailing in many parts of the world. More than 840 million people throughout the world, most of them in developing countries, are chronically hungry; millions of people are suffering from famine as the result of natural disasters, the increasing incidence of civil strife and wars in some regions and the use of food as a political weapon. ... Fundamentally, the roots of the problem of hunger and malnutrition are not lack of food but lack of access to available food, *inter alia* because of poverty, by large segments of the world's population (*para. 5*).

At the normative level, the General Comment provides an interpretation of the right to food which is wide in scope and also clearly reflects a notion of food *security* encompassing both *access* and *adequacy*:

> The right to adequate food is realised when every man, woman and child, alone or in community with others, have physical and economic access at all times to adequate food or means for its production. The right to adequate food shall therefore not be interpreted in a narrow or restrictive sense, which equates it with a minimum package of calories, proteins and other specific nutrients. The right to adequate food will have to be realised progressively. However, States have a core obligation to take the necessary action to mitigate and alleviate hunger as provided for in paragraph 2 of article 11, even in times of natural or other disasters (*para. 6*).

> The concept of adequacy is particularly significant in relation to the right to food since it serves to underline a number of factors which must be taken into account in determining whether particular foods or diets that are accessible can be considered the most appropriate under given circumstances for the purposes of article 11 of the Covenant. The notion of sustainability is intrinsically linked to the notion of adequate food or food security,

implying food being accessible for both present and future gene-rations. The precise meaning of 'adequacy' is to a large extent determined by prevailing social, economic, cultural, climatic, ecological and other conditions, while 'sustainability' incorpo-rates the notion of long-term availability and accessibility (*para. 7*).

Clearly, this requires more than what is normally implied in the simple notion of 'food security' at the national level, usually under-stood in terms of mere food energy or calories. The following termi-nology crystallises the *core content* of the right to adequate food:

> The availability of food in a quantity and quality sufficient to satisfy the dietary needs of individuals, free from adverse sub-stances, and acceptable within a given culture;
> The accessibility of such food in ways that are sustainable and that do not interfere with the enjoyment of other human rights (*para. 8*).

The General Comment explains each concept embedded in this core content in a way which will greatly help in setting precise benchmarks and developing appropriate indicators for the monitoring of the reali-sation of the right to food.

The General Comment goes on to consider the obligations of states to help ensure this right, offering a consolidated framework for work-ing out such obligations and for identifying what broadly constitute violations of economic, social and cultural rights in general;[5] this should inspire more specific elaborations regarding when the right to food can be said to be violated (or not complied with). Finally, it pro-vides a background for understanding the role of the international community in a human rights and obligations perspective.

The reader is referred to the full text of the General Comment,[6] and is now invited to join in a review of the processes leading to its com-pletion and adoption in May 1999.

---

5. Building on the Maastricht Guidelines on Violations of Economic, Social and Cultural Rights drawn up in January 1997 by a group of experts including members of treaty bodies, to assist mechanisms that monitor economic, social and cultural rights. The Guidelines are published in *Human Rights Quarterly*, Vol. 20, No.1, 1998; in the *Netherlands Quarterly of Human Rights*, Vol. 15, No. 2, 199; and in 'SIM Special' No. 20, published by Netherlands Institute of Human Rights.
6. See footnote 2.

II. THE 1970S: A PRELUDE TO THE INTEREST IN THE HUMAN RIGHT TO FOOD

The early 1970s saw the start of a new policy-oriented food and nutrition debate based on a number of growing concerns at the time: that increased food production did not by itself guarantee a reduction in hunger and improved human nutrition; that many technological solutions proposed had been based on reductionist and insufficient analysis of the problems; and that a greater role and responsibility on the part of the state authorities were essential for the prevention of hunger and the promotion of the nutritional well-being of their people [*Berg et al., 1973*].

Arguments were developed to attract the attention of statesmen and planners as well as promoters of agricultural development, many of whom were at the time merely advocating higher food production as the solution to hunger.[7] Contemporary sectoral approaches were criticised for their lack of mutual integration within a holistic understanding of the problems and their causes. National and programmatic cost-benefit estimates were used to expose the futility of investing large sums in education when children might not be intellectually fit for learning due to malnutrition, or in health services where children were repeatedly exposed to infectious diseases due to bad environmental sanitation [*Michanek, 1972*]; hence the imperative for the state to take hunger and malnutrition much more seriously as a major obstacle to national development.

With the impact on national development in focus, various models for centralised food and nutrition planning were brought to the fore within international food and nutrition-oriented development circles [*Joy, 1973; FAO/WHO, 1976*]. These models were later criticised and rejected for their top-down approach and thus their non-feasibility in practice [*Field, 1977; Jonsson and Brun, 1978; McLaren, 1978; Schuftan, 1978*]. Community-level development approaches to 'participatory food and nutrition planning' emerged as an alternative [*Pines, 1982*]; however, 'participation' and 'bottom-up' planning were still loaded words for many governments who associated them with radical critique of the system rather than with effective contributions from non-governmental actors. Yet others confused participation with conventional 'community development programmes' without making the link to 'civil society action' and the state creating 'an

---

7. The award of the Nobel Peace Prize for 1970 to the plant breeder and 'father of the green revolution', Norman Borlaug, was an illustration of such a simplified perception of the causes of hunger.

enabling environment' for this by means of 'good governance' and 'state accountability' – now all household terms in modern development thinking and generally accepted as prerequisites for democracy and the observance of human rights [*UNDP, 1998*].

In a global perspective, a major concern was the impact of the activities of multinational corporations in the area of food production, processing and marketing. Well ahead of today's globalisation debate and its effect on human conditions, the threats of the 'global supermarket' were already being pointed out during the 1970s [*George, 1976; Lappé and Collins, 1978*]. The radical concern with the political economy of food and nutrition towards the second half of the decade very much centred on the negative impact of multinational corporations. At the same time, there were few constructive ideas about what the state could do to counteract these global corporate economic tentacles. The fixation on an exclusively negative analysis of worsening global and national food systems thus appeared to leave little hope for change. A universal framework within which to identify space and to support positive action seemed to be lacking.

In 1976, the Covenant on Economic, Social and Cultural Rights came into force. The notion of the relationship of human rights with economic and social development began to surface among some human rights experts and a few interested governments. Via a spill-over effect the idea of an approach to food and nutrition policy and planning through human rights began to ferment among some nutrition policy analysts. There was a growing feeling that fundamental ethical principles, transformed into human rights norms under international law, might help to underscore the argument for state responsibility for adequate human nutrition for all. Human rights might offer a new opportunity for advocacy and action to improve good nutrition as a critical factor in human and social development. Analysis based on this approach needed to go beyond a mere identification of causality and exposure of 'the guilty', by applying human rights principles to identifying the nature of the gap between 'the normative and the reality' and the obstacles to closing that gap.[8]

But while food and nutrition 'norms' in the narrow sense were reasonably well agreed among the experts, very little agreement existed regarding what would be desirable behaviour of governments to help achieve these norms. To define the right to food and nutrition both in

---

8. It may be symptomatic that Leonard Joy, who in the early years of the decade was considered one of the gurus of food and nutrition planning before the critics dismissed the centralised character of the leading view at the time, in 1981 re-examined his own former thinking to advocate a more normative approach [*Joy, 1981*].

terms of the content of the right as such and its corresponding state obligations, was therefore seen as a new challenge.

III. THE 1980S: CONCEPTUAL INITIATION AND MATURATION

A first opportunity to discuss how to approach this challenge came with a United Nations University symposium in 1981 on 'The right to food as a human right'. This brought together human rights experts and food/nutrition developmentalists – two groups of people who had previously hardly met professionally and were now faced with the task of laying the foundations for a bridge between food and nutrition development concerns and goals, on the one hand, and the system of human rights norms and implementation on the other [*Eide, A. et al., eds., 1984*]. A second meeting organised a few years later by the Netherlands Institute of Human Rights (SIM) addressed more specifically the legal aspects of the right to food [*Alston and Tomasevski, eds., 1984*]. The two volumes remain important sources of information, ideas and vision concerning the linkages between economic and social rights and economic and social development. The second also set an agenda for the years to come, which in retrospect by the turn of the century has been met on a number of points, though major challenges still remain.

Two principal dimensions emerged from these events as being in need of further conceptual development and operationalisation: firstly, a more precise definition of what it is one has the right to with regard to food, and secondly, an approach to defining the corresponding duties or obligations for implementing the right to food. A new terminology gradually opened up for people working with food and nutrition in development: the hungry would no longer be seen as passive recipients of charity from the dominant groups who might or might not find it appropriate to allocate resources for their benefit. They would become *rights-holders*, which means they can in principle claim that their rights be fulfilled, while an external party – primarily the state – by definition becomes the corresponding *duty-bearer* with obligations to help fulfil the rights. States' compliance with their obligations could in turn be monitored by the international community via the UN. This was new and attractive language to many of those who had been participants in an increasingly frustrated nutrition policy and development debate about the responsibility of the state, in which the imperative of non-interference in the internal affairs of sovereign states seemed to exclude all thoughts of international monitoring.[9] However, obligations remained a touchy subject, given the considerable misunderstandings prevailing around economic, social and cultural rights, with many perceiving the role of the state as that of a mere provider. To redress this notion became a major focus in the debate which was to follow. Obligations of the state clearly ought to be defined in more nuanced as well as realistic terms, with options for different degrees of involvement by the state authority, and with varying scope of the action implied.

What, then, should be expected of the state as duty-bearer in its contractual relationship with the rights-holders? The notion of the needs to *respect*, to *protect* and to *facilitate/fulfil* the human right to food opened the way for a flexible approach to defining state obligations according to needs and circumstances [*Eide, A. et al., eds., 1984*]. A matrix was proposed which combined these three levels of obligations with the elements of a framework for household food security as the substantive normative context in which the right to food could be realised [*Eide, A., 1989; Oshaug et al., 1994*]. The framework includes sub-norms related both to the notion of adequacy of the food mix, or *diet*, and to the stability and sustainability of the supply of food and of access to food. In line with the universality of human rights, all categories in the matrix would be generally applicable, but subject to further precision and specification in each given context. This matrix format has since proved its worth both as an educational and an analytical tool, embraced by a number of scholars for the elaboration of certain other rights – notably the right to education [*Coomans, 1995*] and the right to health [*Toebes, 1999a, 1999b*], as well as by some NGOs [*FIAN, 1996*] and by a few country-level teams that have embarked on national exercises to outline the nature of obligations in their specific situations [*Thipanyane, 1999; Valente et al., 1999*]. In southern Africa in 1999 UNDP made use of the basic idea of the matrix format in training UN teams under the UN Development Assistance Framework (UNDAF) in several countries in the region in co-operation with the regional representative of the High Commissioner for Human Rights.[10] In other agencies similar interest

9.   In this connection it is interesting to note that a recommendation by the World Food Conference in 1974 for an *international* global nutrition surveillance system failed for many years to be put into operation due in part to fear on the part of many governments about releasing basic data for international consumption and possible political use. In 1996 the World Food Summit adopted a recommendation that a global Food Insecurity and Vulnerability Information and Mapping System (FIVIMS) should be established. Beginning in 1997 both an international and national FIVIMS are currently being developed by a UN inter-agency working group and member countries, with FAO hosting the secretariat for this endeavour.

10.   Van Weerelt, P., 1999, personal communication.

has been shown informally and an increased use of the matrix concept as adapted to their needs is envisaged.

A broadening of the understanding of the causality of hunger and malnutrition that evolved during the 1980s is significant for the perception of scope and terminology regarding the right to food and related rights. A proposal for a hierarchy of causal factors developed and field-tested by UNICEF greatly helped to organise information relevant to the generation of hunger and malnutrition in a logical and sequential manner [*UNICEF, 1990*]. It consolidated the notion of 'nutrition' as the broader concept superimposed upon food, which would be only one element – albeit an important one – in the complex set of factors determining the ultimate human nutritional status. In particular, *health* and *care* conditions are seen to combine with the nature of the *intake of food* to generate the ultimate physiological state that can be observed and measured at the level of the individual, in its worst manifestation in the form of outright hunger. This immediately extends not only the interrelationships of the parameters of causality, but also their ramifications to broader analytical and operational development concerns and needs and subsequently to rights.

IV. THE 1990S: MAKING SPACE FOR THE RIGHT TO ADEQUATE FOOD ON THE INTERNATIONAL DEVELOPMENT AGENDA

In the light of the two parallel conceptual developments during the 1980s, a broader discussion of the right to food could be introduced into the international food and nutrition development agenda of the 1990s. There was an equal need to trigger the interest in pursuing the human right to adequate food beyond the particular technical and policy circles concerned with food and nutrition. In particular, the institutional mechanisms and procedures for monitoring the implementation of human rights by UN member states seemed essential to efforts to operationalise food and nutrition security in a human rights perspective.[11] Nevertheless, a first aim was to reach the professional food and nutrition development circles.

---

11. Short of remedies to accommodate individual complaints by people whose right to food is being breached, such international monitoring aims at establishing a dialogue with those states that can be shown deliberately to violate this right, or – more commonly – *to omit pursuing an explicit policy towards the realisation of the right to food.* As underlined by Alston, there may be obstacles that should be identified and acted upon through constructive dialogue [*Alston, 1997*]. The institutional mechanisms in question include, in particular, the relevant human rights treaty bodies, notably the Committee on Economic, Social and Cultural Rights, the Committee on the Convention on the Elimination of All Forms of Discrimination Against Women, and the Committee on the Convention on the Rights of the Child.

An initial effort to promote the right to food as a human right at the intergovernmental level was made by a lobby of NGOs, scholars and a few governments at the International Conference on Nutrition held in Rome in 1992 and organised by FAO and WHO. The time and climate were not yet ripe, however [*Oshaug and Eide, 1998*]. There was strong resistance already in the preparatory stages – ranging from vigorous efforts especially by the United States to prevent it getting on the agenda (in line with that country's general reluctance to ratify important human rights conventions) to those for whom the idea was unfamiliar and yet others who misconstrued the notion of a right to food as the unconditional duty of the state to provide food to all irrespective of its limited resources.[12]

The United Nations nevertheless remained the most viable environment for a gradual educational and promotional effort in which both member states and UN agencies could be reached. The World Conference on Human Rights in Vienna in 1993 contributed to a better climate in which to address all human rights. However, with the exception of UNICEF, none of the UN agencies had by the mid-1990s shown much interest or capacity to go beyond rhetorical statements about food as a basic or inalienable human right. The UN human rights bodies had generally not performed strongly on economic, social and cultural rights.[13] In the Committee on ESCR efforts were made to improve the guidelines for States Parties' reporting on the implementation of economic, social and cultural rights, including the right to food, in their countries. But until the UN system could demonstrate a concerted front in its relationship with member states regarding how to use ESCR actively as guiding principles for development in general, there seemed to be limited scope for a breakthrough.

Consequently the focus turned to the UN specialised agencies, funds and programmes. An appropriate channel was the existing inter-agency arrangement, under the UN Administrative Committee on Co-

---

12. Part of the resistance must also be understood against the background of the Cold War and what remained as ideological overtones even after it was over, with polarised perceptions of human rights as either civil and political freedom rights as in Western democracies *or* economic, social and cultural rights for all as often promoted by authoritarian regimes (see, *inter alia*, Marchione [*1996*]). This contributed to blocking neutral human rights analysis in international development organisations for many years as was still evident in the early 1990s.

13. Some efforts were made by the then Centre for Human Rights (note: since 1999 the secretariat of the High Commissioner for Human Rights is called Office of the HCHR) in the early 1990s to strengthen the work on indicators with a view to more effective monitoring, but the interest and response by the relevant development agencies failed to materialise.

ordination (ACC), for harmonisation and co-ordination of nutrition within the UN system: the ACC/Sub-Committee on Nutrition (ACC/SCN).[14] Following a proposal by UNICEF in 1992, the SCN decided to set up a special Working Group on 'Nutrition, Ethics and Human Rights'. Chaired by UNICEF, the group met for the first time in 1994. During its early years, it experienced a similar resistance from some UN agency representatives and observer countries to that demonstrated at the International Conference on Nutrition [*Oshaug and Eide, 1998*]. The successive annual gatherings, reports and recommendations of the Working Group slowly made the agencies more familiar with the concept and led them to see the potential value of a human rights approach to food and nutrition policies and programmes [*WANAHR, 1998*].

Efforts so far have culminated with the 1999 session of the ACC/Sub-Committee for Nutrition in Geneva in April, which was hosted by the UN High Commissioner for Human Rights, and preceded by a thematic symposium on 'The Substance and Politics of a Human Rights Approach to Food and Nutrition Policies and Programmes'. The symposium, which was attended by high-level representatives of a number of UN member agencies in addition to the usual technical representatives from these agencies,[15] provided an opportunity for a deeper consideration of a number of the issues that had been the cause of earlier concern and questioning. Sceptics were made to see a human rights approach to food and nutrition policies as an opportunity, and not primarily as an unrealistic demand on resource-poor governments. The success of the symposium is beyond doubt; it opened new doors and helped clear the way for more practical advances by UN agencies and democratic governments.

V. THE ROLE OF THE WORLD FOOD SUMMIT AND THE MANDATE GIVEN TO THE UN HIGH COMMISSIONER FOR HUMAN RIGHTS

The demonstrable turning of the tide within the relevant UN agencies and as regards the attitude to the right to food by a number of democratic states during the years 1996–99 can be explained by a number

---

14. Operative since 1978, the ACC/SCN currently has 17 UN agencies as members, while 10–12 donor countries and an increasing number of NGOS usually meet as active observers in this forum, which since 1999 has been subtitled the 'UN Forum on Nutrition'. See http://www.unsystem.org/accscn/ for more information.
15. Besides two heads of agencies, Mary Robinson as the host of the meeting and Gro Harlem Brundtland, Director-General of the World Health Organisation, giving substantive keynote speeches, FAO, the WFP, UNICEF, the High Commissioner for Refugees and the World Bank were also represented by high-level panellists.

of factors, but one event stands out: the World Food Summit held in Rome in November 1996. In the initial paragraph of the *Declaration* issued by the Summit it is stated:

> We, the Heads of States and Government, or our representatives, gathered at the World Food Summit at the invitation of the Food and Agriculture Organization of the United Nations, reaffirm the right of everyone to have access to safe and nutritious food, consistent with the right to adequate food and the fundamental right of everyone to be free from hunger [*FAO, 1996*].

This might have been taken as what some would call the usual rhetoric of high-level conference declarations, were it not for the Summit's *Plan of Action* which includes, in Commitment 7, Objective 4, a specific call for a better definition of the right to food and of the steps needed to realise it [*FAO, 1996*]. Given this double perspective, and the fact that two constituencies – human rights experts and developmentalists alike – needed to sharpen their mutual insight and tools, there was a particular advantage in the WFS giving the specific responsibility for co-ordinating the follow-up of Commitment 7.4 to the UN High Commissioner for Human Rights, as this would ensure the professional quality of the further work with food as a legal human right. Furthermore, because the *Plan of Action* was adopted by Heads of States it was bound to be addressed by the intergovernmental human rights body in the UN, the Human Rights Commission. As the Commission's primary concern had been with civil and political rights at the cost of attention to economic, social and cultural rights, this was an opportunity to begin to redress that situation – starting with the right to food.[16] In principle system-wide collaboration would be guaranteed by the formulation that the High Commissioner act '... in consultation with the relevant treaty bodies, and in collaboration with relevant specialised agencies and programmes of the UN system and appropriate intergovernmental mechanisms'.[17]

The following years 1997–98 saw a number of initiatives, including two expert consultations on the right to food held by the Office of the High Commissioner for Human Rights.[18] Extensive reports including

---

16. It was especially fortunate that the new High Commissioner for Human Rights, Mary Robinson, who had taken office in Geneva only a few months before the Summit, had from the outset expressed her particular interest in economic, social and cultural rights and had committed herself to work towards an equal place for these alongside political and civil rights, in the human rights work of the UN system.
17. World Food Summit Plan of Action, Commitment 7.4 (e) [*FAO, 1996*].
18. Geneva, 1–2 December 1997; Rome, 18–19 November 1998, co-hosted by FAO.

recommendations from these consultations were submitted by the High Commissioner to the UN Human Rights Commission, and resolutions adopted on this basis by the Commission, that have helped stimulate attention to this right and recommended practical work to be undertaken. The Commission's expert Sub-Commission on the Promotion and Protection of Human Rights also paid considerable attention to the right to food during this period, by having a special report prepared on the right to adequate food and to be free from hunger. Such a report had first been prepared and presented to the Sub-Commission in 1987, to the Commission in 1988, and subsequently published in 1989. A new and updated version was prepared on request by the Sub-Commission in 1997 and submitted to it in 1999 [*Eide, A., 1999b*]. It will be submitted to the Human Rights Commission in 2000.

VI. FURTHERING THE WORK WITH THE RIGHT TO ADEQUATE FOOD AS A HUMAN RIGHT

1. UN Agencies

The success of the April 1999 SCN symposium referred to above must to some extent be seen in the light of a generally improving climate for human rights within the UN system as a whole. The Secretary-General's reform process which culminated in the programme launched by Kofi Annan in July 1997 [*UN, 1997b*] was particularly clear on the need for a fundamental restoration of the mandate contained in the UN Charter to pursue human rights throughout the system. This was to take place in close conjunction with the strengthening of the other two pillars of the Charter – those of peace and of economic and social development. There was a general appeal to all institutions and staff in the UN to incorporate a human rights dimension into their daily work:

> By virtue of its worldwide membership, the Organization provides a unique institutional framework to promote human rights and to develop the legal, monitoring and operational instruments that can better uphold their universal character while maintaining a full understanding of, and respect for, the broad range of national and cultural diversities. A major task for the future will be to enhance the human rights programme and integrate it into the broad range of the Organization's activities, including in the development and humanitarian areas.

The attendance and active participation of several UN agency leaders at the ACC/SCN symposium in 1999 may be understood as an opportunity taken by them to meet each other in a specialised forum, where the modalities concerning some selected rights could be explored with regard to the implications for their agencies.

From principle to action, however, is often a big step for agencies not yet prepared for the practical implications. It is therefore pertinent to ask what verbal commitments will lead to in practice in the work of the relevant UN agencies.

UNICEF falls into a special category, with its systemic efforts since its Executive Board decision in 1996 to have the provisions of the Convention on the Rights of the Child guide all its policy and field work and experiences emerging from country programming.[19] What can be expected of the others? A policy statement by UNDP on Sustainable Human Development and Human Rights [*UNDP, 1998*] brings together critical development concepts such as good governance, transparency, participation and accountability, with the possibilities for strengthening national and international legislation, monitoring and implementing the universal human rights norms and thereby the realisation of human, social and economic development. With the *UNDP Human Development Report* in 2000 focusing on human rights, it is probably only a matter of time before all agencies will have explicitly committed themselves to a human rights approach as related to their specific mandates.

Excellent initial work has been done by FAO especially through its Legal Office to begin to sensitise the organisation to a human rights perspective. Shortly after the World Food Summit contact was established with the High Commissioner for Human Rights, and in the same year the two secretariats signed a memorandum of understanding. FAO co-hosted the second consultation of the Office of the HCHR, held in 1998 in Rome. FAO contributed to the marking of the 50th Anniversary of the Universal Declaration on Human Rights in 1998 by publishing a booklet on *The Right to Food in Theory and Practice* [*FAO, 1998*]. While an all-organisational human rights vision has not been established, an in-house interest is growing. Of particular interest in the potential comparative advantage of the organisation in advising interested member states in drafting so-called 'framework legislation' towards the implementation of the right to food in domestic law and administrative practice, this would be supportive of policies and programmes for achieving food and nutrition

---

19. Zimbabwe is the first country in Africa south of the Sahara where this has been carried out in full.

security. Furthermore, as host of the emerging inter-agency efforts to establish a international Food Insecurity and Vulnerability Information and Mapping System, FIVIMS, and assist member countries in setting up national ones, FAO has the opportunity to introduce human rights dimensions in this important context and thus also help enrich and strengthen human rights monitoring overall.[20] At the end of 1999, the Secretariat initiated activities to study possible further activities of FAO towards a rights-based approach to food security.[21]

WHO introduced a human rights perspective already several years ago into its work to prevent HIV/AIDS and protect affected victims, but did not make any broader commitment to the right to health until the new Director-General, Gro Harlem Brundtland, made a first move in that direction on the occasion of the 50th anniversary of the UDHR.[22] The commitment was reinforced by her more specific commitment to nutrition as a human right, linking the right to food and the right to health, at the April 1999 SCN/HCHR symposium. She then stated that 'human rights begin at home', meaning within WHO and the other relevant agencies themselves:

> If we are to take human rights seriously, we have to become familiar with the difference that a human-rights perspective brings to our diverse missions, policies and activities in a development context... An explicit human-rights approach to health and nutrition means that mechanisms and procedures are gradually put into place to ensure that the values we advocate are underpinned in international human-rights law, are subsequently incorporated into national laws, and thereby have a chance of becoming reality for greater numbers of people. ... There are serious imperfections of the current system of human-rights implementation. But I would counter pessimism by saying that we have barely begun to use the opportunities that this road of action offers.

During Ms Brundtland's first official visit to the Rome-based food agencies in June 1999, she emphasised human rights as an issue that cuts across political and technical priorities. She saw considerable potential for FAO and WHO to explore jointly 'the most direct and

---

20. See: http://www.fivims.net
21. In part as an initiation of this process the author of the present chapter was invited to spend two months at FAO as Visiting Scientist in November–December 1999 preparing a draft conceptual paper, 'The Right to Food in 2000 and Beyond. On the further work of FAO in the nexus of food, nutrition and human rights' (provisional title).
22. See www.who.ch Director-General's speeches, 8 Dec. 1998.

effective means of giving practical effect to a central human-rights axiom – that human rights are not only interrelated, they are also interdependent and indivisible'. And she was even more specific:

> We should ensure that a human-rights culture permeates all our agencies. We can do this by creating working environments where staff will be continually challenged to explore two interdependent avenues: How they can make effective use of human-rights norms, and their implementation systems, in accomplishing their daily tasks, and how they can contribute to the still wider, and more effective, application of these norms through the daily tasks they accomplish.[23]

These considerations could become a platform on which to elaborate further the contributions by the various agencies and programmes. The transition from general commitment and principles to implementation will need time, however, and there are indeed stumbling blocks ahead, both as regards international 'implementation' – clarifying and further developing the normative instruments and ensuring the efficiency of the institutional system and procedures – and at the level of the States Parties themselves. Political obstacles have been demonstrated time and again: respect for human rights often goes against dominant economic interests and power elites. Even in democratic states the debate on whether economic, social and cultural rights are real rights, reflects a long and frustrating discussion among human rights experts, where the conservative view holds that only those rights that are fully justiciable are 'real' rights. This view begins to lose ground as the understanding grows of the more nuanced role of the state in respecting, protecting and facilitating/fulfilling the right, according to circumstances. Another frequent misconception is the notion that the realisation of the right to food and other economic, social and cultural rights is particularly costly compared with the observance of civil and political rights. The UN Study on the Right to Adequate Food considered such a notion to be erroneous, based on the very narrow concept of the state as a direct provider rather than as

---

23. WHO held its first internal consultation in December 1999 to begin to explore systematically the implications of a rights-based approach to health for the organisation. The intention is to repeat such consultations regularly in order to pull out ideas from the various groups and professions within the organisation in a fully participatory environment, where staff will learn together and from each other as well as from external resources. Continued contact and co-operation with the Office of the High Commissioner for Human Rights is considered indispensable. (Personal communication based on participation by this author at the consultation as a resource person.)

a facilitator for primary action by others. Civil and political rights can also be quite expensive, e.g. the right to fair trial, with effective legal representation and an independent judiciary [*Eide, A., 1989; 1999*].

2. Academic Discourse and NGOs

Academic work on the right to food was slow to develop. For a long time the three publications cited above from the 1980s [*Eide, A. et al., eds., 1984; Alston and Tomasevski, eds., 1984; Eide, A., 1989*] were almost the only ones that discussed this right in an interdisciplinary theoretical fashion but with a view to practical implications and indicating future direction. Human rights was in general not yet 'in' as an academic subject relating to food and nutrition and few picked it up as such, apart from some university-based and in part NGO-linked programmes.[24]

As reviewed by Messer [*1996*], the situation changed in the 1990s. Of practical importance was the further development of the right to food 'matrix' concept [*Eide, A. et al., 1991; Oshaug et al., 1994*], which elaborated a methodology for conceptualising and organising work to identify state obligations in given settings. Jonsson [*1996*] has provided essential theoretical contributions drawing also on the re-conceptualisation and field-testing of programmatic approaches within UNICEF's nutrition-related work. Robertson [*1996*] examined, from the perspective of the human right to food, the concept of 'resources' contained in an important provision of the Covenant on Economic, Social and Cultural Rights relating to the state obligation '... to take steps ... to the maximum of its available resources, with a view to achieving progressively the full realisation of rights recognised in the present Covenant...'. Some larger conferences on human rights in general occasionally also brought out papers on the right to food [*Robertson, 1993; Eide, A., 1993*]. In 1996 the journal *Food Policy* issued a comprehensive Special Issue on Nutrition and Human Rights [*Eide, W.B. et al., eds., 1996*], while the *International Journal of Children's Rights* carried a similar special issue in 1997 [*Kent, ed., 1997*]. Other recent contributions include Haddad and Oshaug [*1998*], who examine the implications for research, especially economic research, of a right to food approach; Buckingham [*1998*] who discusses the challenges following the World Food Summit and the possi-

---

24. Among these was Brown University's Hunger Program, and, more recently, the University of Oslo's Nutrition and Human Rights programme and the Department of Political Science at the University of Hawaii. There may be other academic activities going on or being under development not known to this author at the time of writing and further initiatives may be expected as the subject attracts more attention.

bilities for a future legally binding instrument in the form of a food security treaty, Maxwell [*1999a*] who summarises some of the dimensions of a development environment that need to be in place for the right to food to be realised, while Vidar and Watkins [*1999*] juxtapose opposing arguments often heard among human rights advocates and economists through a mythologically imagined debate between Mammon and Minerva.

As regards NGOs, attention to economic, social and cultural rights was for a long time remarkably absent within the international NGO community. To most human rights activists, human rights have meant civil and political rights, while many development NGOs concerned with fighting hunger and malnutrition have been unfamiliar with the human rights 'potential' to strengthen their work. With the development of an academic interest in the right to food and the strengthening of the conceptual basis, NGO involvement in the promotion of this right tended to increase. Current linkages established between some academically based groups and NGOs contribute to a theoretically more consistent and at the same time realistic development.[25]

(i) Draft International Code of Conduct on the Right to Adequate Food as a Human Right: Shortly after the World Food Summit, FIAN, together with the World Alliance for Nutrition and Human Rights and Institut International Jacques Maritain, began drafting a

---

25. First and foremost among the still relatively few NGOs directly active in promoting the right to food is FoodFirst Information and Action Network – FIAN – with its network of affiliated national organisations in many countries. Based in Heidelberg and focusing on 'the right to feed oneself', FIAN is a long-standing actor in the relevant human rights forums of the UN. It played a central role in the NGO lobby for the right to food at the World Food Summit as well as at the parallel NGO Forum. Also Bread for the World has for a number of years pressed for the right to food but may have been less occupied with its legal aspects. The World Alliance for Nutrition and Human Rights – WANAHR – was initiated at an international meeting in Oslo in 1992 and formally inaugurated in Florence in 1994 at a meeting hosted by UNICEF. It brings together academics, NGOs and members of international organisations to review the state-of-the-art and indicate priorities and strategies for future work. The aim of the Alliance is to serve as a linkage network between human rights and development organisations relevant to improved food and nutrition conditions as a development goal and as a human right. The Rome-based Institut International Jacques Maritain has a specific commitment to the right to food and helped organise an international conference with interested Latin American states held in Venezuela in 1996 as part of the lobby for a strong human rights outcome from the World Food Summit. A national example is the Brazilian 'Ágora – Project against Hunger' which explicitly addresses food and nutritional security through a human rights approach, and will, as WANAHR Focal Point for Latin America, through its co-ordination of the extensive web-based Global Forum on Sustainable Food and Nutritional Security, help spread knowledge about how a human rights approach can strengthen advocacy and practical efforts of other NGOs.

Code of Conduct on the Human Right to Adequate Food following a decision by the parallel Global Forum. The draft was discussed at an NGO seminar held in Geneva later in 1997 and by 1999 was endorsed by more than 800 NGOs. It is intended to be brought before the relevant international bodies for their consideration at an appropriate time. The Code of Conduct responds to the two components of the call by the World Food Summit: to clarify the content of the right to adequate food and the fundamental right of everyone to be free from hunger, and to give particular attention to the implementation and full and progressive realisation of this right as a means of achieving food security for all. It sets out the normative content of the human right to adequate food, the corresponding obligations of states at the national and international level, the responsibilities of international organisations, and the regulation of economic enterprises and other actors. It deals with the national framework for monitoring and recourse procedures, and with international reporting and support mechanisms, and sets out the responsibilities of civil society actors.

In substance there is a close relationship between the Draft Code of Conduct and the General Comment of the Committee on ESCR, but they fulfil different functions. The Code of Conduct has a broader perspective. While it primarily addresses states (all states, not only the parties to the Covenant on Economic, Social and Cultural Rights), it also addresses, directly or indirectly, international organisations, including the banks and funds (World Bank, IMF and others), and transnational corporations. It is recognised that the primary responsibility rests with the home or host state, but transnationals, international organisations and financing institutions are called upon not to undermine the regulatory capacity of the state in ensuring the right to food. On the contrary, they should actively support such measures [*Eide, W.B. and Kracht, 1999*].

There is a distinction between the Draft Code of Conduct on the Human Right to Adequate Food and the various codes in existence regarding appropriate conduct during emergency relief operations. The former has been drafted in response to the reference by the World Food Summit to 'voluntary guidelines' for states and other actors to realise the right to food as an instrument in achieving food security. There are other codes of conduct such as that of the Red Cross and the Sphere project which direct themselves primarily to non-governmental organisations and personnel to ensure their best performance under international humanitarian law *vis-à-vis* beneficiaries during crisis situations (see Chapter 13). Human rights and humanitarian law need, however, to be considered more systematically in relation to each other, possibly by developing new instruments integrating both parts [*Kracht, 1999*].

(ii) Other NGO-driven exchange of information and strategies: The position of active development NGOs regarding economic, social and cultural rights is clearly essential. It is therefore rewarding to observe the emergence of strategies for a human rights approach to food and livelihood by some leading development NGOs, notably CARE International [*T. Frankenberger, 1998, personal contribution*]. It is also essential that NGOs – small and big – remain alert to developments that can threaten human rights in general and the right to food in particular. The Global Forum on Sustainable Food and Nutritional Security, established after the World Food Summit to strengthen the South–South voice in the Summit follow-up, distributes substantive news relevant to food security and the right to food through its electronic information network.[26] The NGO 'People's Decade for Human Rights Education' (PDHRE), while aiming at more comprehensive approaches to 'building a human rights culture' [*Koenig, 1998*], may be a potential channel also for specific right-to-food approaches.

The right to food and nutrition is part of the broader right to an adequate standard of living set out in the Universal Declaration of Human Rights, Article 25, the International Covenant on Economic, Social and Cultural Rights, Article 11, and the Convention on the Rights of the Child, Article 27. In addressing in some depth the rights to food and nutrition, all actors can take advantage of methodologies offered by nutrition sciences and practice for precise measurements of the enjoyment of key aspects of an adequate standard of living [*Eide, A. and Eide, W.B., 1999; Eide, W.B. and Valente, 1999*].

3. UN Member States

While development in the UN is critical to advocacy, standard-setting and guidance to member countries in adopting a human rights approach, it is essential that country-level initiatives be developed to explore ways of advancing domestic legal and administrative implementation. Conditions differ widely between countries and the most appropriate ways and means of ensuring freedom from hunger and implementing the right to adequate food therefore vary considerably. Each state party to the ICESCR and the CRC must nevertheless take the measures required under the particular conditions prevailing in their country to ensure that everyone is free from hunger and, there-

---

26. www.globalforum.org.br

upon, move as quickly as possible to a situation where everyone can enjoy their right to adequate food. Two countries that have specifically embarked on defining what would be implied in a human rights approach to food and nutrition security policies, deserve mention: South Africa [*Thipanyane, 1999*] and Brazil [*Valente et al., 1999*]. Their experience might provide useful lessons for other countries.

VII. THE RIGHT TO FOOD FOR ALL – *FATA MORGANA* OR FOUNDATION FOR FOOD AND HUMAN SECURITY?

It is submitted here that concerted creative thinking and testing of new ways of addressing old problems under a human rights perspective, may effectively enhance political and practical action towards the realisation of food security for all. There are many obstacles to this of a varying nature – ranging from the Goliath-like power of some of the generators of globalisation, international finance and trade, for whom human rights are currently clearly a constraint on economically effective performance, to the continued gaps in communication and understanding between human rights advocates, on the one hand, and many development analysts and practitioners, on the other. The first is of growing concern not only to many developmentalists but also in human rights circles [*McCorquodale (with R. Fairbrother), 1999; Oloka-Onyango and Udagama, 1999*]. Many aspects of globalisation can be a threat to the promotion and protection of human rights including the right to food, unless corrective measures are taken. They should be looked at not as unsurpassable obstacles, but as incitement towards an intensified *universalisation* of human rights as perhaps the only counterforce against the threats of globalisation in protecting human freedoms, needs and dignity and ensuring food and human security [*Eide, A., 1999*].

There are also communication problems across disciplines, such as sometimes between legal human rights experts and those trained in the social science tradition of development research [*Maxwell, 1999b*]. An open mind is needed to transgress established ways of thinking within different scholarly traditions and practical experience. Mutual training is one way to bridge the gap between the two camps [*Eide, W.B. et al., 1996; Kent, 1999*].[27]

---

27. In this context it is worth citing Amartya Sen: 'Do people have a right to be free from hunger? This is asserted often enough, but what does it stand for? It is, of course, tempting to say: Nothing at all. But that piece of sophisticated cynicism provides not so much a penetrating insight into the practical affairs of the world, but merely a refusal to investigate what people mean when they assert the existence of rights

As pointed out by Kracht, much remains to be done for development efforts in the third millennium to be guided by ethical and human rights imperatives as much as economic reasoning. Experience with the juridical and legal enforcement of economic and social rights is still in its infancy [*Kracht and Schulz, 1999*]. The concept of good governance in terms of appropriate state action in tandem with civil society initiatives needs to be better worked out for food systems and food security. This is the realistic framework in which to define the agenda for further work to advance the right to adequate food and nutrition as a human right [*Eide, W.B. and Oshaug, 1999; Maxwell, 1999a*].

And here the circle can be brought back to General Comment No. 12. It is clear that this Comment will be of considerable help in establishing both the common normative understanding and improving the institutional approaches to policy and action with appropriate benchmarks for each given situation, and corresponding indicators and procedures for monitoring progress as a basis for constructive dialogue about the removal of obstacles to the enjoyment of the right to adequate food for different groups of people, and measures for its realisation. To this end, cross-disciplinary and institutional capacity-building will be a critical dimension, as will empirical and policy research on processes of implementation of a human rights approach to food and nutrition policies and programmes, nationally and internationally. The two tasks should to a large extent develop hand in hand, in a process of joint learning-by-doing.

REFERENCES

Alfredsson, G. and A. Eide, eds., 1999, *The Universal Declaration of Human Rights. A Common Standard of Achievement*, The Hague/Boston/London: Martinus Nijhoff Publishers.

Alston, P., 1997, 'The Purposes of Reporting', in UN [*1997a*].

Alston, P. and K. Tomasevski, eds., 1984, *The Right to Food. International Studies in Human Rights*, Stichting Studie- en Informatiecentrum – SIM, Utrecht, The Hague: Martinus Nijhoff Publishers.

Berg, A., N. Scrimshaw and D. Call, 1973, *Nutrition, National Development, and Planning*, Cambridge, MA: MIT Press.

Buckingham, D., 1998, 'Food Rights and Food Fights: A Preliminary Legal Analysis of the Results of the World Food Summit', *Canadian Journal of Development Studies*, Special Issue, Vol. 19.

---

that, for much of humanity, are plainly not guaranteed by the existing institutional arrangements' [*Sen, 1982*].

Coomans, A. P. M., 1995, 'Clarifying the Core Element of the Right to Education', in A.P.M. Coomans and G.J.H. Van Hoof, eds., *The Right to Complain about Economic, Social and Cultural Rights*, Utrecht: SIM Special 18.

Eide, A., 1983, 'The Right to Food', in Mahoney and Mahoney, eds.

Eide, A., 1989 (updated 1999), *The Right to Adequate Food as a Human Right*, Special study for the UN Sub-Commission on the Prevention of Discrimination and Protection of Minorities, UN Studies in Human Rights No. 1, New York and Geneva: United Nations.

Eide, A., 1993, 'Strategies for the Realization of the Right to Food', in Mahoney and Mahoney, eds.

Eide, A., 1999a, *The Right to Food and to be free from Hunger*, an updated study prepared for the UN Sub-Commission on the Promotion and Protection of Human Rights, by A. Eide, UN/C.Sub.51/12.

Eide, A., 1999b, 'Globalization and the Implementation of the Human Right to Adequate Food', in Ogunrinade *et al.*, eds.

Eide, A. and W. B. Eide, 1999, 'Article 25', in Alfredsson and A. Eide, eds.

Eide, A., W. B. Eide, S. Goonatilake, J. Gussow and Omawale, eds., 1984, *Food as a Human Right*, Tokyo: UNU Press.

Eide, A., A. Oshaug and W.B. Eide, 1991, 'Food Security and the Right to Food in International Law and Development', *Transnational Law and Contemporary Problems*, Vol. 1, No. 2.

Eide, W. B. and U. Kracht, 1999, 'The International Code of Conduct on the Human Right to Adequate Food: Stepping Stone on the Road to Rights-based Development', Institut International Jacques Maritain, Notes et Documents, XXIVième année.

Eide, W. B. and A. Oshaug, 1999, 'The Nature and Levels of State Involvement in Governance Towards Food Security. A Conceptual, Normative Approach With Practical Implications', in Ogunrinade *et al.*, eds.

Eide, W. B. and F. L. S. Valente, 1999, 'Operationalising Rights and Obligations in the Fields of Food, Nutrition, Water and Health – and their Interconnections', in UNDP [*1999*].

Eide, W. B., G. Alfredsson and A. Oshaug, 1996, 'Human resource building for the promotion of human nutrition rights. A cross-disciplinary challenge', *Food Policy*, Vol. 21, No.1.

Eide, W. B., U. Kracht and R. Robertson, eds., 1996, Special Issue on Nutrition and Human Rights, *Food Policy*, Vol. 21, No. 4.

FAO, 1996, *The Rome Declaration on World Food Security and The World Food Summit Plan of Action*, Rome: FAO.

FAO, 1998, *The Right to Food in Theory and Practice,* Rome: FAO.

FAO/WHO, 1976, 'Food and Nutrition Strategies in National Development', Ninth Report of the Joint FAO/WHO Expert Group on Nutrition, FAO Nutr. Meeting Rep.Ser. No.56/WHO Techn. Rep. Ser. No. 584, Rome: FAO; Geneva: WHO.

FIAN, 1996, 'The Relationship between Food Security and the Human Right to Adequate Food', Part I of *Food Security and the Right to Feed Oneself,* FIAN Dossier, Nov., Heidelberg: FIAN International Secretariat.

Field, J. O., 1977, 'The soft underbelly of applied knowledge', *Food Policy*, Vol. 2, No. 3.

George, S., 1976, *How the Other Half Dies: The Real Reasons for World Hunger,* Montclair, NJ: Allanheld, Osmun & Co.

Haddad, L. and A. Oshaug, 1998, 'How does the human rights perspective help shape the food and nutrition policy research agenda?', *Food Policy,* Vol. 23, No. 5.

Jonsson, U., 1996, 'Nutrition and the Convention on the Rights of the Child', *Food Policy*, Vol. 21, No.1.

Jonsson, U. and T. Brun, 1978, 'The Politics of Food and Nutrition Planning: A Preliminary Working Paper on Its Socio-economic Content', in L. Joy, ed., *Nutrition*

Planning: The State of the Art, Surrey, UK: IP Science and Technology Press Limited [for the US Agency for International Development].

Joy, L., 1973, 'Food and Nutrition Planning', Reprint No. 107, Brighton: Institute of Development Studies.

Joy, L., 1981, 'Food and Nutrition Planning Theory: Current Conceptual and Methodological Advances', in *The Process of Food and Nutrition Planning*, Proceedings of an international conference held in Antigua, Guatemala: Institute of Nutrition for Central America and Panama (INCAP).

Kent, G., ed., 1997, Special Issue on Food and Nutrition Rights, *International Journal of Children's Rights*, Vol. 5, No.4.

Kent, G., 1999, 'Fundamentals of the Human Right to Food and Nutrition: A web-based interactive tutorial', in preparation on behalf of WANAHR, http: // www2.hawaii.edu/~kent/.

Koenig, S., 1998, 'Creation of Human Rights Communities as a Means to Fight Hunger and Malnutrition', in Special Report: The Right to Food is a Basic Human Right. *Hunger Notes*, http://www.worldhunger.org/special.htm

Kracht, U., 1999, 'Human Rights and Humanitarian Law and Principles in Emergencies – An Overview of Concepts and Issues', a study prepared for UNICEF/Eastern and Southern Africa Region, Nairobi.

Kracht, U. and M. Schultz, 1999, 'Food Security and Nutrition at the Threshold of the Third Millennium', in Kracht and Schultz, eds.

Kracht, U. and M. Schultz, eds., 1999, *Food Security and Nutrition – The Global Challenge*, Berlin Series on Society, Economy and Politics in Developing Countries, New York: St. Martin's Press.

Lappé, F. M. and J. Collins (with C. Fowler), 1977, revised edition 1978, *Food First. Beyond the Myth of Scarcity*, Ballantine Books, New York: and Toronto: Houghton-Mifflin Company.

McCorquodale, R. (with R. Fairbrother), 1999, 'Globalization and Human Rights', *Human Rights Quarterly*, Vol. 21, No. 3.

McLaren, D. S., 1978, 'Nutrition Planning Day Dreams at the United Nations', *American Journal of Clinical Nutrition*, Vol. 31, Aug., pp. 1295–1299.

Mahoney, K. E. and P. Mahoney, eds., 1993, *Human Rights in the Twenty-first Century*, The Hague: Kluwer Academic Publishers.

Marchione, T., 1996, 'The right to food in the post-cold war era', *Food Policy*, Vol. 21, No. 1.

Maxwell, S., 1999a, 'Can We Finally Implement the Right to Food: Solutions Outside the Box', in UNDP [*1999*].

Maxwell, S., 1999b, 'Can We do Anything Sensible with a Rights-Based Approach to Development?' Summary of a talk given at Overseas Development Institute, London, by Julia Häusermann and Jeremy Swift (March). See http://www. oneworld.org/odi/speeches/hauser.html

Messer, E., 1996, 'The Right to Food 1989–1994', in *The Hunger Report 1995*, Langhorne, PA: Gordon and Breach Science Publishers.

Michanek, E., 1972, 'Opening speech at the 1971 Dag Hammarskiold Seminar on Nutrition as a Priority in African Development', Uppsala, Sweden, in Vahlquist, ed.

Moore, G. and M. Vidar, 1999, 'FAO and the Right to Adequate Food', Institut International Jacques Maritain, Notes et Documents, XXIVième année.

Ogunrinade, A., R. Oniang'o and J. May, eds., 1999, *Beyond Bread: Food Security and Governance in Africa*, Proceedings of the TODA Institute HUGG Symposium Food Security and Governance in Africa, Durban 19–21 June, Johannesburg: University of Witwatersrand Press.

Oloka-Onyango, J. and D. Udagama, 1999, 'Human Rights as the Primary Objective of International Trade, Investment and Finance Policy and Practice', Working Paper submitted at the 51st Session of the UN Sub-Commission on the Protection and Promotion of Human Rights, E/CN.4/Sub.2/1999/11.

Oshaug, A. and W. B. Eide, 1998, 'The World Food Summit: A Milestone in the Development of a Human Rights Approach to Food', in Special Report: The Right to Food is a Basic Human Right. *Hunger Notes*. http://www.world-hunger.org/special.htm

Oshaug, A., W. B. Eide and A. Eide, 1994, 'Human rights: a normative basis for food and nutrition-relevant policies', *Food Policy*, Vol. 19, No. 6.

Pines, J., 1982, 'National nutrition planning: lessons of experience', *Food Policy*, Vol. 7, No. 4.

Robertson, R. E., 1993, 'The Right to Food in International Law', in Mahoney and Mahoney, eds.

Robertson, R. E., 1996, 'Nutrition, human rights and resources', *Food Policy*, Vol.21, No. 1.

Schuftan, C., 1978, 'Nutrition planning – what relevance to hunger?', Food *Policy*, Vol. 3, No.1.

Sen, A., 1982, 'The Right Not To Be Hungry', in G. Floistad, ed., *Contemporary Philosophy*, Vol. II, The Hague: Martinus Nijhoff.

Thipanyane, T., 1999, 'A National Framework for the Promotion and Protection of the Rights to Food Security and Nutrition: a Case Study by the South African Human Rights Commission', presented at the UN ACC/Sub-Committee for Nutrition Symposium on 'The Substance and Politics of A Human Rights Approach to Food and Nutrition Policies and Programmes', Geneva (April), *SCN News* No. 18, Geneva: UN ACC/SCN Secretariat. See http://www.unsystem.org/accscn/.

Toebes, B. C. A., 1999a, *The Right to Health as a Human Right in International Law*, Netherlands School of Human Rights Series, Vol. 1, Antwerp-Groningen-Oxford: Intersentia-Hart.

Toebes, B. C. A., 1999b, 'Towards an Improved Understanding of the International Human Right to Health', *Human Rights Quarterly*, Vol. 21, No. 3.

UN, 1997a, *Manual on Human Rights Reporting*, by P. Alston, ed., Geneva: Office of the High Commissioner for Human Rights, HR/PUB/91/1(Rev.)

UN, 1997b, *Renewing the United Nations: A Programme for Reform*, Secretary-General's Report – 14 July, A/51/950, New York: United Nations.

UNDP, 1998, 'Integrating Human Rights with Sustainable Human Development', a UNDP policy document, New York: United Nations Development Programme.

UNDP, 1999, *Human Development and Human Rights*, Report from the UNDP/ UNHCHR/Royal Norwegian Ministry of Foreign Affairs Symposium, Oslo, 2–3 October 1998, New York: United Nations Development Programme.

UNICEF, 1990, 'Strategies for the Improvement of Nutrition of Women and Children in the 1990s', Executive Board Document, New York: UNICEF.

Valente, F., N. Beghin, M. Immink, D. C. Coitinho, D. Shrimpton, M. Rondó and K. C. L. Valente, 1999, 'Understanding Human Rights Approaches to Food and Nutritional Security in Brazil', presented by D. C. Coitinho at the UN ACC/Sub-Committee for Nutrition Symposium on 'The Substance and Politics of A Human Rights Approach to Food and Nutrition Policies and Programmes', Geneva (April), *SCN News* No. 18, Geneva: UN ACC/SCN Secretariat. See http://www.unsystem.org/accscn/.

Vahlquist, B., ed., 1972, *Nutrition as a Priority in African Development*, Stockholm: Almquist & Wiksell.

Vidar, M. and B. Watkins, 1999, 'Discussion Notes on the Right to Food', Institut International Jacques Maritain, Notes et Documents, XXIVième année.

WANAHR, 1998, 'The Promotion and Protection of the Human Right to Food and Nutrition by ACC-SCN Member Agencies. Obligations and Opportunities', paper prepared by the World Alliance for Nutrition and Human Rights for the fourth meeting of the ACC/Subcommittee on Nutrition Working Group on 'Nutrition, Ethics and Human Rights' in conjunction with the 25th Annual Session of the ACC/SCN, Oslo (March). Available from the SCN Secretariat in Geneva.

15

Revisiting the Food Aid Debate: Taking a Closer Look at the Institutional Factor

MARTIN DOORNBOS

Revisiting the debates about food aid, as the EADI Lysebu Workshop on Food Aid and Human Security in April 1998 allowed us to do, is instructive in several respects, and prompts a variety of observations and lessons. At one level, the debate, as it was being conducted towards the end of the millennium, remains strongly reminiscent of that of the 1970s and 1980s. In fact, the continuity and repetition of the arguments produce a kind of 'déjà vu' effect: there is ongoing discussion about the 'additionality' versus 'fungibility' of food aid; about food aid as a 'resource' as opposed to a 'tool'; about food aid for 'relief' as opposed to 'development'; on the pros and cons of monetisation; on the risks of disincentive effects and chronic aid dependency as opposed to enhancing agricultural self-sufficiency and national food security; and on a range of related questions. With respect to most of these issues, the arguments advanced have remained essentially the same and appear to have become routinised; when revisiting the discussion one is struck by how little the debate has moved forward over a period of roughly two decades. Significantly, also, one notes that food aid continues to be a topic that has its 'supporters' and 'critics'.

At another level, though, there is noticeable change in the terms of the debate. This has less to do with changing appreciations of the merits or demerits of food aid *per se* (though there seems to have been a 'critical' shift of emphasis in this respect), but rather with changes in the broader context and conditions under which the discussion is being conducted. In particular, the availability of food aid from agricultural surpluses in Northern countries is no longer as assured a given as it had been in earlier periods, and hence a fundamental element of uncertainty about the future of food aid as it has come to be constituted has entered the equation [*Clay et al., 1998a: 5–8*]. Clearly, this uncertainty has an unsettling effect on the arguments used in the debate thus far, for, if the lifeline to the practice of aid is itself endangered, any debate about it necessarily becomes more abstract and academic.

In addition to the basic factor of the prospect of surplus commodities running out (and concurrently the alternative of buying food aid commodities on the market becoming too expensive), contextual changes also include shifts in the nature of the donor–recipient relations governing food aid. Among other things, questions have increasingly been targeted at the role earmarked for food aid as a development tool in the hands of donor organisations [*Fritschel, 1998: 7*]. Recipient countries have become increasingly vocal and critical at being relegated to the receiving end of the line, and would like to have a greater say on the preconditions under which food aid programmes are to be implemented. Also, various receiving countries now have their own expertise available for assessing needs and issues, and they feel this should be involved in the dialogue. Moreover, food aid, in its classical sense of the donation of concrete commodities, has evolved in many different directions, with concessional imports, triangular commodity purchases, monetised commodity inputs on food markets, and other such mechanisms having been developed. Several of these have actually become quite difficult to distinguish from 'normal' imports, especially when government agencies are still involved in the latter. Again, as compared with the patterns prevailing some decades ago, other more sophisticated support arrangements are now available for recipient countries, such as the annual meetings on budget support (which could well include an item for food purchases if it was deemed necessary) organised for various countries in Paris and other venues. In principle, these meetings allow for more wholesale approaches to issues of aid, as well as being more 'chic'. Several of these changes have sharpened the questioning as to whether there is still a place for international food aid at the end of this millennium, or whether we should prepare for a fresh start without it in the next.

I. THE INSTITUTIONAL FACTOR

Even though there is increasing discussion, and more and more questions are being raised about the future of food aid, it is important to be specific as to what is meant by this, and what exactly is at issue. Food aid *per se* is a time-honoured phenomenon, with the first recorded food aid dating from the time of the Crimean War, and with other possibly even older instances. In this respect, one would seem quite justified in assuming that food aid, already with a respectable historical record, will have a future in many circumstances where there is a pressing need for it. Indeed, a point of consensus today is that relief aid in emergency situations is, and must remain, beyond question [*Clay et al., 1998b: 41–3*].

Current questions about the 'future of food aid', however, appear to carry a more restricted and specific connotation. Food aid in the late twentieth century has come to denote a whole complex of institutional arrangements involving donor–recipient relations with numerous countries in the South, which finds (or, perhaps, found) its point of departure in the availabity of surplus agricultural commodities in the North in need of an outlet for disposal. It is this availability, which for many years could be taken for granted, which is now no longer guaranteed, and by implication questions about the future come to concern the entire range of institutional structures, and their modes of operation, which have been developed towards the allocation, distribution and delivery of food aid.

This general set-up was based on a number of premises, which themselves have been subject to continuous debate. Central has been the belief that the world is producing sufficient food to provide nutrition for the entire population, so that what would be required would essentially be the establishment of suitable bridging mechanisms between supply and effective demand. In this perspective, it was believed that food aid could serve as one such mechanism, until such time as global market integration could effectively replace it. In the end, however, the operational starting point was that food aid was a disposable resource at the discretion of donor agencies, implying that, with this resource to hand, they attempted to search for appropriate applications and to look for 'the best way of making use of it' [*Fritschel, 1998: 1, 6*]. In practice, this meant trying to identify recipient countries where donor criteria and conditionalities could be expected to be met, or where wider policy objectives as formulated on the donor side might seem attainable with the use of aid commodities as an incentive. Hence this practice of food aid has been essentially resource- and donor-driven. It has also led to prolonged debates about its potential disincentive effects on local production and other implications and the extent to which these could be overcome.

II. 'CRISIS' AND RESPONSE PATTERNS

The impending changes in context with regard to the continued availability of food aid commodities could not fail to provoke profound uncertainties in various quarters involved with the provision of food aid. Indeed, the relevant prospects have already prompted reactions ranging from directly defensive postures to readiness to re-examine missions and objectives. A closer look at actual and potential reactions may therefore be useful, with an eye on the look-out for future roles.

First, when examining the situation of organisations thus examining themselves, it is important to bear in mind how closely a number of them, such as the World Food Programme (WFP) and NGOs like CARE and Catholic Relief Services, have been involved institutionally with the above patterns and mechanisms of food aid procurement and disbursement [*Christian Michelsen Institute, 1993*]. The connection is so complete and direct, especially on the North American scene, that, without agricultural commodities to be disposed of, the agencies concerned immediately tend to lose their basic rationale as well as their means of survival.

What do institutions do when they are under threat of losing their key functions? A number of strategies can normally be expected. Predictably, one immediate response is almost certainly a defensive one, namely to argue 'we have always acted properly'. To substantiate this, the relevant institutions will produce figures and feedback intended to underscore their record of effectiveness in accomplishing their mission. Significantly, the need to do this may be felt particularly strongly in cases where such effectiveness in the past had remained unclear or had not been entirely undisputed.

A second line of defence, potentially closely related to the first, is to seek strategic support from relevant bodies: parliaments, the press, real or imagined constituencies at the receiving and/or giving end (among the latter, for example, farmers' lobbies, shippers' organisations, church bodies, experts). The messages formulated at this level are likely to be loud and clear, leaving no doubt about the vital role the organisation in question is performing, and pointing to the untold dangers that would follow if its operations were to be interrupted.

Sooner or later, these lines of response may be followed by seemingly even more serious and 'objective' efforts to set the record straight: mobilisation of (positive) evaluations, ostensibly neutral, intended to produce the kind of base-line documents that will impress funders and/ or political decision-makers and thus help to give the institutional activity a new lease of life. As the stakes are high in institutional evaluations, there are strong chances of complex 'politics of evaluation' syndromes coming into play. Sensitive issues in these engagements tend to arise around questions such as who is to appoint whom as evaluators, who is to formulate and decide on the terms of reference, what conclusions and recommendations are to be put forward, either with or without amendments, and whether these should be accepted as legitimate and politically acceptable outcomes. As the very survival of the institution may be at issue, such instances of micro-politics may at times become notably tense and conflict-ridden, as has in fact been illustrated more than once within the broader area of international food aid arrangements [*Doornbos and Terhal, 1993*]. The much-publicised Indian dairy development programme Operation Flood, implemented on the basis of massive donations of European dairy aid to India, has more than once given rise to particularly pronounced positions within the arena of the politics of evaluation [*Doornbos et al., 1988*]. Multi-donor engagement in the programmes concerned, and multi-agency involvement in their assessment, may at once render these processes even more complex but their outcomes nonetheless more assured, given the likelihood of a mix of interests playing a role on the donor-cum-assessors side.

At times, defensive strategies may recognise the impending demand for more radical reorientation but try to get away with marginal adaptations. In such instances it may be worth reading between the lines and trying to decipher the codes. The message may contain distracting measures of 'reform', claims of 'novel' approaches, and the praise of wise men in evaluations. But once the documents are filed, there may be an intention to try and get back to business as usual.

More serious, though not necessarily more common, are a basic preparedness and determination among institutions to take an honest look at their role in the face of changing circumstances, and to try and strike out in new directions on the basis of radical adaptations of their mandate and programme activities. The most courageous among the latter type of reactions, but by far the most rare, would be for some institutions to decide to wind up their activities in the light of contextual changes which have rendered their core role superfluous or problematic. The problem with either kind of resolution is that it would depend on being formulated and proposed from within the respective institution itself, which runs contrary to normal institutional instincts for survival.

A number of such strategies, in various possible combinations, are currently already becoming manifest on the food aid front, as also transpired at the Lysebu Workshop. Indeed, several international NGOs and some UN agencies, in particular the World Food Programme, appear to have good reasons to re-examine their mandates in the light of changing circumstances. For many such agencies, the issue is as much one of institutional longevity as about the safeguarding of food aid as such. It is ironic that such struggles are often particularly pronounced in the case of organisations that were originally set up as temporary bodies. The latter may have been readily set up, with broad initial enthusiasm and institutional support from various sides, and seemingly clear original objectives, but in the end turn out to be extremely difficult to dismantle, especially in the case of multilateral agencies with their rather diffuse ownership. Again, one factor tending to enhance the 'staying power' of such institutions is the practice of multi-donor evaluations, which often include one party or another prepared to neutralise any proposals for radical reorientation.

III. REVERSING THE ORDER?

In rapidly changing contexts, such as the one the world of food aid is currently facing, there may be a need for far more radical reorientation or restructuring than has been under consideration thus far. Paradoxically, some such initiatives may actually do more to help the institutions concerned to stay in business. Dutch NGOs, for example, have for some time been studying the options for 'aidless' NGO activities, anticipating a time when there will be less finance available to sponsor international aid programmes in the South. For NGOs and other organisations operating in the specific field of food aid, it may similarly be worthwhile to consider options other than those related to their present activities. One precondition for any such reappraisals becoming meaningful, however, must almost certainly be their serious consideration of severing their own direct 'dependency' on food aid commodities as a basis for their operations.

As an alternative scenario to the way in which food aid has predominantly been disbursed thus far, which basically placed the initiative for project activities in the hands of the food aid donor agencies, the possibility of reversing the key steps might be given due consideration. A reverse order might start (and should perhaps in the past have started) from a reconnaissance of priorities in terms of enhancing food security in a given situation (for example, by means of raising productivity, improving marketing possibilities, considering additional technological or financial inputs, safeguarding equitable distribution, etc.). Such an alternative starting point might allow a more reliable determination of possible needs for temporary or longer-term food aid support, based on careful scrutiny of the conditions under which aid might be 'safe' and useful, and possibly in conjunction with other interventions. Calls for support, which would thus emanate from situations in need of food supplements, would in turn presuppose donors being prepared to take on a more 'recipient' role, ready to receive such kinds of requests. Such alternative scenarios have been followed only in rare instances, however, and seemingly without much enthusiastic support from the key institutions engaged in handling food aid. Nevertheless, there may be a point in giving them a closer look.

Essentially, reversing the order might entail one or more of the following elements and steps, in different possible combinations:

(a) reversing the donor–recipient hierarchy, and with donor agencies accepting the role of being 'on demand' rather than 'in command'; in particular with regard to the food aid and food security field, genuine partnership should replace sensitive notions of 'donors' and 'recipients';

(b) donor agencies, themselves dependent on the food aid lifeline, considering merging or at least liaising closely with other organisations which have a different entry point into the overall problematique, as a way of enhancing the potential for institutional and operational responsiveness. For example, the WFP might seek to liaise or integrate its activities more closely with those of FAO, among others, on the production side; precisely because it is a 'single commodity' organisation, a merger of the WFP with other organisations might make it easier to weigh different alternatives and determine when food aid might be resorted to, if at all, in conjunction with other strategies;

(c) significantly widening (even after any possible mergers) the dialogue on operational priorities and choices in the field by including other actors, internal as well as external, in principle including all those that would be relevant for the identification and resolution of a complex set of issues. In practice this could mean fora in which Ministry of Agriculture staff within a relevant country as well as farmers' bodies, marketing organisations, NGOs with an interest in the area concerned, and other multilateral agencies might participate, each bringing its own expertise and comparative advantage;

(d) collectively studying and defining key issues and strategies for attaining food security, with a broadened focus on relevant variables such as employment and income generation, enhancing agricultural production, paying due respect to rural as well as urban nutrition aspects, and other factors. Such collective involvements should yield more informed views as to when and how it might be advisable to have recourse to food aid to compensate temporarily for unavoidable gaps or set-backs in attaining food security, and how a possible food aid intervention is likely to impact on other policy efforts being made in this regard.

A reorientation in this vein might bring about a number of things at once, namely (i) giving due recognition to the complexity of the interplay of factors affecting food security, which has often been highlighted in critical reviews of food aid practices; (ii) by juxtaposing different lines of expertise and resources on a common set of problems, avoiding undue reliance on one specific type of intervention, such as food aid, for solving problems which may require more multi-dimensional approaches. By implication, it would minimise the risk of one-track interventions ultimately prolonging rather than serving to attenuate the problems faced. There would also be the benefit of being able to draw on a sizeable literature that has already focused on several of the complexities involved, thus making 'positive' use of analyses and commentaries that have too often been regarded as 'negative'.

IV. TOWARDS ALTERNATIVE SCENARIOS: AN EXAMPLE

It has become commonplace to note how inert the UN and other multilateral agencies have been vis-à-vis urgent calls for reform. Normally, therefore, there would be little chance of reorientations such as the above being given much serious attention. At the present time, however, the 'threat' of disappearing surpluses may have the interesting effect of 'far-fetched' ideas being taken more seriously. As regards the above suggested reversals, experience to date with a modest precursor project, namely the War-torn Societies Project (WSP) initiated by the United Nations Research Institute for Social Development (UNRISD) in 1995, suggests that these would not necessarily be a step in the dark.

The focus of WSP projects, which to date have been undertaken in Eritrea, Mozambique, Guatemala and Somalia, has been on post-conflict reconstruction, to which WSP seeks to make a contribution by means of action-oriented research activities intended to lead up to informed policy dialogue [UNRISD, 1994]. In each of these countries, research was initiated on what were perceived to be the key issues in reconstruction – mapping out what was being done, and what needed to be done, in such areas as demobilisation, integration of returnees, provision of food security and basic needs, establishment of justice and governance structures, and other areas. The choice of themes would be made by a Project Group, comprising all parties, national and international as the case might be, interested in the project as a whole. Invariably, though, national views would gain priority in the making of these choices. The ensuing research would be carried out in several successive phases according to a particular common scenario, and would be executed exclusively by teams of well-qualified and well-accepted national researchers [*Doornbos and Tesfai, 1999*].

Around each chosen research theme, a working group of up to 10–12 members would be formed, consisting of representatives of national and international agencies with a special interest in the respective theme. On food security, for example, a working group might comprise members from the Ministry of Agriculture, farmers' organisations, the food processing industry, NGOs involved in the provision of food aid and rehabilitation schemes, FAO or WFP representatives wherever applicable, the World Bank country mission, etc. On refugee resettlement issues, similarly, one would have representatives from the main national organisations responsible for returnee programmes, UNHCR, international and national NGOs engaged in resettlement schemes, UNFPA, and others with an involvement or interest in the field. These working groups would meet regularly, approximately once a month, giving both direction to the research activities and feedback to the field data and results. In this sense, the research was a kind of participatory action-research, but with the active participation here of people from various agencies with a stake in the broad policy field, and thus more a matter of participation at a macro rather than the usual micro level of participatory action-research.

In these various pilot projects, the setting up of working groups associated with selected research themes became significant in two major ways. First, the research material collected often constituted the first compilation and stocktaking of relevant and up-to-date information on the given field in the country in the new situation, and thus was of direct relevance to many of the parties involved [*Doornbos and Tesfai, 1999*]. But second, and at least as important, was the dialogue that ensued in most working groups in connection with the research. This was dialogue fed by research and in turn feeding into the research, but it was also a research-induced dialogue among various stakeholders in the respective policy area itself, which in a number of cases turned out to be highly valuable. Indeed, involvement in informal WSP working groups enabled representatives from different ministries, agencies, political parties or other organisations to compare notes and get a better understanding of other members' involvements and perspectives, of the rationale for certain policy positions, or of the shortcomings of particular policy measures. In several instances these confrontations with new perspectives and research data did actually lead to adjustments or rethinking of policy. In Mozambique, for example, local-level research data collected through the project on the impacts of structural adjustment on agriculture and food security gave the actors concerned, notably the

World Bank, reason to adapt their policy approaches. In Eritrea, WSP discussions and research helped clarify a long-standing policy stalemate between external and internal actors that had arisen over the government's policy of monetising food aid commodities. Invariably, in all four pilot cases, judging by the numerous expressions of interest by the participants concerned, the dialogue aspect has turned out to be a striking feature of these WSP projects.

From the experience with these projects, therefore, there does indeed appear to be scope for action-oriented research playing a constructive role in generating policy dialogue and better understanding. While the focus here has been on societies emerging from prolonged conflict and devastation, there seems to be no reason *a priori* why similar kinds of approaches should not be applicable to other policy contexts with important external as well as internal involvements, or to certain sectoral areas in which similar kinds of issues recur. Clearly, the particular modalities to be followed might need to be quite different in other areas, but the key element would be to build on action-research as a strategy towards broader deliberation with the inclusion of all relevant actors whose inputs it would be important to have.

Returning specifically to the food aid field, adopting this kind of approach might (i) help change the external–internal actor dichotomy from which it appears to suffer so pronouncedly, and (ii), by bringing in other relevant actors, local and external, might provide a better basis for determining optimal mixes of agricultural production incentives and aid components – as long as the latter can be made available. It would certainly not be true, as has sometimes been suggested, that no relevant counterparts would be available and ready to participate in any such common endeavours, in turn leaving the field basically open to donor-initiated actions. On the contrary, it would be essential not to bypass potential counterparts, but to engage them in the process from the onset. The WSP pilot projects seem to have demonstrated that it is in principle possible to generate meaningful policy dialogue on the basis of collective action-research at a macro level. Having passed this basic viability test, it may now be useful to develop appropriate methodologies for different kinds of policy contexts, notably that concerned with issues of food security.

V. CONCLUDING REMARKS

Looking back again at the debates about food aid over the past several decades, one cannot fail to notice a certain shift in the nature of these debates. First, during the postwar dawn of food aid arrangements, much of the discussion was on technical and operational aspects, though by and large remaining non-controversial in nature: the pros and cons of particular approaches were largely debated on the basis of acceptance of the need for food aid in a number of circumstances. Almost imperceptibly, however, food aid subsequently became a more 'permanent' proposition, and areas for its possible application were extended as Northern surplus commodities made this possible, if not compelling. In debate, these links to overproduction – of grains, milk and meat – were seriously questioned, and the nature of the exchanges became increasingly adversarial and controversial. On the side of the industry during this episode, criticism and alternative suggestions were not particularly welcomed. They would hardly be listened to, and rather risked being dismissed out of hand or being accused of having been inspired by ulterior motives to damage a 'just' cause.

At present, with the imminent decline of available surpluses for disposal as food aid, a change in the climate for discussion again appears to be in the making. One senses a greater preparedness to reconsider issues and involvements, priorities and alternatives, at least among some of the staff and sections of the agencies involved. Others, however, remain as sensitive to criticism as before, if not more so. As suggested above, this is not too surprising, but appears perfectly explicable in terms of struggles for institutional survival (be it that these often happen to be focused on a short rather than a longer horizon). Nonetheless, more meaningful internal dialogues on alternative futures may ensue within the key agencies engaged in food aid activities. If these do come about, then conceivably they may create a broader orientation on food security with correspondingly new approaches by the organisations involved, thus allowing suitable institutional complementarities within the limited space for policy engagement that remains.

REFERENCES

Christian Michelsen Institute, 1993, *Evaluation of the World Food Programme: Final Report*, Bergen: CMI.

Clay, E.J., N. Pillai and C. Benson, 1998a, *The Future of Food Aid: A Policy Review*, London: Overseas Development Institute, June.

Clay, E.J., N. Pillai and C. Benson, 1998b, *Food Aid and Food Security in the 1990s: Performance and Effectiveness*, London: Overseas Development Institute, Working Paper No. 113, Sept.

Doornbos, M., M. Mitra and P. van Stuijvenberg, 1988, 'Premises and Impacts of International Dairy Aid: The Politics of Evaluation', *Development and Change*, Vol. 19, No. 3, pp. 467–504.

Doornbos, M. and P. Terhal, 1993, 'The Limits of Independent Policy Research: Analysing the EEC–India Dairy Aid Nexus', in A. Hurskainen and M. Salih, eds., *Social Science and Conflict Analysis*, Helsinki: Helsinki University Press.

Doornbos, M. and A. Tesfai, 1999, *Post-Conflict Eritrea: Prospects for Reconstruction and Development*, Lawrenceville, N: The Red Sea Press.

Fritschel, H., 1998, 'The Changing Outlook for Food Aid', *2020 Vision News and Views*, Washington DC: International Food Policy Research Institute, Nov.

United Nations Research Institute for Social Development (UNRISD), 1994, *Rebuilding War-torn Societies: Problems of International Assistance in Conflict and Post-Conflict Situations*, Geneva: UNRISD, Aug.

16

Food and Human Security: Retrospective and an Agenda for Change

EDWARD CLAY AND OLAV STOKKE

There continue to be two competing views on global problems of food and human security and of how these might be addressed. The traditional view is that the food problem is fundamentally one of supply. This is associated with the long-standing emphasis on food self-sufficiency as the way to ensure food security. This policy was embraced by many European industrialised countries in postwar reconstruction and afterwards by most developing countries. There is still the problem of those countries that are unable to produce enough food and those people who are unable to afford enough food.

The traditional view then involves an intuitively obvious leap – to use global surpluses of food to address directly the problems of hunger and under-nutrition. That strategy rests on contrasting plenty with need – 'tackling hunger in a world full of food' [*WFP, 1996*]. The implied international policy is that food should be transferred as food aid from surplus to deficit countries and then targeted as food assistance on the hungry and malnourished in these countries. That view is finding decreasing support, as indicated in the actual declarations of the World Food Summit, the parallel statement of NGOs and the many contributory statements by governments [*FAO, 1996*]. Nevertheless, many, especially in developing countries, are still strongly committed to seeking the greatest degree of local, national and regional self-sufficiency in food as the only way for people to guarantee their food security and achieve autonomous development. This perception of the unacceptable economic and political risks involved in reliance on international trade is strongly reflected in policy advocacy by civil society institutions around the 1996 World Food Summit and subsequently the WTO. This equation of self-reliance with self-sufficiency implies that many are still committed to a form of supply-side analysis of food security.

The alternative, counter-intuitive view on problems of global food security reflects increasingly complex conceptions of the nature of food insecurity and the ways in which problems of hunger and malnutrition are addressed. Those who are short of food will only be able to obtain it in the long run if they can pay for it, leading to the concept of food self-reliance at the economy-wide or household level. This view has highlighted the importance of employment and markets, as well as increased food production and availability. The food security issue is about effective demand, access and people's ability to assert their entitlement to food [*Drèze and Sen, 1989; Maxwell, 1996, Shaw and Clay, 1998*].

I. GLOBAL FOOD PROBLEMS AND INSTITUTIONAL ARRANGEMENTS

There are, as Pandya-Lorch in Chapter 2 indicates, continuing world food problems. These are problems concerned with ensuring adequate production and stability of supplies. The predominant opinion, reflecting many exercises exploring the future food situation in the early twenty-first century, is that global food production will probably continue to outpace population.

But there is a second, equally important question: whether the distribution of available food as determined by effective demand through trade and market processes will meet the needs of deficit regions and countries and vulnerable social groups. Here the assessments are far more pessimistic. The projections in Chapter 2 suggest that food security for all will be far from ensured: large groups are expected to suffer hunger and malnutrition in the twenty-first century, simply because they cannot afford to buy the food which is available. There is no international food security regime with a capacity to compensate for this lack of effective demand, nor do regimes exist at the national level in many low-income developing countries to ensure that the potentially food-insecure and malnourished are able to satisfy their needs.

Recent research has also demonstrated three other necessary conditions for minimising child hunger and malnutrition [*Smith and Haddad, 2000*]. One is universal basic education for all women as part of improving women's status relative to men. A second is an improved health environment. The third is addressing the broader problem of livelihood security. It is impractical to address problems of hunger or under-nutrition and malnutrition as if these were separable and targetable clinical conditions. Some narrowly defined vitamin deficiencies might be addressed in this way but not broader problems of stunted growth and increased risk of ill-health and shortened life expectancy.

In an increasingly liberalised global economy, there are also potentially serious issues of short-term variability in production that will be amplified through their impact on prices (Chapter 3). Recognising these problems, the Uruguay Round trade agreement made special provision for addressing the food problems of food-importing countries, particularly the poorest, linked to existing arrangements for food aid. The WTO is responsible for follow-up, but the problem with the decision is that no responsibility for doing anything is actually vested anywhere. On the evidence of actions since the Marrakesh Agreement, little of substance is likely to materialise in the foreseeable future.

The special dispensation for food aid within the Uruguay Round agreement could be criticised as industrialised countries giving themselves more freedom to address their internal agricultural problems, with the justification of the need to make special provision for developing country food import problems and humanitarian assistance. In 1998, confronted with declining prices, a build-up of wheat stocks and drastically reduced import capacity in major markets affected by economic collapse, notably Indonesia and Russia, the US Department of Agriculture used food aid arrangements to address its problem of overhanging stocks. In the run-up to the 1998 mid-term elections, surplus commodities were redirected to food aid, doubling budget lines for FY 1999. Much of this additional aid has been provided as emergency support to countries affected by economic crises and natural disasters (see Chapter 1, Box 1.3).

The international institutional arrangements for food aid, and food security more broadly, have been inherited from an era of structural agricultural surpluses in which food aid was seen to have a major humanitarian and development role. The Food Aid Convention emerged as the arrangement intended to provide a floor level to food aid, linked to assessments in the 1970s of minimum annual global requirements (Chapter 4). The Convention drew aid donors who were not agricultural exporters into a burden-sharing arrangement that committed them to provide minimum quantities of aid in the form of cereals. It has had some limited impact in reducing downward fluctuations in food aid levels, but only in 1993–94 and 1996–98. As major food aid donors were typically setting food aid levels substantially above minimum obligations, the short-term effects of price variability and the export supply situation continued to impact on food aid, but above floor levels over a 20-year period. Then, confronted with budgetary pressures and higher prices, the major cereal exporters – Australia, Canada and the US – were first able to reduce their obligations unilaterally and then the US failed to meet these lower commitments in a tighter market situation. The European Commission, in the throes of food aid policy reconstruction and without agricultural pressures to export grain, also underfulfilled EU commitments in 1997/98. The Convention has proved to be only partially effective in its primary function (Benson in Chapter 4).

To anticipate with a high degree of certainty medium-term trends for even 3 to 5 years ahead is an uncertain enterprise, particularly when the point of departure is the rapidly changing political and economic situation in the 1990s. The likely scale and nature of the humanitarian crises with related food insecurity problems are difficult to anticipate. Expectations are too easily influenced by very recent events. The early 1990s brought an upsurge of regional and local conflicts, so that the focus of humanitarian relief became, by mid-decade, dominated by complex emergencies (Chapters 5 and 6). Then, to confound expectations, the decade ended with a sequence of large-scale natural disasters. The threat of a descent into political anarchy across much of the developing world was partly replaced by the casual linking of every catastrophe to climatic change or the El Niño-La Niña or ENSO phenomenon. The actual crises had widely spread geographical locations and posed different food assistance and international aid requirements.

The extrapolation of trends in food aid is also increasingly difficult, as short-term variability in quantities provided has become more pronounced. There is the continuing, but possibly weaker, link between the levels of stocks and international food prices.[1] There is also the enhanced risk under the new WTO regime that prices will be more volatile, noted in Chapter 3. There is also evidence that the policy responses of the major donors to the changing short-term situation are diverging. Events since the Lysebu meeting underscore these developments. In 1998 and 1999 US food aid commitments increased sharply, both because of the effects of lower prices of grains and oil-seeds and because of extra funding by USDA under the most flexible Title 1 (loan) and Section 416 (grant) budget lines (Chapter 1, Box 3). But in

---

1. This may be inferred from a close reading of the statistical analysis in Chapter 4 and a comparison with earlier and similar exercises, e.g. Benson and Clay [*1998*], and reported by FAO statisticians in private communications.

contrast the EU food aid allocations were little affected by lower prices as the policy of shifting from commodity aid to financial aid to food security was sustained. Of course, the EU might react again to a sustained period of lower prices and higher stocks, as it did in the early 1990s, by using export credit lines to shift surplus food to customers experiencing financing difficulties, such as Russia [*Benson and Clay, 1998*].

The implication of recent experience is that food aid is becoming a more uncertain resource for relief and development. If there is any element of additionality because of supply-side agricultural and trade policies, then these extra resources are at best contingent and short-term. Such resources are not equivalent to the structural surpluses of earlier decades that provided a relatively assured basis for WFP development projects. It is notable that donors no longer talk as they did between c. 1975 and 1985 of the multi-year programming of food aid as budgetary or balance-of-payments support. Therefore it makes sense for those that see a potentially positive role for food assistance projects and safety nets to ask if there are other politically based sources of additionality or advantages of easier targeting and disbursement that will still provide a continuing basis for food aid (Schulthes in Chapter 10).

As the Food Aid Convention draws in a wider group than would otherwise earmark funds for providing food aid on an annual basis, the question is, does it have the effect of making food aid institutionally an additional resource? Since some food aid had to be in the form of food every year, donors, individually and collectively, have had to find ways of making the best use of what they have agreed to provide. Thus the Convention provides part of the underpinning for the WFP as a humanitarian and development agency. At a bilateral level, the predictability of tied food aid also provides a basis for the actions of some NGOs. US legislation mandates minimum levels of food aid for private voluntary organisations (PVOs) and the Canadian Food Grains Bank has also emerged as a way for NGOs to use tied food aid on a regular basis.

The overall additionality of food aid, beyond what would otherwise be available as development aid, appears now to be limited, mostly applying only to the United States, and unpredictable. The imperative to respond to humanitarian disasters would necessitate some response even by the US, if food aid were not available. Rather, food aid has become institutionalised as a separate and therefore additional resource, from the perspective of those involved – international agencies, NGOs, and individual recipient countries in their aid negotiations. The rationale for providing food aid has changed from the original one of making an additional resource (food in kind) available for relief and developmental purposes. Now the maintenance of institutions – US private voluntary organisations and the WFP in particular – has increasingly become part of the rationale for keeping up food aid in kind. The argument that food in kind represents an additional resource, increasing total aid for development and relief, has become increasingly unconvincing.

II. HUMAN SECURITY AND HUMANITARIAN FOOD AID

There are dimensions to the problems of food insecurity beyond those captured by growth curves and variability in production and prices. These sources of insecurity are interwoven with political and social insecurity and the effects of economic shocks. There are international and internal conflicts; some nation states are collapsing. The wider conception of human security recognises that these problems are interrelated. According to UNDP [*1994: 23*], human security means, first, safety from such chronic threats as hunger, disease and repression and, second, protection from sudden and hurtful disruptions in the patterns of daily life – whether in homes, in jobs or in communities.[2] A danger which this concept shares with other wider concepts which aim to be all-inclusive and to obtain universal acceptance, is that it is not easily operationalised and therefore difficult to implement. Nevertheless, it follows that in many situations, food and nutritional security cannot be successfully addressed as a separable technical problem, but has to be considered as part of the wider issue of human security, as Kracht, for example, argues in Chapter 5.[3]

---

2. According to the *Human Development Report 1994,* the concept of security has for too long been interpreted narrowly: as security of territory from external aggression, or as protection of national interests in foreign policy or as global security from the threat of a nuclear holocaust. It has been related more to nation states than to people. The legitimate concerns of ordinary people who sought security in their daily lives were forgotten. The notion of human security has four characteristics: (i) it is a *universal* concern; many threats are common to all people – such as unemployment, drugs, crime, pollution and human rights violations – which all represent a threat to human security; (ii) the components of human security are *interdependent*; when the security of people is endangered anywhere in the world, all nations are likely to get involved – famine, disease, pollution, drug trafficking, terrorism, ethnic disputes and social disintegration are no longer isolated events, confined within national borders; (iii) it is easier to ensure through *early prevention* than later intervention; and (iv) it is *people-centred* – concerned with how people live and breathe in society, how freely they exercise their many choices, how much access they have to market and social opportunities, and whether they live in conflict or in peace [*UNDP, 1994: 22*].
3. For a recent, useful overview of the literature, see Grundel [*1999*]. See also the recent attempt to redefine the limits of humanitarian aid by the Dutch Advisory Council on International Affairs [*AIV, 1998*].

Food aid, particularly in emergencies, is generally considered politically uncontroversial: food, along with other kinds of humanitarian aid (medicine, shelter, etc.), is provided to people who suffer from hunger and other forms of human deprivation. Reality is not always that simple. In conflict situations, humanitarian aid, including food, may sometimes function in a way that is inconsistent with the intentions of the donors. It may even turn into a tool of the oppressors and thereby nourish and prolong conflicts and increase the suffering of victims. This was demonstrated in the Sudan as well as in the Great Lakes region in Central Africa (see, *inter alia*, de Waal [*1997*], Esman [*1997*], Prendergast [*1996*], Slim [*1997*] and Stokke [*1997*]).[4] It goes without saying that this may create both an ethical dilemma and awkward practical issues: how can aid that runs the risk of being misused be defended? That dilemma is not new, nor restricted to relief operations. Aid from well-intentioned donors may cause harm as well as good.[5]

---

4.   Esman [*1997*] maintains that several efforts by donors to achieve distributive justice on behalf of low-status, disadvantaged groups may prolong conflicts and cost lives, arguing that donors should prepare ethnic impact statements before intervening in areas of potential ethnic conflict. He also points to the humanitarian assistance to the refugee camps in Goma, Zaire, close to the Rwandan border, distributed through 'leaders' who proved to be officers of the Hutu militia, using the camps and the supplies for conscription, training, re-supply and sustenance in preparing for the re-invasion of Rwanda and the renewal of the war against the Tutsi regime. Prendergast [*1996*] maintains that aid may sustain conflicts in three major ways: it can be used directly as an instrument for war, it can be indirectly integrated into the dynamics of the conflict, and it can exacerbate the root causes of war and insecurity. With illustrations from several conflict areas, particularly in the Sudan, Ethiopia and the Great Lakes region, he shows how the conflicting parties, and the host government in particular, are able to manipulate and blackmail donor agencies to serve their own objectives, particularly through denial of food aid, manipulation of the distribution of aid in order to gain favours and support and even to maintain a military presence, and direct diversion of humanitarian aid to sustain their capacity to fight. Aid may also increase the resources of the conflicting parties by way of indirect 'taxation' and 'humanitarian structures' may even be hijacked.
      Alex de Waal [*1997*] provides a fundamental critique of relief operations, claiming that 'international humanitarianism', the way it operates, is an obstacle rather than an aid to conquering famine in Africa. 'Sending relief is a weapon of first resort: popular at home, usually unobjectionable abroad, and an excuse for not looking more deeply into underlying political problems. At worst, supporting humanitarianism is a smokescreen for political inaction' [*ibid.: 134*]. A core argument is that 'its power is exercised and its resources dispensed at the cost of weakening the forms of political accountability that underlie the prevention of famine' [*ibid.: 4*]. This argument is in line with similar warnings related to aid conditionality: the effects of external initiatives in promoting 'good governance' might, paradoxically, be to reduce rather than to strengthen Third World governments' capacity for policy-making and policy implementation as a consequence of their loss of policy initiative [*Doornbos, 1995; Stokke, 1995*].
5.   Hugo Slim [*1997: 3*], discussing the risks involved in a humanitarian intervention, notes that getting involved 'is bound to lead the helper into an encounter with

However, these broader political perspectives aside, food assistance continues to be the primary response to a range of social assistance needs of refugees and internally displaced people. Humanitarian relief is geared to providing basic physical infrastructure, shelter, water supply and health care and transfers of food in kind. Much of the food continues to be tied aid, and that adds an additional layer of inflexibilities in terms of what is an appropriate, adequate and assured response.

The weaknesses of this approach are highlighted by a few specific and continuing problems (Chapter 6). When rations are disrupted or only partially provided, those providing and evaluating assistance press for additional rations to replace those forgone. Those affected by ration shortfalls are presumed to have had to sell assets, draw down cash balances or increase indebtedness and incur other obligations. Additional food assistance enables them to meet other needs and improve their asset indebtedness position through selling rations or repaying obligations in kind.

Blended foods and the fortification of vegetable oil and milk products are a consequence of a limited range of commodities, again partially linked to aid tying. From a clinical nutritional perspective these are potentially satisfactory solutions. But such foods pose social problems of acceptability and also technical problems in organising satisfactory, intensive and supplementary feeding.

There are many practical difficulties in providing humanitarian assistance, problems of logistics security and social organisation of assistance in the initial phase of a crisis, as in Rwanda in 1994, or in the immediate aftermath of Hurricane Mitch in 1998. In physically difficult environments and situations of continuing insecurity and uncertainty, such as the Great Lakes region or the Horn of Africa, failures in relief and problems of malnutrition, morbidity and increased mortality cannot be entirely avoided. Are these then issues for continuing improvement in practice, or is a more radical reconstruction of emergency aid appropriate? If humanitarian assistance is an overwhelming priority, and there are unavoidable technical and financial problems of collective response, then tied aid would appear to be an unreasonable additional constraint. Favouring a subset of producers, processors and suppliers in the donor countries introduces an additional constraint that increases costs and brings in inflexibilities which,

---

humankind at its worst, as well as its best. In such situations, helpers soon find themselves dining with the devil. And in doing so, no matter how long the spoon, they will tend to finding themselves feeding on moral compromise and getting dirty hands'.

on the available evidence, appear to detract from the effectiveness of humanitarian assistance (Chapter 6).

III. LIBERALISATION AS AN INTERNAL REALITY

The experience of SADC countries during the 1990s indicates the importance of recognising the effects of internal market liberalisation and the reduction in obstacles to legal trade and traffic on a regional basis (Chapter 7). When affected by drought shocks, SADC countries do not so much need food aid as finance for food imports and, in some cases, additional support besides food for drought relief. The increasing willingness of international and regional financial institutions and some donors to respond accordingly indicates a partial but significant adaptation in donor practice. Stronger regional institutions and the addressing of political sources of conflict make possible both preparedness against natural disaster shocks and more effective, integrated responses to mitigate their effect.

There is also an issue of confidence-building at a regional level involving donor agencies and aid-recipient countries. The importance of establishing a process within which the reduction in programme food aid could be managed and liberalisation of internal marketing supported is illustrated by the experience of the Sahel countries and OECD's Club du Sahel in sustaining a food security dialogue (Chapter 12).

IV. FOOD AS A RESOURCE FOR ECONOMIC CRISIS MANAGEMENT AND DEVELOPMENT

The process of reassessing food aid since the late 1980s has taken place during what is a truly difficult period of rapid change and considerable uncertainty. There has been considerable volatility in markets and levels of surpluses, moves to liberalise trade and major economic and humanitarian crises. The reassessment appears to be resulting in increasingly divergent practice. The collapse of the Soviet Union's purchasing capacity and massive surpluses of cereals coincided with the El Niño-linked drought in southern Africa and natural disasters elsewhere between 1991 and 1995. There was a relatively conventional response involving large-scale food aid, highly concessional export credits and the redirection of aid from politically lower priority recipients. Subsequently, the WTO liberalisation, budgetary restraints and a tighter international market situation produced a widespread re-examination of institutional arrangements, modalities of food aid and finance for food. That re-examination has highlighted the high transaction costs or inefficiency of programme food aid as reported in the 1990s evaluations reviewed in Chapter 8.

All the major donors, apart from the US, appear to have abandoned programme food aid as an aid instrument. This change in policy is suggested by the response in 1998/99 to economic crises in East Asia and the former Soviet republics. Only the United States amongst major donors has responded with large-scale programme food aid to crisis-affected countries exploiting what might be positively described as a 'window of opportunity' provided by the extra resources available because of a weak market and the build-up of domestic pressure to assist farmers (Chapter 1, Appendix Tables A1.1 and A1.2). However, the alternative cynical interpretation is that this is a return to opportunistic surplus disposal made possible by the exclusion of food aid from WTO restraints. These actions appear to have been made with little regard for impacts on markets and rural livelihoods in importing countries such as Indonesia [*Poh and others, 1999*].

V. FOOD FOR DEVELOPMENT IN QUESTION

In our earlier joint volume, we drew attention to the way in which policy analysis, evaluations and research had narrowed the areas of controversy surrounding the usefulness of food aid [*Clay and Stokke, 1991: 6*]. The contributions in the present volume by Pillai (Chapter 8), Faaland *et al.* (Chapter 9), Schulthes (Chapter 10) and Thirion (Chapter 11) indicate that this process of reducing the areas of professional disagreement has continued.

The different ways in which agencies themselves are responding to the challenges of budgetary constraints and increasing donor ambivalence suggest that strategies are also opportunistic, reflecting the uncertainties and constraints of their food aid sources.

The WFP [*1996, 1999*] emphasises the special enabling role of food assistance in targeting the poorest, particularly women through their control of food distribution within households. Food aid should be used to support projects in which feeding of undernourished people is a primary and direct objective. The selection of projects should contribute to the building of a resource base for beneficiaries. As Faaland *et al.* comment, this strategy is not really new, but a restatement of already established objectives for the use of food aid in supporting development, but it is still very ambitious in the light of past performance and the institutional constraints in the donor and recipient agencies (Chapter 9).

In contrast, US PVOs have lobbied effectively for changes in the legislation, most recently in the 1995 Farm Bill, to allow them to use a higher proportion of food aid to generate local currencies for a wider range of almost entirely rural-based social development projects. Consequently, by FY1998, almost 40 per cent of project food aid under the US PL480 Title II Programme was monetised. Some PVOs, for example Africare, only used development food aid for monetisation. Others had wholly monetised some of their country programmes, for example CARE's component of the rural works programme in Bangladesh.

Changes in the kinds of food provided could increase the amount of calories and protein available to the poor and food-insecure people in developing countries without increasing the cost to the donor government. This way of increasing the nutritional transfer efficiency of food aid was identified, for example by Pinstrup-Andersen [*1991*], in a review of Danish food aid that might involve the substitution of peas, wheat flour and vegetable oil for canned meat and cheese. Responding to this recommendation, by 1997 the Danish contribution to the WFP contained six times more calories and three times more protein at a lower real cost than in 1990 and still drew on Danish sources of supply. This potentially increased the numbers able to receive a notional daily ration of 1800 kcl per person from 46,000 to 290,000 [*Colding and Pinstrup Andersen, 1999*]. However, as Shoham and his colleagues note in Chapter 6, European and Canadian rape-seed oil is likely to be nutritionally less satisfactory than lower-cost palm oil, and may require costly fortification.

The selection of foods to provide, on the basis of income transfer effectiveness, the highest ratio of the monetary value to the recipient and cost to the donor, is another well recognised way of manoeuvring within the constraints imposed by both the practicalities of delivery and the restrictions of the donor food basket [*Reutlinger and Katona Apte, 1984*]. However, there have been few reported examples of situations in which the package of food assistance has been modified on the basis of such calculations. Rather, the main effect of this approach has been to provide a rationale for simpler baskets of food assistance, often only wheat or maize, which do not attempt to meet nutritional requirements in a balanced way.

There has also been a substantial shift from direct food aid to financing the local acquisition of food and triangular transactions (Chapter 1, Table 1.3 and Chapter 12). However, the shift to untied acquisition appears to have reached a ceiling of around one-fifth of all food aid in the mid-1990s. The scope for such operations may be severely circumscribed in some emergency situations such as a drought or where local markets are severely disrupted. There is also apparently a lack of political will to attempt to untie finance in the face of domestic agricultural interests in major agricultural exporting countries, particularly the USA, Canada and Australia. Instead, the aid agency response has been to reduce funding for food aid. Even USAID did not fight vigorously to retain its main programme aid budget, Title III (see Chapter 1, Box 1.3).

These attempts to increase the effectiveness and efficiency of food aid by juggling commodities and seeking increased flexibility can achieve marginal and, in a few cases, striking one-off gains in efficiency. However, even in humanitarian relief, excepting perhaps a purely nutritional crisis, such a purely technical focus on resource transfer efficiency is difficult to reconcile with increasingly complex conceptualisations of poverty and food insecurity which point to enhancing people's capacity to assert their own entitlements.

These are practical, well-established strategies of attempting to improve performance within broadly well established areas of activity or finding a margin for manoeuvre, making the resource more flexible. In economic terms, they might be characterised as strategies of local optimisation within a wider environment that is accepted as difficult to change.

VI. MODEL T FOOD AID

Robert Chambers, in a critique of conventional approaches to rural development and technology transfer, suggests that these imply: North over South dominance, normal professionalism, normal careers and normal bureaucracy undertaking top-down, centre-outwards transfer of knowledge and resources [Chambers, 1997]. He recalls the statement attributed to Henry Ford that the customer can have a Model T car of any colour so long as it is black.

Donor food aid programmes and arrangements have been relatively inflexible and standardised and open to similar criticism. Food aid in practice meant the commodities that donors had in surplus or had chosen to provide, such as US yellow maize and corn-soya mix from dedicated processors, Italian rice or skim-milk powder from the EU, Canadian canola (rape-seed oil), Danish cheese and Norwegian fish. Food aid involved starting from technical nutritional requirements of calories, protein and minor nutrients to putting together a basket of commodities from what the donors put on offer. The challenge for operational agencies was to respond to emergencies making the best use of these resources and the WFP, the Red Cross and many NGOs became skilled at doing this. The development challenge was to find opportunities to promote development, again with this predetermined basket of resources and within the layers of donor legislation and bureaucratic regulation.

In looking forwards the editors, in their conclusion to the earlier volume, envisaged that the distinction between food aid and aid more widely would gradually disappear through increasing flexibility and untying [Clay and Stokke, 1991: 33]. The realities of food aid have gradually been modified to some degree. In particular, those who were never traditional major cereal exporters have increasingly been willing to finance untied food purchases as well as meet transport costs and other complementary distribution arrangements. In humanitarian crises, financial resources are more readily available, enabling the WFP in the late 1990s to acquire approximately half of the food it supplies in developing countries. But the continued insistence of some major donors on tying aid to their products remains a serious constraint on humanitarian activity (Chapter 6). The 1999 Food Aid Convention is a further modest step in the direction of flexibility, allowing 10 per cent of the value of obligations as non-cereals for humanitarian assistance after two years of negotiations (Chapter 4). The European Union reforms from 1996 onwards make it no longer necessary for NGOs to think in terms of monetisation. Budget lines can be used directly to finance social development and human development projects. These reforms leave the future role of food aid in kind for development as much more uncertain (Chapter 11).

As Schulthes makes clear in Chapter 10, the Model T issue is ultimately about additionality. The traditional role of the operational food agencies was opportunistic, to look for the most effective ways of using food aid as an additional resource. The sources of that additionality were twofold. There was the availability of exportable surpluses of some food commodities. An associated 'political additionality' has been the apparent greater willingness of some donor countries to provide food to support hungry people and disaster-affected countries [Reutlinger, 1999; Shaw and Singer, 1996]. The operational challenge was to make the best opportunistic use of this additional resource.

The alternative approach to this process of adaptation is to return to first principles and to ask what is the comparative advantage of food assistance. When is it more appropriate to provide specific groups with directly distributed food or an income transfer tied to food? Then to follow up with a supplementary question and ask where and when might finance for food or food aid in kind be the more appropriate way of supporting these food assistance actions. The critical distinction is that between food assistance actions and food aid as an international instrument for supporting these actions.

In most circumstances, financial aid is preferable to programme food aid for general development purposes. This holds true whether aid is being provided for balance-of-payments or budgetary support. When the intention is to support the food and nutritional security of specific groups, then the choice of finance or food should take into account their circumstances and their definition of their problems and how these might be addressed [*Chambers, 1997*]. Even in an emergency and, particularly, a long-term humanitarian relief situation, it should not be assumed that food aid is automatically the appropriate response.

The contributors to this volume indicate a range of situations in which food assistance *is* an appropriate way of addressing food insecurity and the best means available of providing a safety net for the poorest and most vulnerable. Issues of gender and the way in which income and food are controlled in the household will affect strategies (Chapters 6, 8, 10). In the past, food aid was frequently seen as the only supporting instrument available. However, with the increasing commitment to poverty alleviation and eradication, there is now a wider range of options. For example, the World Bank operational guidance now allows the inclusion of food assistance components in IDA financing of human resource development activities.

When then is food aid likely to be an appropriate response? This is most likely when there is market collapse and also institutional weaknesses. In some limited circumstances of high food insecurity a combination of social and technical reasons makes food aid the best of the practical options available. This implies some combination of the following:

- high incidence of chronic moderate to severe under-nutrition;
- endemic micro-nutrient deficiency disorder;
- lack of purchasing capacity on the part of vulnerable households;
- markets which are incomplete or volatile; and
- availability of commodities which are especially appropriate to the needs of the food-insecure combined with delivery of targeting capacity.

In these circumstances the choice of food aid instruments should also reflect considerations of technical cost-efficiency balanced with an assessment of risk.

The review of recent donor polices reveals that such considerations have had a substantial impact on food aid. The shift to acquiring food in developing countries and the provision of finance for food assistance operations are an important aspect of this change. Nevertheless, there is considerable diversity of practice, which adds unnecessary complexity, and there are still areas in which the practice of official donors and NGOs is organised around the treatment of food aid as a separate and apparently additional resource.

VII. INSTITUTIONALISED ADDITIONALITY

The strategy of US PVOs in successfully lobbying for wider monetisation reflects their assumption that food aid is, *de facto*, an additional resource for their activities. It implies that there is extremely limited scope for persuading those who legislate on agriculture and aid to make available more cash instead of surplus food for PVO operations.

The institutionalisation of food aid in practice also makes for additionality from the perspective of recipient countries. A distinct set of agencies are offering another, separate form of aid. The recent experiences of some of the large, continuing and former large recipients are thought-provoking on this issue of additionality (Chapter 1, Table 1.3 and Appendix Table A1.2). Even Asia's nuclear powers – China, India and Pakistan – have been willing to make use of that additional resource when they are in turn providing food aid. Large-scale food aid to Egypt, for 20 years the largest recipient, was phased out in the early 1990s during the process of liberalisation of the agricultural sector. This was without apparently major effects on poverty, malnutrition or the wider economy [*Bonnavie et al., 1996*].

A pragmatic argument made in favour of development food aid projects is that they provide the basis for an effective response to crises, because these are likely to occur in low-income countries and regions within these countries that are extremely vulnerable to disaster (Chapter 9). The validity of this argument is an empirical matter.

Hurricanes Georges and Mitch in 1998 and the Turkish earthquakes in 1999 occurred in countries which did not have substantial food assistance programmes. The Orissa Cyclone in 1999 involved massive food assistance, but India has little need for food aid to support these actions. Recent conflict-related emergencies have arisen in countries of West Africa and the Great Lakes region of central Africa that were neither traditionally drought-prone nor substantial food aid recipients (Chapter 6). This is also the case for Kosovo, East Timor and the Caucasus in 1999. Equally importantly, these humanitarian operations do not appear to have been seriously delayed because of the absence of an existing infrastructure of food aid supported projects. Where food aid is institutionalised, for example in Ethiopia, there are in practice considerable difficulties in using food aid flexibly in an emergency (Chapter 8). Recent experience suggests that this role for food aid as a form of risk insurance, providing a basis for disaster response, does not represent a general argument for retaining development projects in a large number of low- and middle-income countries. The institutionalisation of food aid as part of disaster preparedness needs to be related to specific countries and requires further action to be effective.

VIII. NORMATIVE AND PRAGMATIC APPROACHES TO FOOD SECURITY AND HUMAN SECURITY

Food aid – in its many forms – should be need-driven and provided in order to directly reduce human suffering and enable people to sustain their livelihoods. That normative statement finds an echo in many policy declarations of international bodies and donor agencies. However, the actual mix of motives may vary from one actor to another, reflecting altruistic concerns as well as self-interest. In this, food aid is not different from other forms of aid [*Stokke, 1996*]. Gradually the predominant policy perspective has become more holistic. Food aid is increasingly considered as one means among many to attack the wider problem of human insecurity, including poverty. But it is probably not the most effective tool, with the possible exception of some humanitarian crises and in circumstances of high food insecurity, as noted above (Section VI).

The ultimate objective – to prevent human suffering, hunger and malnutrition in the short term, and to escape the longer-term consequences of these conditions – involves, in the first place, policies in the societies concerned at both macro and micro levels. Thus, the assurance of food availability depends, *inter alia*, on the agricultural policy that is pursued at national and regional levels, as well as globally. Except in (temporary) emergencies, policies that influence agricultural production, processing and marketing in these countries are more critical for the availability of food than is food aid. Support for agricultural development has always been prominent on the agenda for development co-operation. However, there are also issues of effective demand, access and entitlement. These demand side issues are further highlighted by the trend towards economic liberalisation: even if markets could adequately meet the food and nutritional requirements of all, a large proportion of the population may remain hungry and undernourished because people cannot afford to buy the food that is available. And human security, as briefly outlined above, depends on the development of human capacities, peace and good government, too.

Human suffering, whether man-made or caused by nature, calls for urgent relief actions both from within the societies directly concerned and from the international society.[6] The difficulties of agreeing and organising common or consistent international action are formidable in an immediate crisis. These difficulties multiply in moving to address persistent, chronic structural problems of human insecurity involving poverty, failures in developing human capacity, systematic exclusion and repression.

Strategies followed by 'the international society' to alleviate human misery and ensure human security vary: some are universal in scope, others are more limited in their perspective, attuned to the particular needs of specific organisations in fulfilling their mission. What they may have in common are commitments to alleviate suffering, to ensure or improve food security that can be built upon through establishing and developing internationally agreed norms. Efforts to build normative approaches range from seeking to elaborate a human rights basis for food security to establishing 'good practice' in providing aid.

One strategy is to transform the predominant values that have become associated with humane internationalism[7] into globally agreed norms and standards. The Universal Declaration of Human Rights adopted by the UN General Assembly in 1948 and a series of international charters and agreements ratified later, represent the prime point of departure of such efforts.[8] The key documents define

---

6. The notion of 'the international society' goes beyond international organisations (global and regional) and their member governments that have a mandate to intervene in situations of serious crisis of the kind identified (often referred to as 'the international community'). It also includes individual governments as well as their 'civil societies' (in particular, organisations active in providing humanitarian relief) and international non-governmental organisations (INGOs), which may act on their own, particularly in humanitarian crises, but even in violent conflicts (intra-state conflicts in particular).

7. For definitions of the concept of humane internationalism (and its various forms), see Pratt [1989, 1990] and Stokke [1989, 1996]. For a condensed discussion of the concept, see Stokke [1996: 20–25].

8. The 1948 declaration was followed by the International Covenant on Civil and Political Rights and the International Covenant on Economic, Social and Cultural

human rights over a broad spectrum, including the most fundamental of them, namely the right to life, freedom from torture and from arbitrary arrest and imprisonment, civil and political, then extended to include economic and social rights, such as employment, shelter, health and education. In 1986, the UN General Assembly included the right to development among these universal rights. A right to food for all is now considered as part of this set of norms. In Chapter 14, Wenche Barth Eide describes attempts to ensure and improve food security by integrating the right to food among the universal human rights.

The Red Cross movement (the ICRC and the Federation of Red Cross and Red Crescent Societies) has a long record in the field of international humanitarian operations in troubled areas and in war zones and is global in its scope. Its mission is, basically, to ensure human security and to provide relief. To fulfil its mission, the ICRC depends on an internationally agreed legal framework. With this as a basis, more detailed guidelines are worked out in order to facilitate the work in the field, where conflicting parties most often rule the ground. In 1993, the international Red Cross movement as well as a wider group of international NGOs agreed on a code of conduct for disaster relief, including measures to ensure food security. Alain Mourey describes this initiative and the subsequent efforts to implement the code (Chapter 13).

More pragmatic efforts have been made to develop codes of good conduct for food aid. This approach requires agreement on a normative ranking of objectives and a shared view of process that is empirically based. Seeking to learn from a shared interpretation of experiences from the mid-1980s, food aid donors and governments in the Sahel region agreed on a statement of what represented good practice and joint arrangements for monitoring performance. These efforts are described by Robin Jackson (Chapter 12). They are shown to have practical possibilities for strengthening disaster preparedness and countering some of the potentially negative effects of food aid operations.[9]

These various approaches and strategies represent steps towards a future human security regime, with a focus on food security as assur-

---

Rights. In addition, other treaties deal with specific categories of people, such as children, women, and the mentally ill, or malpractice, such as torture, discrimination and disappearances. These treaties are ratified by most governments, although some governments have expressed reservations with regard to individual sections.

9.   There are other efforts at establishing a code of conduct on food aid and human security. See, among others, EuronAid [*1995*].

ing all people's right to food. It is difficult to know with any certainty what avenue, the normative or the more pragmatic, will prove to be the more effective in promoting and ensuring human security. Perhaps these are mutually reinforcing. Progress along the normative route may be boosted by successes in addressing immediate, practical problems, and vice versa.

However, there is still a long way to go before anything close to an international food security regime is established.[10] So far, there is no general agreement even on norms and objectives – considered to be the first and easiest steps on the difficult road.

Vision is necessary for reformers; it may give perspective and guidance to more pragmatic institutional reform. The normative approach provides such a vision. However, vision needs to be followed up by sustained, practically oriented actions. There is ample scope for practical reform and improvement of the emerging, feeble food security regime (see Chapters 3 and 4). Although globally agreed objectives, a fundamental precondition for an international regime, have not been established, international commitments to reduce the number of people who are exposed to absolute hunger (under-nutrition) have been made in general terms and targets indicated. Vague as such commitments certainly are, they could become a point of departure for restructuring arrangements that have become unsatisfactory. The Food Aid Convention is a potential candidate for shifting to a rights based formulation of international responsibilities. Benson in Chapter 4 has described how the obligations of the Food Aid Convention were linked to an assessment of 'needs' reflected in the 1994 World Food Conference Target of 10 million tonnes. But when in the 1990s some donors reduced their commitments and more flexibility was allowed in meeting obligations, the basis of these obligations was no longer clear. This increasingly vague formulation could be replaced by a commitment linked to a rights based definition of entitlements set out in a code of good conduct. The responsibility of signatories would be not to make minimum annual physical contributions of food or

---

10. An international regime is characterised by a system of norms, objectives and rules, formalised through some sort of international agreement between most of the actors in the policy area; there are procedures for the implementation of these rules, including negotiation, mediation and conflict resolution; and there are institutions responsible for policy decisions, monitoring and enforcement of the rules set. For a mainstream definition (although attacked for being too vague), see Krasner [1982: 185]: 'International regimes are defined as principles, norms, rules and decision-making procedures around which actor expectations converge in a given issue-area.' See also Rittberger, ed. [1993], in particular Keohane [1993: 28]: '... regimes can be identified by the existence of explicit rules that are referred to in an affirmative manner by governments, even if they are not necessarily scrupulously observed.'

finance for food. Instead they would make a commitment to 'assure' these entitlements in situations of humanitarian crisis associated with conflict and/or natural disaster.

The specification of rights and responsibilities could also become a point of departure for regular monitoring (evaluation) of the state of affairs and trends, globally and in individual countries, with regard to the prevailing food security, and the performance of the relevant individual governments and aid donors. Evaluation (monitoring) of performance constitutes, as noted, an important component of an international regime. It may even be instrumental in a process that leads to more precise objectives, since monitoring of performance presupposes clear objectives. Institutions to evaluate the performance of official development assistance are already established (OECD DAC) and these institutions may be adapted to the monitoring of food security (FAO) and even to the wider concept of human security (UNDP). Although far from what we conceive of as an international food security regime, systematic and improved monitoring may represent a small, pragmatic step in the right direction.

IX. INSTITUTIONAL CHANGE

Several contributors to this volume point to the need for institutional reform, involving changes to food aid institutions and within the international community more generally. Broadly three types of response are discernible.

First there are declaratory changes in terms of policy objectives and targets. As Doornbos indicates (Chapter 15), there are real dangers that such statements are purely rhetorical, at worst tactics for evading more substantive change in actions and mandates. The World Food Summit and preceding UN-sponsored international conferences exemplify this approach – problems are defined, targets are set but responsibility is diffuse, spread across many agencies and assigned to national governments. Issues of resources and institutional change have been avoided [*Shaw and Clay, 1998*]. Such international conferences and the declarations that result, like the Marrakesh Accord, have a role in clarifying and moving the agenda for policy but they can also be exercises in defending established interests and the evasion of responsibility.

The second option is adaptation. There is considerable evidence that institutions are modifying modalities and practices, but more in response to short-term influences than as part of a longer-term strategy. The gradual change in WFP resources from predominantly development project aid to humanitarian assistance is a striking example. This change was not envisaged and not planned in any long-term way, but came about in response to changing demands on the organisation. Another example is the World Bank's modification of its operational guidance to allow funding of food for human development and the use of IDA emergency recovery credits for crisis food imports. The continued *ad hoc* modification of arrangements to deal with problems as they arise through existing mechanisms is perhaps the dominant response to the changing environment, signalled in Chapter 1, elaborated at the global level (Chapters 3 and 4) and at a regional level (Chapter 7), and in relation to humanitarian problems (Chapters 5 and 6). Much of this adaptation is useful, and increases the effectiveness and efficiency of humanitarian aid and food assistance. But the slowness of adaptation and the apparent limits to change make it difficult to respond adequately to the consequences of major changes in the political and economic environment.

The third, more ambitious, option is to reconfigure the architecture of international institutions. The establishment of the WTO was such an opportunity, but is it being dissipated? Faaland *et al.* suggest in Chapter 9 that the mandate of the WFP perhaps should be revised from a focus on food aid as a resource to a role that combines humanitarian assistance and the alleviation of hunger. If, as Maxwell, for example, suggests [*ODI, 1999*], there were a wider blueprint for the sequencing of incremental changes, this could move international institutions towards more effectively addressing short-term humanitarian problems and the longer-term challenge of continuing widespread chronic hunger and malnutrition.

It would be unrealistic to expect that radical institutional reform in order to cope with such challenges will emerge from within the international agencies concerned with food aid and food security. The World Food Summit in 1996 and other international conferences under the UN avoided such issues. This indicates that the best that can realistically be hoped for is that they will adapt to the new realities and challenges, with some delay and after pressure from their governing bodies in which governments are represented. That is the way institutions normally behave. It may also be realistically hoped that they will make stronger efforts – beyond rhetoric – at co-ordinating their activities better than has been demonstrated in the past, for example during the complex emergencies of the 1990s.

Sustained pressure for change from outside and from national government representatives in the governing bodies of the organisations concerned will be needed. Governments will need to co-ordinate their positions, each government within its national setting and the member governments among themselves, in order to make policies more coherent.[11] That point emerges clearly from Chapter 3 on the WTO and Chapter 4 on the FAC and has been underlined by the apparent failure to establish an agenda for agriculture at the WTO meeting in Seattle in December 1999.

If more radical change in the existing international system is to be achieved – to restructure it to the present and future challenges of human security, including food security – initiatives have to come from outside the established agencies: from the governments that pick up the bill. This presents a regional organisation, such as the EU, with a special challenge. There is necessarily a US dimension – food aid began with, and has recently become again, a predominantly US concern. There is also a critical Southern dimension to the matter of institutional change. International agencies provide Southern governments with an opportunity to present their perspectives and promote their interests on a global stage. Radical change should not be seen as simply a Northern agenda for rationalising, in other words, cutting contributions to global institutions.

Or is the attempt at unified international action to be abandoned in favour of actions based on variable geometry – seeking coherence amongst the internally constrained, even inflexible actions of the major players? That is what has been happening and, as documented here and elsewhere, it fails to achieve even a 'good enough' outcome.

X. HUMAN SECURITY AND THE POLITICS OF FOOD AID

The first challenge is that there is a lack of consensus on goals, objectives and broader means of achieving these. A fundamental issue is whether there is a separate hunger problem that can be addressed by providing aid from food surpluses or by acquiring this food and distributing it to hungry people. Or can the food entitlements of the poor only be effectively assured as part of a wider strategy for providing livelihoods, personal security, health, education; that is, as an aspect of wider human security? The balance of argument in this volume is

---

11. Politics tends to be compartmentalised. One consequence is that different government representatives may adopt contradictory positions in the various governing boards in which the government is represented. Often, representatives give emphasis to the more particular interests of 'their' organisation and its stakeholders rather than to the overall objectives of their government. However, a coherent national policy is not always in place. In order to pursue overall objectives in an effective way, co-ordination and a coherent policy are imperative.

heavily in favour of the latter, widely accepted, contemporary perspective on the indivisibility of human security.

However, powerful interests in a few industrialised countries, particularly the US, see no contradiction between simultaneously addressing humanitarian and hunger problems and promoting domestic agricultural and other commercial interests. This represents a problem today as it did in the past.

The Model T approach is to accept and to use opportunistically the resources that are politically and institutionally available as food. There is also scope, in some cases substantial, for adaptation and localised increases in efficiency. That implies working to modify the small print of international agreements and unpicking some of the web of regulations and procedures that tie aid at an individual donor level. The more challenging approach and the one that is most difficult to realise, is envisaging food as a human right; and then that the international community should encourage and support the initiatives of people and countries to ensure their entitlements.

Looking forward, the second challenge lies in the sequencing of change. The next US Farm Bill might be regarded as both an opportunity and an obstacle to the further evolution of international arrangements. How and when should the issues of food and human security be taken up to planning the next round of WTO trade negotiations? As part of a rights-based approach, a consistent international position on the untying of humanitarian aid might facilitate change at an individual UN member country level. Do either the US internal process or the trade talks provide an opportunity to pursue this issue of untying of humanitarian aid?

An attempt to rethink how the mandates of the UN and related institutions should be reconfigured to address problems of hunger and rights to food may be a precondition for institutional change. In the absence of such a coherent, wider blueprint, adaptation and local optimisation become the only viable strategy for change. On the evidence of the last decade the results of such a strategy may well be positive, but are unlikely to make a substantial impact on global problems of hunger, poverty and human insecurity.

Recognition of the need for institutional change is a necessary first step, but the problem is not solved by rhetoric. Again, it would be somewhat futile, and flying in the face of what we know about how institutions work, to expect that this problem can be left to the agencies involved alone. They all have their own vested interests to defend – in extreme cases even their survival as institutions may be at stake, affecting those that staff them as well. The ideas and the pressure for change therefore have to come from and be sustained from the outside, in particular from donor governments and the major players amongst the developing countries, and from those who influence what these governments attempt to do – in civil society, in the media, in academia, on the boards of Exxon and Monsanto, and on the streets of Seattle, Beijing and Calcutta.

REFERENCES

AIV, 1998, *Humanitarian Aid: Redefining the Limits*, The Hague: Advisory Council on International Affairs (Nov.).

Benson, C. and E.J. Clay, 1998, 'Additionality or Diversion? Food Aid to Eastern Europe and the Former Soviet Republics and the Implications for Developing Countries', *World Development*, Vol. 26, No. 1, pp. 31–44.

Bonnavie, H. *et al.*, 1996, *Egypt: The Extended Study* (Evaluation of EU Programme Food Aid), London: Overseas Development Institute.

Chambers, R., 1997, *Whose Reality Counts? Putting the Last First*, London: Intermediate Technology Publications.

Clay, E. J. and O. Stokke, 1991, 'Assessing the Performance and Economic Impact of Food Aid', in Clay and Stokke, eds.

Clay, E. J. and O. Stokke, eds., 1991 (reprinted 1995), *Food Aid Reconsidered: Assessing the Impact on Third World Countries*, London: Frank Cass.

Colding, B. and P. Pinstrup-Andersen, 1999, 'A six-fold increase in the impact of food aid: Denmark's contribution to World Food Programme', *Food Policy*, Vol. 24, No. 1, pp.93–108.

de Waal, A., 1997, *Famine Crimes, Politics and the Disaster Relief Industry in Africa*, London: Africa Rights & The International African Institute in association with James Currey (Oxford) and Indiana University Press (Bloomington and Indianapolis).

Drèze, J. and A. Sen, 1989, *Hunger and Public Action*, Oxford: Clarendon Press.

Doornbos, M., 1995, 'State Formation Processes under External Supervision: Reflections on "Good Governance"', in Stokke, ed.

Esman, M. J., 1997, 'Can Foreign Aid Moderate Ethnic Conflict?', *Peaceworks*, No. 13, Washington DC: United States Institute of Peace.

EuronAid, 1995, *Code of Conduct on Food Aid and Food Security*, Brussels: Liaison Committee of Development NGOs to the European Union and EuronAid.

FAO, 1996, *Rome Declaration on World Food Security and World Food Summit Plan of Action*, Rome: Food and Agriculture Organisation of the United Nations.

Grundel, J., 1999, *Humanitarian Assistance: Breaking the Waves of Complex Political Emergencies – A Literature Survey*, CDR Working Paper 99.5, Copenhagen: Centre for Development Research (August).

Keohane, R.O., 1993, 'The Analysis of International Regimes: Towards a European-American Research Programme', in Rittberger, ed.

Krasner, S.D., 1982, 'Structural Causes and Regime Consequences: Regimes as Intervening Variables', *International Organization*, Vol. 36, No. 2.

Maxwell, S., 1996, 'Food security: a post-modernist perspective', *Food Policy*, Vol. 21, No. 2, pp.155–70.

ODI, 1999, 'Global Governance: An Agenda for the Renewal of the United Nations', *ODI Briefing Paper* 1999 (2) (July).

Pinstrup-Andersen, P., 1991, 'Food Aid to Promote Economic Growth and Combat Poverty, Food Insecurity and Malnutrition in Developing Countries, and Suggestions for How to Increase the Effectiveness of Danish Aid to the World Food Programme', Report prepared for the Ministry of Foreign Affairs, Denmark.

Poh, L.K. and others, 1999, 'Manufacturing a Crisis: The Politics of Food Aid to Indonesia', *Development Report*, No. 13, Oakland, CA: Institute for Food and Development Policy.

Pratt, C., 1989, 'Humane Internationalism: Its Significance and Its Variations', in Pratt, ed.

Pratt, C., ed., 1989, *Internationalism under Strain*, Toronto: Toronto University Press.

Pratt, C., 1990, 'Middle Power Internationalism and Global Poverty', in Pratt, ed.

Pratt, C., ed., 1990, *Middle Power Internationalism: The North–South Dimension*, Kingston and Montreal: McGill-Queen's University Press.

Prendergast, J., 1996, *Frontline Diplomacy. Humanitarian Aid and Conflict in Africa*, Boulder, CO and London: Lynne Rienner Publishers.

Reutlinger, S., 1999, 'From "food aid" to "aid for food": into the 21st century', *Food Policy*, Vol. 24, No. 1, pp.7–15.

Reutlinger, S. and J. Katona Apte, 1984, 'The Nutritional Impact of Food Aid: Criteria for the Selection of Cost-Effective Foods', *Food and Nutrition Bulletin*, Vol. 6, No. 4, pp. 1–10.

Rittberger, V., ed., 1993, *Regimes in International Relations*, Oxford: Clarendon Press.

Shaw, D. J. and E.J. Clay, 1998, 'Global Hunger and Food Security after the World Food Summit', *Canadian Journal of Development Studies*, Vol. 19, Special Issue, pp.55–76.

Shaw, D. J. and H.W. Singer, 1996, 'A future food aid regime: implications of the Final Act of the Uruguay Round', *Food Policy*, Vol. 21, No. 4/5, pp. 447–60.

Slim, H., 1997, 'Doing the Right Thing. Relief Agencies, Moral Dilemmas and Moral Responsibility in Political Emergencies and War', *Studies on Emergencies and Disaster Relief*, Report No. 6, Uppsala: The Nordic Africa Institute in co-operation with SIDA.

Smith, D. *et al.*, 1997, *The State of War and Peace Atlas*, London: Penguin with the International Peace Research Institute, Oslo.

Smith, L. and L. Haddad, 2000, 'Explaining Child Malnutrition in Developing Countries: A Cross-Country Analysis', *Research Report*, Washington DC: IFPRI.

Stokke, O., 1989, 'The Determinants of Aid Policies: General Introduction', in Stokke, ed.

Stokke, O., ed., 1989, *Western Middle Powers and Global Poverty*, Uppsala: Scandinavian Institute of African Studies.

Stokke, O., 1995, 'Aid and Political Conditionality: Core Issues and State of the Art', in Stokke, ed.

Stokke, O., ed., 1995, *Aid and Political Conditionality*, London: Frank Cass.

Stokke, O., 1996, 'Foreign Aid: What Now?', in Stokke, ed.

Stokke, O., ed., 1996, *Foreign Aid Towards the Year 2000: Experiences and Challenges*, London: Frank Cass.

Stokke, O., 1997, 'Violent Conflict Prevention and Development Co-operation: Coherent or Conflicting Perspectives?', *Forum for Development Studies*, Oslo: NUPI.

UNDP, 1994, *Human Development Report 1994*, New York and Oxford: Oxford University Press.

WFP, 1996, *Tackling Hunger in a World Full of Food: Tasks Ahead for Food Aid*, Rome: World Food Programme, Public Affairs Division.

WFP, 1999, *Time for Change: Food Aid and Development*, Rome: World Food Programme (April).

Glossary

ACC/SCN	Administrative Committee on Co-ordination (UN)/ Sub-committee on Nutrition (co-ordinating body for UN agencies involved in nutrition)
ACF	Action (Internationale) contre la Faim (AICF)
ADAB	Australian Development Assistance Bureau
AGRHYMET	Regional Centre for Training and Operational Application of Agrometeorology and Hydrology Information and Analysis
AICF	Action (Internationale) contre la Faim (ACF)
AIDS	Acquired immune deficiency syndrome
ATPSM	Agricultural Trade Policy Simulation Model
BMFS	Bonos Mujer Jefe de Familia (Honduras)
BMU	Bundesministerium für Umwelt, Naturschutz und Reaktorsicherheit (Federal Ministry for the Environment, Nature Conservation and Nuclear Safety) (Germany)
BMWi	Bundesministerium für Wirtschaft (Federal Ministry of Economic Affairs) (Germany)
BRAC	Bangladesh Rural Advancement Committee
BRCS	British Red Cross Society
BSD	Bistånd i siffror och diagram (Foreign Aid in Figures and Graphs) (Sweden)
CARE	Cooperative for American Relief Everywhere
CCC	Commodity Credit Corporation (USDA)
CCFF	Commodity Contingency Financing Fund (IMF)
CD	Country Director
CESAR	Centre for Environmental Studies and Resource Management (Oslo)
CFA	Committee on Food Aid Policies and Programmes
CFA	Communauté Financière Africaine (African Financial Community – Franc zone)
CFS	Committee on World Food Security (FAO)
CGIAR	Consultative Group on International Agricultural Research
CIDA	Canadian International Development Agency

CILSS	Comité Inter-Etats de Lutte contre la Séchesse dans le Sahel
CLC	Cash-in-lieu-of commodities
CLONG/UE	Non-governmental Organisation/European Union Liaison Committee
CMI	Christian Michelsen Institute (Bergen)
CMR	Crude Mortality Rate
CO	Country Office
COMECON	Council for Mutual Economic Assistance – Communist organisation
CPF	Counterpart Fund
CRC	Convention on the Rights of the Child
CRS	Catholic Relief Services
CRS	Congressional Research Service
CSB	Vitamin-enriched corn-soya blend
CSO	Country Strategy Outlines
DAC	Development Assistance Committee (OECD)
DANIDA	Danish International Development Agency
DFID	Department for International Development (UK)
DG	Directorate General (of the European Commission)
DHA	Department of Humanitarian Affairs (UNDP)
DIAPER	Permanent Regional Project for Diagnosis of Food Security in the Sahel
DPR	Democratic People's Republic (of Korea)
EADI	European Association of Development Research and Training Institutes
ECHO	European Community Humanitarian Office
ECOSOC	Economic and Social Council (UN)
ECSR	Committee on Economic, Social and Cultural Rights
EGS	Employment Generation Scheme (India)
ENSO	El Niño – Southern Oscillation
EU	European Union
FAC	Fond d'aide et de coopération (Fund for Aid and Co-operation) (France)
FAC	Food Aid Committee
FAC	Food Aid Convention
FAO	Food and Agriculture Organisation of the UN
FAOSTAT	FAO Statistical Data Base
FCR	Full Cost Recovery
FFW	Food-for-work
FIAN	FoodFirst Information and Action Network

FIVIMS	Food Insecurity and Vulnerability Information Mapping System
f.o.b.	Free on board
FSCR	Food Security Commodity Reserve
FSG	Food Studies Group
FY	Fiscal Year
GATT	General Agreement on Tariffs and Trade
GDP	Gross domestic product
GIEWS	Global Information Early Warning System
GNP	Gross National Product
GTZ	(Deutsche) Gesellschaft für Technische Zusammenarbeit (Germany)
HCHR	(UN) High Commissioner of Human Rights
HEWS	Humanitarian Early Warning System (UN)
HO	Humanitarian Ombudsman
HIV	Human immunodeficiency virum
HP	High Protein
HQ	Headquarters
ICESCR	International Convenant on Economic, Social and Cultural Rights
ICO	International Coffee Organisation
ICRC	International Committee of the Red Cross
ICVA	International Council of Voluntary Agencies
IDA	International Development Association (World Bank)
IDP	Internally displaced person
IDPM	Institute for Development Policy Management
IDRC	International Development Research Centre (Canada)
IDS	Institute of Development Studies (University of Sussex, Brighton)
IEFR	International Emergency Food Reserve
IFAD	International Fund for Agricultural Development
IFADP	Integrated Food Assisted Development Project (Bangladesh)
IFPRI	International Food Policy Research Institute
IFRC	International Federation of Red Cross and Red Crescent Societies
IGAD	Intergovernmental Authority for Development ('Greater Horn of Africa')
IGC	Inter-governmental conference – EU. The first one took place in 1991 and resulted in the signature of the Maastricht Treaty, the second took place in 1996 and

	resulted in the signature of the Treaty of Amsterdam in 1997
IGO	Intergovernmental Organisation
ILCA	International Livestock Centre for Africa
ILO	International Labour Organisation
IMF	International Monetary Fund
IMPACT	International Model for Policy Analysis of Agricultural Commodities and Trade
INGO	International non-governmental organisation
InterAction	American Council for Voluntary International Action
IRA	Immediate Response Account
IRIN	Integrated Regional Information Network (UN regional/country networks)
ISTI	International Science and Technology Institute
ITSH	Internal transport, storage and handling
IWC	International Wheat Council
LDC	Less developed country/least developed country
LIC	Low Income Country
LIFD	Low Income Food Deficit
LLDC	(List of) Least Developed Countries (UN definition)
LMIC	Lower middle-income country
MCH	Mother and child health initiative/programme
MDD	Micronutrient deficiency disease
MOH	Ministry of Health
MSF	Médecins sans frontières
MST	Movimento dos Sem-Terra (Brazil)
NAR	Nationale Adviesraad voor Ontwikkelingssamenwerking (National Advisory Council for Development Co-operation) (The Netherlands)
NFI	Non-food-item
NFIDC	Net Food-Importing Developing Country
NGHA	Non-Governmental Humanitarian Agency
NGO	Non-governmental organisation
NORAD	Norwegian Agency for International Development/ now Norwegian Agency for Development Co-operation
NUPI	Norsk Utenrikspolitisk Institutt (Norwegian Institute of International Affairs) (Oslo)
OCHA	(UN) Office of the Commissioner for Humanitarian Relief
ODA	Official development assistance
ODI	Overseas Development Institute (London)

OECD	Organisation for Economic Co-operation and Development
OLS	Operation Lifeline Sudan
Oxfam	Oxford Committee for Famine Relief
PAI	Population Action International
PCIA	Peace and Conflict Impact Assessment
PDHRE	People's Decade for Human Rights Education
PFA	Programme Food Aid
PRO	Protracted Relief Operation
PRRO	Protracted Refugee and Relief Operations
PRIO	Peace Research Institute, Oslo
PVO	Private voluntary organisation
REWS	Regional Early Warning System
RHU	Refugee Health Unit
RMP	Rural Maintenance Programme (Bangladesh)
RNIS	Refugee Nutrition Information System
RRN	Relief and Rehabilitation Network
RUNS	Rural–Urban North–South
SADC	Southern African Development Community
SADCC	Southern African Development Co-ordination Conference
SCF	Save the Children Fund
SCHR	Steering Committee for Humanitarian Response
SCN	Sub-committee for Nutrition (ACC)
SCP	Sub-committee on Projects (CFA)
SFP	School feeding programme
SFP	Supplementary feeding programme
SIM	Studie- en Informatiecentrum Mensenrechten (Netherlands Institute of Human Rights)
SIPRI	Stockholm International Peace Research Institute
SPHERE	Minimum Standards in Humanitarian Response (a Programme of the Steering Committee for Humanitarian Response and Interaction)
SSA	Sub-Saharan Africa
SSR	Self-sufficiency ratio
TB	Tuberculosis
TFP	Therapeutic Feeding Programme
UDHR	Universal Declaration of Human Rights
UK	United Kingdom
UN	United Nations
UNCTAD	United Nations Conference on Trade and Development

UNDAF	United Nations Development Assistance Framework
UNDP	United Nations Development Programme
UNFPA	United Nations Fund for Population Activities/United Nations Population Fund (renamed 1988)
UNHCR	United Nations High Commissioner for Refugees
UNICEF	United Nations (International) Children's (Emergency) Fund
UNRISD	United Nations Research Institute for Social Development
UNU	United Nations University
UR	Uruguay Round
US	United States (of America)
USA	United States of America
USAID	United States Agency for International Development
USDA	United States Department of Agriculture
USSR	Union of Soviet Socialist Republics
VGF	Vulnerable Group Feeding
VIDC	Vienna Institute for Development Cooperation
WANAHR	World Alliance for Nutrition and Human Rights
WB	World Bank/IBRD
WFM	World Food Model
WFP	World Food Programme
WFS	World Food Summit
WHO	World Health Organisation
WIDER	World Institute for Development Economics Research (Helsinki)
WMO	World Meteorological Organisation
WSP	War-torn Societies Project
WTO	World Trade Organisation

Notes on Contributors

Charlotte Benson is an independent economist and former Research Fellow of the Overseas Development Institute, London. She has been involved in a number of studies on food aid, including most recently a report commissioned by the UK Department for International Development on *Food Aid and Food Security in the 1990s: Performance and Effectiveness*; and a *Joint Evaluation of European Union Programme Food Aid*, commissioned by EU member states and the Commission.

Roger Buckland, formerly Policy Adviser, SADC Food Security Technical and Administrative Unit, Harare, has returned to Canberra, Australia where he has semi-retired.

Edward Clay is a Senior Research Associate at the Overseas Development Institute, London and has extensively researched and written on natural disasters and food security and advised many international agencies and governments on food aid policy. He was formerly Director of the Relief and Development Institute, London, and a Fellow of the Institute of Development Studies at the University of Sussex.

Martin Doornbos is a Fellow of the Institute of Social Studies, The Hague, and Professor of Political Science. He is editor of *Development and Change*, and has published extensively on development issues, with particular reference to the role of the state and food aid. Among his recent publications is *Post-Conflict Eritrea: Prospects for Reconstruction and Development* (with A. Tesfay, 1999).

Graham Eele was Regional Training Adviser, SADC Food Security Technical and Administrative Unit, Harare from 1996 to 1998 and is now with Oxford Policy Management Ltd in the UK where his activities include food security analysis, poverty alleviation and the development of statistical agencies.

Wenche Barth Eide is an Associate Professor at the Institute for Nutrition Research/School of Nutrition, University of Oslo. Her professional interests are in the field of public and global food and nutrition security problems and policy analysis especially as related to agricultural and rural development, and the linkages to human rights. She has been Technical Advisor in Nutrition to the International Fund for Agricultural Development (IFAD) in Rome, and is a member of the Board of Trustees of IFPRI (International Food Policy Research Institute).

Just Faaland, an economist, has published widely on issues of development and aid. He was for many years Director of Research of the Chr. Michelsen Institute and has also been Director of the World Bank Resident Mission in Bangladesh (1972–74), President of the OECD Development Centre (1983–85) and Director General of the International Food Policy Research Institute (1990–92). He has had long-term advisory assignments in Pakistan and Malaysia and has worked in many other countries in Asia, Africa and Latin America; most of these were sponsored by UN and other international and national development agencies.

Robin Jackson is a socio-economist working in the Policy Division at the World Food Programme. Previously, she worked with the Food Security and Crisis Prevention group at the Club du Sahel, OECD, Paris.

Jim Greenfield graduated from the London School of Economics in Economic Theory in 1962 and subsequently worked at the School in the Economics Research Department before joining FAO in 1966. Following an initial assignment on the FAO/ICO/IBRD Joint Coffee Study, he joined the Commodities and Trade Division working on commodity market analysis and projections methodology. After a secondment to the World Food Council he resumed his career in the Commodities and Trade Division working on rice, roots and tubers and grains. Since 1989 he worked extensively on Uruguay Round-related topics publishing a number of articles on the subject. Since 1996 he has served as Director of the Commodities and Trade Division.

Panos A. Konandreas has a Ph.D. in Agricultural Economics, University of California and a M.Sc. in Engineering, National Technical University of Athens. Until 1998 he was Chief in the Commodities and Trade Division of FAO, directing the work of the impact of the Agreement on Agriculture on commodity markets and policy implications for developing countries. Presently, he is at the FAO office in Geneva focusing on the interests of developing countries in the next round of negotiations in agriculture. Prior to joining FAO in 1982 he worked at IFPRI and ILCA. He is member of the editorial board of *Food Policy* and co-edited a special issue on *Implications of the Uruguay Round for Developing Countries.*

Uwe Kracht is an independent development consultant specialising in sustainable, human-centred development, with emphasis on food and agriculture, nutrition and poverty elimination. He is also Co-Co-ordinator of the World Alliance for Nutrition and Human Rights (WANAHR) and has worked extensively in the field of ethics, human rights and development in a globalising world.

Diana McLean, an agronomist, has worked in a poverty and rural development programme as a project manager in Mali and as Regional Agronomist for West and Central Africa for the United States Agency for International Development (1979–86); as an institutions analyst, management trainer, and monitoring and evaluation specialist for the International Service for National Agricultural Research (1986–88); and as a consultant in institutional assessment, rural development, policy, project development and evaluation for CIDA, IDRC, CARE, USAID and others (1988 to present). She has extensive field experience in sub-Saharan Africa.

Reggie Mugwara is Director of the SADC Food, Agriculture and Natural Resources Sector Development Unit in Harare.

Alain Mourey is a nutritionist with the ICRC's Health and Relief Division, presently in charge of the Economic Security Unit of that Division. He graduated in Biochemistry and later specialised in Human Nutrition at the London School of Hygiene and Tropical Medicine (1981–82). Since then he has developed nutrition and assistance policies for the ICRC, using his experience gathered through numerous field missions tackling famines and nutritional emergencies linked to armed conflict all over the world.

Ole David Koht Norbye, an economist, began to work on problems of development in poor countries as adviser in Pakistan from 1959 to 1961. Since then until retirement, he was Senior Research Fellow at the Chr. Michelsen Institute, and had numerous assignments in developing countries, including long-term ones in Kenya, the Sudan and Bangladesh, and worked for ILO, FAO, UNCTAD, UNDP, the World Bank, OECD Development Centre, the Ford

Foundation and Nordic aid agencies. He has published many articles and mongraphs as well as studies and reports, including evaluations, linked to his various assignments.

Fiona O'Reilly has had ten years of experience in the emergency sector and has a background in public health. After spending five years working in emergency programmes in Eastern Africa she took up the post of Co-ordinator and Co-director of the Emergency Nutrition Network, based in Trinity College, Dublin.

Rajul Pandya-Lorch is Head of the 2020 Vision for Food, Agriculture, and the Environment Initiative at the International Food Policy Research Institute (IFPRI). Before taking her current position, she was special assistant to IFPRI's Director General. Her recent research has focused on trends in and prospects for global food security and on policies to alleviate and prevent food insecurity, poverty and environmental degradation.

Nita Pillai is a Food Policy Officer at Consumers International, formerly Research Officer with the Overseas Development Institute, London. She is a microbiologist and nutritionist and has worked on public policy issues relating to food aid and food security.

Jens Schultes, Dr.jur., University of Cologne 1967, joined the UN World Food Programme in 1969 and served as Director of the WFP Regional Bureau for Asia and the Pacific from 1992 until retirement in 1997. His publications include 'The Effectiveness of Aid as a Problem of Bureaucratic Management', in Clay and Shaw, eds., London, 1987; 'Monetisation of Project Food Aid?', in *Counterpart Funds and Development*, IDS, 1992; 'Neuorientierung in der Ernaehrungssicherung', in *Entwicklung und Laendlicher Raim*, 4/92 and 'From Activities to Entitlements', IDPM, University of Manchester, 1997.

Ramesh Sharma, a national of Nepal, is a Senior Economist in the Commodities and Trade Division of FAO in Rome which he joined in 1991. In FAO he has worked on food security issues, food policy analysis and agricultural trade issues. Since 1995, he has been involved heavily on the analysis of the Uruguay Round Agreement on Agriculture, including its consequences on the policy and economy of the developing countries. He has a M.A. degree from the

University of New England, Australia and a Ph.D. in Agricultural Economics from Stanford University.

Jeremy Shoham has been working at operational, training and research level in the field of emergency food and nutrition for over 15 years. He is currently Co-director of the Emergency Nutrition Network and a partner of NutritionWorks.

Olav Stokke is a Senior Researcher of the Norwegian Institute of International Affairs, Oslo, where he previously has served as the Director of Research, Deputy Director and Acting Director and for years been in charge of the Department of Development Research. He is the editor of *Forum for Development Studies* and, since 1979, the Convenor of the EADI Working Group on Aid Policy and Performance.

Marie-Cécile Thirion is a Programme Leader with Solagral. An agro-economist by training, she has specialised in food security. She is responsible for the co-ordination of the European Food Security Network (Resal) and follows, on a regular basis, the donors' food aid policies, food security policies in developing countries, and the impact on food security of international negotiations and food aid practices of countries in the North.

Jane Wallace worked for five years as the Co-ordinator of the Refugee Nutrition Information System in WHO, Geneva, and has recently taken up a post as Programme Officer in the Department of Emergency and Humanitarian Action in WHO. She is currently working on the Health Information Network for Advanced Planning.

Index

INDEX

IGAD region 289
IMF 6, 24, 185, 344; CCFF 24, 40
imports, food 7, 21, 26, 33, 55, 61–2, 64–7
  passim, 81–2, 84, 86–92, 182, 212, 292,
  293, 295, 365 *see also* NFIDCs; guarantee
  schemes 194
incentives, farmer 73
income 59, 60, 62, 64, 66–8 *passim*, 72, 83–
  4, 129, 132, 135, 144, 182, 188, 189, 200–2
  passim, 357; transfer 22, 171, 172, 198,
  200, 207–10 *passim*, 215, 259, 372, 376
India 23, 25–6, 29, 35, 54, 61, 66–7, 214,
  375, 376; EGS 200–2 *passim*, 204;
  Operation Flood 25–6, 26n7, 355
Indonesia 35, 38, 46, 54, 132, 365
inflation 129, 204, 205, 216
information 178, 187, 188, 191–3, 281, 294–
  8 *passim*, 301, 303;
  FIVIMS 340; IRIN 134, 135
infrastructure 63, 67, 73, 98, 125, 185, 189,
  190, 193, 199, 200, 244, 263, 264
Ingram, James 267
insecurity, food 8, 22, 23, 58, 71–3 *passim*,
  120, 124–34, 145, 158, 224, 364, 366, 376,
  378
Institut International Jacques Maritain 343
institutions 1, 5–6, 9, 19, 42–6, 170–75, 177,
  178, 261, 353–61 *passim*, 365–6, 374;
  reform 10, 17, 20, 42, 380–3; regional 192–
  3
International Grains agreement 42; Council
  43
investment 3, 14, 64, 67, 73, 98, 188, 190,
  193, 261–4 *passim*
Iraq 124
irrigation 125, 183, 200
ISTI 215
IWC 103, 107

Jackson, Robin 9, 289–308, 380
Jackson, T. 209
Jamaica 208
Japan 26, 28, 30, 31, 51, 170, 177
Jaspars, J. 159
Jaspars, S. 157, 171
Jiang Zhongyi 204
Jones, S. 187
Jonsson, U. 330, 342
Jordan 35, 53; region 132
Jost, S. 25, 292
Joy, L. 330

Kagame, P. 128
Katona Apte, J. 371
Kent, G. 132, 342, 346
Kenya 155, 156, 174, 176

Koenig, S. 345
Konandreas, Panos 7, 38, 76–101
Koning, A. 27
Korea, North 18, 26, 31, 35, 38, 46, 54, 168,
  251; South 26, 51
Kosovo 40, 129, 276, 287, 376
Kracht, Uwe 7, 8, 40, 120–48, 344, 345, 368

labour 173, 200, 202, 263, 264, 269
Lancaster, Carol 15
land 125, 127, 130, 135; reform 130, 144
La Niña 69, 366
Lappé, F.M. 331
Latin America 58, 60, 69, 127
law, international humanitarian 124, 137–40,
  142, 158–9, 310, 315, 318, 326, 344
Leach, I. 45
Leader, Nick 10, 124, 142, 302, 303
least developed countries 76, 77, 82–92, 98,
  100–1, 224, 227, 240, 242, 281
liberalisation 47, 377; market 63, 67, 80, 185,
  187, 206, 371–2; trade 5, 14, 40, 47, 67, 73,
  80, 98, 106, 185, 371–2
Liberia 18, 52, 124, 125, 139, 151, 154, 157,
  161
LIFD countries 233, 240–1, 250, 281
life expectancy 72, 365
literacy 209, 210, 269
livelihoods 22, 69, 135, 197–211, 364, 384
livestock 60, 65–7 *passim*, 79, 281
loans 24
local purchases 21, 24, 36, 45, 105, 167–8,
  225, 231, 278–83 *passim*, 292, 294, 297,
  299, 300, 373–4
Lodgaard, Sverre 10

Ma, G. 64
Mackintosh, K. 134, 139, 140
maintenance 235, 264
maize 61–3 *passim*, 68, 157, 166, 167, 171,
  183, 189, 373–4
Malawi 52, 201–3 *passim*
Mali 52, 130–31, 291, 299, 301
malnutrition 47, 57, 59, 60, 62, 120, 122,
  152, 153, 171, 188, 224, 252–4 *passim*,
  268–9, 334, 370, 383
Malthus, Thomas 63, 68n5, 69
marketing 158, 184, 185, 190, 253, 356, 379
markets 63, 66, 73, 77, 80, 98, 109, 168, 185,
  187, 190, 194, 205, 210, 224–5, 291, 292,
  376 *see also* liberalisation
Marr, A. 38
Marrakesh Decision 5, 7, 40, 42, 76, 77, 82,
  92–8 *passim*, 365, 382
Marshall Plan 17, 18, 46

403

Maxwell, Simon 10, 22, 205, 342, 346, 347, 364, 383
McClelland, D.G. 2, 19n2, 196, 198, 207, 208, 212, 213, 215
McCorquodale, R. 346
McLean, Diana 9, 221–55
McLaren, D.S. 330
meat 60, 62, 63, 66, 78, 84
Mei, F. 64
Mensbrugghe, D. van der 77
Messer, E. 124–6 *passim*, 342
Metz, M. 204
Mexico 130
Michanek, E. 330
micronutrients 150, 152, 154–6, 162, 163, 211–12; deficiency disease 153–6 *passim*, 376
Middlebrook, P. 204
migration 14, 136, 189, 200, 203
milk powder 106, 370, 374
Mirghani, Z. 160
Missiaen, M. 116n1
Moffitt, R. 203
monetisation 25–6, 171, 197, 206, 212, 227, 231–2, 240, 271, 278, 282, 297, 351, 352, 360, 373, 375, 376–7
monitoring 169, 173, 232, 234, 281, 284, 286, 293, 297, 381–2
Mora, J. 215
moral hazard 190
Moren, A. 156
Morocco 53, 132
mortality 152, 153, 188, 211, 212, 369
Moss, R.H. 132
Mourey, Alain 7, 9, 309–25, 380
Moyo, S. 200
Mozambique 35, 52, 124, 126, 156, 166, 183, 186, 244, 358, 359
MSF, Holland 162
Mugwara, Reggie 8, 181–95
multinational corporations 331, 344
Mursal, H. 162

Nafziger, W. 129, 144
Namibia 184, 186, 187, 194
Nepal 54, 156
Netherlands 9, 37, 177, 223, 293; NAR 128; Operations Review Unit 159; SIM 332
NGOs/PVOs 7, 9, 31, 36, 51, 134, 139–42 *passim*, 160, 197, 201, 252, 263, 268, 274–88, 293, 310, 312, 318, 343–5, 355–9 *passim*, 363, 367, 373, 375, 377
Nicaragua 34, 53
NFIDCs 7, 40, 76, 77, 82–92, 98, 100, 111, 364–5
Niger 52, 131, 200, 301; River region 132

Nigeria/Biafra 270
Norbye, Ole David Koht 9, 221–55
Nordic UN Project 229
Norway 9, 28, 37, 39, 51, 177, 223; Ministry of Foreign Affairs 10; NORAD 252n9; PRIO 129–30
NUPI 10, 131
nutrition 125, 149–54, 161–3, 167, 177, 178, 210–16, 221, 266, 326, 330, 331, 334, 340, 341, 357, 373, 374 *see also* ACC/SCN; International Conference on 335–6; status 17, 57n2, 150, 171–2, 217; World Alliance for (WANAHR) 336, 343

objectives, aid 15–17, 22, 28, 94, 117, 196, 266, 382, 384
OCHA 6, 43
ODI 10, 19, 32, 151, 154, 158, 161, 164, 174, 176, 383; Relief and Rehabilitation Network 172
OECD 15, 30, 371 *see also* DAC
Oloka-Onyango, J. 346
O'Neill, Helen 4, 48n13
O'Reilly, Fiona 8, 149–80
Oshaug, A. 333, 335, 336, 342, 347
ownership 6, 16, 201, 235, 243, 298
Oxfam 142, 155, 163, 274, 310

Pakistan 35, 54, 202, 203, 244, 375
Pandya-Lorch, Rajul 7, 38, 55–75, 364
Papua New Guinea 131
parastatals 184, 185
Parry, M.L. 70
participation 16, 185, 232, 235, 268, 330, 339
patronage 190
Payne, L. 151, 175
peace-building 120, 143, 145, 148; keeping 16, 18, 145
Pelletier, D.L. 211
People in Aid 314
Peru 35, 53
pests 194
Philippines 130
Philips, M. 215
Pillai, Nita 7, 8, 41, 196–220, 372
Pines, J. 330
Pinstrup-Andersen, P. 7, 36, 38, 69, 122, 134, 143, 197, 198, 373
planning, ration 157, 160–63, 178
Poh, L.K. 35, 372
Poland 35
political factors 129–30, 136, 170, 175–7, 242–3, 374, 384–6
population 160–61; growth 59, 63, 68, 69, 83, 191; - Action International 70

404

EADI BOOK SERIES